tear here

The Complete Idiot's Reference Card

Traveler's Check List

- ❏ Set out airline tickets and travel documents
- ❏ Water the plants
- ❏ Unplug all appliances
- ❏ Stop delivery of newspapers
- ❏ Go to Post Office to put a temporary hold on your mail
- ❏ Order special meals on flights for the kids
- ❏ Leave keys and itinerary with family, neighbor, and/or work
- ❏ Arrange for transportation to the airport
- ❏ Adjust thermostats
- ❏ Take pets to kennel or find sitter
- ❏ Have neighbor cut lawn or shovel snow so house doesn't look vacant
- ❏ Close all windows
- ❏ Lock all doors
- ❏ Set house alarm
- ❏ Pack snacks and games for the kids
- ❏ Keep all medication out and pack in a carry-on bag
- ❏ Call airline to reconfirm seats 24 hours prior
- ❏ Call airline day of departure to confirm flight times and avoid unnecessary delays at the airport
- ❏ Set all lights on timers; vary the times
- ❏ Clean out the refrigerator
- ❏ Take out all garbage
- ❏ Get traveler's checks
- ❏ Review and pay bills that are due while you are gone
- ❏ Pack camera and film
- ❏ Take travel journal or pad of paper and pen
- ❏ Get dollar bills for miscellaneous tips
- ❏ Suspend any regularly scheduled domestic services; do not tell them you are away on vacation (such as house cleaning, baby-sitters, water delivery, and so on)
- ❏ Pack several plastic zip-lock bags, both small and large sizes
- ❏ Call to obtain the limit on your credit cards
- ❏ Make sure all luggage has an identification tag, including your carry-ons

alpha
books

Our Travel Itinerary
& Important Phone Numbers

Flight Information _____

_____

_____

Airline & Flight # _____

Date _____

Times _____

Destination Airport _____

_____

_____

_____

_____

Accommodations _____

_____

_____

_____

_____

_____

Dates _____

_____

Where We're Staying _____

_____

City _____

Phone _____

Fax _____

_____

_____

_____

Itinerary/Sightseeing/Tours _____

_____

Day 1 _____

_____

Day 2 _____

_____

Day 3 _____

_____

Day 4 _____

_____

Day 5 _____

_____

Day 6 _____

_____

Day 7 _____

_____

Travel Agency Information _____

_____

Agent Name _____

Agency Name _____

Agency Phone _____

Agency Fax _____

_____

Other Important Information & Instructions

_____

_____

_____

_____

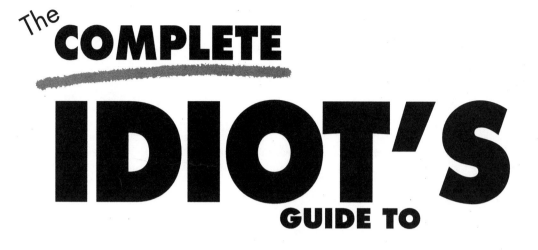

The COMPLETE IDIOT'S GUIDE TO

the Perfect Vacation

by Scott Ahlsmith

alpha books

A Division of Macmillan Publishing
A Prentice Hall Macmillan Company
201 W. 103rd Street, Indianapolis, IN 46290

Dedicated to the memory of my sister, Sana Kay Danielson. Your loving spirit touches every page.

©1995 Alpha Books

International Standard Book Number: 1-56761-531-7
Library of Congress Catalog Card Number: 94-72725

97 96 95   8 7 6 5 4 3 2 1

Interpretation of the printing code: the rightmost number of the first series of numbers is the year of the book's printing; the rightmost number of the second series of numbers is the number of the book's printing. For example, a printing code of 95-1 shows that the first printing of the book occurred in 1995.

Printed in the United States of America

Publisher
Marie Butler-Knight

Product Manager
Tom Godfrey

Product Development Manager
Faithe Wempen

Managing Editor
Elizabeth Keaffaber

Production Editor
Michelle Shaw

Copy Editor
San Dee Phillips

Cover Designer
Karen Ruggles

Illustrator
Judd Winick

Designer
Barbara Kordesh

Indexer
Jeanne Clark

Production Team
*Gary Adair, Angela Calvert, Dan Caparo, Brad Chinn, Kim Cofer,
Dave Eason, Jennifer Eberhardt, Rob Falco, David Garratt, Erika Millen,
Angel Perez, Beth Rago, Bobbi Satterfield, Karen Walsh, Robert Wolf*

*Special thanks to Lan Sluder for ensuring
the technical accuracy of this book.*

Contents at a Glance

Contents

Preface

What I Did on My Summer Vacation

I've been preparing to write this book since I was six. My research began on the eve of our first family vacation. Mom and Dad were taking my sister Sana and me to Cass Lake, Minnesota. We were returning to the rustic cabin where my parents spent their honeymoon. I learned my first bit of travel jargon on that vacation. I learned that "rustic" means no indoor plumbing, and I learned a whole new use for outdated Sears & Roebuck catalog pages. We were recycling—we just didn't know what to call it then.

The night before we left our Vinton, Iowa home, we had the 1949 dark green Oldsmobile 76 serviced, packed to the rafters, and ready to head north. I remember Mom tucking me into bed, making sure I'd said my prayers, and reminding me that tomorrow night I'd be sleeping in a different state.

Now that bit of news had about the same effect as a cup of sugar and a quart of caffeine poured into the average hyperactive six-year-old Iowa farm boy. I fought off sleep and kept trying to visualize exactly how the state line would appear. How thick would it be? Would it be straight or crooked? Which state owned it since it was exactly on the border between two states? Would it be tall like a wall or short and flat like it appears on a map?

If curiosity were brains, I'd be a Ph.D. instead of a travel agent. But I have no regrets. I still remember crossing the Iowa-Minnesota state line. My dad even stopped the car so I could inspect the sign that said Welcome to Minnesota on one side and Welcome to Iowa on the other. I thought that was pretty cool. Oh, I was slightly disappointed not to find an actual line like I'd seen on the map, but I did see a wire fence. My dad explained that was easier to maintain than a painted line. I understood. Dad always knows best.

That family vacation was the thrill of a lifetime, and I've been fortunate enough to have had almost 40 years of vacation and travel thrills since then. I've been truly blessed because I've never felt like I've had to work to earn a living. I've always been able to do what I loved: travel. I'm looking forward to sharing my love and passion for travel with you. And yes, I still get a chill and a thrill whenever I cross a state or country boundary.

Introduction

What's It All About?

One of my first experiences as a trip director convinced me that this book needed to be written. I was a young pup back in 1972 who acted like he knew it all. The following experience showed that, while I wasn't necessarily an *idiot*, there was a lot I didn't know about the world of travel and those who traveled in it.

As a trip director, I was supposed to cater to every want and desire of every participant who had won the incentive travel award. The participants who won these awards were sharp. They were always the best and brightest in their company. They sold more insurance policies, more vacuum cleaners, more mufflers, or more carpeting than anyone else. They were the best of the best.

I lived in fear of these participants. At any moment, they were capable of asking a question that would show my ignorance and inexperience. They would make me look like an *idiot*. Well, now you know why I was selected to write this book. It happened.

A fresh group of incentive award winners had just arrived from the airport and were checked into the hotel without incident. My supervisor had great confidence in me and left me in charge of the hospitality desk for a few hours. Actually, I found out later he really didn't have too much confidence in me. He just wanted to grab a couple of quick hours by the pool. He figured nothing could go wrong since all the guests were busy unpacking and getting ready for the evening's festivities.

Five minutes after he left, the phone at the trip director's hospitality desk rang. I answered with a false air of confidence and heard a panic-stricken voice cry, "I can't get out of my room." I was a mess. Here I was, alone and faced with a situation I couldn't handle. Why couldn't he have just wanted to know where dinner was being served, or what time the golf tournament began tomorrow? I knew that stuff, but "I can't get out of my room" wasn't in my notes. I didn't have a clue.

I remembered being trained to ask a question to confirm that I fully understood the client's request. So I asked, "Well, you got into your room, didn't you?" Brilliant, Scott. Of course, he got into his room. Then it dawned on me. He was trying the wrong door. He was probably trying to open the door to the adjoining room. Those doors have locks on both sides to avoid embarrassing incidents.

So I boldly asked, "Are you sure you're trying the correct door?" My client, who was also the top salesperson of the group and had VIP plastered all over his name on the rooming list, sounded more than slightly irritated when he responded, "Yes, of course I remember which door I used to enter my room. I've only been here for 15 minutes." Being from Iowa and having mastered an acute grasp of the obvious, I asked, "What's the matter? Is the door stuck?" And the response I received taught me a very valuable lesson about travelers.

The VIP client, the best of the best in his company said, "No! The door's not stuck. It has a "Do Not Disturb" sign hanging on the handle and I'm afraid of opening it." I learned right then and there that traveling was one of the great equalizers. No matter how many insurance policies someone sold, no matter how many yards of floor covering someone sold, they were extremely vulnerable when they left the safety and security of their environment. No matter how successful and talented, they became novices the moment they left home.

I explained the function of the "Do Not Disturb" sign, reassured our client that he could safely open the door to the hall without offending anyone, and thanked him for calling and being concerned about disturbing the other guests in the hotel. At that time, I had a much better understanding of Moses' comment, "I am a stranger in a strange land."

The remainder of that trip went very smoothly and I never forgot the lesson I'd learned, "As soon as we leave home and begin our travels, we become a guest and we should always behave like one." It's just really nice when you can pick up the phone and get a ruling on the signs.

As we go through the following pages, I want you to think of this book as that friendly voice that can answer those questions that always surface when you leave home. That's what this book is about...helping you behave like an informed guest.

To help you feel more comfortable and less strange when you travel, this book is organized into parts. "Part" is a technical publishing term that loosely translates into putting things that look and sound the same in the same area. I don't fully understand the term, but I trust my editors and they assure me it'll all make sense in the end. Each part contains four or more chapters, and each chapter contains a bunch of paragraphs that are really complete thoughts masquerading as sentences.

Anyway, enough of these publishing paradigms. Here's a quick summary of the parts that make up the whole of this book.

Part 1: The Perfect Vacation for You. We're living in a market in which one size no longer fits all. Each of us wants to be treated like an individual. We no longer want mass-produced anything. Even Levi Strauss is offering custom-tailored jeans; just give them your measurements. Travel is under the same pressures to celebrate the individual. This section helps you pick the right kind of vacation for you.

Part 2: Choosing the Perfect Ingredients. Here's where you'll find the nuts and bolts of your vacation. We open the hood and take a good look at a vacation's components. This section rolls up its sleeves and talks about going, staying, eating, and doing.

Part 3: Making the Perfect Arrangements. Up until this section, we had this gigantic jigsaw puzzle called a vacation strewn around a table top. This section shows you how to take a piece from here and there and, after a little shaping and molding, produce a vacation ordered just to your liking.

Part 4: Enjoying Your Perfect Vacation. Too many travelers ruin their own vacations because their unrealistic expectations bear absolutely no resemblance to reality. This section helps keep you from being your own worst enemy and puts you in a place where you can deal with and actually look forward to the unexpected.

Special Rest Areas

Everyone needs a periodic break from the riveting words and phrases found on the following pages. To help you avoid literary burn-out, we've constructed a few rest areas throughout this book. These areas come in three different versions. You won't want to miss any of them. And like all good rest areas, we offer ample free parking, expensive, high-fat-content food, and restrooms that are regularly inspected—not cleaned, just inspected. Look for these cultural oases along your journey through this book:

Caution
Warnings about things that can ruin a vacation. You'll also find safety issues in these boxes.

Insider Tips
Helpful hints from travel professionals.

Off the Beaten Path   Top-secret destination and activity suggestions that you may not find without some help.

A Brief History of Travel

We all enjoy a historical perspective or, in some cases, a hysterical one; we like to know who slept where and whose footsteps we're following. Vacationers were not unknown even 4,000 years ago (you could spot them instantly, traveling in little groups with their mouths open, gawking in amazement at one of the Seven Wonders of the Ancient World) when visitors bought souvenirs and had their likenesses etched on clay tablets with the Egyptian pyramids in the background.

For thousands of years, professionals have traveled to conduct their business. Some of these professionals were explorers who took money from their rulers for going out and discovering new territories and staking a claim to that new land in the name of their ruler. They didn't have title companies back then so it really didn't matter that the land belonged to someone else.

If the inhabitants of the land didn't agree with the explorer's claim, the second group of professional travelers was called into action. These, of course, were the soldiers. They never bothered looking for "Do Not Disturb" signs. They just barged in, made their point, reconfirmed the authority of the explored, pillaged a little here and a little there, and then left.

The third group of professional travelers were called bandits on land and pirates on the seas. These travelers didn't have royalty to fund their explorations or armies to back them up, so they just arrived on the scene and took what others had discovered, claimed, and fought to own. Due to their low self-esteem and lack of popularity, thieves and pirates never had a place to call home. They were kind of like airline flight crews: two or three strange cities in a day, followed by a few hours in a strange hotel room, and then up bright and early the next morning for more of the same. The major difference between thieves and pirates and most flight crews was compensation. Being a thief or a pirate paid much better than working for an airline.

The fourth and last group of professional travelers consisted of merchants. Yes, even hundreds of years ago, the traveling salesman was alive and well. Instead of selling aluminum siding, they were selling frankincense and myrrh, but the jokes were probably the same.

Vacation travel as we know it today is a relatively new invention. Place yourself in merry old England around 1830. The good country life was being threatened by railways. Sir Isaac Coffin said in the public record at the House of Commons, "The rail system will destroy the beauty of the countryside and the comfort of a gentleman's estate, and fox hunting."

It was the destruction of fox hunting that persuaded doctors to denounce traveling by train. They said it was injurious to health, not because of the massive amounts of smoke and cinders, but because of the rush of air caused by traveling at such outrageous speeds. Others suggested that the railways were detrimental to the industrial revolution because they encouraged the working classes to travel, which distracted them from their main duty, which was to work.

In 1841, a temperance leader and Baptist preacher named Thomas Cook had a revelation. He thought he could improve the cause of temperance by selling outings by train. He reasoned that if people were on trains in the countryside, they couldn't be in the taverns in the city slums. On July 5, 1841, he organized a day trip from Leicester to Loughboro in England and sold more than 500 one shilling tickets.

The trip was only 10 miles in each direction, and the entertainment consisted of speeches and a brass band in Loughboro's central park, but the enormous success of the trip began what is known today as "the Cook's tour." This was the first time that travel was made affordable to the working class, and marked the beginning of travel for leisure. In the following years, John Mason Cook, Thomas' son, joined his father and built a travel empire that reached around the world. They owned and operated fleets of steamers on the Nile, organized Moslem pilgrimages from India to Mecca, and went around the world just as Jules Verne's *Around the World in Eighty Days* was being published.

In 1927, leisure travel was shifting from the rails to the air, and Thomas Cook, the company, was offering an air tour from New York to Chicago to see the Tunney-Dempsey boxing match. In a flyer promoting the flight to the fight, the traveler was promised, "observation windows in the planes from which to view landscapes, clouds, and strange light effects." The flight departed Curtis Field near Garden City at 8:00 a.m. and arrived in Chicago "early the same evening." As you can see, airlines were not as concerned with on-time performance in 1927 as they are now.

The Tunney-Dempsey package cost $575 per person and included ringside seats at the fight and a room at the "new and magnificent Hotel Stevens, the world's largest hostelry."

Immediately after World War II, tourism began growing at colossal rates. There was a new feeling of social equality that combined very nicely with a new increase in disposable income created by the post-war-economy. Trains gave way to planes and the family car. The U.S. highway system was becoming the best in the world and vacations quickly became annual events.

Vacations Today

Today, we see massive and positive political change sweeping the world, the breakdown of the cold war barriers and economies, and authoritarian governments turning democratic. Disposable incomes for citizens of many of the poorest countries are rising. Rising incomes and more *open* destinations encourage more people to travel. All of these events make travel and tourism expenditures a leading economic force in the United States and around the world.

Tourism creates a large number of jobs and is the second largest employer in today's economy. It also has a positive effect on the United State's balance of trade by attracting millions of foreign tourists to our country. The U.S. government is just beginning to understand the gigantic return on investment generated by travel and tourism dollars. If you don't believe this, just look at the taxes added to your airline ticket, hotel bill, and rental car invoice.

Technological advances make travel easier and more necessary. At one time, teleconferencing and all the latest gadgets were predicted to cripple travel. People would just stay at home and interact with their computer-television-telephone thing in their living room. And although some couch potatoes are trying to keep this dream alive, the truth is that we don't get much satisfaction from a purely *high tech* world. We need and search for an ample dose of *high touch*. Travel, especially vacation travel, provides us with the opportunity to interact with others, and this is a priority for most of us.

Technology changes the way we plan travel, the way we buy travel, and the way we move from place to place. We see a constant explosion of technological advances in the travel industry. Virtual reality, for instance, gives you an opportunity to sample different destinations and methods of travel before you leave home. What it doesn't do is let you sit at that small table at Café du Monde in New Orleans and enjoy the aroma of café au lait and freshly made beignets with the opportunity to lean over and introduce yourself to the family seated at the next table.

I'd like to believe the café au lait and beignets side of vacations will always be more satisfying and alluring than technology and virtual reality. The following pages accent my belief. In this book, we'll acknowledge and learn about the new travel technologies, but we'll always return to our needs as human beings. In other words, we'll supplement all the *high tech* glitz with an equal, or sometimes greater, dose of *high touch*. Welcome to the joy and excitement of a perfect vacation. Sit back, relax, turn the page, and let's get started.

Acknowledgments

Every book is the result of a collaborative effort. No man is an island, and no man can write a book without the help of a great many people. I wish I could acknowledge everyone I've had the joy of meeting in the travel industry. Unfortunately, I was never very good with names, and I doubt if you would really enjoy reading through several thousand names of folks you've never met.

To my mentor and idol, Fritz Wanlund: your humility will never let you admit the profound influence you've had on my career. Except for the night we passed out on the Dorado, Puerto Rico beach in our rented tuxes with a bottle of champagne tucked under each arm as the tide was coming in, I've always thought your advice was dead-solid-perfect. I still find myself asking, "Now how would Fritz handle this?"

Thank you to the entire Alpha Books staff, especially Tom Godfrey and Faithe Wempen. Tom, you put a great deal of faith (no pun intended) and trust into a "maiden voyage." You also kept my confidence high when I needed the extra boost. Faithe, your steadiness and clear vision always provided the beacon I needed to find the end of the project. Michelle Shaw and San Dee Phillips—your combined senses of humor triggered a couple of aftershocks here in southern California.

There are also all my friends who make TRAVA (our Chicago-area travel agency) and TRAMS (Lee Rosen's Los Angeles-based travel software developer) such great places to work and play. Without all of you picking up the slack, I would never have had the time to begin, let alone finish, this book. Thank you all.

My parents, Gene and Eleanor, deserve an award. They've spent years wondering where on earth their son could be now. They're getting even by frequently firing up the motor home, disconnecting their cellular phone, and leaving Indianola, Iowa for parts unknown. Thank you Mom and Dad for your steadfast love and support. Happy trails to you.

"Thank you" doesn't even dent the tab I have running with Diane. She's that remarkable combination of best friend, lover, and business partner. Honey, without you, none of this would mean a thing.

Part 1
The Perfect Vacation for You

Whatever you thought about vacations before you bought this book, be prepared to change. We're going back to basics and learning how to achieve vacation nirvana: a state of perfect blessedness to a Buddhist.

How are we going to do that? Good question. We're going to follow the very simple formula of finding out what you want from a vacation and help you plan to do a lot of that; while at the same time, we're going to find out what you don't like about vacations and eliminate those activities altogether.

Pretty cool, if we can pull it off, eh? Well, let's get started. Fasten your seat belts, and keep your arms and legs inside the vehicle; it's going to be a thrill a minute.

YEAH!

Chapter 1

Vacation 101— Are You Ready for Some Fun?

In This Chapter

➤ What is a vacation?

➤ Unraveling the mysteries of a vacation

➤ Getting started

➤ Finding help

This chapter introduces you to the concept of "the perfect vacation" and how going on one can enrich your life, make you more popular, and prevent tooth decay. Okay, calm down—the part about enriching your life isn't really relevant. This chapter lays the foundation for planning your perfect vacation. We're not going to get into any heavy theory (astral projection, magic carpet travel, demolition derbies) in this chapter. Here, we're just getting started.

What Is a Vacation?

Have you ever thought about the similarities between the words vacancy and vacation? I'm not sure what this really means, I just want to give you something to mull over.

Let's begin with what a vacation is supposed to do: give you a break from your normal day-to-day activities. This could mean a break from your job, school, children, or washing your dog (you'd have to have a fairly big and dirty dog, however, for it to need washing every day).

If you're not familiar with vacations, you may be thinking that a coffee break could be termed a vacation. You'd be right, in a sense. It's just a little difficult to visit the bridges of Madison County or jet to New York to catch a couple of Broadway plays during your coffee break. (Although I once had an employee who could have taken in at least one play on her break time—don't worry, Julie, I'm not talking about you.)

For our purposes, a vacation is a break from your normal activities long enough for you to pack a bag and go someplace.

Get Ready, Get Set, Go Somewhere

If you bought this book—I'm going out on a limb here—you are probably interested in going somewhere. You may not know where, or when, or why (sounds like my journalism professor), but you probably have the urge to travel. Well, you're in the right place. We're going to talk about vacation travel and all of its components.

Most people I meet who are relatively new to this vacation travel thing are slightly apprehensive. You may be, too, and that's just fine. When you finish reading this book, you'll be ready to get up and go. All you have to realize is that most of your apprehension is fear. Not the kind of spine-tingling fear you feel when you watch a scary movie, but the kind of fear you experience during your first day at a new job. Everyone around you seems to know what they're doing, and you're afraid you may look silly or incompetent because you don't have a clue.

We'll spend some time making you feel competent and comfortable so you can get a clue and move beyond your initial fear. One of my jobs as a travel professional is to replace your fear with sheer excitement. I want you to get so full of anticipation about wading in the Gulf of Mexico or golfing at PGA West that you have a few sleepless nights just before you leave on your vacation.

Beware—I love to travel, and I fully intend to share my affliction with you. If you don't want to know my passion for traveling, put this book down, go out and buy another bag of chips, rent a couple of movies, and continue your project of creating a permanent impression of your body's frame in your favorite couch or chair. Otherwise, you'd better start packing, because we're getting ready to go.

Vacations Are Easy—Just Use Common Sense

Unfortunately, a number of travelers like to play the, "I've Got a Secret" game. This means they know just enough about travel to be dangerous. To avoid looking like a bag of hot air, they try to tell you how difficult or complicated traveling can be.

You've probably encountered these folks at cocktail parties. It seems that after a drink or two, they take great pride in telling you about the time and effort they put into finding that elusive VXAP21NR airfare to Boise last summer. They relish taking the simple and converting it into the complex. Usually, they do this because they want to hide the fact that they're not too well-versed in travel.

By the time you're done with this book, you'll be able to turn to them and say, "Oh, I got the same fare from my travel agent. It took less that eight seconds for her SABRE airline reservation computer to evaluate more than 3,000 fare combinations and give me the three lowest-priced flights. We used a new software product developed by SABRE called Bargain Finder. How did you find your VXAP21NR fare? I hope you didn't spend a great deal of time calling each one of the airlines directly. You know those fares change so quickly, the lowest ones might be there and gone between your second and third phone call." Congratulations, at this point, you've just won the first round of "I've Got a Secret." And if you'll stand over here, Monty will tell you what you've won!

Top Ten Vacation Myths

10. **You Have to Travel Great Distances**   One of the best vacations I've ever had was a trip to Boston. I stayed at the stately Copley Plaza, walked the Freedom Walk, and explored the Harvard campus. Since I lived in Foxboro, Massachusetts, my trip consumed less than 50 miles.

9. **Travel Agents Charge Lots of Money**   Sometimes, travel agents request a service charge when their expenses (telephone, fax, delivery, and so on) are not covered by the commission they earn from airlines, cruise lines, and tour operators. This charge is usually less than $35, if it exists at all.

8. **You Have to Spend Lots of Money**   Many times, you will have a richer vacation experience if you stay in less expensive Bed & Breakfasts and buy provisions at grocery stores for a wine and cheese picnic in a park.

7. **You Must Find the Best Deal**   I've never seen any correlation between the cheapest vacation and the best vacation. Many times, the "cheapest deal" ends up costing a fortune due to all the service charges, taxes, and fees that are not included.

6. **You Have to Stay in the Best Hotels**   Lavish hotels can be fun and make you feel very pampered, but we tend to remember what we did, what we saw, and where we ate much more vividly than where we slept.

5. **Any Hotel Will Do**   On the other hand, a great vacation can be ruined by a bad hotel experience. If the hotel isn't safe and clean, it's no bargain at any price.

4. **Reservations Restrict Your Freedom**   Quite the opposite. Reservations enhance your freedom because you have the comfort of exploring your destination without worrying about where you're going to eat or sleep. Plus, with proper advance notice, reservations can be changed to fit your wants and desires.

3. **You Have to Schedule Every Waking Moment**   Part of a good vacation is doing nothing. Too many reservations can be confining and cause you to cut short some pleasurable experiences.

2. **Tourists Are Welcome Everywhere**   Unfortunately, tourists have earned bad reputations. It happens when they forget they are guests and expect, or worse yet, demand that someone pay attention to them.

1. **Nothing Will Go Wrong**   Murphy's Law was created for vacations. Our goal is to plan a vacation so that when things change, they are not considered "going wrong," but rather going in an interesting direction. Changed plans often lead to the most memorable and pleasant experiences of a vacation.

Your First Step to a Perfect Vacation

You've probably heard the old adage, "Every great journey begins with a single step." Well, that applies to vacation travel and is the key to planning your perfect vacation. Too many people grab the first vacation opportunity that lands in their mailbox or that flashes across their TV screen during a Wrestling Mania commercial. Unfortunately, these impulse vacation buys will generate little satisfaction.

Buying a vacation travel package without some planning is like calling a department store and ordering a new dress or business suit without ever going to the store, looking in a catalog, or knowing your correct size. You'll probably get your clothing, but your chances of receiving much satisfaction from this transaction are slim. Disappointment is inevitable when the "first step" is replaced by a "giant leap."

First steps are not only a good place to start, they are the only place to start. I remember taking a much-needed vacation to the Colorado Rockies. I had just finished a very difficult period at work. I had had several major projects with tight deadlines staring me in the face and had been working more than 16 hours every day just to stay current. I didn't just *want* to take some time off after the last deadline; I *needed* some time off.

As soon as my last deadline passed, I stuffed some clothes in a bag and pointed the car toward Colorado. That was my fateful giant leap, and every step after that was just a little more disastrous. To shorten a long and painful story, working 16 hours a day was much more pleasant than this impromptu vacation. In fact, it was a disaster and a huge waste of time and money.

My first mistake was going to the Rockies in March without a reservation. Sure, I knew it was ski season, but I also figured there had to be rooms available. There were, but I quickly learned the difference between available and desirable.

Next, I discovered that I had packed—no, that's not the right word, stuffed is better—all the wrong clothes in a duffel bag. Don't ask me what I was thinking, but I had eight dress shirts, two ties, a pair of shorts, and an ample supply of socks that matched nothing, including each other. This wardrobe did not earn me "best dressed" honors in Aspen.

Finally, I had left in such a hurry that I had no time to make arrangements for someone to care for my cat, Fishbreath. I figured, no problem, he can travel with me. We quickly learned that Aspen is pretty boring for a feline so he decided to amuse himself by shredding the drapes in my less-than-desirable room.

I learned a big lesson from this trip. I'm still a very carefree, spontaneous traveler, but I now know to plan a few key elements in advance so my desire for spontaneity can be fed by opportunities rather than necessities.

If you've ever experienced a vacation that didn't quite meet your expectations, the culprit can always be traced to how you got started—that first step. You may think the trip was ruined by the canceled flight, the rude car rental agent, or the over-sold hotel and the corresponding night you spent in the rental car. Certainly, these events played a significant role in the quality of your vacation, but the effect of every one of them could have been softened with a little contingency planning.

I'm reminded of a seven-day fall foliage tour we planned throughout four New England states. As you may know, these tours are very popular. For a few weeks each autumn, every hotel, every restaurant, and every motorcoach in New England is sold out. The key to planning a successful fall foliage vacation is gaining a firm understanding of Murphy's Law about things going wrong at the worst possible time and then planning activities to take advantage of misfortune. I believe this has been called the "lemons into lemonade" principle.

We knew something was going to go wrong on this trip and if this unknown disastrous event caused us to get off our schedule, we could miss a lunch or dinner and have a full motorcoach of unhappiness. So we practiced a little PPA (Potential Problem Analysis). PPA means sitting around a table and writing answers to the question, "Okay, what's the worst thing that could possibly happen?" Once your list is fairly extensive, you need to ask yourself, "Okay, and what will I do if this happens?"

With our fall foliage trip, one of our PPAs was that the motorcoach was going to break down. Our plan to address this problem was to pack red and white checkered table cloths, wicker-covered Chianti bottles, candles, cheese, wine, and fruit every morning before the motorcoach departed. If we had a breakdown (the bus, not us), we'd transform the bus into an Italian bistro and have a "Motorcoach Is Broken Down Party."

Well, as Murphy predicted, it happened. Actually, not quite as we'd anticipated, but close enough. Instead of breaking down, we managed to get the motorcoach stuck in the mud (don't ask) and needed to find two very big tow trucks to fix the problem.

When we realized these 619 tow trucks weren't available at your regular neighborhood gas station, we started the "Motorcoach Is Stuck in the Mud" party. It was such a success that no one complained about missing their lobster dinner that evening. We continue to be asked for information about that broken-down motorcoach Italian café tour. It's the first time fall foliage has ever played second fiddle to a bunch of empty Chianti bottles stuffed with candles.

Finding Help (Not the Psychiatric Kind)

Planning is easy if you find someone to help you. You need someone with experience and a keen understanding of what you want. You must be careful not to confuse what you want from a vacation with what is available. Travel vendors spend millions every year for printed, exquisite brochures. These are designed to sell and promote a company's vacation product. They give you lots of facts and features embedded in flowery language.

What they don't give you is a way of understanding how you will benefit if you take this tour, that package, or this cruise. All of us travel for different reasons; we all have different tastes. The most important first step in finding the right vacation for you is finding some good advice to go along with the pretty brochures and slick advertisements.

Travel professionals and other travelers are your best sources of help as long as you feel they are telling you what *you* will find enjoyable. If they constantly focus on the features of a vacation that were enjoyable to them, move on and find better advice.

Chapter 2 will help you pinpoint what you really want from a vacation. It'll help you take the right (or left if you're so inclined) first step of your journey.

The Least You Need to Know

Planning and taking a vacation is exciting and not too difficult if you approach it carefully. Just remember, you've worked very hard to earn the break from your normal routine. Now you want to invest some of your hard-earned money in an activity that should give you pleasant memories for many years to come. The difference between acquiring pleasant memories and acquiring nightmares is a fine line, and your best insurance policy is good advice from people who know what you want.

> ➤ Plan to learn enough about traveling to develop a passion for it, because once you discover how fun travel can really be, you'll want to do a lot more of it.

> ➤ Don't feel like you have to spend a lot of money, because the best vacations are measured by the memories, not the budget.

> ➤ Never buy a vacation under pressure, or you'll wind up somewhere you never wanted to be for far too long.

> ➤ It's not a good idea to hop into your car and drive to the Rocky Mountains without even a map. Planning is important. It helps you choose a vacation that's just right—maybe even perfect—for you.

> ➤ Practice PPA (Potential Problem Analysis) to gain the confidence to handle—even thrive on—the unexpected.

Chapter 2

So Many Vacations... So Little Time

In This Chapter

➤ Select the right advice

➤ It's your vacation; do what you want

➤ Is the price right?

➤ Evaluating your vacation needs

So You Want to Go on Vacation?

Outwardly, you've made the decision to do something different for your next vacation. Inwardly, you haven't got a clue where to begin, and the last thing you want to do is make a mess of your vacation. Don't worry, I have these same fears when it comes to hanging wallpaper. I know what I want, but I don't have a clue as to how to go about getting it done.

This is our mind's natural response to any situation where the number of questions outdistance the number of answers. Just like I need someone (any volunteers?) to help me select appropriate wall paper, determine how much to buy, tell me which tools to get... ah forget it; I'd rather think about your vacation. We'll spend this chapter showing you ways to sift through all the vacation ideas and pounce on the one that is just right for you.

Part of the challenge of planning the perfect vacation involves filtering the advice you receive from others. You know, the friend at work who insists, "Oh, you simply have to go to the Whatchamacallit Museum in Toledo. Their collection of bone china refrigerator magnets is awesome." Or your neighbors who have invited themselves over for dinner to share their special bottle of dandelion wine and their 186 slides of the butterflies they collected during their two-week stay in the Poconos.

The problem with bone china, dandelion wine, and butterflies is that they probably interest other people a lot more that they interest you. You need a plan to take everyone's vacation recommendations, and find just the one for you. Let's get started.

How to Read the Sunday Travel Section

The first principle of Sunday Travel Sections springs from a short lesson in economics. I promise this will be really short, because I'm about to tell you everything I know about the science of economics and I have an entire department of professors at the University of Kansas to verify that I know precious little about the subject.

Sunday Travel Section—Economic Principle #1

These sections exist in almost every Sunday newspaper across the United States (except *The New York Times* Travel Section and a few others) because they generate large sums of advertising revenue.

Now, armed with this solid piece of economic perspective, are you going to view the advice and suggestions found on these pages quite so seriously? Do you think they'll really tell you that their biggest advertiser's newest Hawaiian tour is a real bust? Probably not. Do you think you'll find a brutally unbiased comparison of every cruise ship sailing a Western Caribbean itinerary? Probably not. Travel writers get paid to write articles that please the editors of these travel sections, and travel editors get paid to please the advertisers that pay big bucks to support the newspaper.

This doesn't mean you should never read the Sunday Travel Section ever again. It just means you should read it to get vacation suggestions, not to make your decisions. You should also read the advertisements. If someone decided to spend a bunch of money to buy the space for the ad, they probably have a pretty good suggestion.

Should I Cruise, Tour, Fly, Drive, Trek, or Just Stay Home?

Most newspaper travel sections give you enough vacation suggestions. The challenge is finding the right one for you. The first skill you'll need is a vacation advertisement budget monitor. If you haven't already noticed, most ads for travel products focus on price. That's because you and I have told the media researchers that price is the most important factor in choosing a vacation. We just don't want to overpay.

The travel industry has only itself to blame for our concern about overpaying. We've all experienced or heard the stories about two people on a _____ (fill in the blank with plane, train, cruise, or tour) who started discussing when and where they purchased their trip and how much they paid. Anyone who has had this experience knows that the price they paid for their vacation probably bears little resemblance to the price paid by their seatmate. Unfortunately, the advertised price is probably different from the final amount paid. Let's look at a typical Sunday Travel Section advertisement. I'll show you what I mean.

Eight Days Waikiki—$399 or $22 Per Month

Our budget-oriented mind thinks, "Wow! This is great. We can instantly feel the gentle trade breezes tugging at the napkin beneath the tropical fruit drink the waiter just delivered to our lounge chair anchored in the soft warm sand of Waikiki beach. And all this for $22 per month. Let's go!" This sounds like it could be cheaper than staying at home. Maybe, at these prices, I could work two weeks and vacation the other fifty.

Not so fast. Let's learn this together. Repeat after me, "I will never get too excited about an advertised price for a vacation until I've read the small print." Now, just for practice, here's the small print that went with the $22 per month Waikiki ad.

Rates are per person, based on double occupancy. Prices subject to change and to Holiday/seasonal supplements. Availability may be limited and some restrictions may apply. Call for applicable dates. Prices do not include a $12 per person departure tax or any Passenger Facility Charges that may apply. Financing charges are additional.

Let's study this a little closer. What's this "double occupancy" thing? How much is it if I want to go by myself? Or, what if there are five of us? Do we have to buy two double occupancies and one single? Good questions.

Next, "prices are subject to change." That's fine. Every advertiser has to say that because their attorney makes them, but what about this "Holiday and seasonal supplements" stuff? For starters, this can add hundreds to the advertised price.

The next one is my favorite, "Availability may be limited." Of course, it's limited. What are they going to do, strap someone on the wing when all the inside seats are taken? Maybe they'll attach two big tow trucks to each end of the hotel when it gets full and stretch it just enough to accommodate the extra guests. I don't think so.

Prices do not include departure tax and Passenger Facility Charges. This, folks, is our government at work, even while we're trying to vacation. If you want a jolt of reality, take a look at your next airline ticket. The total taxes on a domestic airline ticket are frequently more than the commission earned by the travel agent that issued the ticket. We're all fairly accustomed to paying sales taxes. You know, that 4 to 8 percent that's tacked on to a purchase at the cash register. Well, for starters, taxes on tourism purchases start at about 10% and go up from there.

So why are the advertised prices so much different from the actual purchase price? It's because rooms, seats, cabins, cars (you name it) are subject to yield management pricing. This is our second (and last, thank goodness) little economic principle.

Travel Pricing—Economic Principle #2

Empty airplane seats, hotel rooms, and cruise cabins do not generate any revenue. Some revenue is better than none. Ergo, price the travel product as high as you can without losing the sale.

The fancy name for this brilliant piece of logic is, "Yield Management Pricing," and it is responsible for these irritating conversations between seatmates concerning who paid how much for what.

> Just Say No! Good travel agents are trained to automatically reject the first few prices offered by the reservation agent for the cruise line, the tour operator, the car rental company, or the hotel if they sense the travel supplier has more capacity than they have customers. We teach our agents the phrase, "Do you have anything less expensive? I'd like to give you this booking, but I know my client won't pay that much."

These conversations can lead to some rather comical outcomes, like the business traveler who received the "Honeymoon Package" because one of our agents kept asking for a lower rate. Not only did he receive a rate that was less that half of the originally quoted rate, but he was upgraded to a suite, and received a complimentary bottle of champagne from the hotel's general manager. Unfortunately, he was traveling alone and was on a business trip.

Now, let's try another travel ad's small print. Remember, focus on what you think you'll actually pay rather than the lure of the romantic copy. Here's an ad from the same travel section as the previous example.

Seven Glorious Days Sailing the Caribbean—from $740

Double occupancy. $740 per person based on calculated 2 for 1 discount, stateroom category "M," on the 2/18 sailing. Airfare not included. Available to residents of and travel agents in Southern CA. Not combinable with other offers and does not apply to groups. Port charges $102.

First of all, that $102 port charge should jump right off the page. Without reading any further, you know we're dealing with an $842 vacation rather than a $740 one. Next, you might have noticed that airfare is not included, and since this ad appeared in a Southern California newspaper and the cruise sails from Ft. Lauderdale, we have an additional expense for airline tickets or a four-day drive. Also notice that this offer is available only for category M on the February 18th sailing.

Now you're starting to get the picture. Just as "All that glitters is not gold," all prices in travel advertisements are meant to be increased.

How Do I Sort Through All This Clutter?

The first step is understanding what you want and how much you're willing to spend to get it. We've just learned a little about how to translate an advertised price into reality. Next, we're going to learn how to translate our own expectations into reality. When we're finished, we'll have a custom-tailored vacation that gives us exactly what we want at a price we can afford. The only surprises will be the pleasant ones we find in every travel experience.

Flying May Be Cheaper Than You Think

Thanks to Herb Kelleher, Chairman, CEO, and President of Southwest Airlines, you can fly from Los Angeles to Tucson for two (makes sense, otherwise they would have named it Oneson) for about $120, stay at AAA-rated Smuggler's Inn for about $66.50 (including tax) a night, and rent a car for about $24 (including tax) a day and you have a nice weekend vacation for about $300 plus meals and entertainment.

Similar bargains are available in other cities served by Southwest. Southwest has a backlog of city fathers who are begging them to begin flying to their city. The additional tourism revenue generated by inexpensive airfare is a big boost to communities like Tucson, Tulsa, Little Rock, Corpus Christi, and others.

Dreams, Wishes, and Goals

Although the price of the vacation is at the top of most everyone's list of priorities, it is not the only criterion for planning the perfect vacation. We need to understand what it is that we want from our vacation—not what the travel editors or advertisers tell us we want, but what we truly want. Once we know that, we can really begin to have some fun.

Although the following questions look like a test, they're really not. It's just a survey to help you understand your vacation expectations. Please complete the survey below by placing a check mark in the box that best describes your preferences (1 meaning most describes you and 4 meaning least describes you):

1   2   3   4

❑   ❑   ❑   ❑   I love to escape on vacation: no phones, no newspapers, no television.

❑   ❑   ❑   ❑   The idea of sitting on a beach bores me to tears; I have to keep moving for fear I'll miss something important around the corner.

❑   ❑   ❑   ❑   The more people I meet on vacation, the better; I love the excitement generated by groups of people.

❑   ❑   ❑   ❑   I'd be happy with no set plans, sleeping under the stars if I have to, just to be in touch with nature.

❑   ❑   ❑   ❑   Vacation means luxury to me. I want all the comforts of home and more: the best restaurants, the best entertainment, the best accommodations.

❑   ❑   ❑   ❑   I'd rather drive than fly to see each site along the way. Getting there is most of the fun.

❑   ❑   ❑   ❑   The thought of hot sun, soft sand, and cool drinks sounds perfect to me.

❑   ❑   ❑   ❑   I don't want to think while I'm on vacation. I just want to get up and have my entire day planned for me.

❑   ❑   ❑   ❑   I'm into sports; the more physical my vacation, the better. Hiking, skiing, running, and jogging are my way of releasing stress and relaxing.

❑   ❑   ❑   ❑   As long as the kids are occupied and happy, I don't care where we are; that's what's most important to me.

❑   ❑   ❑   ❑   This is my time and I like relaxing days and active nights. I want nightclubs, theater, gourmet dining, and dancing until dawn.

❑   ❑   ❑   ❑   I love history; it's important to see the things that made our country great and relive those famous historical moments.

❑   ❑   ❑   ❑   Finding a hidden treasure is what excites me most. A little-known get-a-way or best-kept secret that I discovered and can call mine. It doesn't have to be glamorous, just warm and friendly.

❑   ❑   ❑   ❑   Vacation is really about all of us. We have to have something to appeal to each one of our needs. Adult activity as well as something for the kids. It's important to have a good balance.

17

In Chapter 3, I'll show you how to score the results of this profile. This will give you a better understanding of what you want from a vacation and how much it is going to cost. Armed with that information, we'll be able to begin constructing your perfect vacation.

The Least You Need to Know

➤ Your vacation needs are different from those of your neighbors or your friends at work.

➤ The advertised price probably needs a few things added to it before it begins to reflect reality.

➤ No one knows what you want better than you.

➤ Once you understand what you want from a vacation, there are plenty of people who can help you with the arrangements.

Chapter 3

Interpreting Your Dream (Vacation, That Is)

In This Chapter

➤ Scoring the Vacation Profile Survey from Chapter 2

➤ Activity level: White-water rafting, or vegging on the beach?

➤ Structure: Minute-by-minute itinerary, or just wingin' it?

➤ Interaction: Make new friends, or bond with your loved ones?

➤ Understanding the importance of a vacation budget

If you've been following along up to this point, you are probably thinking: *Oh boy, can't wait to find out the results of the survey I just took!* If you flipped to this page by chance, you're probably wondering, *"What survey?"* If you've been having this really interesting dream and you're hoping someone's going to tell you what it means, you're in the wrong book. We're interpreting dream vacations here, not dreams.

If you didn't complete the little survey at the end of Chapter 2, what follows will make about as much sense as a calculator in an abacus factory. On the other hand, if you want to just make up a score from the survey, you'll be about as accurate as most vacationers who haven't thought much about where they want to go.

And the Survey Says...

If you began visualizing different vacation scenes while you answered the survey, you're on the right track. The survey is a little tool to start you thinking. These questions are similar to the ones a professional travel agent asks. We're beginning to determine your vacation profile.

I know a vacation profile sounds really scientific. If you'd feel more comfortable, go ahead and slip on your white lab coat and grab your fancy clipboard with the stopwatch. You really don't need these props if you're anxious to get started, or if your best lab coat is at the cleaners. What you *do* need is a desire to know which vacation format is most compatible with you.

Don't worry; this is going to be fun. To get you started, we're going to arrange your survey answers into three categories: activity, structure, and interaction. These categories represent the three major components of a vacation.

The Activity Component

The activity component of your vacation determines how much motion or commotion you want during your vacation. Do you want to wake up early and go, go, go? Or do you want to sleep late, spend some serious pool time, and then take an afternoon nap before doing some leisure reading?

As with the other two components, there is no right or wrong. Depending on your schedule during the past year and even your current mood, you may be ready for a highly active or a rather sedate vacation. Just because this profile suggests one level of activity over another, doesn't mean all future vacations have to be founded on the same activity component.

Normally, I enjoy a very active vacation. Seeing, doing, playing golf, trying a new restaurant for dinner, and staying at a different hotel every night is usually fine with me. This year, though, I opted for a different activity component. I wanted to practice and perfect my two-toed sloth imitation. One week in a deluxe open-air villa with no telephones, no fax machines, no televisions, planted in the middle of the Costa Rican jungle overlooking the Pacific sunsets matched my vacation needs. It was consistent with my profile at that time. Next year, I'll try something with more activity.

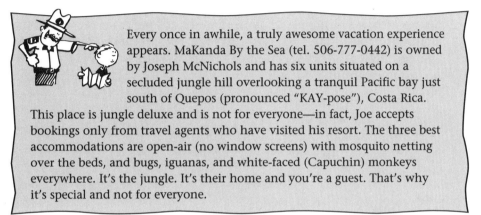

Every once in awhile, a truly awesome vacation experience appears. MaKanda By the Sea (tel. 506-777-0442) is owned by Joseph McNichols and has six units situated on a secluded jungle hill overlooking a tranquil Pacific bay just south of Quepos (pronounced "KAY-pose"), Costa Rica. This place is jungle deluxe and is not for everyone—in fact, Joe accepts bookings only from travel agents who have visited his resort. The three best accommodations are open-air (no window screens) with mosquito netting over the beds, and bugs, iguanas, and white-faced (Capuchin) monkeys everywhere. It's the jungle. It's their home and you're a guest. That's why it's special and not for everyone.

Let's score your activity level. In the table below, record the numeric answers you checked on the survey in Chapter 2.

Survey Questions	Your Numeric Responses	
#1	+	_____
#2	–	_____
#6	–	_____
#7	+	_____
#9	–	_____
Total		_____

Next, total the numeric response column, paying careful attention to the plus and minus signs. It's okay if the result is a negative number. Also, don't feel bad if you need a calculator to complete this task. I've always considered addition and subtraction to be higher math, which explains a lot about the condition of my checkbook.

If your score was lower than –10 or higher than +5, you goofed. Try again and pay careful attention to the plus and minus signs.

In general, a lower score means you like less movement and commotion in your vacation. A –5 or less indicates you would be happiest with a one-destination, package-type vacation. If your score settles in around the –10 range, you not only want a one-destination package; you also want a hotel with 24-hour room service.

As your score increases, you want to select destinations for their sightseeing or theme park attractions, but you would be more comfortable staying at one hotel and not having to keep packing and unpacking. If your score is between –5 and 0, a cruise would be compatible. Scores above zero mean that you must have ancestors belonging to nomadic tribes. You like to go, rest for a few moments, and then go again. Frequent short vacations or extended tours covering an entire region are right up your alley.

Whatever your score, you now have an idea about how much activity you desire from your next vacation. This is an important beginning to planning the perfect vacation. But wait—we're not done. Activity analysis (sounds impressive doesn't it?) is just the first step. Next we move to structure.

The Structure Component

Yes, I know, "The Structure Component" sounds pretty threatening. Like we're going to study "The Structure Component" of an atom. Don't worry, not in this book. That's my next book, *The Complete Idiot's Guide to Splitting Atoms and Hairs*. In this case, "The Structure Component" (isn't that fun to say?) refers to the organization of your vacation.

If you knew me, you'd know that it's ludicrous for me to even type the word "organized," let alone use it in a sentence. However, in the vacation business, miracles happen every day, and here we're going to gauge the amount of organization you want in your vacation.

As you did with your activity level, complete the following table with your responses to the corresponding questions in your Vacation Profile Survey in Chapter 2.

Survey Questions	Your Numeric Responses
#4	+ _____
#11	+ _____
#12	– _____
Total	_____

Total your numeric responses. Remember to pay attention to the plus and minus signs. If you don't, they can easily get their feelings hurt, so please don't ignore them.

The range of acceptable answers for "The Structure Component" is from –2 to +7. If your total is lower or higher, please take a minute and recalculate. If your total is between these two numbers, you're in the game and ready to play.

If your total is about +2, you're fairly normal. Well, at least as far as your need for structure and organization in a vacation goes. A "Plus Two," as we like to call them in the ol' vacation laboratory, likes to balance planned activities with sufficient free time. "Planned activities" probably means you have an airline ticket and hotel reservations for the duration of your trip. You probably also have an "idea" of where you would like to eat at least a few meals and what you would like to see or do.

When your score hovers around the –2 area, you don't have a clue where you're going, what you're doing, or where you're staying. And the best part is, you like it that way. Brings back memories. Watching the sunrise through the steam of one of those hot and humid Kansas mornings, I decided to brush my teeth and point my pickup east (easy to find because of the sunrise) and head for a little town called Woodstock, New York. I didn't have a clue (still don't), but I had a great time. That's a pure "Minus Two" thing to do.

So what does a +7 want in a perfect vacation? We're talking about a structural and organizational frenzy. These folks want breakfast at 7:45 a.m., whale watching at 9:00 a.m., and dinner at Admiral Risty's at 8:00 p.m. They know what they want. They want it all planned and buttoned down (a technical term, I believe), and they want to savor every moment of their perfect vacation knowing that everything is prearranged. Cruises and escorted tours appeal to the "Plus Seven."

What do you think happens when a "Minus Two" and a "Plus Seven" try to take a trip together? Nothing short of nuclear fission, which is an interaction of sorts, and that leads us to our next component.

The Interaction Component

As my cardiologist, Dr. Allan Lew, likes to say when he's reviewing my stress test results, "I don't know exactly what this means, but we'll take a closer look at it because it's really fascinating." I feel the same about this Interaction Component. It's truly interesting, but I'm not really sure what it means.

Anyway, you paid for this book (I hope) and I'm here to give you your money's worth. We'll give this our best shot and try to figure out what this means for you. So, out with your pencils and complete the following matrix. Since this is the third time we've done this little exercise, I don't expect you want me to go through the instructions again.

Survey Questions	Your Numeric Responses
#3	– _____
#8	+ _____
#10	– _____
#14	– _____
Total	_____

The acceptable range for your total is between –11 and +1. If your total is lower than –11, higher than +1, or contains a decimal point, you need to try again. Don't hurry; we'll wait until you're finished.

If your total Interaction Component is a "Minus Five," that means you're smack dab in the middle. You probably figured that out without my help, didn't you? It also indicates you want to meet others when you vacation. That's part of the lure and pleasure a vacation holds for you.

A low number, such as a –11, doesn't mean you're antisocial. It simply means your vacation gives you a chance for a little peace and quiet or that this is a good time to bond with your family.

A high value, if you can consider +1 to be a big number, means you travel to broaden your

Have you ever thought of whom you'd like to travel with on your vacation? An Amtrak survey shows Oprah Winfrey, Kevin Costner, Erma Bombeck, Charles Kuralt, Cindy Crawford, Demi Moore, and Eddie Murphy as top favorites. Amtrak also found that 43% of Americans want to travel with a good conversationalist. In addition to maintaining a good conversation, this person had better smell good and be upbeat and peppy.

network of acquaintances. Meeting and getting to know new people is just as important to you as seeing new sights.

Putting It All Together

Now that you're armed with activity, structure, and interaction values, what the heck are you going to do? As you've probably figured, good numbers do not a good vacation make. We need to apply this information to the vast variety of vacation opportunities. That's what the remainder of this book is about.

Your newly acquired Vacation Profile Component Values have another use. They make for great lunch or cocktail party conversation. Just imagine how amazed your co-workers will be when you tell them you're making plans to attend Macy's Thanksgiving Day Parade in New York City. Especially when you tell them this is all due to your "Plus Five" activity component, your "Plus One" interactive value, and your low requirement for organization and structure.

Gotta Pay the Piper

If you're really astute or an accountant, you've already noticed that question #5 was not included in the Activity, Structure, and Interaction Analysis. It wasn't that we harbored any deep anger or hatred for #5; we just wanted to give it special emphasis.

Question #5 gives you an idea about how much you want to pamper yourself. It's okay to want to spoil yourself a little while you're on vacation. A splurge can be fun. On the other hand, some of the best vacations I've organized have been produced on a very tight budget.

The most important message here is to take a very realistic look at the funds you have to invest in your vacation and don't overspend. You don't have to. Great vacations are measured by how they make you feel, not by how much they cost.

Different Strokes for Different Folks

Now that you know how to analyze and determine what you want from a vacation, you can begin finding out what your vacation-mates want. Compromise is an acquired trait, and it reaches a pinnacle of importance when a family plans a vacation.

Just think what happens when a low-activity, high-structure traveler finds himself in the same hotel room with a high-activity, low-structure partner. It's not pretty.

The place to compare your vacation needs and wants with your family's needs and wants is in the comfort of your living room. When you're in an inflatable raft hurtling through the frigid white-water rapids, it's a little too late to begin explaining that you really wanted a beach, a palm tree, and a good book. Makes it easier to understand why some families opt for separate vacations, doesn't it?

The Least You Need to Know

➤ What you want from a vacation changes as your needs change.

➤ Knowing what you desire for a specific level of activity, interaction, and structure will help you plan a perfect vacation.

➤ Going around saying that you have a Plus Two Activity Component will baffle your friends and irritate complete strangers.

➤ Getting a family to agree to a vacation that satisfies every member's need for the three basic vacation components may require a diplomacy mission from the UN.

Chapter 4

Coming Up with the Plan

In This Chapter

➤ Discovering your "vacation purpose"

➤ Putting the "R & R" in relaxation and recreation

➤ When a vacation incorporates a special event

➤ Mixing friends, relatives, and vacations

My friend and business partner, Lee Rosen, credits his substantial success to a very simple axiom: "If you want to make something happen, write it down." This simple act helps your mind define the goal and begin arranging steps to accomplish the desired results. Without this definition, our minds deal in generalities and generally nothing gets accomplished.

The "write it down" technique applies to personal goals just as readily as business goals. One of your goals could be to cruise Alaska's inner passage next year; or drive to San Antonio, show the kids the Alamo, and explain its role in forming the southern boundary of the United States; or to make a weekend getaway to Memphis and look for Elvis (okay, now settle down; I too believe he's still around—I was sure I saw him at the Memphis airport a year or so ago eating donuts near a pay phone).

In this chapter, we're going to take the likes and dislikes you discovered in Chapter 4, put them in writing, and attach a purpose. Yup, I said purpose. You know, a reason for going on vacation. The best answer to the question, "Why?" The feeling you want to have when you return home. All of these things contribute to your vacation's purpose.

We'll wait a few moments before getting started so you can find a sheet of paper and a pencil. A crayon will do, but you have to write really big letters, otherwise they all smush together (technical term). Crayons are also good for creating notes of apology. How can you get mad at a spouse who leaves you a hastily scrawled note in crayon saying, "Sorry honey, broke your favorite vase. Gotta go bowling. I'll be home early," followed by a big, red, hand-drawn crayon heart? Some things a word processor will never replace.

Okay, did we stall long enough? You've got your paper and writing instrument? Here we go....

We're Off to Find a Purpose

Of all the ingredients used to cook up a perfect vacation, none is more important and more frequently overlooked than purpose. That "why" thing? If you ask most people to think about the causes for their disappointment with a vacation, they'll tell you they didn't get what they expected. The hotel didn't come close to resembling the brochure photographs; they just weren't ready for all the homeless people sleeping in Jackson Square across from the White House; the weather was miserable. Nobody told us it was too cold to sit by the pool in Las Vegas in March.

The prescription to prevent vacation disappointment is a clearly written purpose. Something that says, "Here's what we want from our vacation and here's why we're going". Otherwise, how much fun can you expect to have stuffing all your comfort-of-home things (including Mr. Bear) into a 27"×20"×10" suitcase, going someplace where the water tastes funny, and you don't know anyone?

Next, we're going to look at five vacation purposes. You will undoubtedly create your own, but I find most vacations start with one of these five purposes.

According to The American Traveler Survey prepared by Plog Research, Inc. of Los Angeles, here's why vacationers vacation:

Reason	Percent Choosing
Beautiful/scenic	66
Weather/climate	63
Lots to do	48
Been there before	47
Spouse/friend wants to go there	45
Heard about it from friends	40
Very relaxing	35
Airline ticket price	35
History/educational	33
Good for family	26
Nightlife entertainment	22
Lifelong desire	18
Travel agent recommended	12
Can gamble	11
Book or novel I'm reading	6
Saw it in a movie	4
Time-share	4

Plog Research is a leading travel marketing, research, and consulting firm. The American Traveler Survey involved 13,526 U.S. travelers.

Relaxation

Many vacations have relaxation as their primary or secondary purpose. Our work ethic culture elevates the importance of balancing work with pleasure. From childhood, we've learned, "All work and no play makes Jack a dull boy." After meeting Jack, I realized no amount of play was going to help. Sometimes, dull is just dull.

If you choose relaxation as the purpose of your vacation, what you're really saying, is, "Everything I plan for this trip should be soothing, calming, and pleasurable." We all find relaxation in different activities. Some may be totally relaxed after running 10 miles, others may just be totally exhausted. To me, golfing is relaxing; to others, it is stressful competition. Some find tennis relaxing; others liken it to fighting a battle.

The point is, you will have a perfect vacation if relaxation is your purpose and you can honestly say when you return home, "Wow, I feel so relaxed. What a fantastic trip." The only way I know to achieve that result is to stop and ask yourself as you plan your vacation's itinerary, "Will this enhance or detract from my goal of total relaxation?" Obviously, you want to include those activities that enhance and exclude those that detract.

Recreation

Like relaxation, recreation is a very popular purpose for a vacation. It too can come in different shapes and sizes. The trick is to know and understand what *you* call recreation.

Entering a backgammon tournament, playing badminton with the grandchildren, and collecting shells from the beach in Sanibel can all be classified as recreational activities. For you, however, recreation may be hiking and camping in one of our National Parks, or whale watching off the coast of Maui. Only you and your travel companions can select the right type of recreation to fulfill your vacation's purpose.

Now you're probably saying, "Hey, wait just a minute. I find playing golf both relaxing and recreational." That's great, and as long as your vacation's purpose is consistent with the way you feel when you play golf, go for it. The purpose issue arises when the purpose of your vacation is to rest and relax by playing golf and you choose Palm Springs in November. Many of the courses are being reseeded at that time in preparation for winter play. Along the same lines, though, you probably would not want to plan a restful, relaxing beach vacation to Ft. Lauderdale during Spring Break.

Educational

Most of us spend a good portion of our lives trying to get out of school. Once we're out, we (for unknown reasons) spend the rest of our lives trying to become better educated. Vacations and travel are perfect vehicles to help us achieve our quest for more knowledge. If learning is your desire, then you need to select vacation destinations and activities that are compatible with this purpose.

One of the newest educational vacation trends is *ecotourism*. This type of travel implies a conscious approach to preserving the natural world and sustaining the well-being of the human cultures that inhabit it. Richard Bangs, president of Mountain Travel/Sobek, an El Cerrito, California-based, environmentally aware tour operator, says his clients are the "kinder and greener visitors who immerse themselves in the trackless travel experience and come back deeply connected, wiser and concerned, educated and motivated."

Ecotourism may involve birdwatching and nature study, or it may simply be a new style of biking, trekking, and rafting. Unlike traditional tourism, ecotourism accents the traveler's responsibility and makes sure visitors take nothing but photographs and leave nothing but footprints.

Educational travel opportunities are everywhere. Some of them are more formal than others, but then we learned in Chapter 4 that some vacationers need more structure than others. You can choose from a very diverse offering, such as spa vacations that teach heart-healthy cooking, dude ranches that let you re-enact Billy Crystal's *City Slickers* fantasy, and baseball fantasy camps that let you learn what it might have been like if the big league scout had just attended your little league games. Of course, if labor disputes continue in professional sports, you may have an opportunity to turn your educationally oriented vacation into a full-time profession.

Again, remember the importance of combining compatible vacation activities with your purpose. Blending nightclub hopping into the wee hours of the morning with your health-conscious cook-ing classes at the spa produces conflict, not vacation.

Special Events

Sometimes, the purpose of your vacation may be to attend a special event. If this is the case, make certain the activities you plan and the expectations you cultivate are compatible. I've personally witnessed several vacation disasters that could have been avoided if the travelers had reached a consensus of purpose *before* leaving. Most of these disasters stem from a small misunderstanding about time allotted for shopping and fine dining versus other activities associated with a special event like the Super Bowl. Golf clubs and honeymoons can precipitate similar results.

In cases like these, a good travel agent can save a vacation and is much less expensive than the subsequent marriage counselor.

Walt Disney World in Florida will offer a dream-come-true wedding beginning in the fall of 1995. You can be married, happily-ever-after, in their new, multi-million-dollar Fairy-Tale Pavilion—a glass-enclosed Victorian summer house built on an island in Seven Seas Lagoon with a view of Cinderella's Castle.

Disney staff will help the bride-to-be select everything from music to munchies and flowers to fantasies. Speaking about fantasies, how about the ultimate Cinderella's Ball wedding package, where the bride arrives in a glass carriage drawn by six white ponies, while a costumed fairy godmother and stepsisters mingle with your guests. Oh goody! And, as a grand finale, dessert is served in a white chocolate slipper. That's a very innovative way to keep souvenir-hunting guests from stealing the dishes. The reception is over before midnight... or else.

Visit Friends and Relatives

Of all the reasons for taking a vacation, visiting friends and relatives is the most tricky. In the travel industry, where we give everything an acronym, Visiting Friends and Relatives trips are referred to as "VFR" vacations. The reasons VFRs can be tricky is that most folks just don't know how much of Aunt Sally's hospitality they can endure. You can usually get a good clue by asking yourself, "When was the last time we visited Aunt Sally?" If the answer is calculated in decades, you may have forgotten the very good reason why you haven't been to see her.

On the other hand, many of the most pleasurable vacation memories you will ever cultivate come from reunions with family and friends. My parents travel every year to visit their college classmates and other circles of friends they've made over the years. These can be very rewarding trips if the purpose is clearly defined and the expectations are realistic.

...And There's Much, Much More

We've touched on a few of the most popular reasons for vacation travel. I hope you've written down a few thoughts as we've gone along. Remember, that's the first step to getting this planning process off to the right start. In Chapter 5, we'll explore the different formats available for your vacation and how specific formats are more compatible with specific purposes.

The Least You Need to Know

➤ Take a moment to agree, and then commit to writing down the purpose of your vacation.

➤ A disastrous vacation is usually a result of unrealistic expectations.

➤ Choose vacation activities and destinations that are compatible with your desired goals and results.

Chapter 5

Tour B or Not Tour B

More species of tours exist than orthopedic surgeons at a football game. Shakespeare immortalized the dilemma of selecting just the right tour when he couldn't decide whether to take Tour B or plan his own itinerary. Whichever choice he made, he still took a tour. Whether it was escorted, independent, or packaged, it was still a tour.

Somewhere in travel history the word "tour" received a bum rap. Folks associated it with rigid structure and the herding of cattle. If you believe this, you're missing some awesome vacation travel experiences. Plus, tours don't have to be enjoyed in groups. A fly/drive tour through California's Napa and Sonoma valleys can be enjoyed by yourself just as easily as by a family of four. Substitute a motor home for the car, and your tour group grows larger yet.

Let's explore different types of tours and see if we can give this vacation type renewed respect.

May I Escort You to Your Table?

I've traveled with escorted tour groups and I've traveled with my dog in a '57 Ford pickup. And I liked them both. Well, of course I liked my dog more than the pickup, but here I'm talking about liking the two different types of tours: escorted and independent. The stereotype of escorted tours attracting only older clientele with walkers and canes is not true. For certain types of vacations, an escorted tour is not only the recommended way to travel, it's the only way to travel.

Escorted Tours

The major benefit of an escorted tour is the tour escort. Now I know this is not a Nobel Prize winning observation, but this person makes the difference between having just *traveled* to a destination and having truly *experienced* a destination. Maybe your tour escort knows the certain part of a secluded bay that is just perfect for viewing Orca whales. Maybe he knows an off-the-beaten-path café that serves the best crab cakes you've ever tasted. Maybe she brings a rather sterile-looking civil war battlefield to life with a vivid narrative of what really happened on the very spot where you are standing and how these events shaped the outcome of the battle and forever changed the course of history. Now if this sort of insider knowledge bores you, forget an escorted tour and plow through your next vacation from beginning to end so that when it's over, you can say, "Whew! I'm glad that's over and now I can get back to work."

According to the 1994 World Travel Awards in which travel agents select the companies that deliver the best services, Tauck Tours was voted the "Top American Tour Operator." Gogo Tours and Maupintour finished second and third.

A tour guide friend of mine knew the special magic a good escort can bring to a tour group. He would spend months researching an itinerary. Once he had an idea of how the sequence of experiences should flow, he'd take the trip himself. He'd keep copious notes while interviewing bellmen, waitresses, and just about anyone else who would talk with him. He inspected countless hotel rooms, and generally immersed himself in an itinerary until he knew how to make every tour participant's vacation come alive. His clientele traveled with him wherever he went, not because he picked the most exotic destinations, but because he always gave them experiences that they could never have on their own.

I'm reminded of his Cajun Bayou Tour. He escorted his group of devotees through Cajun restaurants that ranged from five-star gourmet Creole palaces to dilapidated bayou Cajun shacks. The fact that he even located some of these treasures was worth the price of the tour. People are born, raised, married, and buried in New Orleans and Acadiana without ever experiencing these spots.

A spectacular and nearly religious experience is Alaska's aurora borealis, commonly called northern lights. I can't explain the source of this multicolored light show, but it has something to do with errant electrons and protons and the earth's gravitational field. I can tell you that the best times to view the northern lights are during the spring and the fall.

What really made his dining derbies magical was not so much the meals; while they were outstanding, the truly awesome part was arriving at each restaurant in the afternoon and meeting the chef. If you've never sat around a few *linen-free* restaurant tables during the middle of the day with several wines for tasting and an animated chef explaining his or her art, you've never been on an escorted tour. When you return to that same restaurant for your evening dinner reservation, the food tells a story and the memories last forever.

When I was at Cartan Tours, one of the largest and most respected escorted tour companies operating in Hawaii, Canada, and Mexico, we would constantly survey tour groups to determine their age and reasons for taking an escorted tour. We were continually amazed that about 10% of our Hawaii and Canadian Rockies tour participants were under the age of 25.

Cartan also enjoyed a significant number of honeymooners. When we asked these young, newly married participants why they chose an escorted tour, they unanimously agreed that they wanted every detail covered so they could enjoy each other.

Be Safe, Not Sorry

Most travelers choosing an escorted group tour for their vacation usually do so because of previous outstanding experiences. They also feel very secure traveling with a qualified escort. Would you feel comfortable white-water rafting down a strange river's rapids without an expert? How about trekking down the steep trails leading to the bottom of Arizona's Grand Canyon? Or would you feel comfortable exploring the wilds of Alaska's Denali National Park without someone to show you the way?

When we leave home, we all look for security in our new surroundings, and an escorted tour provides a high level of security.

Comfort and Convenience in the Strangest Places

No one plans to be uncomfortable or inconvenienced during their vacation. Canceled flights, oversold hotels, and rental car taxes and surcharges manage to provide ample discomfort and inconvenience. While escorted tours won't eliminate all the potential disruptions, they do make life much easier. Consider, for instance, Backroad Tours bicycling trips. Their itineraries not only include experienced escorts, they also include a van with every group. The van which carries spare bicycle parts and everyone's luggage is driven by a trained mechanic. It's also equipped with bike racks so those who find a hill just a little too steep can ride in the van and join the rest of the group at the top.

No Hidden Charges

Escorted tours include many expenses that are all too frequently overlooked when you are developing a budget for your vacation. Little things, such as gratuities for baggage handlers, waitstaff, and chamber maids, have a substantial impact on your budget. Add to these expenses the taxes, surcharges, entrance fees, and event tickets, and you can easily increase your vacation's total cost by another 20 percent.

You work hard earning your vacation dollars; you deserve to be able to plan your vacation's expenses so you can splurge a little. If your budget is blown by unexpected expenses, a carefully planned vacation can turn into a torturous nightmare. Most escorted tours are priced to include all the essentials and to avoid any potential surprises.

Making Friends and Influencing People

One of the most popular reasons for traveling is meeting people and making new friends. Structured tours provide an exceptional venue for socializing. Since tours also tend to attract people with similar interests, you generally meet people with interests similar to yours. For instance, a four-day golf tour of the best courses along Mississippi's gulf coast is probably going to attract more golfers than cricket enthusiasts. Just as a tour of New York City's rock music haunts will attract more Guns 'n' Roses fans than New York Philharmonic season ticket holders.

The Rock and Roll Tour of New York and the Hard Rock Café offer a comprehensive tour of more than 50 sites where rock history was made and where rock stars wrote, performed, partied, and died. The tour includes a look at the Peppermint Lounge, Filmore East, and Shun Lee Palace (Paul McCartney's favorite Manhattan restaurant). Advance reservations can be made through your travel agent or by calling (212) 807- ROCK.

Local Customs and Other Secrets

Many tours supplement their escorts with local guides. These guides give each city, museum, or side trip special meaning. Earlier, I mentioned a friend who planned tours and I told you about his special talent as a tour developer and escort. One of his cardinal rules was to always find the best local tour guides and include them in his itineraries. These guides add a "hometown" dimension to every tour and many times are some of the more colorful people you will ever encounter.

Top Ten U.S. Tour Itineraries

This Top 10 list is in no particular order. The only reason I numbered the list is so you could monitor your progress as you read through it.

10. Branson, Missouri

9. Lake Tahoe and Yosemite, California

8. New England Fall Foliage

7. Washington, D.C. and Skyline Drive

6. Anchorage, Homer, and Seward, Alaska

5. Albuquerque and Taos, New Mexico in October for the Annual Balloon Festival

4. Asheville, NC and the Smoky Mountains

3. New Orleans Plantations

2. Salt Lake City and Bryce Canyon National Park

1. Kohala Coast and the Big Island of Hawaii

Is It a Tour or a Cruise?

Sometimes, it is very hard to tell the difference between a tour and a cruise. Many escorted tour itineraries operate a cruise on wheels. Cruises are popular because their price usually includes air transportation, airport transfers, sleeping accommodations, and food. Many escorted tours include exactly the same components. A cruise usually visits a variety of ports just like an escorted tour. The biggest difference between escorted tours and cruises is the sleeping accommodations. On a cruise ship, you are assigned a specific cabin and you unpack and live there for the duration of your cruise. An escorted tour, however, frequently changes hotels, which requires unpacking and packing. On the other hand, hotels rooms are usually more spacious than cruise ship cabins—especially the bathrooms.

If it appears that I am evading stating my preference and not suggesting a cruise over an escorted tour or vice versa, you're right; I can't decide. In my mind, the benefits of both are equal. So I guess I'm suggesting that you alternate. How's that for a very biased non-opinion?

When a Packaged Tour Fits the Bill

Sometimes, your vacation doesn't justify an escort. This happens for several reasons:

1. You've traveled to this destination before. Let's say, like when you visit your vacation home on the lake.

2. The vacation you've selected includes all transportation, accommodations, meals, and sightseeing. This could be a cruise, a Club Med vacation, or another type of *all-inclusive* destination.

3. The vacation destination you've chosen isn't included in any tour operator's offering. This would be the case if you decided to spend a week in Indianola, Iowa. Not that there is anything wrong with Indianola, it was a great place to go to high school and my mom and dad continue to call it home. It's just that the August Indianola Hot Air Balloon Classic hasn't caught the attention of tour operator marketing types.

When an escorted tour isn't appropriate, you may want to consider a packaged tour. Tour packages contain most of the same ingredients as an escorted tour except the escort. Sometimes, the escort is replaced by a host or hostess who has a local phone number in case you need assistance. Packaged tours give you the same price-saving benefits as escorted tours. The only missing ingredient is the escort.

How Much Is That Package in the Window?

We're going to pause here for just a moment for a little economic lesson. You'd see the immediate humor in this if you knew the struggles I had with *price elasticity* and the *velocity of money* in my college Economics class.

I think an economist would call this, "understanding economies of scale," but I'm not sure I mastered that principle either. I do know that packaged tours attract millions of vacationers every year because of their low price and relatively high value. The economic stuff comes into play when a package operator has enough customers to charter an airplane, arrange for motorcoaches to transfer customers between the airport to the hotel, and buy blocks of 50 or more hotel rooms every night.

The price charged for this air, land, and accommodation package is usually much less than the price you'd pay if you bought your airline tickets on a regularly scheduled flight, booked your hotel room directly with the hotel, and paid for a taxi between the airport and the hotel. Quantity purchasing in the packaged tour business leads to very good prices. Okay, class dismissed.

Plenty of Packages to Choose From

Packaged tour operators are ants at a picnic. Because these operators buy in bulk or operate charter flights, they tend to specialize in regional markets. MTI Vacations, Funway-Funjet Holidays, Travel Impressions, and Apple Vacations are four of the largest regional operators.

American Airlines owns a packaged tour operator, Fly AAway Vacations; and Delta Airlines owns Certified Vacations. Both airlines sell blocks of seats to other tour operators. If you think these airlines appear to be directly competing with their customers, you're right. It's just one of those travel industry quirks. The good news is it works, and as a vacation traveler, the price you pay is affected by competition.

A Package Just for You

Certain destinations attract packaged tour operations. Las Vegas, Orlando, and Cancun are three top package destinations. They are equipped to handle charter flights and large groups of arriving passengers. These destinations also have thousands of hotel rooms and many other prospering tourist attractions. In the travel business, we say these destinations have a "sophisticated tour and travel infrastructure." Some may translate this as "tourist trap," but to keep prices low, packaged tour operators deal in volume. Remember our economics lesson earlier in this chapter?

If the low price of a tour package is appealing, look through the Sunday travel section of any major newspaper. You'll see many advertisements. Many times, you'll also see the names and telephone numbers of travel agencies listed below these ads. These are called tag-on ads and travel agencies pay to have their name appear in those listings. This doesn't mean that only these agencies can sell the tour operator's packages. It just means those agencies paid the tour operator for the privilege of being included in the listing.

Travel agents offer three options to their single clients. Traditionally, singles could travel alone and pay a single supplement which adds as much as 50 percent to the cost of a vacation, or the tour operator could try to match the single traveler with a complete stranger. The third option and most viable is a service called Travel Companions. For a flat fee of $239 for a year's worth of unlimited matching, this company offers the single traveler a civilized way to meet others with similar interests. For additional information call 800-FUN-4-TWO or see your travel agent.

Some package operators accept bookings directly from the traveling public, but most prefer to distribute their product through travel agencies. The price of dealing direct is the same as using an agency, although an agency may know of a special that one operator is running because they have a few unsold airline seats or hotel rooms. A good travel agent will always shop around for the best deal among all the tour operators serving your selected destination.

Independent Touring—Doing It Your Own Way

Independent tours are a lot like going to a restaurant and ordering à la carte. You order only what you want, and you expect to pay a little more for each item. Your total meal tab, however, may be less expensive than a prix fixe meal because you order only what you want.

Look for the Tour's Label...

To instill a little discipline in the independent form of travel, the industry's name creators developed FIT, GIT, and DIT. These labels, other than contributing ingredients to travel jargon alphabet soup, separate independent travel into three broad categories:

1. Foreign Independent Tour (FIT)
2. Group Independent Tour (GIT)
3. Domestic Independent Tour (DIT)

Each of these formats is similar to their escorted and package cousins. The major difference is that these vacations are highly customized. I've constructed independent tours for groups of two. The itineraries followed the same path as an escorted itinerary and several of these independent groups of two included an escort during the entire trip. This is not the cheapest way to travel, but if you want an escort, a high degree of flexibility, and freedom, it sure beats staying home.

The Least You Need to Know

Whether you choose Tour B or not, escorted, packaged, and independent tours are good vacation options. They all offer structure, destination assistance, and security. Selecting a tour is a very personal choice. Each tour format has advantages. If you're having a difficult time deciding what is right for you, ask around. Friends and neighbors are good places to start. Travel agents are also a good source of information. If they haven't traveled with a specific tour operator or to a specific destination, they can refer you to another one of their clients who could give you a first-hand opinion.

➤ Escorted tours add new dimensions to your vacation.

➤ Tours allow you to combine adventure with safety and security.

➤ Eliminate unexpected charges for taxes and surcharges by selecting an all-inclusive tour.

➤ Some destinations are better served by tour packages rather than escorted tours or independent travel.

➤ Independent vacations maximize flexibility and freedom.

Chapter 6

Selecting a Destination

In This Chapter

➤ The season's the reason for the rate

➤ Selecting sun, sand, and surf spots

➤ Choosing a city package that's just right for you

➤ Theme parks and other fun destinations

By definition, vacations have one mandatory ingredient. You do have to *go* somewhere. You don't have to go far. You don't have to stay very long. You don't have to do anything. But, you do have to *go*. In my case, other people have been telling me where to go for years.

For most of us, choosing a vacation destination is our most difficult decision. The problem is not that there are too few places to go, the problem is that the options are so numerous it's hard to make up our minds. The challenge is to narrow the possibilities and make a decision that is compatible with your vacation profile (Chapters 2 and 3) and your purpose or goal (Chapter 4).

In this chapter, we'll highlight a few, and I mean just a *few*, places to go. We'll sort these highlights into three categories with the intention of getting you on the right track. After all, only you can select your destination, because only you know your vacation expectations. As Yogi Berra, the famous baseball player and coach, used to say, "You have to be very careful if you don't know where you're going, because you just might not get there."

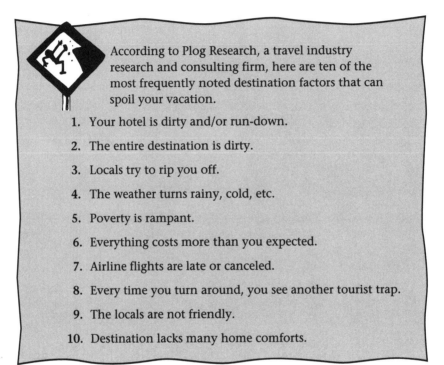

According to Plog Research, a travel industry research and consulting firm, here are ten of the most frequently noted destination factors that can spoil your vacation.

1. Your hotel is dirty and/or run-down.

2. The entire destination is dirty.

3. Locals try to rip you off.

4. The weather turns rainy, cold, etc.

5. Poverty is rampant.

6. Everything costs more than you expected.

7. Airline flights are late or canceled.

8. Every time you turn around, you see another tourist trap.

9. The locals are not friendly.

10. Destination lacks many home comforts.

Just the Right Amount of Seasons

Almost every destination has three different seasons and three corresponding rates: High Season (high rates), Shoulder Season (lower rates), Low Season (lowest rates). Usually, weather determines the season and the rate. For instance, the combination of Aspen and February yield High Season rates. Move closer to the middle of April, which is Shoulder Season, and you'll see the rates decrease. You'll also see the snow melting.

Hawaii's rates are governed more by holidays than by weather. This is because it's always a beautiful day in paradise. Their High

Season is during the Christmas and New Year holidays. Their Shoulder Season rates surround these holidays by two to three weeks.

According to the American Automobile Association, the busiest and most popular High Season of the year is Thanksgiving, when more than 40 million people try to get out of one location and into another. Of these, about 5 million travel by plane, train, or bus. Gas station owners must know this, because their prices usually increase during this week.

According to the 1994 World Travel Awards for which travel agents select the top North American destinations, Florida ranked first and was closely followed by California and New York.

Less than 25 percent of the Thanksgiving week travelers stay in hotels. They prefer to mooch off their friends and relatives. This means airfares may reflect High Season rates, but certain hotels may offer substantial Low Season discounts. Usually, hotels catering to the business traveler need your business the most during Thanksgiving and will therefore offer the most attractive rates.

The best day to fly is Thursday—Thanksgiving Day. Most people eat enough turkey to raise their L-tryptophane to nap-inducing levels. The airlines know this and offer incredible deals for flights between Thanksgiving afternoon and Saturday evening. How about $25 round-trip between Los Angeles and San Francisco?

The worst days to fly, unless you want to try to get bumped and earn a free ticket (see Chapter 8), are the Tuesday and Wednesday before Thanksgiving and the following Sunday and Monday.

Sand, Sun, and Surf

In an underdeveloped country, don't drink the water; in a developed country, don't breathe the air.

—Changing Times Magazine

We mentioned in Chapter 4 that many vacationers travel to enjoy rest, relaxation, and recreation. One destination type offering ample doses of the 3 R's is the sun, sand, and surf spots. (I realize I have exceeded my alliteration quota for the entire book in the last two sentences. I promise to actively avoid another alliteration outburst.)

My Ten Favorite Caribbean Islands

Although very few of the Caribbean Islands affiliate with the United States, they collectively provide some of the best sun, sand, and surf destinations in the entire world. A brief sketch of ten of the most popular islands follows. They are arranged in alphabetical order because we don't want to offend anyone's favorite island.

Anguilla (pronounced "an-qwill-a")

If you crave 36 miles of powdered-sugar beaches, quiet nights, and crystal-clear water and reefs packed with tropical fish, go out and buy a huge aquarium or travel to Anguilla. This place is a well-kept secret, so enjoy, but don't tell anyone else about it.

Barbados

This is about as prim and proper British as you're going to find in a Caribbean island. Barbados doesn't have the best of anything, but neither does it have the worst of anything. It's almost like someone towed Bermuda into the Caribbean. It's a good compromise.

British Virgin Islands

Take the 1,800 acres that are called the Peter Island Resort and Yacht Harbour, add 50 private rooms, five private villas, and a private beach, and you have a romantic paradise. A bottle of Veuve Clicquot, your favorite significant other, and a trip to the Baths at Virgin Gorda make the BVI unforgettable.

Dominican Republic

Friendly Latin people combine bargain prices with great nightlife to make DR a popular destination. Even though this country shares the island of Hispaniola with Haiti (You don't believe me? Go look it up.), you'd never know it. It's a democratic nation and you'll feel safe wandering around at night.

Puerto Plata is a favorite destination for tourist crowds seeking a well-known resort. If you're looking for something more secluded, try Punta Cana or Samana Peninsula.

Grand Caymans

If you like diving, snorkeling, white sand beaches, and lots of other people who enjoy the same thing, go to the Caymans. Like Belize and Bonaire, this is a favorite stop for folks with a passion to breathe under water.

If you're not into diving and snorkeling, you'll be bored stiff and begin wishing you were back at work. Well, maybe not at work, but at least some other place.

Grenada

If you look up "Caribbean Island" in the dictionary, you'll see a picture of Grenada. After all, their major crop is nutmeg. What more does a Caribbean paradise need?

The capital city of St. George's was built in 1732 and their harbor is so clean you can see tropical fish swim by. You can't even see the *buildings* in some of *our* capitals.

Guadeloupe

If you're looking for gobs of French tourists, mediocre beaches, and great Caribbean cooking, you've found it on Guadeloupe. It also has its own rain forest (Basse Terre), abundant nightlife, and gobs of French tourists.

Jamaica

Jamaica is not really one of my favorite islands, but I include it in this list because it is so popular. It suffers from political violence and crime against tourists. If you stray from the confines of your all-inclusive resort, prepare to be hassled about everything from having your hair braided to buying drugs. Some of these hucksters make the telemarketer selling aluminum siding during your dinner hour appear amateurish.

Carry $6 in one pocket and $150 in the other. When a mugger asks for your money, take the $6 out, throw it on the ground, and then walk quickly in the opposite direction. The majority of muggers will go for the money and leave you alone.

On the bright side, Jamaica has great beaches (Negril), nightlife (Ocho Rios and Montego Bay), and Rastafarians (everywhere).

Puerto Rico

Direct flights to and from Puerto Rico make this Caribbean island popular for short stays. San Juan, the Caribbean's largest capital, boasts a raucous nightlife and credit-limit raising shopping. I recommend staying in San Juan only long enough to see Old San Juan, the beautifully preserved example of Spanish colonial architecture.

If old buildings and history don't thrill you, get out of the city; try the two Hyatt properties at Ceremar or a guest house on the nearby islands of Vieques or Culebra.

St. Barthelemy

I saved the best for last, even though I did have an argument with myself about placing St. Barts under the B's or the S's. Obviously, the S's won so I could use the "best-for-last" line. This is another secret spot, so please don't tell others.

Getting to St. Barts involves either a ferry or a commuter plane from St. Martin. Once you're on the island, you can rent a mini-moke, which is like a golf cart with no place to store your clubs. And before I forget, the beach at Grande Saline is "clothing optional." That's a politically correct phrase that means the people on this beach are naked. This is probably why St. Barts is one of the most expensive islands in the Caribbean.

Mexico

Although the focus of this book is United States destinations, it's not fair to talk about sun, sand, and surf and not talk about Mexico.

The stories you've heard about drinking the water in Mexico are more or less true. Our bodies react in strange and mysterious ways to different kinds of water, especially Mexican.

Rather than putting you through another Top Ten List (no offense Dave, okay?), I'll highlight two popular Mexican resort cities. There are many others, but these are great places to start your sun, sand, and surf sojourns. (Sorry).

Cancun

Talcum powder is coarse compared to the white sand beaches found at this Yucatan Peninsula altar for the sun worshiper. Technically, Cancun City, once a sleepy little fishing village located a few miles from what most tourists call Cancun, is now a bustling city of 70,000 employees of the tourism industry. The tourist part of Cancun is relatively new and was the first Mexican city designed and built for tourism.

It is strictly a relaxation and recreation destination. You'll see mile after mile of hotels, restaurants, and night clubs. No one really goes to the night clubs until after midnight. This is recreation for a party animal that makes the beach the next morning a place for recuperation, oops, I mean relaxation.

Aculpulco

Cancun and Aculpulco are on opposite sides of the country of Mexico and, in many ways, they are on opposite ends of the sun, sand, and surf spectrum. Cancun is young. Aculpulco is mature. Cancun is sunrises. Aculpulco is sunsets. Cancun is clean and orderly (for Mexico). Aculpulco is sexy and a little raunchy. They are two great world-class resorts separated by a common language and a lot of terrain.

I've traveled to Aculpulco for years and have watched this destination change and return to its original condition. I've seen the beaches packed with wildlife (two-legged, scantily clad variety), and I've seen the beaches deserted except for automatic weapon toting militia. It all depends on the mood of the natives. When they realize how much tourism means to their economy, they're outstanding. When the tourism dollars become bountiful, they become greedy and, in some cases, corrupt.

Now is a good time to visit Mexico, they've just completed their elections and the peso is dropping, which means our dollar goes farther. Oh boy, cheap margaritas, olé!

City Packages

If you like your vacations short, sweet, and frequent, consider a city package. Although some packages last for an entire week, most come in the 3–4 day variety. Just enough time to feel like you've had a break, but not so much that you need a decompression chamber to re-enter the work force.

The arrival of the low-cost air carriers, such as Southwest Airlines, has made long-weekend city packages affordable and popular. A recent promotion offered round-trip airfare between Cleveland and Washington, D.C. for $28. When your airline ticket is cheaper than your taxi to the airport, you know you have a great deal. This promotion made flying to Washington for lunch and a quick stroll through the Smithsonian a fiscal delight.

Here are a few cities that lend themselves to package weekends. There are many, many more. These will start you thinking about the possibilities.

Boston—Bean Town

The history virtually oozes through every footstep (wear old shoes) as you walk along the Freedom Trail and then pay your respects to Norm and the gang at the Bull & Finch Pub at 84 Beacon Street, the inspiration for the television series *Cheers*.

Bring your appetite and visit The North End for an authentic and memorable Italian dinner. The North End neighborhood is as close to Italy as you'll get without your passport.

Hop across the Charles River to Cambridge and practice saying, "I parked my car in Harvard yard." Be careful with those R's. Feel free to absorb whatever higher education you find on the Cambridge side of the river. It's one of the most expensive and most prestigious you'll find anywhere in the world.

Chicago—The Windy City

From the world-class shopping along the Magnificent Mile (Michigan Avenue) to restaurants that put the experience back into dining, Chicago is still, "The City That Works."

One of Chicago's best breakfast bashes begins every morning at 5 a.m. at Lou Mitchells, 563 W. Jackson Blvd., 312-939-3111. The juice is fresh-squeezed and the eggs have double yolks (must be tough on the chickens). Omelets served in sizzling iron skillets with thickly sliced

Greek bread make you come back for more. Get there early for a seat at one of the old-fashioned Formica-topped tables. A Lou Mitchells cult thing happens every Saturday morning. If you have the time and the patience, standing in line with the natives makes the food taste even better.

Lincoln Park contains one of the premiere zoos in the world and Halstad Street is Chicago's off-Broadway theater district. The city is safe, clean, and a tribute to the renewed vitality of America's cities.

You've done a really good job of keeping the secrets I've told you so far, so I'm going to trust you with Chicago's *best-kept* restaurant experience: Zaven's, 260 East Chestnut. 312-787-8260. It's a quick three-block walk from the Water Tower Shopping Mall on North Michigan Avenue, and you'll swear I gave you the wrong address when you're standing in front of this high-rise condominium building. The restaurant's entrance is just to the right of the doorman's desk in the building's lobby.

The food is good (continental gourmet with a middle eastern flair), but most diners return to Zaven's because they fall in love with the owner, Zaven Kodajayan. From his Armenian roots, through his training at the George V in Paris, to his remarkable 18 years at the same Chicago location, Zaven charms his guests and treats everyone like they were long lost relatives. Be sure to call for reservations. The restaurant is small, the seating is intimate, and the mood is romantic.

Los Angeles—Tinsel Town

Where else can you drive by OJ's estate, Marilyn Monroe's grave, visit a working movie set/theme park/shopping promenade all within a couple of hours? In many respects, LA is a collection of excesses. You'll find one (and sometimes two) of just about everything you can imagine.

Packed between the beaches and the mountains, Los Angeles sprawls, and sometimes shakes, to a very different drummer. For a great weekend getaway, rent a convertible (you need a car in LA), wear your sunglasses, and cruise.

For a culturally enriching experience stop by Venice Beach. You'll see rollerblading practiced as an art form and street vendors selling every ware imaginable. It's a slice of Americana that fuels dinner conversations for weeks to come.

New York—The Big Apple

If you can make it there, you can make it anywhere... or so says the Chairman of the Board. A weekend in New York is like playing in the big leagues. It's like turning the volume up really high when you have a really good set of speakers. It's not tame and it's not even polite, but from the Broadway shows to shops in SoHo, New York does have it all.

If you can't get a reservation for breakfast at Tiffany's, try the Royal Canadian Pancake House, 145 Hudson St. 212-219-3038. About 50 different kinds of pancakes, 18 varieties of waffles and a dozen kinds of French toast make choosing difficult at this pancake house. Try the oven-baked apple pancakes—light and fluffy.

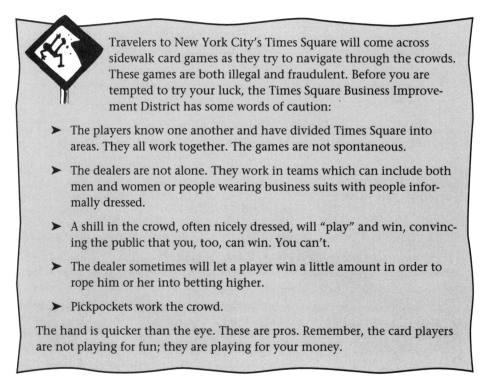

Travelers to New York City's Times Square will come across sidewalk card games as they try to navigate through the crowds. These games are both illegal and fraudulent. Before you are tempted to try your luck, the Times Square Business Improvement District has some words of caution:

➤ The players know one another and have divided Times Square into areas. They all work together. The games are not spontaneous.

➤ The dealers are not alone. They work in teams which can include both men and women or people wearing business suits with people informally dressed.

➤ A shill in the crowd, often nicely dressed, will "play" and win, convincing the public that you, too, can win. You can't.

➤ The dealer sometimes will let a player win a little amount in order to rope him or her into betting higher.

➤ Pickpockets work the crowd.

The hand is quicker than the eye. These are pros. Remember, the card players are not playing for fun; they are playing for your money.

Theme Parks

Coney Island, Cedar Point, Riverside Park—the names of amusement parks bring back memories and inspire us to check out their modern-day equivalents. As Americans, we've had a long-standing love affair with the roller coaster and other contraptions that jeopardize your lunch and put a chill up and down your spine.

Some of the best roller coasters in the world are held in captivity in U.S. theme parks. There is a brand new one at the Buffalo Bill Resort in Stateline, NV. This beast is getting rave reviews from coaster jocks; it's constructed of steel and has a 210 foot drop. The track is bright yellow, and it twists and curves all around the place. As one big, gnarly dude reviewed it, he said, "It's humongous." Kind of says it all doesn't it?

At Cedar Point, near Sandusky, Ohio, which is west of Cleveland, the Mean Streak and Magnum also receive reviews like, "awesome" or "very fast." Coaster reviewers are people of few words. That's because their stomachs are lodged in their throats. The Mean Streak is known as one of the longer coaster rides, and there is a new addition called Raptor. You sit with your legs hanging out and your chair suspended from above. Lots of loops and twists—supposed to be a scream.

Great America in Chicago has a similar coaster which is new this year.

Knott's Berry Farm in Orange County, California, is building a coaster around the entire park. When it is completed, it will be over three minutes long—which is an eternity for coaster nerds. For those of you who want a coaster and want it now, Knott's has Montezooma's Revenge, another yellow coaster (seems to be a popular color) that torpedoes you into a loop and then, after a brief stop, brings you out of the loop… backwards. Also at Knott's is Boomerang, which turns you upside down six times in less than a minute. Coaster fanatics review this one as a "major rush," which used to mean something totally different when I was in college.

Six Flags Magic Mountain, just north of Los Angeles in Valencia, has VIPER, a 70 mph six-loop monster that's over two minutes long. It does have the highest loop in the world according to *The Guinness Book of World Records*. You can also ride Batman, which like Raptor at Cedar Point, leaves your feet dangling and the track above your head.

There are many more coasters around the country. Each has its own cadre of loyal followers. Vacationers have been known to plan their itinerary to include rides on as many roller coasters as they could cram into a week.

Disneyland and Disney World

Only in America can an artist named Walt, with a dream that never ends, convince a group of bankers to loan him buckets of money to build a fantasy land on a soggy tract of land in Anaheim, California. And all of this was to pay tribute to two fictional mice, a dog, a duck, and several other cartoon characters.

Anaheim begot Orlando and Orlando begot Japan and Japan begot France, and today, the name Disney means vacation quality. Walt was a visionary who understood the value of youth, keeping our children enthralled, as we rediscover the child in all of us.

MGM and Universal

Movies entertain and theme parks entertain. So, if movie studios design and build theme parks, we should get entertainment raised to the second power, right? You bet.

The *Central Florida Discount Travel Guide* is available to travelers visiting Walt Disney World or the Kissimmee-St. Cloud area. This helpful central Florida vacation guide contains about 80 pages of information on area attractions and a calendar of events, accommodations, and transportation. Also included are discounts for hotels, condos, restaurants, and attractions. To obtain your free copy, call 1-800-831-1844.

What worked for Disney Studios works just as well for MGM and Universal Studios. High quality, fair price, and a few unexpected surprises are the stuff a good vacation is made of.

The MGM theme park adjacent to Disney World in Orlando offers a nice compliment to the Disney product. Like Disney, MGM is built around themes from popular movies, and the employees at the park are merely actors on a large set. It's easy to get caught up in the action.

MGM recently (mid-1994) opened a theme park/hotel/casino/convention center in Las Vegas. Located near the south end of the Strip, this complex is so large that it has its own private hospital and clinic for its employees and their families. If you like non-stop, 24-hour movie memorabilia, this is a must.

Universal Studios theme parks near Los Angeles and Orlando offer the same movie themes as Disney and MGM, but with an accent on the films released by Universal. The unique and fun part of visiting Universal is that you can combine a tour of the movie lot with a few thrills, such as an earthquake or an attack by Jaws. In addition, if you're not worn out by all of that, you may be able to see the taping of one of the "sitcoms" produced on a Universal sound stage.

Ten Tips for Taking Children to Visit a Theme Park

1. Dress in comfortable cotton clothing that dries quickly after a water ride or a rain shower.

2. Pack sunscreen, lip balm, and a visor for the baby.

3. Visit the park on weekdays when attendance is lightest.

4. Plan ahead. Know which rides and shows your family will enjoy.

5. Always start at the back of the park when it opens unless you think too many others have read this book and know this tip. In that case, proceed to the middle of the park and work your way out in a spiral.

6. Pick up a map at the park's entrance that locates all the bathrooms and diaper-changing and bottle-warming stations.

7. Plan to ride the most popular attractions when the park opens or after 6 p.m. when the motorcoach groups usually depart.

8. If the children become hot or tired, find a show that everyone will enjoy in an air-conditioned theater.

9. Request children's menus and portions when dining out.

10. Wear a fanny pack. These are much easier to take on rides and also much harder to misplace.

Tourist Towns

The latest incarnation of amusement parks turned theme parks are theme cities. These all produce high-quality vacations at affordable prices.

Branson, Missouri

A few years ago, you could have purchased a few acres in this southern Missouri town for next to nothing. Today, Branson real estate prices rival any big city. Branson caught the attention of many Nashville stars. They stopped, bought some land, and built theaters and show rooms that seat thousands. It's the place to be if you're into the Nashville set. If you're into Nine Inch Nails, Branson is guaranteed to disappoint you.

Las Vegas

If you haven't been to Las Vegas lately, you're really missing a quality family vacation opportunity. Wait a minute, did I just say family vacation and Las Vegas in the same sentence? Yes, yes, a hundred, no a thousand times yes.

When Las Vegas felt the competition from Atlantic City, they got a wake-up call. They knew they needed a new image to set themselves apart from the hundreds of casinos that were emerging as local governments learned that gambling revenues were easier to collect than new tax revenues.

Las Vegas started a renaissance. Steve Winn built The Mirage with an erupting volcano that stopped traffic. He followed that with another new hotel that stages an elaborate battle between two pirate ships, and he just announced plans to build a hotel and a lake for water skiing on the Strip in the desert.

According to the 1994 World Travel Awards where travel agents select the world's leading casinos, all three reside in Las Vegas: MGM Grand, Caesar's Palace, and The Mirage.

Not to be outdone, MGM just opened a city (they employ so many people, they have their own hospital) with a full-blown amusement park attached. From there, you cross the street to the Luxor which dwarfs the Egyptian pyramids and has a boat tour through its lobby. By the way, the light pointed toward the heavens from the apex of the Luxor is so powerful, it costs $1 million per year to feed it electricity. Go figure... no, just go to Las Vegas. Oh, by the way, I almost forgot, they still have great casinos, too.

Because there is more to Nevada than just Las Vegas, the 58-page Discover Nevada Guide may come in handy. It contains 132 discount coupons and information on the state's other attractions. Call 1-800-NEVADA-8.

Nashville... Indiana, That Is

Near Bloomington, Indiana, the home of Indiana University, is the quaint, little town of Nashville, set in the picturesque hills of Brown County. Nashville is filled with shops displaying the work (and play) of local artists. A mere two miles from Nashville, you can drive through the Brown County State Park (especially gorgeous during autumn months). Not far down the road is Columbus, Indiana, known for its unique architecture.

Frankenmuth, Michigan

This re-creation of a small Bavarian village boasts an enormous Christmas store and a huge miniature (oxymoron alert) dollhouse store. At one of the Bavarian Inn stores, you can order a doll to your specifications—no, not the inflatable kind. You specify the eye color, hair color, and clothing style, and they'll make you a one-of-a-kind doll. This is a great stop for collectors and saves you sitting in front of the TV for hours waiting for the Home Shopping Network to get to the mass-produced collector's dolls.

Steamboat Springs, Colorado

In the winter, this place is filled with Spandex and down-clad skiers. You may know about their February Winter Carnival where their high school marching band wears cross-country skis in the parade, and horses pull kids on skis. What you may not know is that one weekend in July, this hidden treat (three-hour drive from Denver) has one of the best hot-air balloon rodeos in the country and the Art in the Park crafts show.

The Least You Need to Know

➤ Selecting a destination that is compatible with your vacation needs and wants is a good first step to planning your perfect vacation.

➤ Every destination has different pricing seasons: High, Shoulder, and Low.

➤ Sun, sand, and surf spots offer relaxation and recreation.

➤ City packages are quick, convenient, and satisfying destinations.

➤ Theme parks and cities are great for families and add an entertainment perk not found in other destinations.

Chapter 7

Special Care for Special Vacations

In This Chapter

➤ Travelers with disabilities

➤ Vacationing with children

➤ Traveling with pets

This chapter contains a potpourri (meaning a variety of ideas, not the stuff you pour into a bowl and wait for your bathroom to smell like a grove of pine trees) of special vacation topics for travelers with special needs. Each of the above topics could (some already do) have books written about them. You'll learn a little about each of these special vacations and where to turn if you want more in-depth information.

Dynamic Vacations for Travelers with Disabilities

We have a friend and business travel customer who racks up thousands of frequent flyer miles and takes his wheelchair with him everywhere—he doesn't have a choice; he has to. He doesn't want sympathy. He just wants suppliers of travel services to use common sense.

For instance, a hotel correctly followed our agency's explicit requests and gave our client a specially equipped room for wheelchair guests. The recently remodeled room was beautifully decorated and contained an extra-wide entry doorway, wide spaces between the beds, and grab-rails in the bathroom. Unfortunately, no one thought about widening the bathroom doorway to accommodate a wheelchair or about lowering the closet poles so someone seated could reach the hangers.

Call the Albuquerque Convention and Visitors Bureau at 800-284-2282 and say, "Hello." Next, ask them to send their guide entitled *Art of Accessibility*. This comprehensive guide for travelers with disabilities lists hotels, restaurants, attractions, and other facilities for visitors who have mobility, visual, or hearing challenges.

Consider how *you* might feel about paying $150 per night for a hotel room with a bathroom that you could see but not use and no place to hang your clothes. Sometimes, our good intentions get clobbered by lack of perspective. This oversight could have been prevented if someone had just placed him or herself in a wheelchair and rolled through the room before the renovation plans were approved.

People with disabilities represent a large percentage of this country's population. Unfortunately, we had to pass a law (ADA) to protect their rights to travel and access the natural beauty of our country. It may come as a shock to many that disabled and nondisabled people share more similarities than differences. People with disabilities are proud, contributing members of society who marry, raise families, attend church, throw wild parties, laugh, cry, and tell really bad jokes just like their abled counterparts. While many uninformed citizens complain about the cost of providing access to all public attractions and sights, travelers with disabilities contribute more than $5 billion (yes, that's the one with the "B") annually in tourism revenue.

Americans with Disabilities Act (ADA)

About 7 million of the Americans with disabilities use a wheelchair, crutches, or a cane; about 9 million people are visually impaired; and about 28 million have a hearing loss. Title I of the ADA, implemented in July, 1992, protects the rights and increases accessibility of Americans and travelers with disabilities.

Several travel agencies specialize in vacations for people with disabilities. Some arrange travel for individuals and others plan group departures. More and more tour operators also recognize the demand for itineraries programmed with the disabled traveler in mind. The following organizations cater to travelers with disabilities:

➤ **Society for the Advancement of Travel for the Handicapped (SATH)**, 212-447-7284, promotes respect, legislation, and accessibility for disabled travelers in general and offers advice and assistance to individual travelers. This organization maintains lists of tour operators and other travel firms, collects information about accessible facilities worldwide, and distributes a quarterly newsletter about developments in travel for people with disabilites.

> Write the Airports Council International-North America, Consumer Information Center, Pueblo, CO 81009 for your free 48-page pamphlet called, "Access Travel: Airports." This booklet details facilities, services, and accessible design features at 553 airport terminals worldwide.

➤ **Travel Information Service of Moss Rehab Hospital**, 215-456-9600, which, for the past 25 years, has compiled accessibility information and provides this information by phone for specific destinations.

Tips for Smooth Travel with Limited Mobility

Here are five tips for mobility-challenged vacationers:

➤ Obtain a copy of the Air Carrier Access Act (SATH, listed above, will help you). This document describes your rights and explains what access and accommodations the airlines must provide. One thing you may not know is that airline passengers are allowed to take their manual wheelchair onboard on a first-come, first-served basis. Ask the airline reservationist or your professional travel agent to make the necessary arrangements.

➤ Get to know the different airplane models and their interior configuration. Learn which seats have a moveable aisle armrest, for example, so someone can be transferred to the seat without having to be lifted.

Two newsletters and two books offer suggestions for the vacationer with special challenges. To obtain the newsletters contact: "The Diabetic Traveler," 203-327-5832 and "The Handicapped Traveler Newsletter," 903-677-1260. The books are, *Traveling Like Everybody Else: A Practical Guide for Disabled Travelers* by Jacquaeline Freedman and Susan Gersten (Adama Books, Bellmore, NY) and *Easy Access to National Parks* by Wendy Roth and Michael Tompane (Sierra Club Books).

➤ Research ground transportation at both the departure and destination cities. Learn which companies offer hydraulic lifts with their vehicles. Hydraulic lifts can be difficult to obtain in the Caribbean, but Disney World in Orlando has a good supply.

➤ Ask your travel agent to comparison shop for specially equipped vans. Prices range from outrageous to moderate.

➤ Bypass the hotel reservation agent if you want to learn about a specific hotel's accessibility. Call the property directly and ask to speak with housekeeping or engineering personnel. They're the best qualified to give you answers about how the rooms are arranged. Rather than reading from a computer screen that a particular room is fully accessible, they can tell you whether there is a roll-in shower as opposed to a tub with grab-bars. This makes a big difference to an individual traveler. You'll also find the housekeeping and engineering personnel eager to share their advice. It seems that few others at the property ever ask for their opinions.

Tours and Other Group Activities

Certain tour operators specialize in group departures for the traveler with disabilities. The following list gives you a small sample of the possibilities:

➤ Flying Wheels Travel, 800-535-6790, coordinates tours and cruises worldwide for wheelchair travelers.

➤ Evergreen Travel Service, 206-776-1184, designs programs for wheelchair, blind, deaf, and senior travelers.

➤ Accessible Journeys, 800-846-4537, organizes vacations for mobility-impaired travelers. The firm also maintains a roster of nurses available for hire as travel companions.

➤ Handicapped Scuba Association, 303-933-4864, a nonprofit group sponsoring dive trips and certificates for divers with disabilities.

In addition to these, a host of other tour operators offer itineraries geared to the needs and wants of the traveler with disabilities:

➤ Alaska River Journeys, 907-349-2964, offers fully guided trips with gourmet cooking to some of North America's last remaining wild and scenic river corridors.

➤ Wilderness Inquiry, 612-379-3858, shares canoeing, kayaking, and dogsledding activities with people of all ages and ability levels. Since 1978, their trained staff has lead more than 15,000 people through wilderness adventures.

➤ Al's Wild Water Adventures, 800-289-4534, presents 12 unique, prepackaged river vacations on Oregon's Rogue River and Owyhee River. They welcome beginners and offer a variety of accommodations and water crafts.

➤ Overland Expedition Company, 805-927-5885, combines a motorcoach, hotel, and restaurant into one moveable vacation. Their specially converted Double Decker buses sleep up to 22 passengers and include a full kitchen with living and dining areas. They'll customize a tour for any group and offer scheduled tours through the Southwest, Baja, and Yucatan.

Kids Stay Free!

Never play peek-a-boo with a child on a long plane trip. There's no end to the game. Finally, I grabbed him by the bib and said, Look, it's always gonna be me!

—Rita Rudner

The classic travel paradox begins with responsible, caring parents not wanting to put their kids through the discomforts of travel. On the other hand, those discomforting travel experiences are filled with valuable lessons. Thank goodness my parents opted for the valuable lessons that came with the discomforts of travel.

As a seven-year-old, I vividly remember a hot and humid August day in St. Louis (apologies for the rabid redundancy). We were in the middle of a family vacation that had had its ups and downs. The ups included a spellbinding miniature golf course and the St. Louis zoo. The downs centered on the obligatory visit to some distant relatives. This day, however, was going to be the pinnacle of our vacation. We were going to see our first major league baseball game. The St. Louis Cardinals with Stan "The Man" Musial were playing some other team. Who cared? We had tickets to a game. That's all that mattered.

The valuable lesson began on the way to the ball park when our car made a terrible thumping noise that was followed by a symphony of horn honking. We were stopped in the middle of a very busy St. Louis intersection with our car's drive shaft lying on the asphalt. The valuable lessons were coming fast and furious now.

I learned that universal joints are to drive shafts what knees are to legs. I also learned, if you're going to have problems with a U-joint in the middle of a busy intersection, it's best to also have a gas station on a nearby corner. (This lesson no longer applies since it was learned back in the days before mini-marts, when gas stations employed mechanics and actually repaired cars.)

The next batch of lessons hit all at once. I learned that those events you look forward to the most, like a major league baseball game, can evaporate into thin air. The gas station mechanic then taught me that public transportation can solve a host of U-joint problems and get you to Busch Stadium in time to join in singing the National Anthem. By the way, Stan Musial did hit a home run that day, and I saw it.

Now, should caring, responsible parents subject their kids to the discomforts of travel? You bet. My St. Louis U-joint memory is nearly 40 years old, and I still remember boarding the city bus with renewed hope of seeing that ball game.

And this year's award for the "Best Title for a New Travel Publication Produced by a Tourist Board, Visitors Bureau, or Chamber of Commerce" goes to... drum roll please... the Taos Chamber of Commerce for their publication, *Kids Guide to Taos: What You Really Want to Do 'Cause It's Your Vacation Too!* Aside from having a truly great title, this publication knows what kids like and gives them a fact-filled tour of the town. The guide outlines everything from hiking to picnics to trolley rides to which parks have the best swings. Call them quickly, before you grow up, at 800-732-8267.

Traveling with Kids—A Little Forethought, Please

I've always felt that kids were build for portability—just try to find your two-year-old, who was just here a *minute* ago. This is why they travel so well. The difference between pleasant and unpleasant traveling with children is expecting the unexpected. Sit back for just a minute and picture a jammed airport—your flight has been delayed for hours, the kids are whining, and your spouse is whining louder. What do you do?

If you're visiting friends or relatives, tell them ahead of time what you'll need: a crib and apple juice for the baby and a certain brand of cereal for the older kids, for example. Making small things familiar at your destination helps ease everyone's concerns.

If you have a toddler or baby, gently remind your hosts about keeping pills and poisons locked away. Suggest they move breakables and cover electrical outlets. It's always a good idea to carry a few extra plastic outlet plugs in your diaper bag. You never know when one will come in handy. Just remember, your house may be childproof, but the rest of civilization is probably unprepared for your invasion.

Delays and travel are synonymous whether you're traveling by car, train, boat, or plane. The remedy is to be ready for every eventuality. Travel armed with plenty of "surprise" trinkets, toys, games, tapes, and books. You'll look like a virtual magician pulling distractions and solutions out of a hat.

If you're traveling with an infant, stow plenty of juice, diapers, formula, baby food, and clothes where you can get to them quickly. There is nothing worse than a soaked infant when all the dry diapers are buried in the big suitcase in your rental car's trunk. And speaking of rental cars, don't forget your car seat. Many rental car companies offer them, but what if they overbook or someone doesn't return one on time? Plan ahead for the unexpected.

No matter where you travel on vacation, children are going to spill things and get sick. Too hot, too cold, not enough sleep, and too much rich food—it is no wonder kids get sick. Always pack a thermometer, a first-aid kit, and any medicines your child may need for a chronic condition such as asthma or allergies. Just to be on the safe side, keep an extra change of clothes within easy reach.

Tips for Kids Traveling with Adults

Remember, adults get uptight and restless over little things, such as being late and the prospect of having to sleep on a sofa in the hotel's lobby. None of these has ever bothered you, but when you travel with adults you have to expect the unexpected. Pack your backpack with a couple of favorite books and games. A joke book is a good bet, although watching adult behavior can be just as entertaining. Bring along a hand-held video game and a small tape or CD player, if you have one. These are great for tuning out troublesome brothers, sisters, and, of course, your parents.

Offer to pack your own suitcase. Your parents will flip over your newfound sense of responsibility, and you'll be certain to have your favorite jeans, T-shirts, and sneakers. Don't forget plenty of underwear or the good clothes your mom wants you to wear when you go out to dinner.

Ask for a map so you can help plot the route and help navigate. You never know when the plane's pilot may pin a set of wings on your collar and ask for your assistance. If you're driving, you know how Dad hates to stop and ask for directions. Your map could prevent one of those really long dinners where your parents talk in code and spend a lot of time staring at their food. Look carefully at the landscape you pass. What's different from home? How would it feel to live here?

If you are flying alone to visit your mom, dad, grandma, or grandpa, make certain you have a list of telephone numbers. You should also practice making collect calls while someone is available to coach you. Carry money with you, and plan what you will do if you get stuck in an airport because of bad weather or a canceled flight. Watching the ground crew load luggage on the planes and trying to count the number of bags as they're boarded is still one of my favorite pastimes.

Hotels Can Be a Kid's Best Friend

Although many hotels have waved their magic wands to make children's services available, the growing demands of the *married-with-children* market segment have prompted some nifty innovations. These guests are accustomed to traveling and, now that their lives include children, they expect hotels to serve the children as well as the parents.

The Ritz Kids program at Ritz Carlton properties includes all the standard components, such as a free stay for children up to age 18 who are staying with their parents, plus cribs, high chairs, and baby-sitting. The creators of these programs have become experts in special events, such as teddy bear teas, etiquette courses, and cooking classes. The Ritz knows parents want a safe, fun, and educational environment for their children, and they continually refine their offerings.

Jack Tar Village Beach Resorts offer a Kids Club, which responded to customers' requests. This program appeals to children between the ages of three and 12. The Clubs schedule supervised, age-appropriate activities, so three-year-olds are not doing 12-year-old stuff. Generally, Kids Clubs operate to give parents time to play golf, enjoy the beach, or do whatever parents do while the kids are occupied. Activities include sand-castle building, scavenger hunts, cookie baking, Coke-tail parties, and clown parties. Jack Tar Kids Clubs exist at their resort properties in Puerta Plata, Dominican Republic; Puerto Vallarta, Mexico; and Frigate Bay, St. Kitts.

For Kids Only

Okay, you want to check out the ski resort or hotel. Just make sure your parents know where you are going and about how long you plan to explore. Write down the hotel's address, your room number, and the hotel's main phone number. Put this information in your pocket; use it if you have a hard time finding your way back. Resort hotels tend to sprawl, which makes getting lost pretty easy. You never know when you'll have to help an adult find the main lobby.

Pets and Travel: See Spot Stay!

Although dogs usually act really excited about the prospects of going for a ride, they may not be quite so excited about a long airplane ride. For starters, they get really bummed when they learn they can't put their head out the window. If you have no alternative and your pet has to fly with you, here's what you need to know.

Some airlines will allow one or more pets to travel in the passenger cabin of a plane instead of the cargo hold, as long as advance reservations are confirmed. I once met Benji on a plane. He had his own first-class seat and sat up and saluted each of the passengers as they boarded the plane. Most pets, until they reach Benji's status and income, are required to be kept in a travel cage that must be stowed under the seat in front of you.

According to the conditions established by the Animal Welfare Act, the following must be maintained when transporting pets:

➤ In order to fly, dogs and cats must be at least eight weeks old and must have been weaned for at least five days.

➤ Animals cannot be shipped COD unless the shipper guarantees their return if the animals are refused at their destination.

➤ Animals cannot be exposed to temperatures below 45°F unless they have the written approval of a veterinarian.

➤ Food and water must be provided for puppies or kittens younger than 16 weeks that are being transported for more than 12 hours. For adult pets, food must be provided at least every 24 hours and water every 12 hours.

➤ Cages and pet carriers must meet minimum standards for ventilation, strength, sanitation, and safety.

➤ Dogs and cats must not be brought to an airline more than four hours before departure. A six hour lead-time is permitted if shipping arrangements are made in advance.

Although many animal protection groups, such as the Humane Society of the United States, People for the Ethical Treatment of Animals, and Friends of Animals, issue warnings about animals traveling in airplane cargo holds; statistically, air travel is safe for pets. About 500,000 animals (mainly cats and dogs) travel every year in cargo holds with few injuries or deaths. Still, more than 100 animals died aboard airliners in 1990, the latest year for available statistics. Between 1991 and 1993, the U.S. Department of Agriculture fined six airlines a total of $67,500 for violations of the Animal Welfare Act, which orders airlines to provide humane care and treatment, including protection from extremes in weather, adequate space and ventilation, and veterinary care.

Most animal deaths are the fault of owners who oversedate their pets or fly them during inappropriate times, such as noon on a hot summer day. Professional travel agents recommend against transporting your pet in the cargo hold of an airplane unless absolutely necessary. If your pet must travel with you, it is highly recommended to take a direct flight. Always fit your animal with a permanent identification tag containing your home address, phone number, and a temporary tag with your destination information.

The following literature will help prepare you and your pet for a vacation if the preceding hasn't convinced you to find a good kennel or an accommodating neighbor.

➤ *The Dog Lovers' Bookshop Newsletter*, 9 W. 31st St., NY, NY 10001, 212-594-3601, fax 212-576-4343, offers a listing of books on recreational and leisure activities for dogs and their owners. This free newsletter describes books that you can order through the Bookshop (like these listed below) by referring to their item numbers.

➤ *DogGone*, P.O. Box 651155, Vero Beach, FL 32965, telephone 407-569-8434 ($24 a year for six issues).

➤ *Pets-R-Permitted: Hotel, Motel, Kennel & Petsitter Travel & Pets Directory* lists 4,000 lodgings, 1,000 boarding kennels, day kennels near major tourist attractions, and a bonus mail-in offer for money-saving coupons. Item #1002, $11.95.

➤ *Take Your Pet USA* puts you in touch with almost 4,000 hotels, motels, and inns as well as nearby veterinarians. Item #1003, $11.95.

➤ *Touring with Towser*, long a standard, compensates for its relatively sparse listings by adding coupons for pet-product savings, a roster of dog-friendly chain hostelries, and a free coupon book. Item #1004, $3.

➤ *The Portable Pet, How to Travel Anywhere with Your Dog or Cat* covers all facets of the subject, from air travel to car sickness, from campgrounds to foreign quarantine laws, in a question-and-answer format. Item #1005, $5.95.

Pet Travel Tips

Here are four tips to make flying with your pet a less stressful experience:

➤ Your pet may be able to travel with you on board if its carrier will fit under the seat in front of you. This privilege is limited and only available on a first-come-first-served basis. Make arrangements with the airline reservationist or your travel agent.

➤ Check with the airline well in advance to ensure they will accept your pet for travel. Some carriers do not.

➤ When shipping your animal interstate or internationally, you'll need a current health certificate.

➤ Clip your pet's nails to prevent them from hooking onto the shipping crate.

The Least You Need to Know

➤ Americans with disabilities not only love to travel, their rights to accessible destinations are protected by the ADA.

➤ Children are highly portable and learn by traveling.

➤ If you have to travel with your pet, you can take precautions to help eliminate potential discomforts.

Part 2
Choosing the Perfect Ingredients

A good cooking instructor always stresses the importance of pure ingredients when you are learning to prepare the perfect Chocolate Soufflé. This section stresses the importance of choosing high-quality ingredients for your perfect vacation.

I'll show you how to blend the ingredients of a vacation into a mouth-watering treat. We'll start by taking one cup of transportation and slowly blending it with $1/2$ cup of accommodations. Set this mixture aside to breathe. In a separate bowl, we'll add a dash of restaurant savvy (you can substitute sage if you prefer) and pour in one cup of boiling stuff-to-do. Finally, combine both mixtures and bake for 30 minutes in a 275° oven.

Anyone else hungry?

Getting There Is Half the Fun

Cars and boats and planes are just three methods of traveling. There are hundreds of others. They range from the practical to the practically ridiculous.

Living in Southern California, I have seen with my own eyes that some people consider rollerblades and surfboards viable modes of transportation. If you have trouble understanding how surfboards could be classified as vacation transportation, you're not alone. When I mentioned that they weren't very practical for vacation transportation because they wouldn't go very far, the response I got was, "Well, like yeah, Dude, so what's your point?" So now I understand.

It's one of those Zen things, like, "It's good to plan an end for every journey; but it's the journey that matters in the end." What my surfer friend was saying (I'll translate) was that it's not how far you travel on the surfboard, it's how much fun you have traveling that really counts. The same applies to vacations. Gold vacation stars will not be awarded for the distance traveled, only for the amount of fun you had traveling. If getting there is more than half the fun, you get a gold vacation star.

Getting There by Car

When considering a driving vacation, you have three options:

1. Driving the family car

2. Driving a rental car

3. Choosing a Fly-Drive package

The choice between driving the family car or renting a car involves a mixture of cost, reliability, and convenience. You need to ask yourself, "Self, will the old Chevy in the garage endure 1,400 miles of intense driving or are we better off renting a newer, low-mileage car?" If your "self" answers this question out loud, you may want to check in with a mental health professional. The added expense of renting a car may be less than the repairs needed to make your family car reliable enough to go 1,400 miles.

The other reason for considering a rental car is convenience. A family of five with suitcases packed for a week looks a lot happier in a minivan than in a Honda Civic. Remember, it's not how far you travel that's important, it's how much fun you have while you're traveling.

Many tour operators combine an airline ticket and a rental car into a Fly/Drive option. Usually, the tour operator gets better prices from the airlines and car rental companies than you or I would because they buy thousands of these packages.

The Fly-Drive option lets you jump start your vacation. It's like buying a really trashy romance novel and skimming through the boring parts until you find something steamy and interesting. The Fly-Drive vacation lets you fly over the boring parts and absorb and enjoy the good parts.

For instance, let's say it's February in Cleveland. (Need I say more?) You're ready for a break, so you call your travel agent and reserve a 7-day California Fly-Drive package. You fly from Cleveland to San Francisco, drive south along scenic Route 1, and return to Cleveland from Los Angeles. You could drive that same itinerary, but you'd need more than a week—especially with the winter weather in the Midwest and Rocky Mountains. It's more fun and relaxing to Fly-Drive. Skip the boring stuff and head right for the good parts.

Avoid rental cars with the rental firm's logo affixed to the car. Ask the reservationist if their cars have logos or emblems affixed to them. This does nothing but call attention to the fact that you're away from home, probably lost, and probably carrying cash and credit cards to pay your expenses. Always call ahead to let others know when you're expecting to arrive, and plan your travels during daylight hours on major streets and highways.

An Ounce of Prevention Beats a Towing Bill

Whether you're renting a car or driving your family car, the following pointers will help you survive an extended road trip:

➤ Check the tire pressure each morning. Tires heat up when fully loaded cars cruise for hours at a time at high speeds, and if the tires are underinflated, they can heat up to rubber-damaging temperatures. Measure the pressure when the tire is cold (less than three miles of driving) to get a true reading.

➤ Rest every three hours. Drivers and passengers get a chance to stretch their legs, and the respite prevents fatigue and improves concentration.

➤ Check fluid levels often. Especially when driving in hot weather, proper coolant and oil levels are important. If a car does not have a maintenance-free battery, travelers should check water levels every time they stop for gas.

➤ Use a windshield sunshade (when you're not driving, of course). These cardboard protectors keep the steering wheel and seats from getting too hot to handle.

➤ Don't be too concerned if the car's climatic system seems ineffective on very humid days. Automotive air conditioning both cools the air and removes moisture. On muggy days, the system has to spend more time removing moisture, so it removes less heat. Temperatures inside your car may be 8 to 10 degrees higher on a steamy day than on a dry one.

Kid Tips

Here are some tips for traveling with children in automobiles:

➤ Regulations vary from state to state, but most require that small children use car safety seats, not seat belts. In some states, children up to age five are required to use car safety seats. Fines range from $10 to $500. Car rental company reservationists can advise you or your travel agent of state requirements.

➤ It is considered safer for children to ride in the back seat, preferably in the center.

➤ Infants should be fastened securely into infant car seats facing the rear window.

➤ Car seats should have five-point harnesses and be FAA-approved.

➤ Children should never ride in someone's lap.

➤ Children who outgrow car seats are safer in booster seats than in regular seatbelts designed for adults.

➤ If you do not have your own car safety seat, call a car rental company at least 24 hours ahead of time and reserve one. The cost for renting the seat will vary between $5 to $25 per week.

➤ Combination car seat/strollers are available. These convert easily from one function to the other and eliminate the need to carry separate car seats/strollers.

➤ Always look for car seats that offer both rear-facing seating for infants and front-facing seating for older children.

➤ Allow your children to stretch after being in a car seat for an extended period. There have been cases where children have fallen asleep in car seats and suffered nerve damage due to poor circulation.

➤ Call the National Highway Traffic Safety Administration at 202-366-0123 for more information about car seats and state regulations.

Cultivating Good Passengers

The difference between a fabulous vacation and a long drive in the car is often determined by what goes on in the back seat. (No, I'm referring to backseat activities while the car is moving, the driver has both hands on the wheel, and the children are occupying the backseat. I think you've watched one too many Gidget movies.)

Anyway, a classic passenger pleaser is a bag filled with car games. If you don't believe me, just rent *National Lampoon's Vacation* starring Chevy Chase (the Griswalds made car games an art form).

One or our favorite commercial car game kits is, "Miles of Smiles: 101 Great Car Games and Activities." It sells for $8.95 and is available by calling 510-527-5849. If you're into an old-fashioned, driving vacation and feel buying 101 car games would compromise your family vacation values, here are some of our old favorites:

➤ Counting states on passing license plates.

➤ Identifying things in alphabetical order. (The official rules state that, "A Roadmap" satisfies the requirement for an "R," but is not acceptable as an "A" answer.)

➤ Writing a travel journal. Take a periodic break to gaze off into the distance. It'll make others think you're a pensive writer, and it also keeps you from getting car sick.

➤ Writing postcards. This time let's see if you can be more creative than, "Dear Scott, How are you? I am fine. Having a great time. Wish your were here."

➤ CD or Cassette player with earphones. Let me tell you there is nothing like driving through the Berkshires, viewing pastoral scenes, and cranking the volume on a Nine Inch Nails CD. If you have to ask, "What's a Nine Inch Nail?" you're old enough to drive and shouldn't be wearing earphones.

Pay special attention to the extra charges that can be added to your car rental price. Always ask about these charges when you make your reservations. It's too late to change car rental companies when you're returning the car and are shocked and horrified by the amount of the bill.

Here's a sampling of the tax rates on car rentals at major U.S. cities:

Seattle	15%
Las Vegas	12.5%
Phoenix	10%
New York	8%
Memphis	8%
Tampa	6%
Atlanta	4%

Northern and Southern Exposure

Canada and Mexico have laws, too. Although after driving in Mexico, I'm fairly certain they do not apply to the natives (at least not to the taxi drivers). Here are a few tips to help make your driving vacations in these two countries a pleasant experience:

Driving Regulations for Canada

➤ You need a valid U.S. driver's license. A passport or birth certificate may also prove useful.

➤ You must carry evidence of a minimum amount of liability insurance equivalent to $200,000 CDN in every province except Quebec, where the minimum is $50,000 CDN. The CDN means Canadian dollars rather than U.S. dollars. Currently, one Canadian dollar equals about 75 cents, so $200,000 CDN amounts to about $150,000 USD. The exchange rates for all foreign currency change daily. Be sure to check the financial pages of your newspaper or call your travel agent to obtain a current quote.

➤ Most U.S. insurers cover drivers in Canada. Ask your insurance agent to provide you with a Canadian Non-Resident Inter-Provincial Motor Vehicle Liability Insurance Card. Wow, your agent will need a vacation after saying that a few times.

Driving Regulations for Mexico

➤ Although post-NAFTA changes are still in the works, be prepared for some red tape and frequent changes.

➤ You will need a passport or certified copy of your birth certificate, a valid U.S. driver's license, and a Mexican Tourist Card if you plan to stay longer than three days. You can obtain a Mexican Tourist Card from your airline when you check in for your flight, or from most travel agencies.

➤ If you are taking your own car farther than the immediate border area (loosely defined as within 10 miles of any border crossing), you will need to take the original title and registration. It's also a good idea to take several photocopies.

➤ When you arrive at a border station for cars (about 12 miles inside the Mexican border) you can get your new driving permit by paying $10 with a credit card issued by a bank outside Mexico. If you are driving a company car or a friend's car, bring along a notarized letter authorizing you to drive the car. This letter must be signed by the proper owner or the owner's representative.

➤ Your stateside insurance is probably not valid in Mexico. You will have to purchase Mexican liability insurance from an office at the border crossing or from the U.S. car rental agency. Credit card collision insurance is accepted in Mexico.

Special Tips for Cold Weather Driving

When you rent a car, you're not only preparing to drive a strange car, but you may encounter unfamiliar weather and driving conditions. Be careful and observe the following in cold weather environments:

➤ Be sure to find out how to obtain emergency road service.

➤ Antilock brakes, which should not be pumped, are the best. If the brakes are weak, switch cars.

➤ The gas tank should be at least half-full.

➤ The battery posts should be free of deposits and the clamps should be tight.

➤ Inspect the headlights, turn signals, and brake lights.

➤ Tires should be all-weather radials or snow tires with plenty of tread.

➤ Check the wipers. Do they streak? Is there sufficient fluid?

➤ Test the heater and defroster before you leave.

➤ If you are driving to unpopulated areas, make sure you have chains or traction mats, abrasive material such as sand or salt, a small snow shovel, a snow brush, an ice scraper, a flashlight, cloth or towel, booster cables, a blanket, and warning devices. (And now you understand why we moved to Southern California.)

➤ Cellular phones are highly recommended.

➤ Remember, at 32 degrees, ice forms and stopping distances increase dramatically. Ice is likely to form first on shaded spots, bridges, overpasses, and intersections.

➤ The best way to stop is to brake gently, engage the clutch, or put the car in neutral.

As Americans, we've always had a deep affection for the automobile. In 1992, we racked up over 280 million "person-trips" by car, according to estimates by the U.S. Travel Data Center. A "person-trip" is one person traveling 100 miles or more away from home. Auto travel accounted for over 80% of all summer vacations—about the same as the previous two years.

Up, Up, and Away

Whenever possible, avoid airlines that have anyone's first name in their titles, like Bob's International Airline or Air Fred.

—Miss Piggy

The arrival of commercial aviation, less than 85 years ago, initiated great changes in vacation travel. (And, to eliminate the rumor believed to have been started by Julie, our travel agency's manager, I did not fly the 1924 Imperial Airways Co. inaugural flight between London and Paris.) Most of these changes involved speed and price.

Many travel historians date the first commercial air service to the St. Petersburg-Tampa Airboat Line, which began daily operations on an 18-mile route across Tampa Bay on January 1, 1914. The fledgling airline carried 1,204 passengers (at $5 per trip) before it ceased operations in April.

During the 1920s, speed was the newest status symbol. Cars reached the incredible speed of 200 miles per hour, trains were regularly traveling at more than 100 mph, and cruise ships shortened the Atlantic crossing to just over four days. Even the new dances of the 1920s, like the Shimmy and the Charleston, epitomized this accelerated pace of living. For the traveling public, the speed of the airplane coupled excitement with fear.

And then, an interesting thing happened. As airplanes flew faster and safer, the price of riding in them fell lower and lower. So low that today, a one-hour flight, covering hundreds of miles, frequently costs less than $100. Air travel, which was once the exclusive scene of the wealthy jet-set, quickly became affordable for almost every social and economic group. At the same time, the number of vacation travel options, which had been limited to the range of the family car, were growing by leaps and bounds.

How Safe Is Flying?

According to the latest research, flying is safer than riding your bicycle during a tornado. Here are your odds:

Death By:	Your Odds:
Cardiovascular disease	1 in 2
Smoking (by age 35)	1 in 600
Car trip, coast-to-coast	1 in 14,000
Bicycle accident	1 in 88,000
Tornado	1 in 450,000
Train trip, coast-to-coast	1 in 1 million
Lightning	1 in 1.9 million
Bee sting	1 in 5.5 million
Commercial airline accident	1 in 10 million

Sources: "Achieving Comfortable Flight" Pathway Systems, Natural History Museum of Los Angeles County, Massachusetts Institute of Technology, University of California at Berkeley.

Frequent Flyer Cards

It's true folks, the ultimate preppy status symbol for an infant is an airline frequent flyer card. Never mind that infants can fly free until they turn two years old, as long as they sit on an adult's lap. The lure of future free travel or upgrades to first class are so strong, parents are buying tickets for infants so they can begin racking up those miles.

Originally, the airlines offered frequent flyer mileage bonuses to build brand loyalty. That's the same reason cereal companies dump all that sugar into a box of flakes and nuts. Both are trying to get you hooked on their brand and keep you from trying brand-X. Now that virtually every airline has a frequent flyer program, the goal has shifted from brand loyalty to revenue generation. The airlines are selling their miles to hotels, car rental companies, travel agencies, credit card companies, and just about anyone who approaches them with enough money.

While each airline's frequent flyer program differs, you only need about 25,000 miles to earn a free airline ticket for travel within the 48 contiguous states on any one of them. This may seem like a large amount, but the special offerings and bonuses allow you to accrue mileage and earn free travel very quickly.

All frequent flyer programs are similar. You should choose to participate in one whose sponsors (airlines, hotels, car rental firms, and so on) match your desired destinations. Unless you like overpaying, never select a flight, hotel, or a car strictly because they participate in a specific frequent flyer program. If you want to save money, you should always check all suppliers for pricing and availability. Frequently, you'll find frequent flyer loyalty comes with a hefty price tag.

Frequent Flyer Credit Cards

One way to accelerate the accumulation of airline miles is to get a credit card that earns frequent flyer miles every time you charge. Many credit card companies give one frequent flyer mile for every dollar you charge. If you're a big spender, you'll earn a free ticket without ever flying!

One of our travel agency's clients uses his American Airlines Citibank Visa card to buy all his groceries and pay his son's college tuition. With the price of groceries and college these days, he earns a free ticket for his son to fly home for the holidays. They say it pays to be a frequent buyer.

Here are a few Frequent Flyer Mileage Producing Cards:

American Airlines: Citibank Visa or MasterCard. 1-800-843-0777.

American Express. 1-800-545-5038.

Continental—Marine Midland Visa or MasterCard. 1-800-446-5336.

Diners Club—1-800-234-6377.

Northwest—Bank One Visa 1-800-945-2004.

United—First National Bank of Chicago 1-800-537-7783.

If you decide to acquire one of these cards, make sure you check the annual fees and interest rates before you select a card.

Making Air Travel More Pleasant

Northwest Airlines posted a questionnaire on the Internet (the big computer network that gets all the media attention) and asked subscribers to select from the list below no more than three of the most important things an airline can do to make their travel more pleasant. Here's how they responded:

On-time operations	82.2%
Provide more legroom	54%
Get luggage out faster	30.4%
Offer family fares	28.2%
Provide more entertainment choices	18.7%
Allow more carry-on items	17.2%
Provide greater seating choices	14.7%
Provide destination information	14.4%
Extra staffing	10.3%
Help with children	8.4%
Allow fewer carry-on items	8.4%
Give business travelers preference	5.5%

The Best Airlines

Picking the best airline is risky business. If you fly enough, you generally will find good reason to hate every airline. On the other hand, you probably can't do much about it, because of all the frequent flyer miles you have stored in your account.

Sometimes though, airline personnel rise to the occasion and give stellar performances. One of the best I've witnessed was several years ago on a Friday afternoon flight from New York's Laguardia Airport to Chicago's O'Hare. If you've ever been to Laguardia on a Friday afternoon, you know the culture. It gives new definition to the word zoo.

The flight was boarding and all the first-class passengers boarded early so everyone could look at them as they walked to the back of the plane. The flight was oversold (customary for New York on a Friday afternoon) and the ground crew was doing everything possible to get an on-time departure.

As I boarded the plane, I heard one of the flight attendants tell a plump, obnoxious-looking gent that she'd be glad to serve him another martini as soon as boarding was complete and the aisles cleared. At that point, he screamed at the top of his lungs, "Young lady, I find that (expletive deleted) totally unacceptable. You'll get me a (expletive deleted, again) martini, and you'll get it now! And by the way, do you know who I am?"

The boarding process had come to a complete stop and everyone took a look at the complete (expletive deleted).

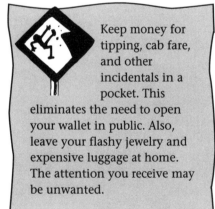

Keep money for tipping, cab fare, and other incidentals in a pocket. This eliminates the need to open your wallet in public. Also, leave your flashy jewelry and expensive luggage at home. The attention you receive may be unwanted.

Without hesitation, the flight attendant grabbed the microphone for the public address system and said, "Excuse me. Excuse me ladies and gentlemen. We have an emergency onboard. Does anyone know the man in seat 1B? He seems to have forgotten who he is!"

With that, the pompous passenger raced off the plane and the flight attendant received a standing ovation. The flight departed on time and the Captain bought all the passengers a drink.

Fortunately, a number of others agree with me, because according to the 1994 World Travel Awards, in which travel agents judge the Top North American Airlines, American Airlines landed the #1 position. Delta Air Lines and United Airlines were second and third.

Have you ever wondered why Delta uses two words, "air" followed by "lines" in their corporate name while American and United use the single combined form of "airlines?"

Well, I called Delta and learned that years ago, airline codes for ticketing purposes consisted of three letters. Delta Air Lines was DAL. American Air Lines was AAL and United Air Lines was UAL. When ticketing became automated, the three letter codes became two letters. Delta became DL, American became AA, and United became UA. Advertising types at most airlines (or is it air lines?) pounced on this insignificant little change and enlarged it to epic proportions by changing their names from Air Lines to Airlines. It was the chic, trendy thing to do.

Delta resisted the temptation to join the crowd and became the champion of Air Lines and the guardian of tradition. So, now you know.

Fasten Your Seat Belts Low and Tight Across Your Lap

Whenever I travel I like to keep the seat next to me empty. I found a great way to do it. When someone walks down the isle and says to you, "Is someone sitting there?" just say, "No one—except the Lord."

—Carol Leifer

Here are 10 things you can do to enjoy a more comfortable flight, courtesy of *Men's Fitness* magazine, November, 1994.

1. Sit in bulkhead or exit row aisles seats. Bulkheads offer extra legroom, and no one can recline his seatback into your face, food, or computer. Remember that you have to store your carry-on luggage in the overhead if you sit in the bulkhead seat because there is no seat in front of you. Exit rows have the luxury of extra legroom also, but you must be able to speak English and open the emergency door, if needed. If you're traveling with your children, they will not be allowed to sit in an exit row.

2. Dress for duress. Wear flat, lace-up shoes so you can loosen them when feet swell.

3. Protect your bags. Checked bags can get lost. Always have an identification tag on the outside and on the inside. Use curbside skycaps to avoid lugging heavy bags though the terminal and having to endure ticket counter lines.

4. Entertain yourself. Bring plenty of magazines—they are lighter than books, and disposable. Don't forget your Walkman and cassettes or CDs. You'll be asked to stow all electronic devices for take-off and landing, but you can use them while in flight.

5. Do "air-obics." A number of airlines offer in-seat exercise routines to help reduce swelling and pain for cramped muscles.

6. Fix your posture. Airline seats don't adjust for relaxed spinal posture. Support your lumbar spine with a rolled-up blanket, and your head and neck with a pillow.

7. Sit up front. Studies show there is less carbon dioxide in the forward seats. During a layover, get off the plane and stretch.

8. Drink eight ounces of water every hour. Airplane air has only 1 to 10 percent humidity, even less than most deserts. Bring your own bottled water and avoid caffeine and alcohol, which are dehydrating diuretics.

9. Eat light. Even if you order vegetarian meals, everything but fruit plates contains too much salt and fat. Bring healthful snacks, and don't overeat, because your internal organs naturally swell due to cabin pressure changes.

10. Use daylight to adjust to a new time zone. Don't try to sleep by going to bed right after you land, or try to stay up just because you gained a few hours.

Things That Go Bump in the Night

A great American pastime is trying to get something for nothing. You'd think a $99 round-trip fare would be a sufficient bargain. But no, some passengers want to try to get the airlines to actually pay *them* to fly. Believe it or not, the airlines will do this on a fairly regular basis. Now you're beginning to understand why some airlines have gone out of business and others have lost so much money during the past few years. The practice of getting the airlines to pay you to fly is officially called overbooking. Unofficially, it's known as "bumping."

Every traveler should order a copy of "Fly-Rights," a consumer guide printed by the U.S. Department of Transportation. This booklet has just been revised, and it reduces federal regulations regarding overbooking, smoking, and refunds to plain understandable English. It has new chapters on travel scams, frequent flyer programs, and helpful hints for disabled travelers. There's a section on bankruptcy protection and restrictions on free flight vouchers awarded by the airlines for overbooking.

The booklet costs $1.75; send your check or money order payable to the Superintendent of Documents, Consumer Information Center, Department 133-B, Pueblo, Colorado 81009. If you're a travel agent or group travel organizer, you'll receive a 25 percent discount for orders of 100 or more.

Passengers are entitled to compensation if they are involuntarily bumped. Current rules on domestic flights specify that if the airline places bumpees (a nontechnical term that I just made up) on an alternate flight that arrives:

➤ Within one hour of the original arrival time: no compensation required.

➤ Within one to two hours: compensation equals the one-way fare to the final destination, with a $200 maximum.

➤ More than two hours later: compensation equals double the one-way fare to the final destination, with a $400 maximum.

➤ On international flights, for delays of one to four hours, passengers are entitled to the one-way fare, $200 maximum; over four hours, compensation doubles. Exceptions apply, and rules pertain only to flights outbound from the U.S., not international flights to the U.S.

If you *want* to get bumped, see Chapter 19 to learn how.

Anchors Away

If you've watched too many *Gilligan's Island* reruns or you're like others who have never cruised, you may be afraid of the excesses and the restrictions—too many people in a small container or too much food and not enough freedom. These are common and valid objections from the first-time cruiser.

These and many other aspects of a cruise can ruin a vacation if the right ship is not matched with the right traveler. I know; it happened to me. The only good thing I can say about my first cruise is that it was short. The dining room was packed, the food was on par with most hotel banquets that serve 800 people at one time, the photographers always wanted to capture a "special moment" and charge for it later, and the other passengers had nothing in common with me and wouldn't have picked me out of a police lineup as a dinner companion, yet we were paired to have dinner together every night. To top this, tipping was not just encouraged, it was virtually mandated.

The World Travel Awards invite travel agents to judge the cruise ships that have given the best overall service. First place went to the QE2. (This award was presented before she alienated every passenger on a December, 1994, crossing from South Hampton to New York. Scheduled renovations were performed during the cruise at great inconvenience to every passenger. As a result, this will probably be the QE2s final World Travel Award.) The Norway and the Crystal Harmony were the second and third place ships.

The easy way around all this is to recommend a dripping-in-luxury cruise, such as Seabourn or Sea Goddess, but then not everyone can afford an $850-a-day cruise. The next option is to find the right ship and the right itinerary among those offered by Princess or Royal Caribbean or any of the others offering a middle of the market cruise product. Here are ten considerations that will help you make the most of your next cruise, whether it's your first or your fifth.

Picking the Best Cruiselines

1. Find a Ship That Matches Your Lifestyle

Cruise lines are like people. They come in all different sizes, shapes, and personalities. A great tactic to help you select the right ship is to ask your travel agent where they would book certain celebrities. This gives you an idea of which ships cater to which personalities without getting too personal.

For instance:

➤ Coach Hayden Fox would enjoy a Windstar cruise. (He's casual and informal, but very active; he can afford the best, but he's not out to impress anyone with his money.)

➤ James Bond would love the Seabourn. (He looks relaxed in formal dinner attire and expects the best service in the most exotic locales, plus he can afford it.)

➤ Jonathan Winters would fit nicely on Holland America. (It is classy without being restrictive, and he'd never feel uncomfortable gathering a small audience to entertain; he'd also enjoy sharing dinner conversation with people in his age group.)

➤ Indiana Jones would thoroughly enjoy a Special Expeditions cruise. (He's into adventure and faraway places that you only read about in *National Geographic*; he'd be right at home in a steamy jungle during the day and an intense lecture on global warming in the evening.)

➤ Roseanne and her television family would be a perfect match for Kathie Lee's, "You should see me now" Carnival Fun ships. (Roseanne would relish eating six times a day, not having to dress up, and shoving Ping-Pong balls down her bathing suit to win a prize.)

➤ Bill and Hillary Clinton would be happy on Crystal. (They're in their forties, affluent but not super-rich.)

You should also consider a ship's daily agenda. If a lengthy dinner every night sounds tiresome, select a ship with a café or pizza parlor where you can eat more quickly and informally. If you don't want to pay an arm and a leg for laundry services, choose a ship with a laundry room. And consider nighttime entertainment. If you prefer films to musical shows, and educational talks to gambling, choose a ship that schedules lectures in the evenings or that has a movie theater or an in-room VCR.

2. Use a Good Travel Agent

A specialist who can match you to the proper ship and help you select accommodations makes the difference between a fabulous vacation and potluck. Make sure the agent you choose has sailed with different cruise lines. Beware of the agent that seems to keep pulling and pushing you back to one cruise line. They could be receiving a bonus or incentive to book that line. Just remember, the cruise should be matched to your best interests, not your travel agent's. A good agent will ask questions about your travel habits and preferences, give customized advice, make special arrangements, offer several viable options, and prepare you for possible pitfalls.

3. Don't Overpack

Closet space is limited, and all you really need for a typical week-long cruise is one formal and one semiformal outfit. In fact, if you pack properly for a seven-day warm weather cruise, you can carry everything onto the plane. This is a wise move, considering how much opportunity there is for baggage to go astray on the way from the airline check-in counter to the baggage-claim area to the ship terminal to your cabin. Also, suitcases must be left outside cabins on the last night so that they can be removed while you sleep and taken to the terminal when the ship docks. If luggage gets lost, damaged, or pilfered and you have not bought baggage insurance, full reimbursement is unlikely; many cruise lines' liability limit for lost baggage is a mere $100 per bag.

4. Avoid the Crowds

If you are worried about being able to nab a secluded deck chair far from the poolside madness, book a cabin with a private verandah. You can typically opt to dine there as well.

Avoid buffet lines by eating in the dining room, which at breakfast and lunch is half-empty. As for public events, you may be better off dodging some completely.

Wherever there are crowds, ships' photographers are close at hand, usually invading your space. Fend them off by stating from the start that you won't be buying any pictures.

5. Plan Shore Excursions in Advance

One of the best aspects of a cruise is that it allows you to survey so many different destinations without packing, unpacking, or worrying about the logistics of getting there. After scouting out six islands in seven days on my Caribbean cruise, I now know which merit further exploration and which I've seen enough of.

Cruise lines offer several different group excursions at each port. Research the ports in advance so you know how you would like to spend your time there. Ask your agent for a copy of the excursions brochure. Then, when you board, you will know exactly what to book and can do so before it sells out. Keep in mind that ship-arranged tours may mean being loaded onto a bus with strangers. You may want to rent a car for the day, or, instead of a group excursion to a public beach, you may prefer cabbing it to a lovely oceanfront resort, lunching by the pool, and lingering there for the afternoon.

Independent excursions can also be economical. On our cruise, a fellow traveler and I explored Barbados by taking the ship's sightseeing excursion in the morning, then hiring a car to drive us around the other half of the island in the afternoon. Had we hired the car for the entire day, we would have spent the same amount and had more freedom. Had there been three of us, we would have saved money. If four or more people are cruising together, don't go with the group from the ship, go by yourselves.

If you're interested in heading for far-flung lands, have your travel agent find out the cost of having the ship arrange private cars. You see the same stuff, only in greater comfort and in half the time. And the cruise line inherits a certain responsibility for the quality and safety of the tour, as well as for making sure you're back before the ship sails.

6. Think of CRUISING As a Spa Vacation with a New View Every Morning

Many people equate cruising with stuffing themselves silly, but a cruise is actually an excellent opportunity to shed pounds—with healthy menus available, the personal dietary requests that most cruise lines will fulfill, and the abundance of fresh fruits and vegetables. Exercise facilities on some of the newer ships are state-of-the-art, and exercise classes are scheduled frequently. Just skip the midnight buffets. By the way, make appointments for massages and other spa treatments first thing, because popular hours fill up quickly.

7. If You Don't Like Your Dining Companions—Move

On most cruises, the dining experience is a crapshoot. Passengers request a specific seating time and table size in advance, but these often are not guaranteed, so upon boarding, confirm with the maitre d' that you have gotten what you requested.

You will probably end up dining for close to two hours every night… with people you've just met. Unless you want to dine alone, parties of two should request a table for at least six. If you decide you can't stand your dinner partners, it will be less uncomfortable to leave a table with two other couples than to leave a table with only one. Do not wait until the second or third night to ask the maître d' to switch you to another table.

If it is important to you to sit at the Captain's table (or to receive other special treatment, such as a tour of the bridge or an invitation to an exclusive cocktail party), send the captain a bottle of Dom Perignon; you'll get anything you want after that. If you are prominent in your profession, ask your travel agent to send the cruise line a short letter noting that you have expressed an interest in dining with the captain.

8. Take Cash for Tips

Certain luxury ships forbid gratuities, but most encourage them by handing out tipping guidelines. On one ship, we were advised to place varying amounts of cash in envelopes, to be handed to certain crew members. We had not brought the proper amounts with us, since the brochures told us about its cashless system (all services could be charged on a plastic card). So on tipping day, we had to wait in a seemingly endless line at the cashier's desk. Find out in advance how much cash you'll need for tips, and take the right size bills.

9. Tip at the Start

Cruise lines recommend tipping at the end of the trip, but you may receive better service if you tip the dining room staff on the first night, and tell them you're anticipating a wonderful cruise. Most lines suggest a very conservative tipping schedule; they don't want the amount to look so egregious that you won't book on their ship. It is advised to add 50 percent to the ship's proposed tipping schedule, presenting half of that amount on the first day, and saying the rest will come later.

10. Avoid Long Disembarkation Lines

The larger the ship, the more bodies trying to get off, the more buses you have to load, the harder the disembarkation. If your schedule permits, be last in line rather than first. If disembarkation is between 8 and 10 a.m., for instance, eat a leisurely breakfast, relax in your cabin, and get in line at 9:45. On the other hand, if your airline arrangements require an earlier exit and you did not book them through the cruise line, tell the purser you have independent flight arrangements and must disembark early. You will be among the first passengers off.

The Least You Need to Know

➤ Getting from place to place is the most important part of your vacation. Make it fun and rewarding.

➤ Driving can be the best way to discover those off-the-beaten-path gems that produce lasting vacation memories.

➤ Flying allows you to make rapid changes in your environment, enjoy a new scene, and still have money to spend at the destination.

➤ The most important part of a cruise is selecting the right ship and the right itinerary.

A Roof over Your Head

As my good friend Al Capp told me a few years ago, the best thing to do with a hotel confirmation slip when you're told there are no rooms available is to spread the confirmation slip out on the sidewalk in front of the hotel and go to sleep on it. You'll either embarrass the hotel into giving you a room, or you'll be hauled off to jail, where at least you'll have a roof over your head.

—Art Buchwald

The most important thing you need to know about selecting a hotel, booking a hotel, or staying in a hotel is that to do these things, you'll have to leave the most outstanding hotel in the world: your home. Once you know this, you'll be a much happier traveler.

Hotels have been around for thousands of years. They've been called boarding houses, inns, lodges, guest houses, hosteliers, resorts, spas, and motels. (If they advertise hourly rates, they go by another name and are beyond the scope of this book.) Whatever their name, they're all pulled together by a common thread: they provide sleeping accommodations, some more deluxe than others, some offering more services than others, and some much larger than others.

The other common link is that they can never replace the experience of sleeping in your own bed. Everyday, people in the hospitality business deal with guests that have been plucked from the comforts and conveniences of their homes and expect the pillows to feel the same, the bathroom light switch to be in the same location, and the morning coffee to taste the same. The difference between an enjoyable and a miserable stay away from home begins with realistic expectations. There really is no place like home, although a room at The Ritz Carlton Laguna Nigel comes pretty close.

Why do people stay in hotels? The typical hotel guest from the 1994 lodging industry profile, prepared for the American Hotel and Motel Association, gives us the following breakdown of the reasons we stay in hotels:

Business Trips	29%
Conferences	26%
Vacations	24%
Visit family	20%

Choosing the Right Type of Accommodations

Places to stay run the gamut from room to suite and from subsistent to lavish. Selecting the right type of accommodation is a matter of matching your vacation itinerary with the availability of various lodging options. To help you sort through the vast variety of accommodation possibilities, here's a description of various types of places to lay down your sleepy head.

Hotels, Motels, and Hostels—What's the Difference?

The differences between hotels, motels, and hostels have more to do with architecture and price than with any other element. The entrance to a hotel room is normally from a hallway, while a motel room entry-way opens to the great outdoors. Hotels and motels usually have private sleeping rooms, while hostels frequently offer dormitory sleeping arrangements. Although you can always find exceptions to the rule, hotel rooms usually cost more than motel rooms. Hostels are the least expensive of the three choices.

Groups, Chains, and Management Companies

Chains, as they relate to hotels, are brand names. Just as the Kellogg's brand has a number of different breakfast cereals, the Holiday Inn brand has a number of different hotel properties. Although they all carry the Holiday Inn name, they are individually owned and managed.

Most of a chain's individual hotel properties are owned by independent companies. These companies sign a franchise agreement with a chain like Ramada Inn, Holiday Inn, or Sheraton. In exchange for their signature, and a bucket of money, the independent company gets to erect a big sign using the chain's name, tap into their central reservation service, and send their employees to training.

Although franchise agreements require strict compliance with specific quality issues, such as maintenance, appearance, and linens, you may find some properties more desirable than others. The local owners have to write the checks and hire the staff to deliver the quality. Some local owners are more skilled at this than others.

In contrast, *hotel groups* are collections of privately owned properties that have banded together to form a marketing alliance. Utell International is an example of a hotel group. They provide marketing, sales, and reservation services for their member hotels. Although a hotel group is concerned about the quality of each of its member's properties, they don't have the influence and control of a chain.

The third type of organization is a *management company*. Hyatt is a good example of this. Most of their hotel buildings are owned by investors. These investors contract with a hotel management company, such as Hyatt, to bring their signs, their personnel, and their standards to the property. The management company is renting the hotel structure from the investors. Since all aspects of the hotel's operations are controlled by the owners of the brand name, the quality is more consistent at these properties.

Top Five Boutique Hotels

Boutique hotels are small, intimate operations, known for their creative eccentricities rather than their standards. They've been described as a hotel with a personality, and I'll accept that. Here are five top boutique properties. There are more, but because these hotels are unique, so is this list. I mean, just because Letterman's lists come in tens, it doesn't mean every list has to have ten items. Okay?

1. Kimberly Hotel—New York, 212-755-0400. Originally built as a luxury apartment building, the 192 rooms and suites in this Manhattan hotel have balconies. The suites (150 of them) have kitchens and are very spacious.

2. Post Ranch Inn—Big Sur, California, 408-667-2200. Overlooking the Pacific Ocean, these 30 guest rooms, each named after the homesteaders in the area, include fireplaces, stereo systems, massage tables, and complimentary beverages. Opened in 1992, it's difficult to decide which you enjoy more: the environmentally correct architecture or Chef Wendy Little's Sierra Mar restaurant.

3. Molly Pitcher Inn—Red Bank, New Jersey, 908-747-2500. Built in 1928 on the shores of the Navensink River, this 106 room hotel resembles Philadelphia's town hall.

4. Phoenix Park Inn—Washington, D.C. 202-638-6900. Located within walking distance from Union Station and within five blocks of Capitol Hill, this hotel tries to make you feel like you never left home. Their 87 rooms allow them to offer a high degree of personalized service. Check out their special weekend packages.

5. The Sherman House—San Francisco 415-563-3600. A big mansion turned into a small luxury hotel. These 14 rooms are situated in San Francisco's posh Pacific Heights residential area. If you'd like to stay in the first hotel opened in California and the fourth in the United States, this is the place.

All-Suite Hotels

A customer once questioned a fax I sent recommending an all-suite property for his family of five's vacation to Phoenix. They were taking advantage of the low airfares and planned to see a few spring-training baseball games. I sensed irritation in his voice as he began complaining about having to stay in such a fancy hotel. He said he had to wear a coat and tie every day to work, and the last thing he wanted to do was stay in a vacation hotel that required him to wear suits everyday.

I realized he was mistaking the word suites for suits and told him this was not an all-suits hotel, it was an all-suites (pronounced "sweets") property. He felt better instantly but then paused and said, "But Scott, I don't think that'll work either. My wife and daughter are on a diet and having all those sweets around would just be too much temptation."

Sometimes, it's best to know when to just fold your cards and move on to a different table.

Each suite at an all-suite property usually has a separate bedroom and a separate living room area. Many times, the living room contains a small kitchenette and a sofa-bed. All-suite properties target families. The two-room configuration gives the kids and the adults some privacy. The pricing of an all-suite hotel is generally lower than two adjoining rooms at a chain property.

A recent advertisement for one of these all-suite properties read, "For about the price or a regular hotel room, you'll receive a free cooked-to-order breakfast, free in-suite coffee, free newspaper, free parking, and free airport shuttle."

You may recognize these all-suite properties. For the names of others, check your local Sunday newspaper's Travel Section or call your travel agent.

➤ Crown Sterling Suites

➤ Embassy Suites

➤ Guest Quarters Suite Hotels

➤ Hawthorne Suites

➤ Homewood Suites

Most of the newer suite hotels are designed from the ground up to accommodate families and vacationers who want a home-like living environment. Their two-room design offers a true living room feeling. Some of the older suite properties were conventional hotels that were later converted by sticking a door between two sleeping rooms. You may want to ask the hotel reservationist or your travel agent about the layout of the hotel before you make a booking.

Budget-Saving Digs

You've probably used the old saying more than once yourself: "You get what you pay for." Well, not always. I've stayed in $500 per night hotel rooms and I've stayed in $50 per night rooms. More than once, I couldn't find the $450 difference.

Several years ago, hotel marketing executives discovered the same thing. They discovered a large number of people wanted a safe, clean room, a work area, telephone, cable TV, and breakfast. This led to the development of the *no-frills* hotel. Examples of this very popular hotel product are:

➤ Clubhouse Inns

➤ Courtyard By Marriott

➤ Hampton Inns

➤ LaQuinta Inns

➤ Signature Inns

One sure-fire, albeit non-scientific, way to gauge the price of a hotel room (other than looking at the sign on the back of the door) is to inspect the bathroom. The size of a hotel room's bathroom is directly proportional to the cost of that room. If the bathroom has a separate tub and shower, hold on to your wallet. If there's a telephone in the bathroom, increase the limits on your VISA, and if there are two sinks and a swivel television mounted on the vanity, you may want to consider a second mortgage. On the other hand, a sink, tub/shower, and toilet with little or no room to turn around is probably cheaper than staying at home.

For their owners, hotels in New York City generate the most annual revenue per room: $47,652, according to the HOST Report, a semi-annual publication of Arthur Andersen. Runners-up included Miami-Hailed ($43,282), San Francisco ($39,084), Boston ($36,028), and Washington D.C. ($35,694). The lowest revenue per room among full-service hotels in major markets was reported by Atlanta ($21,140).

Concierge Levels and Other Luxuries

If you've taken Martin Mull's advice, stayed at a Red Roof Inn, and discovered that austerity isn't your cup of tea, you may want to try a hotel with premium service rooms. Hotels usually upgrade all the rooms on an entire floor and then give the floor a catchy name, like Concierge Level or Executive Club. Many times, these floors require special key access from the elevator. This just heightens the snob appeal of these floors.

Usually, rooms on these floors are not larger than standard rooms, but they do offer extra amenities. They also cost between $30 and $100 extra per night. The amenities include big fluffy bath robes, fancy shampoos and conditioners, and a private lounge that serves breakfast in the morning and hors d'oeuvres in the evening. Many of these floors employ personnel to help you arrange sightseeing, obtain tickets, or make dinner reservations. Some even have a front desk function so you can check in and out without standing in long lines in the lobby.

Resorts and Spas

Resorts and spas are single destination vacations. Frequently, they are the reason for traveling. The amenities and services of many resorts and spas overshadow their destinations. For instance, Palms Springs is a desert. It's rocks, sand, and cacti, but thousands of people flock there on vacation to enjoy their world class resorts and spas.

The difference between a resort and a spa is blurry. Many resorts call themselves spas and vice versa. A resort is generally a large expanse of property that offers enough activities so guests do not have to go elsewhere. These activities usually include golf, tennis, restaurants, and shopping. A good resort is a destination and doesn't have to rely on the surrounding community to attract guests. Disneyland in California is a good example. Vacationers choose Disneyland, not because of the lure and appeal of Anaheim, but because of Mickey, Minnie, and Goofy.

Here are a few of my favorite resorts:

➤ Loews Ventana Canyon; Tucson, Arizona

➤ Monakea; Hawaii

➤ The Grand Wailiea; Maui, Hawaii

➤ The Hyatt Grand Champions; Palm Springs, California

➤ The Homestead; Hot Springs, Virginia

➤ Marriott Sawgrass; Jacksonville, Florida

➤ The Americana Club; Koehler, Wisconsin

➤ Grand Traverse Resort; Traverse City, Michigan

A spa is like a resort with a focus on health and fitness. Resorts may contain spas, but spas seldom contain resorts. The action at a spa is at a morning aerobics session, followed by a demonstration of fat-free cooking, which is followed by a stress-reduction mediation hour. The body massages, mud baths, and other assorted forms of pampering make spa vacations extremely popular. Disney World in Florida is adding a spa and fitness option to their mega-resort.

Here are a few of my favorite spas:

➤ Doral Saturena; Miami, Florida

➤ Canyon Ranch; Tucson, Arizona

➤ The Golden Door; Arizona

➤ The Clairmont; Oakland, California

All-Inclusives

Club Med was one of the pioneers of the all-inclusive concept and is responsible for the popularity of these properties today. To compete with the cruise vacation market, many resorts and spas offer a simplified pricing structure. It's called *all-inclusive*, and it means that all food and optional activities are included in a predetermined price. Sometimes, all-inclusive packages include unlimited alcoholic beverages; other times, these are extra billing items like they are onboard a cruise ship. All-inclusive resorts and spas are very popular because they make vacation budgeting so easy. Once you've paid for your airfare and your all-inclusive resort, the only additional expenses you'll incur are magazines to read on the flight and souvenirs for your friends back home.

We spend billions of dollars on airline tickets, hotel rooms, and food when we vacation, but we're not big spenders when it comes to gifts or souvenirs. A recent Travel Industry Association survey found that 83% of us buy gifts or souvenirs when we travel and spend an average of $80 per vacation.

The survey found that men and women spend about the same; but younger travelers, between the ages of 35 and 44, spend about $92 on gifts per trip.

Resorts for Mature Travelers

Looking for a spot off the beaten path? Here are a few on each coast:

Rosario Resort on Orcas Island, one of the San Juan Islands near Puget Sound off the coast of Washington, can be reached from the mainland by a one-hour ferryboat ride. The resort is listed in the National Register of Historic Places and was built in 1909 as the residence of a shipping tycoon. The resort has an imposing pipe organ with almost 2,000 pipes, and many evenings offer an organ concert and a presentation about the resort's history. Orcas Island boasts a 5,000 acre park with waterfalls, lakes, and picturesque harbors. Rosario Resort offers a seniors' getaway package that includes guest rooms with views, round-trip ferry service, continental breakfast, taxes, and tips. The rate for two, one of whom must be over age 55, is $75 per night. For information, call 800-562-8820.

In Baline, Washington, farther north near the Canadian border, is the Inn at Semiahmoo, a luxury resort hotel with 200 large guest rooms, some with balconies and wood-burning fireplaces. The resort was at one time a lodge for salmon canners. It offers a discount from published rates based on the guest's age. For example, a 70 year-old guest would get a 70% discount. Minimum age is 55 to qualify. Regular rates are $175. Water-view executive suites range from $245 to $375. For information, call 800-996-3426.

On Florida's Gulf Coast, the Park Inn in Bradenton, south of St. Petersburg, is offering senior discounts of 15% to 20% (depending on location of guest rooms) for members of the American Association of Retired Persons (AARP) or those over age 60. Regular per person rates are $90–95, or $115 for a VIP suite with a Jacuzzi. The following extras are included: daily deluxe continental breakfast, two cocktails per adult, one game of bowling for each guest, use of the fitness center, and discounts on miniature golf.

Golfers may prefer the Park Inn's Hole-in-One deal, which includes continental breakfast, cocktails, use of spa, beach towels, and 54 holes of golf, including cart, on four different full-size courses. Package prices from January through April are $310 per person but are sharply reduced to $195 per person from May through October. For information, call 800-437-7275.

The Peabody Hotel in Orlando, Florida advertises itself as the only Five-Duck resort, since it has inaugurated the March of the Peabody Ducks, where ducks waddle through the hotel lobby twice daily. This ducky idea originated at an affiliate hotel with the same name in Memphis, Tennessee.

The Peabody Orlando, with just under 900 rooms, is extending its discount promotion for seniors to run throughout the calendar year 1995. Regular room rates run from $210 to $230 per night but are reduced to $89 for those over 50. The Orlando Peabody is near Walt Disney World, Sea World, and Universal Studios. Public transportation is available to these attractions. For information, call 800-732-2639.

Bed & Breakfasts

If you think a Bed & Breakfast (commonly called a B&B) is just that, a bed and a breakfast, you're in for a great vacation treat.

The best way to describe a B&B vacation is that it's like a trip back to your best childhood memories. Like the smell of toast and coffee as you pad down the wooden stairs in your slippers to be greeted by fresh-squeezed orange juice, the morning newspaper, and the owner's friendly Labrador Retriever.

B&B's are run by a group of special people that love to make new friends and exhibit a brand of hospitality that you'll never find in a hotel setting. There are very few rules at a B&B. You can come and go as you wish. You can make new friends and talk with everyone, or you can simply be by yourself and contemplate your existence.

B&B's truly enhance a vacation destination, especially if you've never been there before. The owners usually know all the little secret and fun things to see and do that never make the guide books, which is why they're still secret and fun.

Top Five Country/Luxury Inns

The Top Five Country/Luxury Inns according to INNovations (201-433-0151), a New Jersey firm providing marketing support of small lodging establishments, are:

Beaverkill Valley Inn, Lew Beach, NY

EastWind Inn & Meeting House, Tenants Harbor, ME

Madrona Manor, Healdsburg, CA

Tranquil House, Manteo, NC

Wake Robin Inn, Lakeville, CT

Top 10 B&Bs

Every year, INNovations inspects more than 1,000 properties and selects a few notables that display high levels of service, hospitality, and amenities. The B&B's they chose are:

1. Balance Rock Inn, Bar Harbor, Maine
2. Barley Sheaf, Holicong, Pennsylvania
3. Curry Mansion Inn, Key West, Florida
4. Inn at Occidental, Occidental, California
5. Inn at Depot Hill, Capitola, California
6. Inn at Long Lake, Naples, Maine
7. Inn on Summer Hill, Summerland, California
8. Queen Anne Inn, Denver, Colorado
9. Seven Sisters Inn, Ocala, Florida
10. Villa Rosa, Santa Barbara, California

Southern California Romantic B&Bs

Not all B&Bs offer *romantic* rooms, and not all romantic rooms are exclusive to B&Bs, but when you find a *romantic* B&B room, you've found a treasure. To classify a B&B as romantic it has to possess certain features, such as:

➤ In-room fireplaces

➤ Private places, such as decks or patios

➤ Breakfast in bed

➤ Tubs or showers built for two

➤ Big fluffy beds and comforters

These are our favorites:

➤ Post Ranch Inn, Big Sur, 800-527-2200 ($300 to $450 per night)

➤ Inn on Mt. Ada, Avalon, 310-510-2030 (about $500 per night)

➤ Hotel Vista Del Mar, Avalon, 310-510-1452 (about $100 per night)

➤ Knickerbocker Mansion, Big Bear Lake Village, 800-785-5535 (about $100 per night)

➤ Horton Grand Hotel, San Diego, 619-544-1886 (about $100 per night)

Special Lodging Experiences

I guess we all became intrigued with experimenting with different places to sleep about the time our parents allowed us to spend the night in the "fort" we built using the card table and a blanket. From there, we graduated to camping in the backyard and then on to more exotic destinations.

Back to School—Staying in a Dorm

The U. S. and Worldwide Travel Accommodations Guide lists low-cost rooms at colleges and universities. Every year, thousands of rooms go vacant on major universities in the United States. For as little as $12 to $24 per night, you can stay at over 375 universities in the U.S. This is simple, clean lodging with use of sports facilities, theaters, and other campus attractions. To receive your copy, write to Campus Travel Services, P.O. Box 8355, Newport Beach, CA 92660.

Dude Ranches

Ever since Billy Crystal's movie, *City Slickers* was a big success, dude ranch vacations have grown in popularity. If you'd like to try your hand at ropin' and ridin', partner, here are four vacation and guest ranch associations that would be darn proud to put you in touch with their members:

> The Dude Ranchers Association, Box 471, LaPorte, CO 80535, 303-223-8440

> Colorado Dude and Guest Ranch Association, Box 300, Tabernash, CO 80478, 303-887-3128

> Alberta Guest Ranch Association, Box 6267, Hinton, Alberta, Canada T7V 1X6 (mail only)

> British Columbia Guest Ranch Association, Box 4501, Williams Lake, British Columbia, Canada V2G 2V8, 800-663-6000

If you're ready to take the plunge, these dude ranch reservations services will answer your questions and reserve your vacation:

> American Wilderness Experience, Box 1486, Boulder, CO 80306, 800-444-3833

> Gene Kilgore's Ranch Vacations, Box 1919, Tahoe City, CA 96145, 800-472-6247

Hotel Etiquette and Customs

I remember my first trip to Chicago with my father. We drove from Iowa, where we grew cattle (always plant them with the feet pointed down) on our farm and were visiting the then-famous Chicago Stockyards. I'd never been inside a hotel until this trip, and I remember feeling very uncomfortable while we stayed at the venerable Stockman's Inn. I didn't know how to act. I'll always remember not quite knowing what to say or do. This next section will help you feel more comfortable when you encounter a new hotel experience.

Staff—Their Care and Tipping

Which would you rather have: a mediocre hotel structure and outstanding service or an outstanding structure and mediocre service? Unfortunately, the latter is in constant supply today. It's the little personal issues that make or break a vacation, and a hotel stay is no exception.

If the bellman that carried your luggage to your room sees you later in the elevator and calls you by name, that's impressive. If the housekeeper notices that you used every last towel in the bathroom and leaves you two extra towels when she cleans your room, that's impressive. And, if the hostess at the restaurant remembers your name and knows you want to be seated as far away as possible from the smoking section, that's impressive. Like I said, these are all little extras that add an enjoyable dimension to your stay.

Hotel staffs are not overpaid, and they do appreciate a gratuity if they add to the enjoyment of your stay. I'm a firm believer in giving monetary tips when they're earned and giving verbal tips (especially to the management) when they're not. A tip is discretionary. I've never seen the Gratuity Police arrest someone who just experienced poor service and refused to leave a tip.

Here are a few guidelines for tipping hotel personnel:

➤ Doorman (hails a taxi or unpacks your car)	$1/contact
➤ Valet (parks and retrieves your car)	$1/contact
➤ Bellman (carries your luggage to your room)	$1/bag
➤ Housekeeping (cleans and straightens your room)	$1/person/night
➤ Waitperson (takes your order and serves your food)	15–20%
➤ Concierge (commits a random act of kindness)	$10 or more for special assistance

Room Service

Hotels compile offbeat statistics during the course of a year. For example, in one year, 252 guests locked themselves out of their rooms at the Novotel New York, a French-owned property in the heart of Manhattan. Of those unfortunate souls, 30% were in various stages of undress, and 70% were women.

Naturally, room service sees a lot of undress, too. The same Novotel survey revealed that 43% of the men and 17% of the women who open the door are not fully dressed. The most common article worn by either gender when admitting room service personnel is a towel.

Regardless, there's something very soothing and romantic about being served a meal in your private room. I think we were born with the fantasy of being waited on hand and foot. Room service doesn't cost that much more ($2–5 surcharge) and it's a nice indulgence.

Suggestions for an enjoyable room service experience:

➤ If you're ordering breakfast and timing is important, place your order the night before.

➤ Remember, the kitchen is not usually next to your room, so order items that will remain tasty even if they're a little cool.

➤ If you're ordering dinner, remember you're going to be sleeping in your dining room. A heavy fish smell in the morning is an unpleasant way to start your day.

➤ Dial room service when you're done to collect your dishes and tray. Dirty dishes and scraps of food are like engraved invitations to a black tie dinner for insects.

➤ Make sure your towel is tightly fastened when answering the door!

Parking for Dollars

A few weeks ago, I overheard a conversation between a hotel guest and a parking garage cashier. The guest said, "No, you don't understand; I don't want to *buy* Park Place, I just *want* a parking place." The cashier had just told him his parking charges for five days, including tax, were $137.73!

Check out a hotel's parking charges before giving your car to the valet or pulling into the garage, especially if the hotel is located in a downtown area. These charges can be steep, ranging from $8 to more than $25 a day. Many times, you can find a parking lot or garage within a few blocks of the hotel that is more reasonably priced. The hotels figure you'll pay for the convenience of keeping your car nearby.

Dialing for Dollars

In addition to escalated parking charges, hotels are notorious for charging you for the convenience of using the telephone in your room. Usually, calls within the hotel are free, but frequently, calls outside the hotel result in charges between 50¢ and $1 each, even if you're calling a toll-free number.

If you use your room phone to place long distance calls and want the charges billed to your room, be prepared for an even greater shock. Hotels frequently contract with long distance service providers whose rates are not regulated by the FCC. A call that would normally cost $3 could cost more than $15. I was stunned when I recently checked out a very upscale hotel in Naples, Florida. The man checking out next to me was arguing about telephone charges that exceeded his room charges and his room had to be at least $135 per night.

One way to prevent telephone robbery is to ask the front desk personnel to explain, in plain English, their telephone charges. If they're exorbitant, use the pay phones in the hotel lobby, and always use the calling access number provided by the long distance carrier you use at home.

Minibar Means Maxi-Charge

Ever wondered about those intensely expensive cocktails, candies, and sodas from your hotel room's Minibar? According to Minibar North America (they evidently sell enough to fund their own association), the top choice is cola and diet cola followed by bottled water, orange juice, light beer, and M&Ms. In case you're interested, in 1993 we consumed 6,700,000 colas and 5,370,000 bottles of water. M&Ms sold 1,240,000 units and were more popular than Snickers and potato chips.

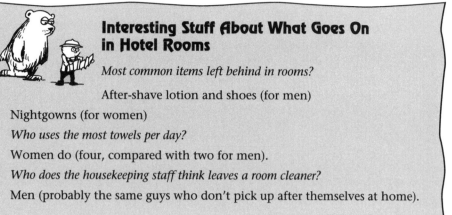

Interesting Stuff About What Goes On in Hotel Rooms

Most common items left behind in rooms?

After-shave lotion and shoes (for men)

Nightgowns (for women)

Who uses the most towels per day?

Women do (four, compared with two for men).

Who does the housekeeping staff think leaves a room cleaner?

Men (probably the same guys who don't pick up after themselves at home).

Safety Issues

No matter where you stay, whether it be the penthouse suite or one of Tom Bodett's "we'll leave the light on for ya" Motel 6 rooms, you need to take precautions. Most of these are common sense. For instance, you probably wouldn't leave $500 cash lying around your house, so why try it in a hotel? Or you wouldn't think of going to bed at home without checking to see that the doors are locked; but I've seen scads of hotel guests not only leave their doors unlocked, but to make entrance even easier, they leave their keys in the lock.

Here's a checklist for lodging safety:

➤ Deadbolt locks on all guest room doors.

➤ Fasten the nightlatches or chains on guest room doors, especially on sliding doors to the balcony or patio.

➤ Always use the viewports in your guest room door.

➤ Store cash, jewelry, and airline tickets in the safety deposit boxes at the front desk.

➤ Avoid parking lots and walkways that are not lighted after dark. Stop at the front desk and ask for an escort if you feel concerned.

➤ Greet and introduce yourself to the security personnel on the hotel property. Ask them how you can reach them in an emergency.

➤ Always, always, *always* plan your primary and secondary exit from your room in case of fire. If you have a difficult time remembering important stuff like this, place a sheet of paper on top of your clothes in your suitcase. This will remind you to take a moment and get familiar with this strange place. There is nothing more frightening than waking from a sound sleep in a strange room filled with smoke.

➤ If you are traveling alone, always request a room near a high traffic area, such as the lobby or an elevator, and *never* open the door for an unexpected hotel delivery without calling the front desk to verify the identity of your visitor.

The Least You Need to Know

➤ Hotels come in all sizes, shapes, and flavors. Choose one that fits your budget and your style, and then realize it will never be like staying at home.

➤ Resorts and spas can be vacations by themselves. Choose an all-inclusive if you're concerned about staying within your budget.

➤ B&Bs range from the exotic to the down-home, and they offer a vacation perspective that is unique unto itself.

➤ Regardless of where you stay, your safety and your family's safety is paramount. Don't cut corners.

Chapter 10

A Traveling Food Fight (er... Food Faire)

In This Chapter

➤ How your diet and your vacation are interwoven

➤ Airplane food; truth or dare?

➤ Vacations are for dining

➤ Regional dishes to spice up your vacation

Never eat in a restaurant that's over a hundred feet off the ground and won't stand still.

—Calvin Trilling

If you're concerned about gaining weight, drink a big glass of water before reading this chapter. It'll make you *feel* full and will allow you to get through all the gastronomic temptations (airplane food excepted) presented while you're on vacation. You have always been told never go to the grocery store on an empty stomach; the same advice holds true for this chapter.

We all store memories by attaching various sensory experiences to an event. For instance, when I recall the first-night baseball game at

Wrigley Field in Chicago, I hear thunder and smell wet wool; the game was rained out and I got drenched. When I think of my favorite South Bay-LA hangout, Fino, I hear Jordan's (the manager) friendly voice coupled with the aroma of garlic used to prepare the extraordinary tapas they serve. The same is true with vacation memories. Our senses prompt recall of past experiences.

This chapter is designed to delight your senses and stimulate your mind's capacity to recall pleasant events... like perfect vacations. I'll share some of my favorite tastes and smells and hopefully prompt you to go out and find some of your own.

Dining at 37,000 Feet

First, remember that you didn't board the airplane to enjoy a gourmet meal. You boarded because you wanted to get someplace in a hurry.

This wasn't always the case, though. Several years ago, Pan Am (tells you right there how long ago it was) offered a First Class amenity called "Upstairs Dining." They offered two seatings and you would "make dinner reservations" when you made your flight reservations. They took the entire upper deck of a 747 and turned it into a restaurant. You actually ate at tables rather than off the little tray attached to your neighbor's seat or buried in your armrest. The flight attendant/ waiter would carve a roast at your table, the wine list was superb, and if they forgot the Grey Poupon, they would turn right around to go get some—well, it's all true except the Grey Poupon bit. As you can tell from Pan Am's demise, "Upstairs Dining" was not a financial success, but it sure was nice... a good dinner, a current movie, a little nap, and you're in London. I miss those days!

An Airplane Eating Scenario to Ponder

Let me paint a picture. This will just take a moment. I promise it won't be a sermon, just one of life's little lessons.

I boarded a six-hour flight from Boston to Los Angeles and I sat next to two gushing honeymooners. I was tempted to give them marital advice, but quickly remembered I wasn't very qualified. So I continued my boarding routine: inflatable neck pillow, shoes removed, reading material organized, computer accessible, a pillow for my lower back, and a blanket to be used when the Captain decides to remind us how cold it was back in Boston. I'd just finished two glasses of water

116

(why? read about it in Chapter 8) and checked with the flight attendant to make sure that the fruit plate I'd requested would find its way to my seat at the proper time.

After take-off, the young couple ordered and inhaled four vodka tonics. They followed this with two glasses of white wine, a plastic plate of fat masquerading as lasagna, and two gooey chocolate chip cookies.

At an altitude of 37,000 feet with reduced cabin pressure, very low humidity, and low oxygen levels, they didn't have a prayer. Before they fell asleep, they'd ordered two more vodka tonics (at least they weren't driving), but the alcohol, fat, and sugar they'd just consumed was too much. Add to that a three-hour time change and they were gonzo. When they awoke, after landing in Los Angeles, they were so sick and hungover that I'm sure they had to postpone their honeymoon for a few days.

The little lesson here has to do with understanding that our bodies can take only so much stress and then they just shut down to repair the damage. Traveling is stressful, and flight compounds this stress. To counteract this stress, we need to eat and drink cautiously.

Special Meal Deals

Most major airlines that offer meal service also offer to prepare a special meal for you. All you have to do is ask. Each airline has a slightly different array of special meal menus, and they aren't available on every flight. The airline reservationist or your travel agent can tell you what's available on your flight and can even place an order for you.

Special meal offerings include Hindu, Buddhist, Muslim, and Kosher plates. I've asked for a Methodist plate, but have never received one. United Airlines teamed with McDonalds to offer special kids' meals on their flight to Orlando. They figure the kids may not get enough fast food at Disney World, so they better start offering it in the air. Other airlines also offer "Kids' Meals." They usually consist of a hot dog, potato chips, and milk.

Many airlines offer special plates for special diets like vegan, low sodium, low sugar, low carbohydrates, and low food. Some of the new "no-frills" airlines consider a bag of peanuts to be your special meal, but you don't need to order these in advance.

Some of my favorite special airline meals (I think that's an oxymoron) are fruit plates, vegetarian, and heart healthy. These meals look so appetizing that I've had seatmates offer to buy them from me. I figured $20 was a fair price. Besides, where else were they going to go?

Getting a Special Meal

If you have ever taken a tour of an airline's flight kitchen, you'll understand why you need to go through the following drill to make sure you get what you order:

1. Request your special meal when you reserve your flight. Be sure your meal is mentioned when your travel agent or airline reservationist reads your itinerary to you.

2. Ask your travel agent to print your meal request on your itinerary that is included with your tickets. This gives you written proof of your request.

3. Call your airline at least 24 hours before your flight departs to confirm departure times and reconfirm your meal request. If your request got lost, the airline will need at least 24 hours to resubmit the order.

4. When you board your flight, tell one of the flight attendants that you ordered a special meal. They're less likely to give it to someone else if you let them know you're expecting one.

5. If you change your assigned seat before the meal service begins, be sure to tell a flight attendant. Most special meals have your name and assigned seat number on a label attached to the serving tray.

6. If you don't get your meal, send a letter to the airline. You'll find their address in the in-flight magazine or one of the flight attendants can give it to you. It doesn't do any good to get mad at the flight attendants; when they arrive on a plane, catering is usually already boarding the food carts. You do want to let the airline management know of their mistake. They can and will review their systems and correct whatever problem caused your meal to disappear.

7. If you're really concerned about having a special meal due to your dietary requirements, you're always wise to bring an apple, some crackers, and cheese from home.

The airlines have done a good job improving their special meal menus and in delivering them. We average about six flights every month and I cannot remember when a special meal was not delivered. Of course, if I change my flight within 24 hours, I don't expect my special meal to catch up with me.

Airport Terminal Dining

Avoid dining at airport food concessionaires if possible. High cost and low quality is the best way to describe what you get. The reason: greedy municipalities that operate most airports. They charge food vendors high rents, and also take a healthy portion of the profits. Unfortunately, most of the people spending time at an airport reside in another city or country and can't vote in local elections. It's the 1990's version of taxation without representation. Tea anyone?

The Anti-Jet-Lag Diet

The Argonne National Laboratory has an anti-jet-lag diet that helps travelers quickly adjust their bodies' internal clocks to new time zones. It has also worked wonders to speed the adjustment of shiftworkers, such as power plant operators, to periodically rotating work hours. (Yes, another miracle diet. No, it doesn't involve eating Twinkies.)

The diet was developed by Dr. Charles F. Ehret of Argonne's division of biological and medical research as an application of his fundamental studies of the daily biological rhythms of animals. Here's how you can use this diet:

1. Determine what a reasonable breakfast time would be at your destination.

2. Do a "feast-fast-feast-fast" at home. Start three days before departure day. On day one, feast: eat heartily with a high protein breakfast and lunch and a high-carbohydrate dinner. No coffee except between 3:00 and 5:00 p.m. On day two, fast: eat light meals of salads, light soups, fruits, and juices. Again, no coffee except between 3:00 and 5:00 p.m. On day three, feast again. On day four (your departure day), fast; if you drink caffeinated beverages, drink them in the morning when traveling west, or between 6:00 and 11:00 p.m. when traveling east.

3. Break your final fast at the destination breakfast time, even if you're not there yet. And don't drink any alcohol on the plane. If the flight is long enough, sleep until the destination breakfast time, but no later. Wake up and feast on a high protein breakfast. Stay awake and active. Continue the day's meals according to mealtimes at the destination.

Here's how it works:

The high protein breakfasts and lunches stimulate the body's active cycle. Suitable meals include steak, eggs, hamburgers, high-protein cereals, and green beans.

The high carbohydrate feast suppers stimulate sleep. They include spaghetti and other pastas (but no meatballs), crepes (no meat filling), potatoes, other starchy vegetables, and sweet desserts.

The fast days help deplete the liver's store of carbohydrates and prepare the body's clock for resetting. Suitable foods include fruit, light soups, broths, skimpy salads, and unbuttered toast. Keep calories and carbohydrates to a minimum.

Dining vs. Eating Vacations

Perfect vacations give you an opportunity to see new sights and to also taste new dishes. To get the most out of your vacation, practice what we call, "Full Five Sensing." This means using all five of your senses: taste, touch, smell, sight, and sound. Five Sensing memories are very vivid and last a long time. Taste and smell are two of the most powerful memory joggers. I still remember a special bakery in Atlanta every time I smell fresh bread baking. My response is automatic and although the memory is more than 20 years old, my recall is vivid because it is stimulated by my sense of smell.

Take time on your vacations to exercise your senses of taste and smell by exploring and searching for local dining experiences. They'll add a new dimension to your enjoyment. I can't imagine having breakfast in Texas without some biscuits and red-eye gravy, or visiting New Orleans without several bowls of Jambalaya. At home, you eat as part of your daily routine. While on vacation, break out of your routine and enjoy some unique dining experiences.

If you're looking for a gastronomic vacation, cooking schools heat up. Enrollment at one- and two-week cooking schools around the U.S. was higher in 1992 than in any other year in the past two decades, according to a report in *The New York Times*. Of the 16 most common daily activities, cooking ranked seventh in pleasurableness, outranked only by love-making, socializing, talking, eating, engaging in sports, and shopping, in that order. Cooking was preferred to watching television or reading. Combining cooking with vacation gives you the best of both worlds.

Restaurant Guides—Fact or Advertising?

How do I find a good restaurant? Can I trust the restaurant guides? How can I avoid the tourist traps and eat where the locals eat?

First, finding a good restaurant takes more skill than luck. You start by asking people who you know do not have a vested interest in recommending one specific restaurant over another. This may be the clerk at a little shop you just discovered, or a flight attendant on your arriving flight. The concierge at your hotel may have some good suggestions, but they normally recommend the restaurants that have just invited them and their significant other for a free meal.

Restaurant guides that you find in your hotel room are almost always advertisements disguised as a food critic's review. Since you'll find these same guides in every hotel room in the city, you'll probably find a good crop of fellow tourists sitting at nearby tables. If you want a more unbiased opinion, buy a restaurant guide from a local bookstore. *Zagat Surveys* is one such guide. They tend to describe a restaurant with a minimum of adjectives and an ample dose of facts. They don't accept advertising, so they have no predetermined pick or pan list.

Top Ten Favorite Restaurants

Restaurants come and restaurants go. Sometimes they go so fast, they're gone before a recommendation gets printed in a restaurant guide. To avoid the embarrassment of recommending restaurants that are no longer available (or worse yet, ones that have changed owners, chefs, and menus, but left the same name on the door just to fool us), these top ten favorite restaurants have been around for a while. They're not old; they've just stood the test of time. They're like old friends: places you must visit whenever you're in town. They're also listed alphabetically because they're all #1 in our book.

➤ Biggs, Chicago, 312-787-0900. Most restaurants maintain an inverse relationship between their food and their ambiance. For instance, as a restaurant's view improves, the quality of their food diminishes. Biggs is one big exception. This restaurant occupies a turn-of-the-century mansion in one of Chicago's trendiest neighborhoods. Peter Salchow, Biggs owner, has meticulously restored the mansion. The food is outstanding and the service is as meticulous as Peter's renovations. Be sure and stop in the lower-level bistro for a nightcap after dinner. The wine cellar is awesome.

➤ Florence's, Boston, 617-523-4480. We were first introduced to this North End gem through a wonderful bottle of La Chryma Christi De Vesuvio, an Italian red wine that's almost as rare as this restaurant. There's nothing really fancy here, but that's the first sign of a great Italian restaurant. This is the type of place where you meet old friends and linger over great food and good conversation.

➤ Fred's Not Here, Toronto, 416-971-9155. Toronto has more than a city's share of good restaurants, so to select Fred's is quite a tribute. I'm not sure I can say what I like about Fred's. It keeps changing. The menu is best described as eclectic and that aptly describes the crowd that seems magnetically attracted to the place. I've never met Fred, but I hear he's never there.

➤ Greens, San Francisco, 415-771-6222. Gourmet vegetarian that will make you say, "Who needs meat?". The view of the Golden Gate Bridge is great, and the inventiveness of the dishes tells you there are some real artists in the kitchen.

➤ Joe's Stone Crab, Miami Beach, 305-673-0365. The absolute best potatoes with onions. We're not talking about good, we're talking about truly, 100% awesome. The stone crabs attract diners from seven continents, and rightfully so, but it's the potatoes with onions that keeps 'em coming back.

➤ The Restaurant in Mansion on Turtle Creek, Dallas, 214-559-2100. Every once in a while you have to splurge, I mean really go all out. I can't think of a better place than The Restaurant in Mansion on Turtle Creek. Not only does this establishment have the longest name of any restaurant in Texas, it is also the only one to have received the coveted Five Stars from the Mobile Travel Guide. Chef Dean Fearing is outstanding and will make this dinner a true vacation memory.

➤ The Saltry Restaurant, Halibut Cove, Alaska, 907-296-2223. Getting to this restaurant is a vacation in itself. First, you have to get to Homer, Alaska, which is Tom Bodett's home, and, as he puts it, "about as far as you can go without a passport." From the Homer Spit (if you don't know, that's another reason to visit Homer), you spend 45 minutes on a private ferry to Halibut Cove, which is nothing like Cabot (*Murder, She Wrote*) Cove on the other side of the world. This place is an artist's colony that redefines the words, "drop out." The restaurant has only two seatings and the food is created on the spot. We asked for the recipe of a dill vegetable soup and were told, "Sorry, we just made it up as we went along." It's that kind of place.

➤ Spago's, West Hollywood, 310-652-4025. We worked for weeks to lower our expectation to a sufficient level that would eliminate terminal disappoint in the Hollywood hangout. After all, no place can be that good that you need to make reservations a full month in advance. Well Spago's is, and the real treat was meeting chef and owner Wolfgang Puck after a memorable dinner. He actually still works there!

➤ The Teahouse, Vancouver, BC, Canada, 604-669-3281. Some restaurants possess magic and this is one of them. Its spectacular view of the Pacific's setting sun takes a backseat to the magic that's worked in the kitchen. Ask for a table in the atrium. It's like dining in someone's greenhouse. Please use caution though, one bowl of the carrot soup and you'll be planning a return vacation to Vancouver before you receive the check.

➤ Zaven's, Chicago, 312-787-8260. When the taxi driver drops you off at 260 E. Chestnut in downtown Chicago, you'll think I misled you. You'll be standing in front of a high-rise luxurious condominium with no visible sign of a restaurant. Don't worry, the entrance is just off the right-hand side of the lobby and inside is one of Chicago's best-kept dining secrets. The food is Continental, the atmosphere is romantic, and the real treat is meeting Zaven.

The Best of the Best

Ever get tired of all the "The Best" lists that deal with things you don't like? Well, this list has been developed over years of traveling using a very subjective and unscientific method. We just asked people to name their favorite treat and tell us where to find it. Here's what we found:

➤ Carrot Soup—Teahouse Restaurant, Vancouver, British Columbia

➤ Deep Dish Pizza—Gino's East, Chicago

➤ Hot Roasted Chestnuts—New York City Street Vendors

➤ Chocolate—Ghiradelli Chocolate Factory, San Francisco

➤ Hot Pretzels—Auntie Anne's, Cleveland

➤ Prime Rib—Lawry's, Beverly Hills, Chicago, Dallas

➤ Desserts—Any Cheesecake Factory Restaurant

➤ Hot Dogs—Wrigley Field, Chicago

➤ Coffee—Cafe DuMonde, New Orleans

➤ Chocolate Chip Fruit Cake—Ya-Hoo Cakes, Texas

How Do You Say... Ethnic?

One of the benefits of living in the United States is that we are truly a melting-pot of races and ethnic backgrounds. For the traveler, this means an opportunity to sample the cuisine and cultures of several foreign countries in just one city. Take San Francisco for example. Their Chinatown is much more than a stop for the tour buses; it's a thriving, bustling center of Chinese culture, commerce, and cuisine. The North Beach area, adjacent to Chinatown, is as close to an Italian village as you can get without visiting Italy. The Fisherman's Wharf business could pass for a Mediterranean Seaport, and San Francisco's Japantown offers the best sushi and shiatsu this side of the Pacific.

Take advantage of these cultural opportunities and explore the neighborhoods offered by different cities. You'll gain an understanding of a fellow human being who is also away from home.

There Seems to Be a Theme...

The latest trend in restaurants is toward an overstated theme. We see menus and interiors resembling chuck wagons, bistros, southern plantations, and speakeasys. The trend says that we want a little entertainment when we dine. The menus at these restaurants are creative and the wait staff usually put on quite a show. Whether you want to be amused or abused, theme restaurants can be a good time.

If you ever stumble across these theme restaurants, they're worth sampling: Ed Dubevics, Benihana, Outback Steakhouse, and The Cheesecake Factory.

To Your Health... and Safety!

If we really are what we eat, we should be extremely careful. Also remember that food poisoning and dangerous bacteria are not limited to rural or underdeveloped areas. Metropolitan areas, large chain restaurants, and cruise ships have contributed their share. It's not enough to carry a roll of Tums or a bottle of Pepto-bismol, you need to be informed. The following places will do just that:

➤ Health Conditions Update. Both travel agents and travelers can receive updates about health conditions by using a new automated fax service inaugurated by the Atlanta-based Center for Disease Control. By calling 404-332-4559, you are able to receive by fax information about travel health concerns. Various reports address everything from vaccination recommendations for different countries (yellow fever shots are advised for most countries in east Africa) to appropriate drugs to use to prevent malaria in Chloroquine-resistant areas (Lariam is top choice).

The system has only recently become fully operational, so you may encounter a few bumps, but service is generally excellent, providing fast, accurate information to help travelers stay healthy.

➤ Center for Disease Control (CDC) Travelers Hotline, 404-332-4559 or 404-332-4555. Automated menu of recorded messages providing information on disease risks throughout the world, by geographic region; vaccine requirements, and food and water precautions, plus recommendations.

➤ Ravel-Health International Inc., 800-659-7361 or 900-454-7525. Vaccine requirements, disease risk, security information, and entry requirements worldwide compiled from CDC, the World Health Organization, and the United States State Department. Callers to the 900 number are changed 95 cents a minute. Callers to the 800 number may charge the reports to their credit card at $7.95 for the first report and $3.95 for each additional report.

➤ U.S. State Department, 202-647-5225. Travel warnings and advisories.

The Least You Need to Know

➤ To avoid being disappointed with your airline meal, gnaw on a piece of tree bark before boarding your flight. Anything will taste good by comparison.

➤ Order a special meal at least 24 hours prior to your departure. You'll be the envy of your seatmates.

➤ Dining (tasting and smelling) should be an integral and exciting part of your vacation.

➤ Break out of your routine; you're on vacation. Eat something you've never tried before.

➤ Safe traveling means healthy traveling. Always be on the lookout for questionable hygienic practices. Be safe, not sorry.

Chapter 11

Activities: What to Do When You Get There

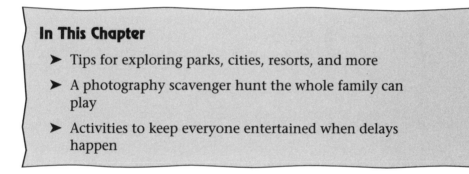

In This Chapter

➤ Tips for exploring parks, cities, resorts, and more

➤ A photography scavenger hunt the whole family can play

➤ Activities to keep everyone entertained when delays happen

This is Chapter Eleven. You know, E-Lev-En. Surely, you remember Eleven. It's just One more. (If you've never seen *Spinal Tap*, you probably think I've lost my mind. I have, but that's beside the point. Run right out and rent *Spinal Tap*; it's great background for this chapter.)

Since getting there is half the fun, what you do when you get there must be the other half. What you do is determined by your destination. If you're enjoying a beach vacation, you'll plan different activities than a theater weekend in St. Louis.

This chapter doesn't give you a list of every activity in every conceivable destination. That's the purpose of local guide books and magazines. Here you will find a series of Top 10 lists, with apologies to

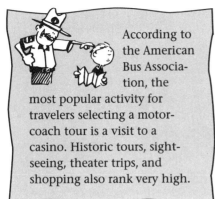

According to the American Bus Association, the most popular activity for travelers selecting a motorcoach tour is a visit to a casino. Historic tours, sightseeing, theater trips, and shopping also rank very high.

David Letterman. The idea is to get your creative juices flowing and to stimulate your best ideas for things to do. We don't ever want to hear this dialogue:

"What do you want to do?"

"I don't know, what do you want to do?"

"I don't know, I asked you first."

Sound familiar? Next time that dialogue gets started, pull out this book and flip to this chapter. There are millions (well, hundreds anyway) of things to do—you just need a little mental nudge to get started.

Top Ten Things to Do in a National Park

We're very fortunate to have so many natural wonders available for our vacation enjoyment. The United States National Parks and Forests provide enormous variety for cost-effective vacations. If you haven't yet become addicted to these great resources, now's a great time. Just remember, "Only *you* can prevent forest fires!"

1. Grab your backpack, sleeping bag, and travel toothbrush, and go camping. Check first to see if the park requires a permit. If you see a sign at the park's entrance that says, "Park closes at sunset," pick another park. Remember to always leave your campsite in better condition than you found it.

   Some National Parks now require reservations to hike certain trails or to camp at various sites. Check with your local AAA representative or your travel agent before you just show up and say, "Surprise, we're here."

2. Grab your backpack, walking stick, and compass and go hiking. If you haven't done this since your Boy/Girl Scout days, you're way overdue.

3. Grab your backpack, a loaf of bread, a jug of wine, and have a picnic. The ants will welcome you.

4. Uncover your bicycle, or rent one, and head for the nearest bike path. Be sure to take or rent a helmet. We've got some really fun ideas coming up and we'd hate for you to miss them.

5. Locate your binoculars, camera, and *Birds of North America* book and go bird watching.

6. Rummage through your attic until you locate your old butterfly net and then go catch some. If you can't find your net, go anyway. You just have to be a little quicker.

7. Go fishing. Remember to take your fishing license with you. The fish don't care, but the park rangers do.

8. Watch others "not feeding the bears."

9. Stand around, preferably with your hands in your pockets, and wait for a geyser to erupt.

10. Take pictures, draw pictures, or paint pictures.

Top Ten Things to Do in Las Vegas

I consider Las Vegas a family resort. It wasn't always, but they've worked really hard to transform a strip of casinos into a wonderful entertainment package. If you haven't been there for a few years, add it to your list. It's not Atlantic City, but I think you'll enjoy it.

1. Take the boat tour of the Luxor Hotel's lobby. You read that correctly, I did say boat tour and hotel lobby in the same sentence. Check it out.

2. Visit the new MGM hotel and its attached theme park. It's about as much fun as the slots and a heck of a lot cheaper.

3. View the live pirate ship battle in the front yard (lagoon) of the Treasure Island Hotel. It's Steve Winn (the hotel's owner) at his very best. Arrive early to get a good view. There are no seats. You stand on the sidewalk for this show.

4. Eat your way through the all-day buffet at the Mirage. You can't miss the Mirage; it's the one with the erupting volcano in its front yard. What will Steve think of next? A hotel with a lake for water skiing? In Las Vegas? Guess you'll just have to wait and see.

5. Check out the Sigfried and Roy show with their white tigers. Over the years this show has earned the label: spectacle. It's kind of like the Rose Parade, 4th of July in Washington, DC, and New Year's Eve at Times Square rolled together. Still good after all these years.

129

6. Take the kids, even the really big ones, to the video arcades at the Treasure Island and Excalibur Hotels.

7. Shop the 250,000 sq. ft. factory outlet mall and watch them add a 200,000 sq. ft addition. This thing is almost the size of Texas.

8. Rent a car, take a bus, or bum a ride to Lake Meade and Hoover Dam. It's not far and it's the most water you'll ever see in the middle of a desert (well, at least until Steve finishes his next hotel).

9. Take a stroll through Caesar's Hotel's shopping mall. It's Rodeo Drive, Michigan Avenue, and 5th Avenue all in one pedestrian-only enclosure. Pay careful attention to the statues by the fountain. You'll have to go there to find out why.

10. Win buckets of money.

Top Ten Things to Do While on Your Honeymoon

Come on now. Do you really need a list for this one?

1. Go on a *second* honeymoon.

2. Go on a *third* honeymoon. Are you starting to get the idea here?

3. Take a ride in a horse-drawn carriage. Bring along a small bottle of champagne and two "real" glasses. Never drink champagne from plastic cups; it ruins the moment.

4. Go to Kauai, the "Garden Isle" of Hawaii. 'Nuff said.

5. Plan a Caribbean cruise. If you don't know which one, take a look at the pictures in the brochures. Couples holding each other while they're standing alongside the ship's rail gazing at the starlit night is a good place to start.

6. Ordering room service—breakfast, lunch, and dinner is fine.

7. Ask your hotel staff (bellman, concierge, front desk clerk) to find a long stem red rose and place it on your partner's pillow with a suggestive note while you're away from your room. Be sure to include a nice gratuity when you pay for the rose.

8. Buy bubble bath, candles, and a can of whipped cream. If you have to ask, you need to buy a copy of *The Complete Idiot's Guide to Having a Great Time in a Hotel Bathtub*. Just kidding; that book's not written yet... is it?

9. Have your picture taken as a couple at every opportunity: at dinner, at the pool, shopping, entering your room for the first time, kissing in front of the hotel, you name it. All you need is to have someone nearby to snap the shutter.

10. Before leaving for your honeymoon, send a picture from a brochure, an article, or a personal note to your spouse or soon-to-be spouse every day for two weeks. Plan the mailings, for they build intensity and enthusiasm.

Top Ten Favorite Things to Do in Orlando

The toughest part of this list is selecting only ten activities. The really cool thing about Orlando is that it is so much more than just Disney World. "It's a small world after all, It's a small world...." Don't you just hate it when that song gets stuck in your head? Come on, lighten up, we're planning the perfect vacation here. Let's have some fun.

1. Have lunch and enjoy the abuse dished out by the wait staff at the 50s diner at MGM's theme park. Probably the only place in America where you can still get an authentic TV dinner and watch Dick Van Dyke reruns. Big fun.

2. While you're at MGM, take the kids, especially the really big ones, to the 3-D Muppet Movie. When it's over, tell me how they do that. Okay?

3. While you're into movies at MGM, see the *Littlest Mermaid*. All I'll tell you is that it is a **total** experience. "Under the sea... Under the sea...." There, that should get rid of the small, small world melody for a while.

4. From the MGM theaters, drop by the Indiana Jones thing. It's action and it's usually packed, so get there early.

5. If you're fortunate enough to stay at the Yacht Club or Beach Club at Disney World, be sure to check out the pool with the water slide disguised as a pirate ship.

6. Go to Sea World. It may be over-shadowed by Disney and MGM, but it's still good entertainment.

7. At Epcot Center, visit France. Enjoy a disgusting French pastry (what you think, they'd serve Belgium waffles?) and see the movie promoting France.

8. While still at Epcot, cross the pond (literally) and visit Canada's pavilion. When you're at this pavilion, talk to people, even total strangers, and end all of your sentences with, "eh? eh?" It's a cute Canadian custom and unlike wearing a beret at the French pavilion, this doesn't mess up your hair, eh?

9. Take the kids (yes, the big one will like this, too) to Norway's exhibit at Epcot. The boat ride sometimes attracts a long line, but it moves quickly and is worth the wait.

10. Visit MGM's newest attraction. I haven't done this yet, but I've watched them build this… this thing. It's called the Psycho Tower and you, like, get into this elevator, packed to the rafters with other people, and, like, it takes you to the top of this like really tall scary hotel-type building and then the elevator experiences mechanical difficulties and this strange music gets louder and then everything falls out of control and….

Top Ten Things to Do at the Beach

1. Apply bunches of sun block.

2. Have someone bury you (up to your neck only, okay?) in sand and then break free and run into the water to wash off the sand.

3. Build a really elaborate sand castle.

4. Practice Yoga.

5. Swim, duh?! (Sort of makes up for the extra activity on the National Park list, doesn't it).

6. Check out the cute _____ (fill in the blank).

7. Splash water on grownups who are taking this beach thing all too seriously.

8. Read a book (magazines are okay, too).

9. Listen to tunes; please use headphones. Your Vivaldi may disturb the Nine Inch Nails experience for your neighbor.

10. Play volleyball, paddle-ball, or Frisbee.

Top Ten Things to Do While Shopping

Am I beginning to sound like Richard Dawson? How's this? "Top Ten Things to Do While Shopping, and the survey says...?"

1. Look for bargains, duh (again)?! No, I'm only going to buy things that are marked up 30 percent above their suggested retail price. Yeah, right.

2. Find a store for kids and buy something for every adult on your list. Uncle Max will love blowing bubbles.

3. Offer to take inventory for an old-fashioned candy store. An Ethel Ms chocolate store is fine, too.

4. Visit any Nordstrom shoe department and ask any salesperson to explain the differences between two different pairs of shoes. Tell them you just can't make up your mind. You'll witness product knowledge at its finest. You could receive college credit for this course if you take good notes and can pass the final. No Al Bundys here.

5. Stop by a really interesting book store and buy a bunch of *Complete Idiot's Guides* for all your gift-giving needs.

6. Buy two copies of every postcard and mail the second one to yourself. If your pictures don't turn out, you'll still have something for your scrapbook. (Plus they're fun little reminders of your vacation mixed in with all the bills.)

7. Find a little shop that serves outrageous dessert treats and splurge. You're on vacation. That's what this is all about.

8. Start a contest to see who can buy the tackiest souvenir. Give the entries to your friends when you get home.

9. Window shop. You never know when you may want to replace that window in the back bedroom.

10. Buy a photo album with the name or picture of your vacation destination.

Top Ten Museums and Other High-Brow Cultural Places

If you're feeling the urge for culture injection, vacations are great places to indulge. Here are ten ideas to get you started. I've kept my editorial and sometimes irreverent comments to myself and just listed your options. I find that people who have a passion for these cultural activities have small senses of humor and are easily offended. Just kidding! Wow, they're also a highly sensitive group.

1. Botanical Gardens

2. Zoos

3. Aquariums

4. Art Museums

5. Historical Museums

6. Planetariums

7. Science and Industry Museums

8. Libraries

9. Legitimate, Off-Broadway, and Dinner Theaters

10. Halls of Fame

Top Ten Things to Do to Make Sightseeing Fun

1. Arrange a half-day city tour. This helps you establish your bearings and gives you a glimpse of the city's major attractions.

2. If walking or jogging is part of your fitness program, try a new route everyday. (Check first with the front desk or bell staff to make certain your planned routes take you through safe neighborhoods or you may be running for something other than your

134

health.) This gives you another opportunity to see the neighborhoods.

3. Try to arrange a walking tour of the city or a neighborhood. These are usually conducted by local historians, environmentalists, architects, or garden club members.

4. Find a tour of an interesting business, such as Quaker Oats, Kellogg's, Stouffer's test kitchens, or Mary Kay Cosmetics.

5. Locate the city's tallest building with an observation deck and take in the view. If you do this after your half-day city tour, you'll be able to trace the tour's path.

I always advise travelers to take time to see the residential parts of a city. Look at the architecture. Check out the landscaping. Survey the general condition of the buildings. To know the places where the inhabitants of a city live, and play, and sleep is to begin to know the soul of the city.

6. Visit a micro-brewery or winery.

7. Attend a sporting event—unless the players are on strike.

8. Buy a regional or city magazine (this is my mother's suggestion) and look in the calendar section for current events that may interest you and your family.

9. Find a friendly looking neighborhood diner, café, or joint; order the day's special. Strike up a conversation with your wait person and you'll begin to get beneath the veneer of the city.

10. Organize a photo scavenger hunt. Buy everyone a disposable camera and have them try to complete a list of pictures about your vacation destination. Take the cameras to a one-hour photo processor and share the pictures over dinner.

Photo Scavenger Hunt Requirements

To successfully complete the scavenger hunt, you must take a picture or have your picture taken in the following situation:

➤ With an English-speaking taxi driver.

➤ With another tourist's family (if the person taking your picture steals your camera, you're disqualified).

➤ In a ritzy jewelry store trying on something you cannot afford.

➤ You with a sign showing the name of the city in the background.

➤ A policeman placing you in handcuffs.

➤ A restaurant chef wearing his hat.

➤ Beneath a movie theater's marquee displaying a current hit.

➤ Trying on hats.

➤ Next to a fountain (not the kind for drinking). You get extra credit if you're actually standing in the fountain. You may be able to combine this with the police-handcuff photo.

➤ Next to a performing street artist, entertainer, or food vendor.

➤ With an identifiable landmark or statue.

➤ With a spoon hanging on your nose. The Jim Petras family members from Euclid, Ohio are world-class record holders in this competition.

➤ A hotel bellman sitting on his luggage cart while you push the cart through the lobby of the hotel.

➤ A piano player and you doing your best Bogart "play it again" imitation.

Top Ten Things to Do While Your Spouse Attends a Meeting

Combining business with pleasure can be a little tricky, but it can also be a great way to stretch your vacation dollar. The best way to prevent the business from getting in the way of the vacation or the other way around is to keep the two separate. Here's how one spouse can be entertained while the other spouse does business-type stuff.

1. Schedule a massage, facial, or manicure. If you're a husband and your wife's attending a meeting, go ahead and indulge. The grooming police won't stop you and ask what you're doing there. You'll be surprised how many men enjoy a massage and a manicure. I do.

2. Buy a memento from the hotel gift shop. You'll probably overpay, but it will anchor memories for your future enjoyment.

3. Discover things about the hotel that your spouse does not know. For instance, find out the name of the hotel's general manager, where he worked before, and whether he lives on property or off. Or learn the names of the chambermaid's children. Or ask for a tour of the hotel's kitchen. If it's not during meal time, most chefs take pride showing you where they work. In general, hotel staffs consist of bona fide characters that can tell you some very interesting stories—much more interesting than what your spouse is learning.

4. Write a hotel postcard and mail it to your spouse. If you want to have some fun, disguise your handwriting and don't sign the card.

5. If your children are with you, arrange for them to see a movie and enjoy pizza while you create a romantic atmosphere in your room that coincides with the end of the day's business session.

6. If you're really bored, ask the driver of the airport shuttle if you can ride along. If you enjoy this and take more than two round-trips, you probably ought to get a life.

7. Make reservations for dinner and arrange for all the staff in the restaurant to greet your spouse by name. Also prepare them with sufficient background that allows them to ask questions that only a really good friend would be able to ask.

8. Do all the traditional hotel stuff, such as reading a book, sitting by the pool, and using the exercise room.

9. Flip through the Yellow Pages and locate a store that caters to one of your special interests or hobbies. Visit the store and enjoy immersing yourself in one of your favorite activities without the interruptions you would receive at home.

10. Visit other hotels and ask the front desk if they can arrange a site inspection.

Top Ten Things to Do When Your Travel Plans Change

You never want to hope for the unexpected, but you do want to plan for it. The following suggestions will help take the sting out of travel plans that are put on hold for one reason or another.

1. When your flight is delayed, take a free hotel shuttle bus to the nearest and nicest hotel or resort. Treat yourself to a nice meal, walk the grounds, or just generally hang out. If the delay is longer than four hours, ask the front desk staff if they have rooms available at the "day room" rate. If the hotel is not sold out, they may offer you a room at a substantial discount and allow you to use their pool and other facilities. When you return to the airport rested and relaxed, all those passengers that were breathing terminal air and sitting on uncomfortable terminal chairs will wonder why you look so calm and chipper. Don't tell them.

2. When your hotel room is not ready, give your luggage and carry-on bags to the bell staff for safekeeping and begin exploring the hotel. Sitting in the lobby and glaring at the front desk staff will not get you a room any sooner. Yelling and screaming will make matters even worse. If the hotel has two rooms available, one adjoining the elevator shaft and the other a Presidential Suite, the person yelling, screaming, and glaring will get the room with the shaft. This is the first principle of front desk management.

3. If your flight is postponed and you don't have enough time to leave the airport, try to find a luggage storage locker for your carry-on bags. Then begin exploring. A shoe shine is a special treat. You might ask if the airport or Air Traffic Control offer any behind-the-scenes tours.

4. If your flight is delayed or your room is not ready, go to a gift shop and buy a magazine that you've never read. Reading and learning about a new subject will make the time you're delayed seem more productive… and less frustrating.

5. Locate the airport chapel and say a little prayer that your flight delay is minimal.

6. Find other travelers that are stranded and make new acquaintances. Misery loves company, but more than that, you may learn

about a great spot for dinner or bargain factory outlet store from your new friends.

7. If the hotel is oversold and wants to transport you to another hotel (referred to as *walking*) for the night, threaten to sacrifice a virgin in the lobby of the hotel. No, just kidding. The practice of overbooking results from people making reservations and then failing to honor them. When a hotel is oversold, there is not much you can do about it except savor the fact that you'll receive a free room for the night and royal treatment when rooms become available. Again, 100 percent of the people who yell and scream at a front desk clerk have never made a hotel room appear out of thin air, and they usually get *walked* to an inferior property.

8. While you're waiting for your flight, your hotel room, or for your car's universal joint to be repaired, give everyone in your family three postcards to send to their friends and insist that every card point out at least three nice things about the vacation. With postcards being relatively small, three positive comments about your vacation will completely fill the message area and not leave room for anyone to dwell on the negative.

9. Grab your camera and have your picture taken with an airline flight crew, your airline gate agent, or the front desk staff at the hotel. Explain that if you're going to be spending so much of your vacation with these people, you'd really like to have them in your scrapbook for years to come.

10. If your flight goes from the delayed status to the canceled status, head for the nearest public telephone and call the airline's reservation center or your travel agent. While others are waiting in line at the gate area to make alternative arrangements, you'll be protected.

The Least You Need to Know

➤ National Parks provide a fabulous backdrop for a perfect vacation at a perfect price.

➤ When you plan vacation activities, be adventuresome, go a little crazy; you'll probably never see any of these people again anyway, and you'll have a great time.

➤ When you're in a new city for the first time, do a few tourist-type things to get your bearings and then go out and do what the local people do.

➤ When your plans change due to unforeseen circumstances, have a contingency plan, and make the most of the new opportunities these changes present.

Part 3
Making the Perfect Arrangements

Do you have reservations about making reservations? Do you place travel agents under dentists in your address book? (You know, those places where you only go when you absolutely have to.) Do you find travel scams appealing?

Well… you've come to the right place. I'm going to lead you through the maze of arranging the perfect vacation. I'll show how to get help when you need it, and you'll know the difference between a dentist and a travel agent by the time you finish this section.

I'll show you how to steer clear of travel scams and other infomercial-type hype, and we'll even spend a little time (shhhh, come closer, I don't want everyone to hear this) talking about using computers to help plan your vacation. Pretty exciting? It'll be our little secret, okay?

THE DANGER OF TICKING OFF AN AIRLINE
ATTENDENT AND THEN USING THE LAVATORY

Chapter 12

Have Your Agent Call My Agent and Let's Do Lunch

In This Chapter

➤ Travel agents come in many different flavors

➤ What a good agent can do for you

➤ When it pays to use a travel agent

➤ How to select a good agent

You could probably build a new house by yourself if you had unlimited time and money. Likewise, you could probably plan your next vacation without the assistance of a professional travel agent if you have unlimited time and money. Of course, if you have unlimited time and money, you probably don't need a vacation; you're already on one. This chapter explains the travel agent's role and how you can locate a good one.

Top Ten Reasons for Not Using a Travel Agent

Many really stupid reasons exist for not using a professional travel agent. The following list presents only the top 10.

10. You love juggling knives.

9. You're incarcerated and not scheduled for parole review for several years.

8. Overpaying doesn't really bother you.

7. You can sleep most anywhere (and probably have).

6. You believe everything you read in those travel brochures.

5. You've memorized the deck plans of 16 different cruise ships.

4. When an airline loses your luggage, you believe they won't sleep until they find it.

3. Most of your vacations take place within two blocks of your home.

2. Your phone is disconnected and someone nailed all the doors and windows shut while you were in your house.

1. You've tapped in to a cosmic force and now prefer astral travel.

Who Pays the Travel Agent?

Many people choose to not use a travel agent's services because they think they'll pay more for their vacation. *This is not correct.* In most cases, you'll pay less when using an experienced travel agent because he or she can access thousands of suppliers, millions of fares, and gobs of valuable vacation information using a computer.

So, who pays for the service? Well, travel agencies usually earn a commission for the reservations they make. The travel service providers (that is, airlines, hotels, tour operators, and so on) gladly pay this commission because it is a very inexpensive method of gaining customers. The average commission is about 10 percent of the cost of the travel arrangements. Hyatt Hotels would rather pay a commission to the 36,000 travel agencies that promote and sell their properties than build and staff 36,000 Hyatt sales offices around the country.

But wait—before you put this book down and rush out to buy a travel agency and begin reaping those 10 percent commissions, let me tell you a little story about the economics of operating a travel agency.

Let's say a customer comes into your travel agency to purchase a $100 something. Your employee makes sure the customer understands everything there is to know about that something, makes reservations, collects payment, and prints documentation. As soon as that transaction is complete, you transmit $90 to the travel supplier providing that something and you put $10 in your bank account. From the $10, you pay your employees, your landlord, the telephone company, the computer reservation company, and so on, and so on.

After paying these expenses, and assuming you are a really good travel agency owner, you'll have $1 left. This means that when you find enough customers willing to buy $1 million of travel somethings from you, you'll make about a $10,000 pre-tax profit as the agency's owner. Owning a travel agency is very rewarding and fulfilling—as long as you measure your rewards in nonmonetary units.

Some travel agencies assess a service charge when their commissions do not cover their costs; for example, if your travel agent reserves a seat at a $99 fare on a Southwest Airlines flight and you want the ticket delivered to your home, the travel agency may ask for a service charge because their commission of $8.91 does not cover the costs they incur. Your alternative is to call Southwest directly, listen to their cute messages-on-hold, make your own reservation, drive to the airport and stand in line at the Southwest ticket counter. Depending on how much your time is worth, a travel agent's service charge of $25 and its associated convenience may be a huge bargain.

Travel Agencies Come in More Than 36,000 Flavors

One of the biggest challenges when selecting a travel agency is knowing which one to choose. The variety can be overwhelming. In the United States, you will find more than 36,000 travel agency locations. If you add to that number the locations where travel agencies are authorized to print airline tickets, you'll have thousands more.

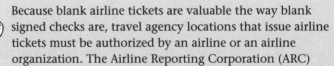

Because blank airline tickets are valuable the way blank signed checks are, travel agency locations that issue airline tickets must be authorized by an airline or an airline organization. The Airline Reporting Corporation (ARC) represents most domestic airlines and grants travel agencies the authority to issue their tickets; the International Airline Transport Association Network (IATAN) does the same for international carriers. These organizations recognize several different types of travel agencies; the four most common are: Home Offices, Branch Offices, Satellite Ticket Printers (STPs), and Electronic Ticket Distribution Networks (ETDNs).

There are four types of travel agencies:

➤ Full-Service

➤ Cruise-Only

➤ Independent Contractors

➤ Consolidators

Full-Service Agencies

Most of the agency locations you see are the Full-Service flavor. This means they print domestic and international airline tickets, make car and hotel reservations, issue train tickets, arrange a cruise or tour, provide you with travel insurance, and still find time to offer a variety of other associated services. These agencies have met the accreditation requirements set by the international and domestic airlines. These requirements include posting a performance bond, demonstrating financial soundness, providing secure storage for blank ticket stock, and employing experienced personnel.

Full-Service agencies may be branch offices of multibillion-dollar corporations, such as American Express Travel or Carlson Travel Network, or they may be truly independent "mom and pop" operations. They may be independently owned franchise locations, such as Uniglobe or Travel Agents International, or they may belong to marketing consortiums, such as MAST or GIANTS. Regardless of their size or affiliation, they all offer a one-stop center for all your travel arrangements.

146

You may not be able to identify a Full-Service travel agency by its appearance. I've seen Cruise-Only agencies that have the term "full-service" plastered all over their display windows. The "full-service" label determines what an agency can do for you, not how it appears. The best way to determine if your agency is a full-service agency is to ask if they are authorized to print airline tickets on their premises. If they have this authority, they fall under the full-service classification. If they can't issue airline tickets, but assure you they can get the tickets for you, they are a Cruise-Only agency or an independent contractor. It is perfectly legal to buy airline tickets from Cruise-Only agencies and independent contractors; you should know, however, that you are not dealing directly with the entity that printed your tickets.

Cruise-Only Agencies

These agencies look like Full-Service agencies from the outside, but they specialize in selling cruises and other leisure travel products. They have not applied for airline ticketing accreditation and, therefore, do not issue airline tickets. In most cases, these agencies are not bonded. Many of the cruises and tours they sell include air transportation, and the tickets for that transportation are issued by the tour operator or the cruise line.

Cruise-Only agencies are highly focused on a select offering of travel products. Some customers feel this focus gives Cruise-Only agents superior product knowledge. They aren't accredited by the airlines for ticketing and have more time to spend learning their cruise and tour products.

Independent Contractors

These agencies are generally home-based businesses. The Independent Contractor (frequently called an IC) goes out to meet customers. Most were travel agents who developed a following and wanted to start their own business without the overhead of an office and a performance bond. Frequently, ICs work with Full-Service agencies to obtain airline tickets and other services that are not directly available to them. The Full-Service agency pays the IC a percentage of the commission it earns on referred sales.

Independent Contractors should not be confused with pseudo-agents. ICs are serious professional travel agents. Most pseudo-agents stumbled across the travel industry through a classified ad offering travel agent ID cards and discounted travel for a one-time fee. Faith healers and loan sharks rank a notch higher on my scale of desirable people to have over for dinner.

Consolidators

What do rotten bananas and airline seats have in common? Both are very perishable commodities. If bananas are not sold before they turn all black and squishy, the grocery store loses the opportunity to earn revenue from them. Likewise, if an airline seat is not sold by the time the airplane door is closed prior to take-off, the airline loses the opportunity to earn revenue from that seat. People in airline accounting departments know this and they know about how many seats are likely to go unsold on a specific flight on a specific day. I don't know how they know—they just know. The fact that sometimes airlines overbook their flights tells us that this is still an imperfect science.

Consolidators are used by airlines to unload these unsold seats before they turn all black and squishy. A consolidator looks like a regular travel agency. The only difference is that they have special contracts with one or more airlines to sell seats that the airline does not think it will sell.

These agencies typically deal with surplus seats on specific flights. The tickets for these seats incorporate heavy restrictions, but the price is often 30 percent or more below the airline's lowest published fare. Airlines know a certain number of seats will probably not be sold on every flight. Empty seats mean lost revenue, so airlines work through Consolidators to sell these seats at a discount—better for the airline to get a little money on each seat than no money at all.

Agreements between some Consolidators and airlines even restrict the names that can appear on the Consolidator's tickets. For instance, a Consolidator for United Air Lines might be limited to selling tickets between the United States and Japan to passengers with Japanese-sounding last names. If your name is Alhsmith or Jones, you don't qualify for the Consolidator's specially priced tickets. The airlines use this restriction to compete with the foreign-owned airlines that offer special pricing to citizens of their country.

Consolidators sell to Full-Service agencies, to Cruise-Only agencies and, sometimes, directly to the public. Most of the time, Consolidators cannot mention the name of the airline providing the service in their advertising or they are limited to soliciting business in specific ethnic markets. The airlines don't want to dilute the demand for their higher-priced seats.

If the low price of a Consolidator ticket appeals to you, consider purchasing the tickets through a Full-Service agency. You'll have someone on your side who knows the reputation of the Consolidator and can help minimize the chances of something going awry.

To prevent buying bogus airline tickets, examine the boxes labeled, "Name of Issuing Agent" and "Place of Issue." If the information printed in these boxes does not match the name and location of your travel agency, you deserve an explanation. Several plausible explanations exist, such as, your agency bought these tickets from a wholesaler to get you a better price, or the tickets were issued by a cruise line or tour operator as part of a vacation package. Nonetheless, you should know who issued your tickets, and if it wasn't your agency, you should know why.

So How Do I Find the Right Agency?

Once you've selected the type of agency, your next question should be, "How do I find a good travel agent?" Always remember, the travel *agency* never makes a booking, understands your special requests, or calls to reconfirm your restaurant reservation for your 25th wedding anniversary. These actions are always completed by human beings—the *travel agents*.

So, to answer the first question, "You find the right travel agency when you find a good travel agent." I constantly remind the agents associated with our agency, "It may be the name on the door or it may be our advertising that attracts prospects, but it's most definitely the personal service you provide that produces customers."

Good travel agents come from a variety of backgrounds and have two distinctive qualities:

➤ Knowing where to go and who to ask for current information.

➤ A passion for travel.

Notice, I didn't say they've been in the business X number of years or that they've visited X number of destinations. Experience plays a role in an agent's development, but the key to a successful relationship between you and an agent is quite simple: Do you like him or her? And do you feel he or she takes the time to get to know you and your family's needs?

What Can a Good Travel Agent Do for You?

Plenty. They make the difference between an expensive nightmare and a dream vacation. A good travel agent saves you money and arranges a better vacation experience than an airline reservationist, a car rental reservationist, and a hotel reservationist could do acting separately.

A good travel agent doesn't just type the numbers into the computer and spit out your tickets; he serves several important roles. So important, as a matter of fact, that I'll tell you about each one.

Counsel and Advise

Good travel agents will find out what you and your family want to do and what you don't want to do. They'll then begin to outfit you with vacation choices that seem tailored to your mood, lifestyle, and budget.

The primary job of a travel agent is to counsel and advise you. If your agent is simply telling you where to go, get another agent. You can find plenty of other people who will gladly tell you where to go.

Shop, Compare, and Negotiate

Frequently I hear, "Why should I use a travel agent? They get paid a commission, so their motivation is to get me to spend as much as possible. My motivation is to get the best deal."

Although I can't speak for every travel agent, I do know a number of very good ones. They are some of the best power shoppers I know. If you ever want professional help negotiating the price of a used Lawn Boy at a neighborhood garage sale, call your travel agent. He will probably get you a rock-bottom price, plus a full tank of gas, and a commitment from the seller to mow your lawn free for the next six weeks.

Good travel agents don't specialize in finding you cheap travel arrangements. They find quality travel experiences designed to satisfy your expectations at a very affordable cost. Now, if you like saving $50 and don't mind being stranded at your destination when your bargain tour operator opts for bankruptcy protection, go ahead and book the cheapest trip you can find. As my Iowan father says, "You get what you pay for."

A Stitch in Time

Did you know that time management experts say a person earning $50,000 per year should value their time at $33.65 per hour? So let's put this $50,000 wage earner on hold waiting for an airline reservationist for about 15 minutes—there goes about $8.40. What if all the low fares are sold out and we have to call another airline? And then two hotel chains and a car rental company? There goes another $25.

From this example, you can see the value of a travel agent. Make one phone call to your agent, who has computer access to schedules and availability for all airlines displayed from lowest to highest price. Your travel agent helps you decide what the best deals are; you make your decision and you're done.

To Serve and Protect

I know this sounds like the motto from your local police department. Don't worry, I'm not going to hit you up for a donation so the less fortunate may attend the annual policeman's ball. I am going to remind you, however, that the world is constantly changing.

Downtown Cleveland is now a great place to spend an evening; downtown Los Angeles and Miami are not. Yugoslavia is off limits at the moment, yet Vietnam is accessible and very popular. Will Cuba make our list of desirable Caribbean islands? Not today, but the trend is pointing in that direction.

The point is that you can no longer rely on a printed guidebook or on a friend's recommendation from two years ago to tell you which destinations are safe and which are not. You need a professional who is connected to the latest electronic travel news. Your travel agent and her reservation computer can give you the latest travel advisories.

With So Many Travel Options, You Need a Professional

Travel opportunities have mushroomed during the past decade. Today, the travel industry is the second largest employer in the United States economy. Travel to our country by citizens of other countries is large enough to create a significant trade surplus. When was the last time you heard those two words in the same sentence?

This growth and explosion of travel options can give you a severe headache. You really need a professional to make sure you maximize your vacation time and dollars. There is nothing worse than returning home and learning that you missed several really interesting experiences because you weren't informed. Ignorance is not a cool state to visit on your next vacation.

The Least You Need to Know

➤ Travel agencies don't make reservations. Travel agents do. Select a travel agent who takes time to get to know you and your family and then matches your desires and budget with a rewarding vacation.

➤ Full-Service, Cruise-Only, Independent Contractors, and Consolidators all want your business. Select the one that makes you feel the most comfortable.

➤ A good travel agent will save you money. Remember there is a big difference between the cheapest vacation and an affordable vacation. Both can be memorable, only one is usually desirable.

➤ Our country is in the middle of a tourism bonanza. This offers you more options and quality vacation experiences than ever before. It also accents the need for professional advice about what's worth seeing and what's not.

➤ No aspect of your vacation is more important than your safety. A professional travel agent is connected to daily events that shape the world. You need this advice to give you peace of mind.

Chapter 13

Avoiding Scams

In This Chapter

➤ Avoid losing your money and your vacation to a scam artist

➤ Learn how to handle telemarketers

➤ Protect your credit cards from fraudulent use

➤ Just say "No" to pseudo travel agent promotions

Travel scams rank among the dubious top five consumer rip-offs, according to a group of consumer protection agencies. (The top positions continue to be held by new and used car dealers and home-improvement peddlers.) Unfortunately, we see newspaper articles such as this on a frequent basis:

> ## Scam Artist Gets 10 Years
>
> Peshtigo, Wis.—Janice Krueger, who operated a now-defunct agency here called Travelers Boutique, was sentenced to 10 years in prison for running a telemarketing scam involving the sale of virtually worthless vouchers for Caribbean cruises and Florida vacations.

Travel scams account for 25 percent of the complaints received by Call for Action, an international nonprofit organization in Washington that tries to settle consumer disputes. Like the newspaper clipping above, most complaints involve travel certificates that were sold over the phone but never received.

You may have received one of these calls. You're told you just won an exotic vacation. Aren't you excited? Or you're offered a travel club membership granting you once-in-a-lifetime guaranteed pricing at various deluxe resorts. Places that cost nonmembers hundreds of dollars per night can be yours for $35 and a small membership fee. Can't wait to part with your money now, can you?

Most of the time, the victim never actually receives the travel documents required to board an airplane. However, some people actually do take the trips, and usually the deluxe five-star property turns out to be the kind of place the traveler never would have chosen. The kennel where they boarded Rover was cleaner and offered more amenities. Their dream vacation becomes their worst nightmare.

It's one thing to get ripped off by an aluminum siding salesman. You can still retreat to the sanctity of your own home and lick your wound privately. When you get ripped off by a travel scam artist, however, you generally learn about your problems when you're thousands of miles from home, in the lobby of a soon-to-be-condemned hotel.

The quantity of reported travel scams historically has increased as the pulse of our nation's economy has decreased. The theory says that people have less money in a poor economy, but they still want to travel. They're on the lookout for bargains, and that makes them an easy mark for the scam artist.

One of the most frequently hit groups are families with children. They receive a call offering a deeply discounted vacation certificate for a family stay at Disney World. They give their credit card number to the slick telephone operator to secure their family's vacation, and bam—they've lost their money. The parents are sad, not just because they lost their money, but because their children are disappointed.

A group by the name of Call for Action, 800-647-1756, was formed 31 years ago to combat scam artists of all kinds. They have 850 volunteers around the country who mediate consumer and business disputes. They claim a 90 percent success rate. This organization is supported by 21 television and radio stations that use the group for story ideas and to resolve people's complaints on the air. If you doubt the validity of a travel promotion, even if you have paid for your certificates or club membership, call the Call for Action group. Maybe they can help.

Congress recently passed a telemarketing-fraud law that makes it easier for the state Attorney General to prosecute out-of-state telemarketers. The law also sets up a clearinghouse to monitor travel scam activity at the Federal Trade Commission. Our experience with stopping, prosecuting, and convicting scam artists has not been promising. The process is slow and money is seldom returned.

We know of one scam operator from Illinois who was reported, arrested six months later, found guilty six months after that, and was released so he could earn money to repay his victims in quarterly installments. Predictably, he fled Illinois, and all the Attorney General's Office could say was that he'll never conduct business in Illinois again. Now, who's scamming whom?

Spotting Scams

Here are a few questions to consider when the ringing telephone interrupts your dinner and you receive the wonderful news that you've just won an awesome family vacation:

➤ Does the price seem too good to be true? If so, it probably is. Say, "No thanks, good-bye" and hang up the telephone. Your dinner barely gets cold and you save a bundle of money and a heap of embarrassment.

➤ Are you asked to give your credit-card number over the telephone? Now stop and think about this one for just a minute. Would you feel comfortable walking into a restaurant, ordering dinner, and paying for it with your credit-card? Of course, we do this all the time. Now, let's say you've just finished your dinner and you decide to take a short stroll to let the effects of your dinner redistribute. You spot a perfect stranger approaching you. They stop and ask for your credit card number so they can mail you a discount certificate for breakfast. Would you give it to them? (We'll pause while you think this one through....) Then why would you give your credit-card number to a perfect stranger over the telephone?

➤ Is the air carrier simply identified as "a major airline?" Or does the caller offer you a collection of airlines without being able to say which one you'll be on?

➤ Are you told that you need to order today, because there is a minimum two-month processing period due to the extreme popularity of this special offering? This is pretty sophisticated, but any waiting period or delay greater than two months should be a clear signal to say, "No thanks and good-bye" and hang up the telephone. You see, the deadline for disputing a credit-card charge is 60 days. Scam artists know that.

➤ On the other hand, use your credit card to protect you. Pay for all travel purchases with a credit card, never with a check or money order. When you pay for purchases with a credit card, you're protected by the Fair Credit Billing Act against fraudulent charges. As mentioned above, you have the right to dispute the charges if you want to change your mind.

Preventive Medicine

Here are some things you can do to avoid becoming a scam artist's victim:

➤ Never put your name in a "prize drawing box" unless you know the sponsor or unless you love "dinner-interrupting" telephone calls from travel promoters, time-share vacation sales people, fitness club peddlers, and home improvement consultants. Just remember, the "prize drawing box" is just another name for a "sales lead generator."

> I'd like to share with you a cute definition of a "consultant." Oscar Wilde once said, "A consultant is an ordinary man away from home giving advice." I like that, but my favorite is, "A consultant is a man who knows 146 ways to make love but doesn't know any women."

➤ Don't be pressured into making immediate decisions. If you aren't given time to check out the offer, it's probably because someone doesn't want you to.

➤ Never give your credit card information to anyone over the phone unless you called them and you know it to be a reputable business.

➤ If someone you don't know calls and says you've won a trip, be very cautious. There are usually several conditions. If the caller asks you to send money before you can claim your prize, say, "No thanks and goodbye" and hang up the telephone.

➤ Always read and fully understand all cancellation and refund policies. Unfortunately, we never think about changing our mind and getting our money back until we can't do either.

➤ Don't believe the travel provider is legitimate just because you see their advertisement in a reputable newspaper or magazine. Newspaper and magazine advertising sales people are more concerned about getting paid than they are about checking the validity of a travel offer. Plus, they'll also throw in that whole thing about First Amendment rights; freedom of speech means you can say and print just about whatever you want and if people send you money and you don't get caught, you can keep doing it.

➤ Ask anyone offering you a special vacation deal exactly what the price covers. Get the names of the hotels, airports, airlines, and restaurants included in the package. Beware of the ones that promote 5-days and 2-nights. (You're going to have to figure that one out on your own—well, okay, see, each day is followed by a night, so it would be a little difficult to buy a vacation that chopped off the nights, wouldn't it?) Contact your travel agent and consumer protection agencies in your area for additional information about the firm offering the arrangements.

157

➤ Always clarify and understand the amount and reason for any additional charges like taxes, surcharges, service charges, shipping charges, fuel charges, port charges, passenger facility charges, custom fees, exit fees, entrance fees, gratuities, and so on. I'm sure you get the idea. The list goes on and on, but one of a scam artist's favorite tricks is to quote an attractive price and then in a softer voice add that, of course, you're responsible for taxes and additional charges. A few years ago, I saw a Hawaii flight promotion for $29. It seemed too good to be true and it was; the service charge was $300 for each flight, giving a total cost of $629.

➤ Determine if the quoted fare is for one-way or round-trip travel. By the way, this little trick is not the exclusive domain of scam artists—legitimate airlines use this ploy. You've probably seen the full-page advertisements for flights to Memphis for $29. The fine print then tells you that the price is based on a round-trip purchase (that means $29 times 2) and is subject to other customary taxes and usage fees. I'm never quite sure what those are, but I do know they increase the price of the trip.

➤ If a deal seems too good to be true; it probably is. Pop quiz: Where have you heard this before?

If you don't get what you expected, complain to consumer protection agencies in your area.

If you've encountered a problem or are suspicious of an offer, call the National Fraud Information Center, a hotline operated by the National Consumers League. The number is 800-876-7060 and can be reached from 9 a.m. to 5 p.m. EDT during the week. You can also call the local Better Business Bureau, the State Bureau of Consumer Protection, and the Attorney General's Office.

A good booklet to read is "Telemarketing Travel Fraud," a free publication of the Federal Trade Commission. Call 202-326-2222 for a copy, or write to Federal Trade Commission, Public Reference Branch, Room 130, Sixth Street and Pennsylvania Avenue NW, Washington, DC 20580.

Travel Free—Like a Travel Agent!

One of the newest scams is what the travel industry terms "pseudo-agent" factories. You'll find direct mail solicitations, infomercials, and telemarketers soliciting your money to become a travel agent so you can travel free or at least at very large discounts. One recent offer promised that you could take the cruise of your dreams for only $35 per day if you'd just send three monthly payments of $98.95.

These offers are not legit, and the travel discounts and identification cards they include are not widely accepted. This is just another way to separate you from your money.

It's true—real travel agents do enjoy free and discounted travel. I've been in the travel industry for nearly 24 years. I own a travel agency that maintains agreements with independent contractors who sell travel and earn commissions. Charlette, Sheila, Denise, and Deanna (my contractors) are not full-time travel agents, but they *are* professional agents and they do earn substantial commission checks every month. They also enjoy free and discounted travel.

They use these trips to improve their destination knowledge and to learn how different travel operators package their products. The result is a benefit to their customers who rely on their knowledge and expertise. Travel suppliers grant these independent contractors free or reduced-rate travel benefits because they consider it a good investment. They know a professional travel agent with a good working knowledge of their destination, hotel, or airline will generate business.

Now, do you think these same travel suppliers are going to offer free or discounted travel to someone buying a three-ring binder, video tape, and an "official travel agent ID card" that unlocks all these fabulous discounts? I don't think so. One of these promoters even hired Robin "Rich and Famous" Leech as their spokesperson, thinking that his endorsement would add credibility to their offer. Robin ought to be embarrassed for trying to mislead people, and you should be wary of offers that appear too good to be true.

The Least You Need to Know

➤ If it sounds too good to be true, it probably is. Okay, are you tired of hearing this?

➤ When you're buying a vacation, you really shouldn't need to buy certificates and memberships.

➤ The quickest way to prevent telemarketing fraud is to hang up the telephone.

➤ Always ask what the total, bottom-line, absolute final price will be. A scam artist will try to make you feel cheap for asking, but you'll eventually learn that your $29 flight to Hawaii really costs $629.

Making Your Reservations

Vacation reservations formalize an agreement between two parties. You and a hotel. You and an airline. You and a restaurant.

These reservations are much different from the reservations you have about your daughter's new boyfriend. Vacation reservations are like glue—they help your plans stick together. They also give you the comfort and security of knowing that arrangements are being held for you at a previously agreed upon price.

A vacation without reservations is a riot. And no, I don't mean riot as in, "ha, ha." I mean riot, as in chaotic civil unrest. The kind of unrest your spouse produces when her expectations of a deluxe hotel room with a spa is replaced by a flea-infested sleeping room with two twin beds and a bath that's shared with six other people.

Balancing Flexibility and Security

Reservations are designed to give you the comfort of knowing that you'll have a table for dinner at 8 p.m. or a seat on a flight between LaGuardia and Boston on Tuesday, or a roof over your head tonight. Reservations give you a feeling of security.

They can also make you feel trapped. Over-planning and over-reserving can make you feel confined and regimented. You get enough of that at work; there is no need to bring that on your vacation.

Like an Olympic gymnast performing on the balance beam, your perfect vacation is a blend of a planned routine with several impromptu creative expressions. If you remain in balance and still demonstrate your flexibility, the vacation judges just may give you a "perfect 10."

How to Make Reservations

All reservations achieve the same result: they secure services for you in the future. You can make reservations by picking up the phone and saying, "I'd like to reserve a table for two next Friday night at 7 o'clock please." Now it helps if you're talking with a restaurant when you say this, but the point is, making a reservation is not difficult. The tricky part is making sure you have all the reservations you need and that the price associated with those reservations is the best that is available. This is when you may want to get a travel agent involved. How do you know your cruise cabin is reserved at the best price? You don't unless you have experience and know a good value from a rip-off.

Reserving the Cheapest Airfare

Your airline reservations usually represent a significant portion of your vacation expense, so it only makes sense to invest the time needed to get the best deal. With some planning and flexibility, you can take advantage of airfare discounts as deep as 80%. Here are some tips.

Schedule your vacation and make your reservations at least two weeks prior to your intended departure. Airlines offer lower fares to vacationers who reserve their flights and buy their tickets early, because this improves their cash flow and allows them to obtain an estimate of the demand for each particular flight. Airline operations need an accurate projection of the number of passengers and baggage on each flight so that they can load the proper amount of fuel, meals, beverages, and flight crew.

Always plan to stay at your destination over a Saturday (and in some cases, Sunday) night. Try to arrange your schedule to allow you to travel during off-peak times. Airlines rely on revenues from business travelers to support most of their routes. If you can travel when the business traveler doesn't, you'll benefit from low prices.

Consider an indirect routing through an intermediate connecting city. For example, the standard one-way fare from John Wayne Airport in Orange County, California, to Chicago's O'Hare International is about $650 round-trip. If you route your itinerary to include a stop in Phoenix, you can sometimes save about 50 percent. Flights that make frequent stops or that require a change of planes (connection) are usually cheaper than non-stops. If you want speed and convenience, you're probably going to pay for it.

Always check the fares for flights originating at nearby airports. Residents of Washington D.C. and Virginia often drive to Baltimore's International airport because fares are cheaper. Flights departing Chicago's Midway airport offer lower fares to the same cities served by flights from Chicago's O'Hare International. Some residents on Chicago's north side even drive to Milwaukee to take advantage of lower fares. Other multiple airport cities include San Francisco, Dallas-Ft. Worth, Houston, Miami, New York, and Denver.

Discount Fares—Some Restrictions Apply

You can typically obtain discounts staying at your destination over a weekend, flying during off-peak hours, and purchasing your tickets at least 7 days prior to your intended departure. These discounted fares are called excursion, discount, or supersaver fares. For example, domestic excursion fares require you to buy your round-trip ticket 7 days, 14 days, or 30 days in advance, and stay at your destination over a weekend (usually Saturday night, though sometimes Sunday night as well).

These off-peak fares may be sold out one minute and available the next. The number of options are mind-boggling. The services of a professional travel agent who knows the tricks of securing cheap reservations and who has mastered a sophisticated computer reservation system with no built-in biases for one airline or airport over any other is usually your best bet.

One way? No way! If your vacation plans require one-way tickets, you will usually find them so expensive that it is cheaper to buy a round-trip ticket and throw the unused portion away.

Certain discount fares also require you to return to your originating city within 30 days. The cheapest of these fares does not allow stopovers and frequently requires that you make a connection before you arrive at your destination. You may also be limited to flying during off-peak hours and on specific flights. Tickets for these low fares are usually nonrefundable and nontransferable, and may either be nonchangeable or require a $35 fee to process any changes. Tickets must usually be purchased within 24 hours of the time you make your reservations.

To obtain the lowest fare, you'll have to return home within 30 days; staying more than 30 days will increases your fare by about 25%. You have to remain flexible about your routing, your departure time and day, and the length of your stay. Off-peak hours are typically before 7 a.m., between 10 a.m. and 2 p.m., and after 7 p.m., depending on the day of the week.

The timing of your reservation can also affect the price you pay. Making your reservations during high (most popular) season may result in high seasonal rates. After the high season passes, airlines generally lower their discount fares to attract more customers. For instance, if you want to travel in May, you should reserve and buy your tickets during the first week in January. If you buy them earlier you'll be paying higher rates because of the holidays. The airlines typically have fare wars immediately after major holiday periods. This is the best time for you to reserve and buy your vacation tickets.

Prices May Vary

If you notice the fare you paid for your flight was lowered after you bought your ticket, call the airline or your travel agent and ask if they can change your reservation and obtain the new discounted fare. If the fare decreases by more than $35, you should exchange your tickets and pocket the refund. Most airlines charge a $35 change fee. Several carriers will waive this fee if you agree to accept your refund in the form of a voucher for future travel.

Fares are always fluctuating. The yield management departments of every airline are constantly trying to maximize the revenues they collect from each flight. Most airlines test fare increases by raising prices on the weekend (Friday night through Sunday night). If the competition doesn't match these increases, or the number of reservations are low, the fares return to normal on Monday. This means you should make your reservations and buy your airline tickets between Monday and Thursday and should avoid buying airline tickets during the weekend.

Please remember, the $35 fee to reissue a ticket applies to all exchanged tickets. You'll have to pay the full difference in price and the $35 fee if you change your itinerary and the new ticket price is higher. Airlines use this measure to discourage passengers from buying tickets during fare wars and later changing the date, time, and destination of their flights. They think of everything don't they?

Stopovers and Circle Trips

If you're flying to two destinations, ask your travel agent about the rates for stopovers and circle trips. A stopover is useful when you want to stay for one or two days at a connecting city, and costs only an extra $20–$50. A circle trip applies when your intermediate destination isn't a connecting city, and costs less than a pair of round-trip tickets, even when your point of origin is a connecting city for the middle leg of the circle trip. This is especially true when one of the stays isn't over a Saturday night.

An Airline Reservation Checklist

Here's a checklist of important considerations that you should review before making your airline reservations:

- ❏ Check the restrictions that may apply to make sure you qualify for the discount rate.

- ❏ Be sure you know what you want. Some discounted fares do not permit changes or cancellations, and those that do will usually assess you a $35 service charge.

- ❏ Check for stopovers. Some airlines permit you to stopover in a city before you reach your destination or before you return home,

165

and they may or may not charge you for the privilege—typically $15–30 per stopover. If you happen to have a friend in the stopover city, a stopover can actually be a nice bonus!

❏ Think about the benefits of round-trip versus one-way. Some discounted fares require that you purchase a round-trip ticket, though there are some that give you lower rates for one-way tickets.

❏ Time your purchase carefully. All fares are seasonal and fluctuate constantly. A travel agent can help you determine the best possible moment to buy your ticket.

❏ Check for minimum or maximum stay requirements on round-trip tickets. The day of departure is not usually included as part of the minimum or maximum stay period.

❏ Take advantage of children's fares, but be aware that a heavily discounted adult fare may be cheaper than the full-price child fare. Children's fares are usually discounted as a percentage off the full coach fare. Children under two travel free as long as they sit on their parent's lap. Always carry proof of age for children whenever they travel.

❏ Check for special discounts for intermediate points. For instance, a ticket from Boston to Chicago passing through Pittsburgh could be cheaper than a ticket from Boston to Pittsburgh! So you buy the ticket to Chicago, and then get off at Pittsburgh, as long as you don't have checked bags.

❏ Use the same airline and the same class of service for all segments of your itinerary. Changing airlines usually adds to the cost of your trip.

❏ Sometimes, fares involving a connection are cheaper than direct flights. So if all the fares are non-stop, ask if flights involving a connection are cheaper. For example, flights from Chicago to Los Angeles that change planes in Denver may be cheaper than non-stop flights.

❏ If you're using a travel agent and they are giving you a fare for just one airline, ask them if there are cheaper fares on other airlines.

Ask about two or three other specific airlines. If all airlines are displaying similar fares, base your decision on the flight's convenience or on frequent flyer miles.

❏ If you are calling airlines directly to get fare quotes, call at least three airlines before making your decision.

❏ If there are multiple airports near your home, tell your reservationist if you're willing to drive a little longer in order to get a cheaper fare. Would you drive an extra 40 miles to save $100?

❏ If you qualify for special discounts (youth, student, senior citizen, clergy, and so on), ask your reservationist about the availability of these discounts. If you don't ask, they won't volunteer the information—they don't know who you are and they can't read your mind.

❏ Tell the reservationist how flexible you can be; can you leave a day earlier or a day later? If you're too specific about the date and time you want to travel and don't say that you're looking for the cheapest possible fare, you may not get the best price.

How to Change and Cancel Reservations

Plans change, for a variety of reasons. It seemed like a great idea to spend 14 days at Disney World, but after 3 days, you may realize you should have planned to visit the Gulf of Mexico, since you're in the neighborhood (sort of). If you have to spend 11 more days listening to "It's a Small, Small World…," you'll be a candidate for shock therapy. What do you do?

The first principle of changing your plans is to always have your new arrangements secured *before* canceling your existing reservations—unless you want to experience 11 days living out of the backseat of your rental car.

The second principle of changing your plans is to always cancel the reservations you are not going to use. You want to do this to avoid any penalties, but also, you want to give the airline, hotel, restaurant, or car rental firm the opportunity to sell your reserved space to someone else.

The third principle of changing your plans is to find someone to do the work for you. Come on, you're on vacation; relax. Your vacation time is too valuable to spend on the telephone making new reservations here and canceling old reservations there. Contact your travel agent, your motor club, or your hotel's concierge and let them do the work. Even if they charge a $25 service fee, your vacation time is too valuable to be spent listening to hold music only to learn that there is no space available and you need to make yet another call.

Finally, you always can and should change your plans to improve your enjoyment of your vacation. Life's too short to spend it doing something you don't enjoy—and your vacation is even shorter.

How to Deal with Sold-Out Situations

Vacation arrangements come in fixed and limited quantities. A 38-passenger motorcoach can transport only 38 passengers—not 39 or 40—just 38. Applying the same logic, a 2,000-room hotel can sell only 2,000 rooms on any given night.

I've overheard many heated and rather comical conversations between vacationers and reservation agents, car rental counter personnel, and hotel clerks in which the traveler insists that the travel supplier can accommodate his request. They plead, "After all, it's just one more. Surely you can squeeze me in. No one will notice." They never seem to understand that their demands do not magically change the number of tables in a restaurant, cars in a rental lot, or seats on a plane.

The best thing to do when you encounter sold-out situations is to relax and remain calm. By doing this, you immediately distinguish yourself from the yelling, screaming, and threatening masses and generally gain the empathy of the travel supplier's personnel. You want their expertise and assistance rather than their defensiveness and resistance. In this situation, the squeaky wheel may get the grease, but the polite and quiet traveler usually gets the assistance. Remember, travel industry employees are not paid nearly enough to take someone's abuse, but they genuinely enjoy helping polite and friendly people. You need their help when everything around you is sold out.

What's your time worth? You can always make your own reservations, but your time is worth something. If your annual salary is $30,000, an hour of your time, including fringe benefits, is worth about $20 per hour or about 34¢ per minute. If you make $45,000 per year, an hour of your time is worth more than $30, and a minute of your time is worth more than 50¢.

There are several alternatives to sold-out situations. Granted, one of them may be sleeping in the boarding area of an airport, but you always have alternatives. First, you should ask to be placed on a priority waitlist. This puts your name in a queue to receive the benefits of any cancellations or no-shows. Another alternative is to alter your itinerary and offer to arrive on a different day, depart sooner, or stay longer. When you encounter a sold-out situation, you need to become creative. Don't rely on the reservation agent to always present the best alternative. After all, it's your vacation, not hers.

The Least You Need to Know

➤ Reserving the least expensive airfare is a complex task and an inexact science.

➤ Generally, reservations made far in advance can always be altered to take advantage of fare wars and other price reductions.

➤ As a courtesy to others, cancel your reservations when your plans change. Don't be a no-show.

➤ When you encounter sold-out situations, solicit the reservationist's assistance through understanding rather than screaming.

Chapter 15

Accessing Online Travel Information

Picture this. It's about 10 o'clock Friday night; you're sitting in your family room with a freshly popped bowl of popcorn, a tall, cold beverage of your choice, and you've just discovered there is nothing good on TV. You have 68 channels, but nothing really interests you so you decide to do a little brainstorming for your next vacation.

With a couple clicks of the mouse (the computer type, not the rodent type—if you still don't know, ask any 10-year-old) strapped to the arm of your favorite recliner, the TV leaves the television network mode and hops into its computer network mode. You click the mouse again when you've moved a little arrow so it points to a graphic image of a bulging suitcase (referred to as an icon, by computer geeks) and you're tapped into a myriad of vacation travel information that will last longer than a month's supply of popcorn and beverage. You're online, you're surfin' the Net, and you're wired, dude.

This scene may read like the prelude to a new episode of "The Twilight Zone," but no Nebraska farmer's going to get hit on his head by an errant chip from a Soviet satellite gone astray. This technology is available today, and we're going to talk about how you can *connect*.

Tapping into Travel Information

If you're new to computers and maybe just a little shy, this section will help you begin. We'll start slowly and stay at that speed throughout this entire chapter. If you're a computer geek, you'll probably be tempted to raise your hand as you read this chapter and interject a number of, "Yeah but, if you connect your *blah-blah* to the reciprocal of your *who-hah*, you'll be able to connect to an *oh-wow* site." Please curb your temptation to interrupt and make this more complicated than it needs to be.

To start, you need four things:

➤ **A computer with some specific stuff attached to it.** This is called *hardware*. It's not the kind of hardware you buy from your friendly neighborhood hardware store. You buy this *hardware* from computer stores. As with a number of computer terms, the word *hardware* gained wide acceptance among computer nerds because it refers to several totally unrelated things and that's confusing. Confusion makes a computer nerd's day. They love taking relatively simple concepts and making them exceedingly complex.

➤ **Specific computer programs.** This is called *software*, but there is nothing soft or fluffy about it. *Software* is nothing more than instructions that tell the computer what to do. Believe it or not, without instructions, a computer is a dumb, albeit expensive, box filled with wires and chips. On the other hand, computer instructions have value only to a computer. So, now you know that *hardware* needs *software* and *software* needs *hardware*; otherwise, you have a huge doorstop and some unintelligible instructions.

➤ **Training.** This is called *training*. Wow, we finally found something in the world of computer jargon that is familiar. Anyway, you need to find a class that will help you learn how to put the software and the hardware together. These classes are held at computer stores, at local community colleges, and at private learning centers that specialize in computer training. If you don't have time to take a class, you can teach yourself—there's a whole line of *Complete Idiot's Guides* designed especially for the computer novice.

➤ **Desire**. This is just what you think it is—nothing technical here. You have to want to learn about computers, and you have to want to connect to loads of online travel information. If you don't have that desire, that's okay; don't waste your time. Chapter 16 teaches you how to build a vacation itinerary, and all you'll need for that is low-tech paper and pencil.

The Right Hardware Stuff

As you've probably guessed, computers come in a variety of shapes, sizes, colors, and brands. Some of the differences among computers are very technical while others are very emotional. The technical differences tend to determine how fast a computer operates or how much information it can store. The emotional differences revolve around brand names and the format of the computer's software (the instructions it needs to run).

Here's the good news. Most computers on the market today let you connect (using your home or office telephone line) to other computers containing a wealth of travel information. The brand name and the technical differences are not that important. What is important is that you buy a current model that you feel you can master.

My recommendation for selecting the right hardware for you is to find an established computer dealer that you trust. Build a relationship with the people in this store and take their advice. Computer technology changes very rapidly. A new batch of smaller, better, and faster gadgets are introduced every six months. You'll appreciate the advice of a reputable dealer who can sort out the *picks* from the *pans* when the new products are released.

Here is the computer system we recommend to thousands of travel agencies using our management, marketing, and accounting software (TRAMS). These agencies also need to access travel information stored on remote networks.

➤ **Any personal computer (PC) containing an 80486 or Pentium processor that can operate Microsoft Windows software**. This eliminates most Apple Computer products and will probably generate screams of anguish from the ranks of loyal Apple fans—they tend to be a vocal lot. You can use an Apple computer to access travel information; however, I recommend Windows-compatible PCs because they are in use by the vast majority of travel agencies and their suppliers. Apple makes a good product that is easy to learn; it just is not installed in enough travel agencies.

➤ **At least 8 megabytes of RAM.** This is an acronym for random-access memory and is what the computer uses to process the instructions given to it through the software. The more RAM you put in your computer (within limits), the more instructions your computer can process. This improves your use of the computer because, unlike my brain, more RAM in a PC lets it perform several different tasks at the same time.

➤ **The biggest hard disk your budget can afford.** The computer's hard disk is where software and information is stored. The bigger your computer's hard disk, the more stuff it can store. Don't accept any hard disk smaller than 500 megabytes. It's just not cost effective. Just like your hall closet, your hard disk—whatever its size—will always be just a little too small.

➤ **A 14.4K modem.** I know this sounds like a foreign language, but here's a simple translation. A modem connects your computer to a telephone line and allows it to share information with other computers (large and small) that also have modems. The 14.4K stuff tells us how fast the modem can transmit and receive information. Modems that are faster than 14.4K currently exist, but they require a telephone line without static or other noise, so I recommend a 14.4K. Most modems also include the capability to send and receive faxes. This has little to do with gathering vacation information from other computers, but it is a nice added benefit.

➤ **Other required stuff.** Your computer will need a keyboard for the same reason a typewriter needs one; a mouse, so you can do things that are slow and awkward to do with your keyboard; a monitor (which looks like a small TV) will come in handy so you can see what you're doing; and a printer so you can show others all the cool travel stuff that you've been able to retrieve.

➤ **Other optional stuff.** As long as we're looking at new computers, we may as well look at another neat toy that we can add to our computer. One of the most popular is a multimedia kit. This additional hardware lets you watch movie clips and listen to sound clips that are stored on CD-ROM discs. Travel information is just beginning to be published in the CD-ROM format, and you'll want to be able to view it on your new PC.

Although prices for computers vary, you should be able to buy a basic computer system, such as the one we recommend, for about $1,500. If you move to a Pentium processor, add more RAM, increase the size of the hard disk, and add multimedia capabilities, plan to spend about $4,000.

The Right Software Stuff

Computer software contains instructions that tell the computer what to do. The variety and quantity of software is awesome so we're only going to focus on software that instructs your computer and its modem how to connect and communicate with other computers that contain valuable travel information. To start, we recommend you subscribe to one of the consumer online networks (sometimes you'll hear them called online services or online systems just to confuse you) and learn the structure, etiquette, and protocols of online communications. These networks also offer their own software that makes it easier for you to connect your computer to theirs.

Online Networks

If you want to break into the electronic age and don't quite know where to start, an online network is a good safe place to put your toe in and test the water. It's also a good place to get hooked and become addicted to the vast amount of free (except for the connect time) information scattered all over the world.

Most online networks are like little cottages in a village. In this village, every cottage has the same three-room design: one room for storing files, one for conducting conversations between visitors, and one for leaving messages for visitors who will drop by later. Although each cottage has the same design, they are each very different from one another. Their differences are evident by the nature of their stored files, conversations, and messages.

If you have a question about stamp collecting, you stop by the stamp collection cottage and leave a little message for anyone that may stop by later. You then stop by the bass fishing cottage to see if any of your old fishing buddies are chewing the fat in the conversation room. No one's there so you leave your buddies a note and head over to the travel cottage to pick up that file about the best restaurants in Fargo. On your way home, you stop by the post office to check your mailbox and grab two messages from mom and one from an old college buddy.

This is what a CompuServe online session is like; you send and receive messages and e-mail (computer geek jargon for electronic mail), you chat with others, and you send (upload) or receive (download) files. Since your online network account is charged for the amount of time you are connected, you generally read and respond to your mail and messages while you are disconnected (offline). Here's a typical request for information on the CompuServe Travel Forum and a helpful response.

```
#: 597516 S3/Hawaii Help Line ·1!·          New      Read
    14-Jan-95  12:36:47
Sb: Hawaii Honeymoon
Fm: Nancy Herron 73554,274
To: All                                              More ↓


I have a couple clients who are thinking about either the Caribbean or Hawaii
in September for their honeymoon.  Their only concern about the Caribbean is
that September is huricane season, so we are looking at Hawaii now.

Does anyone out there know of a romantic, smaller-type property on the beach
for these people?  They want to get away from 'touristy', although they would
like to do some water sport activities (diving, snorkeling, etc.)  She
mentioned huts on the beach so I suggested Kona Village.  But when I told her
how much it is per night I found that $400+ per night was a little over their
budget.  So, we are looking for a nice, moderately priced, non-touristy type
place for them.  Maybe we won't find anything like this in Hawaii.....

Any suggestions?

Thanks,

Nancy
    TRAVSIG.MSG 27/189                       Help=F3  Quit=ESC
```

A request for Honeymoon information on CompuServe's Travel Forum.

```
#: 597808 S3/Hawaii Help Line ·1!·              New       Read
   14-Jan-95  21:19:50
Sb: #597516-Hawaii Honeymoon
Fm: Melanie Hadsell/HNL 76620,3420
To: Nancy Herron 73554,274


Nancy, You might try Colony's Kaluakoi Hotel and Golf Club on Molokai.  It's
right on the beach, but I'm not sure about snokeling and diving.

Aloha, Melanie




TRAVSIG.MSG 28/189                              Help=F3  Quit=ESC
```

A reply with a helpful suggestion to the previous Honeymoon request.

There are three major online networks. Each has advantages over the others, but none dominates the group sufficiently to merit a recommendation. I suggest reading each network's literature and selecting the one that best matches your interests. Here's how you can contact these networks:

America Online	703-488-8700	800-827-6364
CompuServe	614-457-8560	800-848-8990
PRODIGY	800-776-3449	

Each of these online networks has an area dedicated to travel information, such as destination reviews, government travel advisories, and currency exchange rates. These networks also offer varying degrees of access to the now famous Internet where you can find all the travel information you ever wanted and probably some that you didn't want.

Here's an example of a new file available from CompuServe's Travel Forum.

```
#: 596457 S1/Travel In General ·!!·                    New
    12-Jan-95  22:33:19
Sb: NEW FILE:DISABL.AIR
Fm: Dennis Mills /HQM 74774,2451
To: All

A new file titled DISABL.AIR will be available tomorrow morning in the General
Interest Library.

       TITLE: Air travel: passengers w/ disability^M
       Keywords: DISABILITY DISABLED HANDICAPPED AIRLINE DOT WHEELCHAIR

       This is the full text of the U.S. Department of Transportation's
       booklet "New Horizons:Information for the Air Traveler with a
       Disability." It explains the DOT rule that implements the Air Carrier
       Access Act.  Topics include battery-powered wheelchairs as checked
       baggage, on-board wheelchairs, airport and aircraft accessibility, when
       airlines can and cannot require attendants or medical certificates,
       services for vision-and hearing-impaired passengers, and more.

       Uploaded by Tim Kelley


TRAVSIG.MSG 26/174                                    Help=F3  Quit=ESC
```

This CompuServe message announces the availability of a file about air travel for disabled travelers.

Regardless of which online network you select, you'll have a wealth of vacation travel information and assistance at your disposal. You'll also have access to hundreds of other special interest groups as well as stock market quotes, various news services, and airline reservation systems.

Reservation Systems

At one time or another, everyone enjoys being their own travel agent. Through the online networks, you can tap into online airline reservations systems that are a skinny version of the systems used by professional travel agents. These systems allow you to search for availability, check fares, and make reservations for a variety of airlines. Following is an example of an EAASY SABRE screen. They also permit you to order your tickets by mail, have them issued at an airline ticket office, or at most travel agencies.

```
LIST        Z            01-15-95 17:50 ◆ EASYSAB.TXT

                     FLIGHT AVAILABILITY

From:  (LAX) LOS ANGELES, CA
  To:  (ATL) ATLANTA, GA                          THURSDAY  FEB-16-95
---------------------------------------------------------------------------
   Flight   Leave      Arrive   Meal   ST FC Equip  OnTime  Classes of Service**
1*DL5717  LAX  730A  SAN  817A          0  Y  EM2           Y  B  M  H  Q  K  L
  DL 228        855A  ATL  343P   B      0  Y  L10     7     F  Y  B  M  H  Q  K  L
2 NW 646  LAX  645A  MSP 1213P   B      0  Y  757     8     F  Y  B  M  H  Q  V  K
  NW 612        100P  ATL  428P   S      0  Y  72S     7     F  Y  B  M  H  Q  V
3 AA1106  LAX  635A  ORD 1225P   B      0  Y  757     9     F  Y  M  B  Q  V  H  K
  AA1046        125P  ATL  416P   L      0  Y  100     9     F  Y  Q  V  B  M  H  K
---------------------------------------------------------------------------
To SELECT a flight, enter the line number, or          FC = Fast Confirm

  8   View MORE flights            11   View all FARES
  9   CHANGE flight request        12   Translate CODES
 10   View FIRST flight display    13   View LOWest one-way fares

** Quick Tip:  There is no charge for making a reservation on-line.  Let
   EAASY Answers provide you with quick answers to your reservation questions.
   Enter /ANSWER to send a message or call 1-800-433-7556.
Command▶                        Keys: ↑↓→← PgUp PgDn F10=exit F1=Help
```

EAASY SABRE screen displaying flight availability between Los Angeles and Atlanta on February 16, 1995.

Systems allowing you access to their data through an online connection are EAASY SABRE, Travelshopper, traveLOGIX, and Official Airline Guide. Other methods of accessing airline computer reservation systems through travel agencies are just beginning to find their way to the Internet. Currently, the easiest way to connect to one of these airline reservation services is through America Online, CompuServe, Delphi, GEnie, and PRODIGY.

Don't assume that online reservation systems always give you the lowest price. In today's electronic age, too many folks assume that if information doesn't display on their computer screen, it doesn't exist. A good travel agent is often able to find you a better fare than you can find on your own. This is especially true for complicated itineraries and unpublished consolidator fares.

If you like using an online reservation system, use it to identify possible flights and times and to get a feeling for the lowest fare. Then, talk with your travel agent. Be as flexible with your agent as you were with the online system; tell them how much you're willing to modify your travel plans. Don't just give them the flights you found in your online searches; take advantage of their expertise, and ask them to verify that there is nothing cheaper.

The Internet

Internet describes a global network of computers (30,000 and growing) that can be accessed from about 140 countries and boasts more than 25 million users. Sometimes, you'll hear it referred to as simply *the Net*. It's also called the Information Superhighway or just the I-way. Whatever you call it, you'd almost have to be living under a rock not to have heard about it.

The best way to describe the Net is to imagine the U.S. Government stringing a bunch of computer cable between Defense Contractor's offices back in the 1950s to speed development of our response to the Soviet Union's launching of its first satellite. Later, this cable expanded to include other government offices, universities, and private businesses.

Because the U.S. government paid for the cable, no one has been able to charge for the millions of messages and files that travel along the Net every day. Instead, this network of networks has evolved into a pure form of democracy.

Since no one owns the Net, those who use it control it. It has its own set of rules, such as no blatant commercial advertising, and its own method of enforcing those rules, such as *flaming*. Flaming is the act of brutally denouncing someone's behavior or actions by filling their electronic mailbox with thousands of nasty messages. If you normally use your electronic mailbox for business purposes and you have to sift through thousands of nasty messages to find the two or three important business messages, you'll know how effective flaming can be.

The Net is always growing, changing, and active. Sometimes, you can almost hear it breathing. Because communication on the Net is from one network to another, it's easy to be looking through files on a computer at the University of Illinois in Urbana and see a reference to a related topic that is on a computer in Sydney, Australia. Within a few hours, you can travel the world on the Net, and the only cost is what you pay your local service provider for access.

There are numerous ways to connect to the Net, but we're going to focus on connecting through an online network. The connection to the Net using an online network is still evolving. Most of these connections are limited to text messaging, but all of these services are adding the capability of connecting to graphical World Wide Web (WWW) sites. During 1995, you should be able to connect to a WWW site on the Net through your online network. The following figure shows the Hyatt Hotels Corporation's WWW site featuring their resort properties.

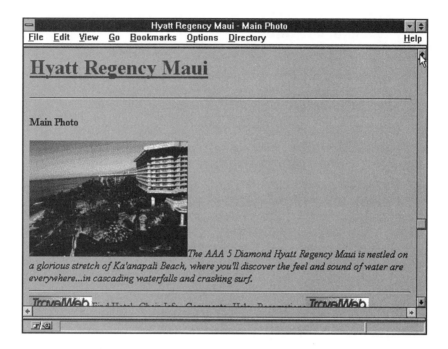

Graphics and photographs of the Hyatt Maui taken from Hyatt Resort's WWW site. The address is http://www.travelweb.com/thisco/common/ search.html

As you can see from Hyatt's Internet address (in the figure caption), getting all the slashes and periods in the right place can be a challenge. Fortunately, the software needed to access the Net is rapidly improving so you won't have to spend your life typing Internet addresses. Here are additional addresses on the Net where you can locate travel information:

➤ Rec Travel
  http://www.mbnet.mb.ca/lucas/

➤ U.S. State Department Travel Warnings
  http://www.stolaf.edu/network/travel-advisories.html

➤ Travel Related Phone Numbers
  http://www.mit.edu:8001/people/wchuang/travel/travel.html

➤ Travel Writing by Philip Greenspun
http://martigny.ai.mit.edu/~philg/travel.html

➤ Travel
http://www.cs.colorado.edu/homes/mcbryan/public_html/bb/
108/summary.html

➤ Global Network Navigator—GNN
http://nearnet.gnn.com/meta/travel/index.html

➤ GNN TC World Travel Watch—South Pacific
http://nearnet.gnn.com/gnn/meta/travel/spacific.html

➤ Travel Forums
http://www.explore.com/Explorer_forums.html

➤ TEN-IO
http://www.ten-io.com

➤ Travels with Samantha Cover Page
http://www-swiss.ai.mit.edu/samantha/travels-with-
samantha.html

➤ THE TRAVEL LANE
http://www.mit.edu:8001/people/kebooth/welcome.html

➤ Explorer Travel Bazaar
http://www.explore.com/Explorer_bazaar.html

➤ Terry Chau's Travel Page
http://www.mit.edu:8001/people/tchau/travel.html

➤ Traveller Information Services Master Index
http://www.traveller.com/

➤ Miscellaneous Travel Information
http://www.mit.edu:8001/people/kebooth/mischome.html

➤ Travel Gems—travel tickets airlines airfares
http://branch.com/gems/gems.html

➤ Surrogate Travel and Mosaic
http://nemo.ncsl.nist.gov/~sressler/projects/nav/surr/
navSurr.html

➤ All Sorts of Fun Travel Info
**http://www.mit.edu:8001/afs/athena.mit.edu/user/p/j/pjb/
www/travel.html**

➤ Travel (Leisure & Recreation)
**http://www.einet.net/galaxy/Leisure-and-Recreation/
Travel.html**

➤ EUnet Traveller
http://traveller.eu.net:80/

In addition to these addresses, several airlines have their own sites on the Internet. These airline addresses are not meant to replace their reservation functions; in fact, they don't offer any reservation functions. They are places where they can post special notices regarding fares and telephone numbers, and where you can leave messages for their customer service departments.

➤ Aeroflot
http://www.seanet.com/bazar/aeroflot/aeroflot.html

➤ Air New Zealand
http://www.iconz.co.nz/airnz/airnz.html

➤ American Trans Air
http://xmission.com/~aoi/fata.html

➤ Ansett/Quantas
gopher: //cis.anu.edu.au

➤ Canadian Airlines International
http://www..cdnair.ca/

➤ Lufthansa
gopher://gopher.enews,com:2100/11/travel/lufthansa/

Or send e-mail to: **lufthansa@enews.com**

➤ Northwest Airlines
http://www.winternet.com/~tela/nwa-info.html

➤ Southwest Airlines
http://xmission.com/~aoi/f0wn.html

This list is courtesy of Marcus Endicott, "The Electronic Traveler," who you can e-mail your thanks to at **mendicott@igc.apc.org**

The Future of Online Travel

Predicting the future in the travel industry is risky business, and predicting the future in the computer industry is laughable because by the time I punctuate this sentence, something has changed. Even so, here are some computer trends that are affecting the travel industry.

Better travel arrangements and more fulfilling vacations will result because the access to better information will continue to improve. I see you sitting in your family room watching video clips of various destinations and even chatting over the online networks with residents of the areas you're thinking of visiting. The days of mass tourism are ending; the days of personal tourism have arrived. Instead of tours comprising one group of thirty vacationers, they'll be designed and operated like thirty groups of one. The computer and its power to store individual needs will give us the ability to do this.

Will some folks want to use this new technology and book directly with the airlines, car rental companies, and hotel firms? You bet; they already book directly now. The only difference is that they will swap their telephone call to a reservation center for a computer modem call that will connect them to an online network.

Once you're online and roaming the Net, here are some of the really nifty-keen vacation things you can bring home:

➤ Notes, suggestions, and warnings from people who actually live at the destination.

➤ A variety of views and opinions about your vacation plans from a very diverse group of travel buffs.

➤ The varied input of thousands of people located all over the world.

➤ Sound bites, video clips, and photos from vacation hot spots to supplement the travel brochures you receive from the various tourists boards and cruise and tour operators.

➤ The weather information at your vacation destination. Of course, you understand that it will probably change by the time you arrive—just like at home.

➤ People contacts—they can either stay just "online friends," or you can plan to meet them at your vacation destination.

The Future Travel Agency

Will travel agencies change? You bet. They will become the distributors of the travel information you want. They will create custom brochures for your vacation planning, and they will match your tastes, wants, and needs with their access to vast pools of information. Travel agents will shift from making reservations and printing documents toward gathering and sifting information about your vacation options.

The Discount Factor

Will travel suppliers discount their products if you make your reservations through them rather than through a travel agency? They may, but since a travel agency's gross margin is around 10 percent, the amount of the discount may not justify your time, effort, and expense.

The TMT Factor

Will consumers flock to the online services and begin booking their future vacations through this medium? Not right away. Online travel services still suffer from two TMT Factors: Too Much Trouble and Too Much Time. As long as the online information is rather difficult to obtain (checkout those Internet addresses), consumers will want someone else to gather the information for them. As long as the consumer airline reservation systems take longer to operate and contain the possibility of overpaying, a quick telephone call to an airline reservation center or to a travel agent will be the preferred method of conducting business.

Interactive Television/Telephone/Computer

Will your television, telephone, and computer become one giant home communication center using the cable that now brings TV programs into your home to make long distance telephone calls and connect your computer to the Internet for interactive communications? Not if the Regional Bell Operating Companies have their way, but over time, yes.

As you have seen, there are still more questions than answers, but the technology is here, and we are smack dab in the middle of the Information Age. The Internet still has Under Construction signs plastered all over it, but it currently attracts more than 25 million users and that's a big market.

We may live in the best of times and in the worst of times, but for me, these are most exciting times. Information is power, and we're able to get just about all of it that we've ever wanted.

The Least You Need to Know

➤ If you want to wade into the wealth of online travel information, you'll need a computer and some software.

➤ The best place to begin tapping into the travel information pool is with an online network.

➤ The Internet is a happening place, and it shrinks the world a little more and brings people and their thoughts and ideas to your personal computer.

➤ The reservation and ticketing part of vacation preparation will be absorbed by technology. The management of the travel information and the planning of the prefect vacation experience will become an art form.

Chapter 16

If It's Tuesday, You Must Be Reading Your Itinerary

In This Chapter

➤ What is an itinerary?

➤ Why itineraries are important

➤ Telling a good itinerary from a bad one

➤ Creating your own itinerary

➤ Distributing your itinerary

There's nothing better than leaning back in your favorite chair, feet elevated, vacation itinerary in hand, and visualizing your upcoming trip. Some people, mainly bosses, call this daydreaming. I call it a necessary part of a good vacation. It's the bridge connecting good planning with good times.

Before you're ready for a little armchair travel, you need this thing called an *itinerary*. In this chapter, you'll learn what you need to do to get your hands on one.

Knowing Where You're Going

So what exactly is this itinerary thing? Well, it's like a map and a calendar rolled into one. It reminds you of what's coming next, just in case you're having too much fun right now. It's also something that tells you what you did last night, in case you had too much fun then. An itinerary tells you where you've been, where you're going, and what time you plan to be there. Although an itinerary doesn't sound too exciting, it's the glue that keeps a good vacation in one piece.

```
                                                              INVOICE

                          TRAVA of Glen Ellyn
   TRAVA                  45 S. Park Blvd., Suite 175
   Incorporated          Glen Ellyn, IL 60137-6203 USA
                          (708) 858-1840  FAX: (708) 858-1846

SALES PERSON: KK        ITINERARY/INVOICE NO. 0047491      DATE: 12 JAN 95
                                          RMAIYB           PAGE: 01

   TO: SCOTT AHLSMITH                 After Hour Reservation Service
       SMART COMMUNICATIONS, INC.
       5757 W CENTURY BLVD STE 605    When you need to change, reconfirm or make a
       LOS ANGELES CA 90045          reservation - Call 1-800-237-7980 to speak to an
                                     agent. Just give your VIT CODE SQ430 and they'll
                                     access your reservations and be happy to assist you.

FOR: AHLSMITH/SCOTT
                                     Airlines often make schedule changes...
                                     Please reconfirm flights prior to departure.

18 MAY 95  -  THURSDAY
   AIR   AMERICAN AIRLINES    FLT:1126    ECONOMY
         LV CHICAGO OHARE                 850A        EQP: SUPER 80
         AR ORLANDO                       1222P       NON-STOP
         AHLSMITH/SCOTT   SEAT-10D   AA-2390716
   CAR   ORLANDO                    NATIONAL CAR RENTAL
         PICK UP-1222
         RETURN-23MAY/1223        1-INTER CAR AUTO A/C
         RATE IS GUARANTEED
         WEEKLY RATE-USD176.99    UNLIMITED MILEAGE
         EXTRA DAY-44.99
         CONFIRMATION NUMBER      1017970821COUNT
   HOTEL ORLANDO
         HYATT GRAND CYPRESS RESORT      5 NIGHTS     OUT-23MAY
         1 GRAND CYPRESS BLVD            1 ROOM       SINGLE WITH BATH
         ORLANDO FL 32836               RATE-185.00 PER NIGHT
         PHONE NBR407-239-1234          GUARANTEED LATE ARRIVAL
                                        CONFIRMATION 12345
   OTHER ORLANDO
         5 DAY THREE PARK PASS FOR DISNEY WORLD RESORT PARKS

23 MAY 95  -  TUESDAY
   AIR   AMERICAN AIRLINES    FLT:1241    ECONOMY     LUNCH
         LV ORLANDO                       1223P       EQP: SUPER 80
         AR CHICAGO OHARE                 213P        NON-STOP
         AHLSMITH/SCOTT   SEAT-9D   AA-2390716


AIR TICKET    AA1146967144    AHLSMITH SCOTT              251.00
                                                       ---------------
                              TOTAL BASE                 222.74
                              TOTAL TAX                   28.26
                                                       ---------------
                              TOTAL AMOUNT DUE            251.00

THANK YOU FOR CHOOSING TRAVA OF GLEN ELLYN....
WE LOOK FORWARD TO SERVING YOU AGAIN SOON
THIS TICKET IS NON REFUNDABLE

            Leaders in Travel & Tourism Innovation℠
            CONTINUED ON PAGE 2
   TERMS: PAYMENT DUE UPON RECEIPT. Please See Reverse Side for Important Information.
```

Create an itinerary so you know where you're going.

Now don't get too defensive; you don't have to list every single little thing you plan to do. I'm not suggesting an itinerary that says, "6:12 a.m. Tie Left Shoe, 6:13 a.m. Tie Right Shoe, 6:14 a.m. Leave Hotel Room for Elevator." An itinerary is simply a set of guidelines, and like all good guidelines, is meant to be broken.

A good itinerary contains specific dates, times, locations, and notes about every major vacation event. It also records information about these events, such as the reservation confirmation numbers we discussed in the previous chapter.

What Makes an Itinerary So Darn Important?

Well, it's like a roadmap. It tells you where you're starting and where you plan to finish. It also gives you a suggested route. Just like a map, however, an itinerary is subject to detours, changes, and alterations. Roads close and plans change. The good part about an itinerary and one of the things that makes it so important, is its capability to get you back on track after you've been handed a detour. The itinerary is always there to remind you where you planned to go, where you planned to stay, and what you planned to do.

Before this begins to sound like a psychology lesson, I want you to know and experience the benefit of an itinerary. On a recent vacation to Washington, DC, I allotted two days to see the museums and monuments in our nation's capitol. By the way, two days is not nearly enough time to see Washington, but I was trying to squeeze in a short vacation in the middle of an East Coast business trip. I knew if I didn't have an itinerary, I'd probably end my two days without seeing what I wanted to see.

The itinerary I created wasn't too fancy; in fact, it was written on the back of the envelope containing my VISA bill. I figured as long as I had to pay the bill, I might as well get a certain amount of satisfaction from recycling the envelope. My itinerary looked like the one on the following page.

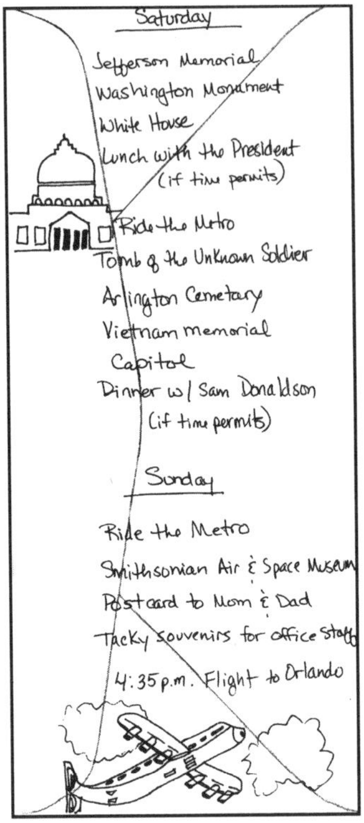

A handwritten itinerary:

Saturday
- Jefferson Memorial
- Washington Monument
- White House
- Lunch with the President (if time permits)
- Ride the Metro
- Tomb of the Unknown Soldier
- Arlington Cemetery
- Vietnam memorial
- Capitol
- Dinner w/ Sam Donaldson (if time permits)

Sunday
- Ride the Metro
- Smithsonian Air & Space Museum
- Postcard to Mom & Dad
- Tacky souvenirs for office staff
- 4:35 p.m. Flight to Orlando

A not-so-fancy itinerary for Washington, DC. The doodles, of course, are optional.

Well, sure enough, bright and early Saturday morning, while standing on the steps of the Jefferson Memorial, the brightness diminished, the heavens opened, and one of those all-day, cold, soaking rains began. As everyone hurried for cover, I could hear the cries, "What'll we do now? Our vacation's ruined. We'll have to spend the rest of the day sitting in our hotel room."

Well, now, doesn't sound like they have itineraries, does it? As for me, I pulled the slightly beat-up itinerary-on-the-back-of-an-envelope from my pocket, smoothed a few of its wrinkles, and headed for the Metro to take a ride to the Smithsonian. I realized I'd probably have to cancel lunch with the President, but with my tight schedule it would have been too rushed anyway (no pun intended Mr. Limbaugh).

So what makes an itinerary so important? Very simply, it's the difference between doing and seeing what you want, or sitting in your hotel room and watching *Gilligan's Island* reruns.

The Zen of Wandering Around

Another important feature of an itinerary is its power to get you to visualize your vacation experience... before you leave home. Everyone enjoys two activities before leaving on vacation. One is thinking or daydreaming about your travels and the other is talking about what you're going to do while you're on vacation. By the way, it's nice to have someone nearby when you're talking about your future travels. Not mandatory, but nice. Have I introduced you to my little imaginary friend?

A good itinerary is one that reminds you of what you want to do and see while making sure you don't miss something really important... like your flight home. A bad itinerary is one that never gets written. A vacation is a series of events. Each event begins as someone's idea. If you don't have a place to catch and store these ideas, they seldom become events. This leads to a lot of sentences beginning with, "I wish we had...." And that's no way to remember a vacation.

Good itineraries are based on the Personal Vacation Profile you prepared in Chapter 3. If you are outgoing and adventuresome, you'll want less structure and ample free time to wander and explore. For me, some of my most memorable vacation moments came from straying off the beaten path and bumping into a sheep shearer who invited me into the shearing shed and coaxed me into trying my hand at removing the sheep's winter coat. Thinking about that experience always makes me feel warm and fuzzy, which unfortunately was quite the opposite of what the sheep was feeling.

Every good itinerary allows time for the unexpected. Whether it's a rainy day in Washington, DC, or an opportunity to shear sheep in Wyoming, a good itinerary accommodates your adjustments and allows you to enjoy yourself while others are overcome by the chaos created by the unexpected.

Creating Your Own Itinerary

Like any good plan, itineraries don't just fall from the sky. Well, during the early part of World War II, when carrier pigeons were used to carry secret messages across enemy lines, the lid on one of the containers strapped to a pigeon's leg came loose and the container's contents (an itinerary) did fall from the sky. But, that's the exception.

Itineraries come in all shapes and sizes. To get yours started, I recommend buying one of those little spiral notebooks. The kind you find in the stationery section of drug stores for around 89¢ should do ya real nice. Don't wait until two weeks before your vacation to buy this notebook. You should begin planning your vacation now, even if you have a year or more before you plan to travel.

The purpose of this notebook is to catch vacation ideas. It's like the bags you attach to a lawn mower to catch all those little grass clippings. This little spiral notebook is your vacation idea catcher. It'll become tattered and worn during the coming months because you'll be carrying it with you wherever you go.

Title the first page, "Things to Do, Places to Go, People to See." When an appealing vacation idea crosses your mind, grab your idea catcher, and jot it down. This is the low-tech approach to building an itinerary. If you want to really impress your circle of friends, carry one of those palm-top computers and make your entries electronically. At 89¢, however, it's hard to beat the value of the notebook.

Months before a recent vacation to Hawaii, I bought an 89¢ idea-catcher and appropriately titled the first page. My entries included: Maui, play golf, sunrise on Haleakala, play golf, inspect Grand Wailea's swimming pools, play golf, read "Heroz" by Byham and Cox, send postcards, and buy chocolate-covered macadamia nuts for the office staff.

We did everything on our "Things to do..." page, except the sunrise on Haleakala. If you've been to Maui, you know the trip up the side of the dormant volcano, Haleakala, is a very small price to pay to see one of the most spectacular sunrises in the world. It is a virtual religious experience. The only drawback was that we'd have to leave our hotel by 4:00 a.m. to catch the show. Somehow, that "Thing to do" looked much different from a nice cozy bed in Hawaii than it had the night we had just finished a great Merlot in Los Angeles and were brain-storming our upcoming vacation. That's okay, though. Remember, itineraries are meant to be changed. And, now we've got an absolutely fabulous reason to return to Maui... as if we really needed another one.

Place a paper clip near the center of your notebook. If you're an accountant or a banker, you'll probably want to count the total pages in the notebook and divide by two and then place the paper clip exactly in the center, but that's not necessary. All we want to do is allow plenty of empty pages to write all our ideas about the "Things, Places, and People" for our vacation. At the top of the paper-clipped page write, "Day 1." Skip a few pages and enter "Day 2." Skip a few more and write "Day 3." Got the hang of this? Yes, you're correct, the next one is "Day 4." If you know the exact dates of your vacation, I suggest writing the day and date directly beneath each page's title. This gives you a better reference.

Next, begin transferring your "Things, Places, and People" ideas from the front of your notebook to this paper-clipped, scheduling section. Don't worry too much about the timing of each activity, you're just trying to get a nice mix of similar activities listed for each day. You want to avoid placing things like; "stand on the rim of the Grand Canyon" with "see Golden Gate Bridge" and "see a Dodgers game" on the same day—unless you have a private jet and a constant urge to cram far too many things into way too little time.

The final step in creating your itinerary is adding times and comments.

A formal itinerary, as opposed to the itinerary-on-the-back-of-an envelope, has specific components. It begins with the date and time each activity starts, continues with a description of the activity, tells who is providing the service, and presents notes about the activity. A formal itinerary is not just for those who fly. It is for everyone interested in enjoying a hassle-free vacation.

Take the itinerary you created to your travel agent. Ask them to type your itinerary entries into your record in their reservation computer system. When the travel agent's computers print your airline tickets, they also print an itinerary. This gives you a neatly printed document listing your complete schedule and activities on one piece of paper.

Who's Going to Receive Your Itinerary?

I know someone who frames her favorite itineraries. She says the price of a great itinerary is less than the price of original art. Her home is now a gallery of vacations. The itineraries are not only great conversation pieces, they also continually elicit memories, which stimulate ideas for her next trip. So the next time you're shopping for that special Van Gogh, remember you could have a Fall Foliage Tour for a fraction of the price. By the way, only "used" itineraries find their way into frames. The new, crisp ones don't have much character until they've traveled. Not unlike you and me.

A secondary purpose of an itinerary is to let others know where you're going and how to contact you. For instance, if you're running away from home, you may want to leave a copy of your itinerary with your parents. If you're running away from your children, you may want to leave a copy with the sitter. Then there are my parents who provision the motorhome with three months of supplies and flip a coin at the end of the driveway to decide if they'll head left or right. Although, if you were my parents, you'd probably look for escape routes with no obvious ways to locate you, too.

Finally, a copy of the itinerary should accompany you as you travel. Now I know this appears obvious, but there is some unknown force that intercedes between the time we begin packing and the time we depart on our vacation. This force not only causes us to forget to pack underwear, but it also causes us to leave itineraries on the kitchen counter. Of course, they're right next to the airline tickets so at least they're in good company.

Place an extra copy of your itinerary inside your suitcase on top of your clothes. If the airline misplaces your luggage and rips your nametag off the suitcase's handle, you have one more way of retrieving your clothes. Also, if your luggage is lost at the beginning of your vacation, you don't want the airline returning it to your home. You'd rather have it join you on vacation. The itinerary helps them find you.

A solution to not leaving home without an itinerary is to tape it to the door you plan to use to leave the house as you start your vacation. Of course, if you have a dog or cat that is highly fascinated by paper fluttering in a gentle breeze, you may want to keep a spare copy of your itinerary in your wallet or purse.

The Least You Need to Know

➤ An itinerary is like a map and a calendar rolled into one. It reminds you what's coming next.

➤ A good itinerary contains specific dates, times, locations, and notes about every major vacation event. It also records information about these events, such as reservation confirmation numbers.

➤ An important feature of an itinerary is its power to get you to visualize your vacation experience... before you leave home.

➤ A formal itinerary begins with the date and time each activity starts, continues with a description of the activity, tells who is providing the service, and presents notes about the activity. A formal itinerary is not just for those who fly; it is for everyone concerned about enjoying a hassle-free vacation.

ON YER' MARK...

Chapter 17

Getting Ready to Go on Vacation

In This Chapter

➤ Making vacation prep fun

➤ Leaving home with complete peace of mind

➤ Packing sensibly

➤ Expecting the unexpected

Planning is not a dirty word. You know that right away because it doesn't have four letters. Now, *plan* is a different story, but we're not talking about the excruciatingly painful process of writing a "plan." No, we're talking about the pleasurable activity known as planning the things you can do before you leave home that will extend the pleasure of your vacation.

If you start this planning activity about two weeks before your vacation, you'll have so much fun that you'll think your vacation has started early. Most perfect vacations begin with the anticipation that comes from reviewing your itinerary and envisioning how each event will unfold. This review is like a dress rehearsal.

Preparing Your Home for Being Left Behind

A key ingredient to a perfect vacation is feeling confident that everything is okay back at the ranch. Here are several suggestions that will help you gain peace-of-mind while you're away.

➤ Give your home a lived-in look while you're away by installing several automatic timers. These are available at most discount stores for about $15 each. Buy the timers with multiple on/off settings. These timers turn selected lights on and off several times during one 24-hour period. If you synchronize your timers, you can simulate movement between rooms. This makes your home a less likely target than homes that have their timers set on a 6:00 p.m. to 11:30 p.m. cycle.

➤ If you install a timer on a radio or television, your home will not only look lived-in, it will sound that way, too. Choose a radio station featuring classical music and turn up the volume. Burglars detest classical music.

➤ Although Mom always taught you to clean up your room before leaving the house, it's best to leave a little clutter when you leave on vacation, especially if you can see the clutter through one of your home's windows. If burglars see a sparkling clean kitchen and family room, they'll guess very quickly that you're away for an extended period. I didn't say that burglars were stupid; I just said they don't like classical music.

➤ Stop all regular home deliveries. All the automatic timers, loud classical music, and messy family rooms are a waste of time if you have a front porch full of newspapers, mail, and milk. Yes, some communities still have dairies that deliver milk to a little insulated box sitting outside your front door. Anyway, the point is that burglars like sour milk and cottage cheese covered with mold. It indicates that you've been away for a long time, and that's good news to a burglar.

➤ Ask a neighbor to stop by periodically and remove those unexpected deliveries that you can not anticipate. These include those lovely little fliers that hang on your door handle asking you to change your oil, apply a new roof, or buy pizza. In a hotel, these signs mean, "Do Not Disturb." To a burglar they mean, "Hey, Look! No One's Home to Disturb Me."

➤ Ask the same neighbor to make sure your lawn gets mowed or your sidewalks get shoveled. The objective, of course, is to make it look like you're at home.

➤ Buy your neighbor a nice gift while you're on vacation. He's earned it.

Making a List and Checking It Twice

Here's a little checklist to use before leaving home. This same list appears on the handy tear-out card in the front of the book, just in case you have an aversion to writing in books.

❑ Water the plants

❑ Unplug all appliances

❑ Stop delivery of newspapers

❑ Stop delivery of mail

❑ Adjust thermostats

❑ Turn off lights

❑ Close and lock windows; partially close drapes

❑ Turn off stove and oven

❑ Turn off water faucets

❑ Set the telephone answering machine to auto-answer

❑ Clean out the refrigerator

❑ Take out the garbage

❑ Activate automatic timers

❑ Make arrangements for pets

❑ Arm your security system

❑ Close and lock doors

Preparing Your Suitcase for Vacation

If you've been to a luggage store recently, you've undoubtedly been bewildered by the massive number of options. Add to this the special promotional stuffers that arrive with your credit card statements offering 18 pieces of matched luggage for just $19.95 per month, and you've gone into luggage overload. Please let me share the condensed version of "My Search for the Perfect Suitcase."

Choosing the Right Suitcase

Luggage manufacturers love me. Over the years, I have purchased just about every conceivable make, style, and size they've designed. Back in 1990 I got a cold, and Samsonite sent me a get-well card.

I was always searching for just the right combination of portability, size, and practicality. I tried modular pieces, soft-sided, hard-to-pack, easy-to-pull, stylish, and U.S. Army issue. None seemed to have everything I wanted. Somewhere, there's a landfill project dedicated to recycling my discarded luggage. I had given up hope of finding just the right pieces until I met Travelpro®.

Travelpro® creates the vertical rectangles on wheels with the telescoping handles that you see following virtually every flight crew member through the airport. They were designed by a Northwest Airlines pilot and are lightweight, durable, and hold a lot of stuff. I lived from mine during a 16-day European trip and arrived home with a clean shirt left over. I promised myself I would not overpack like that for my next trip.

Travelpro® has grown since I bought my first "Rollaboard®" nearly five years ago. They now make garment bags, golf bag carriers, and over-sized catalog cases on wheels for incurable packrats who can't stand to leave anything at home. I love mine!

You can purchase the Travelpro® line at most luggage stores, at the ASU shops in the Dallas/Ft. Worth airport terminals, and if you shop around, you may even find them discounted. ASU (Corte Madera, CA 800-756-1444) will also ship directly to you and guarantee to match any verifiable lower price within 30 days of your purchase.

Be careful—the bungee cords used to strap luggage to those collapsible metal carts can work themselves loose. If they were stretched very tightly and are suddenly granted freedom, the result could be a painful injury. One solution is to buy bungee cords without the metal hooks. A better solution is to buy the carts with web strapping and buckles. These are adjustable and don't have the potential to snap when under tension.

There are also lots of imitations, but I haven't seen any that compares to the real Travelpro® stuff. Mine's in its sixth year and takes at least three trips every month. If a suitcase puts up with that kind of abuse, it's worthy of recommendation.

Traveling Light—A How-To for Efficient Packing

There are many benefits to traveling light. I'm usually reminded of these benefits by the bellman looking for a $12 tip for the two carts of luggage he just coaxed through the lobby, up the elevator, and to my room. One way to lighten your load is to buy miniature sizes of brand name toiletry items. Another way is to get a catalog of small travel cases containing toiletries for men, women, children, and even infants from Travel Mini Pack, PO 571, Stony Point, NY 10980 or call 914-429-8281.

If you buy a "Rollaboard" that fits under the airplane seat in front of you or in the overhead storage compartment, you'll benefit by avoiding lost luggage, eliminating wasted time at the airport, and getting the prime spot on the beach while the rest of the passengers from your flight are still waiting for their luggage to appear on the luggage-go-round at the airport.

Checklist of Basic Stuff You'll Want to Take Along

One rule of thumb for traveling light is to pack only what you can comfortably carry for an entire day. If you can carry an 80-pound backpack without tiring, you'll not only be able to take a lot of junk with you, but you'll also be in darn good shape. For the rest of us, here are some tips for packing light:

➤ An empty backpack, duffel bag, or fanny pack. You never know when you're going to want to carry the little treasures you accumulate along the way.

➤ Small Swiss Army knife—one with scissors. This may sound like an item for a camping trip, but it also comes in very handy when you're roughing it at a five-star resort. Trust me.

To avoid hassles with airport security, make certain the knife's blade length is less than four inches. If it is longer, it will be confiscated and carried in a secure compartment aboard your flight, and you'll have to reclaim it at your destination. Airport security is also required to confiscate scissors that measure six inches or more from the screw or rivet that holds the blades together.

➤ Bottle/can opener and corkscrew combination. Most hotels have one of these hidden somewhere, but having your own saves you the hassle of trying to find the hotel's.

➤ Flashlight. Choose one of those small black metal ones that produce a bright beam and will fit in your purse or fanny pack.

➤ Camera, extra battery, and film. The camera and film are obvious, but without a spare little battery that makes your automatic camera work automatically, you could be picture-less.

➤ Business cards. Meeting others plays a large part in the vacation experience. Continuing your newly formed friendships requires exchanging addresses, and your business card makes this convenient. If you don't have business cards, you might want to have a few personal introduction cards printed at a local copy or print shops (or carry your address labels).

➤ Address book and postage stamps. You'll want to send postcards to friends and family that weren't fortunate enough to join you. This task is much easier if you have your address book and stamps handy.

➤ Sewing kit, safety pins, shoelaces. Buttons always fall off and shoelaces always break at the most inopportune times.

➤ Bandages, first aid cream, cotton swabs, aspirin, vitamins, personal medication, suntan lotion/sunscreen, insect repellent, cough drops, decongestants, lip balm. Always keep items such as medication, aspirin, and vitamins with you. They won't do you much good if they're packed in your suitcase and it's time to take a pill.

➤ Shaving equipment, mirror, toothbrush, toothpaste, mouthwash, deodorant, soap, comb/brush, blow dryer, shampoo, conditioner, feminine hygiene products, masculine hygiene products, dental floss, nail clippers, nail brush, nail polish remover, nail polish, hand lotion. You may want to add your personal favorites to this list. Be sure to place all things that could leak in a sealed plastic bag.

➤ Plastic baggies, adhesive tape, rubber bands, nylon cord. If you don't know why you'll need these, just pack them anyway, and remember to send me a silent "thank you" when you call out, "Honey, did you happen to pack any plastic bags? My shoes are covered with sand and I don't want to turn my suitcase into a portable beach."

➤ Umbrella, raincoat. It even rains in Southern California—when you least expect it.

➤ Alarm clock, ear plugs, night shades, slippers. These things will help you fall asleep and wake up, which may be two of the most difficult things you'll have to do while you're on vacation.

➤ Compass, binoculars. These aren't just for Boy Scouts. Believe me, you'll thank me later.

➤ Small tape recorder, or pad of paper and pens for making notes in your travel journal. You'll be amazed how these will add to your enjoyment of your vacation memories.

➤ Money, travelers checks, credit cards. Make photocopies of the front and back of your credit cards and other important documents, and keep several copies in separate and secure locations to make replacement easier. Bring extra small change—rolls of dimes, quarters, and nickels always come in handy, unless you're vacationing where there are no pay telephones, parking meters, pay toilets, or storage lockers.

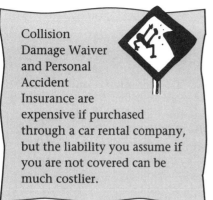

Collision Damage Waiver and Personal Accident Insurance are expensive if purchased through a car rental company, but the liability you assume if you are not covered can be much costlier.

➤ Copies of your insurance certificates and cards. If you're renting a car, contact your insurance agent to determine whether you should accept Collision Damage Waiver (CDW) or Personal Accident Insurance (PAI) from the car rental company or whether your policy provides adequate protection.

How to Pack

Before we get to the details of packing, just stop and think for a moment about what you're about to do. In plain terms, you are going to place things that you cannot live without into a container of questionable strength, and entrust this container to perfect strangers who will drop it, kick it, squash it, and possibly lose it or pilfer from it.

If you always keep this in mind, you'll find it's much wiser to leave many things at home. This will make you an outstanding packer. Now that we have a common understanding, we can get started packing.

Start by placing heavier items such as shoes and toiletries along the edges of your suitcase. Remember, the bottom of your suitcase when it's laying flat for packing is different from the bottom when you're carrying it. The bottom also changes again when the baggage handlers toss your suitcase haphazardly into the cargo hold of an airplane. Since the bottom keeps changing, an edge is about the best protection you'll find.

Roll your clothes rather than fold them. This keeps them from getting creases and from being crushed by heavier items. Rolled clothes require only spot ironing when you get to your destination.

Always pack anything that can spill or leak in sealed plastic bags. Place these bags in an area of your suitcase that protects them from sharp items that could puncture the bags.

Save space by stuffing socks, underwear, and stockings into shoes. Place an old sock (you knew you were saving those for a reason) over each shoe to prevent shoe polish and dirt from getting on your other clothes.

Pack your favorite sun-protection lotions and other toiletries. Not only do they cost more in airports and resort areas, you may not be able to find your favorite brands when you're away from home.

Using Carry-On Luggage Wisely

The first principle of carry-on luggage is that an airplane's cargo hold was built for luggage and its cabin was built for passengers. You should keep your carry-on luggage to a bare minimum. Placing a bag under the seat in front of you limits the space you have for your feet and limits your leg stretching.

Choose a carry-on bag that fits in an airplane's overhead compartment, and fill it with valuables, medications, eye glasses, toothbrush, toothpaste, cameras, jewelry, travel documents, a change of clothing, and anything else that you may need if your suitcase is not available. If your flight is delayed, or your luggage is lost or stolen, this carry-on bag will become your salvation. Pack it with essentials and guard it with your life.

Preparing Yourself for Vacation

Designate a Vacation Stuff Holding Area in your home. Let's call it a VSHA for short. Now that it's an official acronym, I'm going to apply for a government grant to study its effect on the moral fiber of the American family. If granted, you'll probably see a series of government pamphlets about this topic.

For now, and until a government-funded study makes it more complicated, all you need is a fairly large area that does not interfere with the high traffic areas in your house. The bed in the guest bedroom makes a perfect VSHA.

The purpose of a VSHA is to give you a staging area. A place to put things you want to take on vacation as you think of them. For instance, you're in the shower—that great incubator of monumental thoughts—and you remember that you want to take your video camera on vacation. While dripping wet, you can go to the hall closet, grab the camera, put it on the bed in the guest bedroom, and return to the shower to wash the shampoo out of your hair. And while you're thinking about it, take the bottle of shampoo and put it in your VSHA, too. Now, if there is any hot water left, finish your shower.

The idea behind a VSHA is that it provides an area to convert your thoughts, wishes, and good intentions into action. When you come home from shopping for your vacation, you have one place for the clothes and other items you bought. When you begin packing, you'll enjoy having all of the things you want to take with you in one spot.

As you pack, keep a notepad and pencil nearby to create an inventory of the items you're packing. This list performs three functions. First, it answers that frequent question, "Where is my so-and-so? I know I packed it, didn't I?" Second, it helps you complete a lost luggage application if your suitcase goes to Pittsburgh and you're in Phoenix. And finally, it becomes your checklist whenever you re-pack your suitcase while you're on vacation. When you've completed this inventory, place it with your tickets, itinerary, and other valuable documents and place them in your carry-on bag. It wouldn't do you much good to pack your inventory in your suitcase, would it?

Keeping Track of Money Matters

The following tips will help you control your expenses and keep your money safe:

➤ Know the limit on your credit cards before you depart, and stay within that limit. Some credit card companies charge you a fee if you go over your limit, and some refuse the charges if you're maxed out.

➤ Limit your children's spending money. If they are old enough to receive an allowance, try giving them a pre-arranged amount before your vacation so they can learn to manage their own funds.

➤ Carry cash carefully. Wallets should be kept in a buttoned pocket inside a sportcoat or jacket. Purses should be worn with the shoulder strap across your body, no matter how nerdy it may appear.

➤ Consider using ATMs. Many are open 24-hours, and you can withdraw just what you'll need for the next day. As with all ATMs, be security conscious.

➤ Purchase a destination guidebook, and plan an itinerary (see Chapter 16). Having an itinerary for each day will save you time and money.

➤ Prepare a budget for the cash you'll need to cover your daily incidental expenses. If you're not certain about the costs of certain attractions, or whether a restaurant accepts credit cards, call the area's tourist bureau or contact your travel agent.

If You're Leaving the Children at Home

If you're vacationing without your children (my parents tried this frequently, but I always caught up with them), you'll want to leave a copy of your itinerary with your baby-sitter. The tear-out card in the front of this book was designed for this purpose. You will also want to leave the name of grandparents or close family members so the baby-sitter knows who to call if she can't reach you.

Be sure to let your neighbors know that you're leaving, and that your children will be with your baby-sitter, and give them a copy of your children's schedule so they will notice any unusual activity or inactivity.

Leave a signed release for surgery or emergency medical treatment with your baby-sitter. These can be obtained from your doctor or your local hospital.

Let your children's teachers and carpool members know when you're leaving and how long you plan to be away. Also, introduce them to your baby-sitter.

PPP—Potential Predicament Protection

If getting to the airport and boarding your flight just moments before the gate agent closes the plane's door were an Olympic event, I'd be a gold medal contender. This is clearly one of those *Do as I say, not as I do* sections. Timing isn't everything, but when it comes to your vacation, it's miles ahead of whatever is in second place.

You can never prevent certain events from trying to keep you from your plane—they're your karma. What you *can* do is allow yourself enough time to respond and react to them and still arrive at the airport with time to spare. I'm told that having 30 minutes to sit and read a magazine at the boarding gate is a pleasant and desirable activity.

Here are some things that can (and have) happened on the way to the airport:

➤ Flat tire(s)   Make certain your spare tire is fully inflated and that you know where to find your car jack and tire wrench.

➤ Taxi/Limousine driver gets lost   Always have a general idea of the relationship between the airport and your home or hotel. You may think a taxi driver should know the location of the airport, and he may; it may be that he's just more familiar with the location of the airport in Bombay than in your city.

➤ Heavy traffic   Every airport has alternative access, even Boston's Logan Airport that strategically places a two-lane tunnel between you and your flight. Your job is to know the alternatives.

➤ Your car won't start   Have the telephone number of two taxi or limousine companies available. If one can't pick you up in time for your flight, try the other. As a backup, ask a friend or neighbor if they would play chauffeur if you encounter difficulties. Now, if your flight departs at 5:45 a.m., you may want to try another taxi company rather than wake your neighbor.

➤ Inclement weather   Watch the weather forecast the night before your departure. If bad weather is predicted, add 50 percent traveling time to your original estimate. As weather forecasts go, there's about a 50/50 chance you'll need the extra time.

The Least You Need to Know

➤ Preparing and securing your home gives you peace-of-mind.

➤ Choosing the right suitcase is just as important as what you pack inside it.

➤ Every vacation, whether it's two days or two weeks long, requires checklists in case your mind goes on vacation before the rest of you.

➤ Choose a VSHA in your house were everyone places the items they want to pack.

➤ To avoid missing your flight, anticipate and prepare alternatives to keep you on schedule.

Part 4
Enjoying Your Perfect Vacation

Here's what you've been waiting for; you've planned, you've packed, and now you're ready to go. But not so fast, vacation buckaroo. We need to have a little talk first. (Didn't you always hate it when your parents said that?) This will be one of those fun talks. We'll discuss how you may react to things that are different from home and also how you can prepare for the unexpected (such as when an alien clamps onto the ski rack of your rental car and carries you to the planet, Ohno) and make it into the highlight of your trip. By the way, if you get to go to Ohno, would you let me know how you like it? I've never had a chance to go there.

We'll finish our little talk with some fun ways to stockpile your vacation memories and begin racheting-up for your next vacation. It should be fun.

Chapter 18

Now Be on Your Best Behavior— You're a Guest!

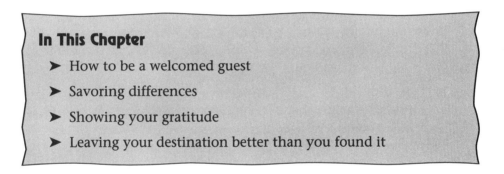

In This Chapter

➤ How to be a welcomed guest

➤ Savoring differences

➤ Showing your gratitude

➤ Leaving your destination better than you found it

To feel at home, stay at home. A new destination is not designed to make you comfortable. It's designed to make its own inhabitants comfortable.

—Clifton Fadiman

Perfect vacations are a time to relax, to go with the flow, and to experience a lifestyle different from your own. Bring along your sense of humor, let your hair down, and have a good time.

The Ugly Tourist

Tourists get a bad rap because they tend to want everything to be comfortable and familiar. It's okay to want that, but to complain about it makes a tourist look pretty silly.

The general manager of a posh New York hotel once told me about a seemingly nice man who became demanding and belligerent because the nightly news aired at 11 p.m. in New York rather than 10 p.m. like it did back home in North Dakota. The man demanded that the hotel do something about this because it was ruining his vacation. He and his wife couldn't fall asleep after staying awake the extra hour to wait for the news.

Can't you just see millions of New Yorkers saying, "Hey, you know Harold and Mildred are in town this week so let's make them feel right at home and cancel NYPD Blue so they can watch the 11 o'clock news at 10 o'clock."

The old adage, "When in Rome, do as the Romans do" will serve you just fine. After all, that's what vacationing is: learning about other people and their surroundings.

Be a Gracious Guest

If my grandmother, Matie Belle Smith, were around today, she'd be lovingly called, "a real piece of work." She always called them like she saw them and never acted her age, which are just two of the reasons we all loved her so much.

I'll always remember her combination welcome and warning to her house guests. It was framed and hung on the wall in the guest bedroom:

Welcome Guest; be at ease
Sit deep and come often; do as you please
Good friends, like wine, grow better with age
House guests, like fish, begin to smell after three days.

She and my grandfather had many friends and a constant stream of vacationing guests, but I don't remember any of them staying longer than three days.

Remember your guest status throughout your vacation and be aware that your presence is disrupting your host's normal routine. While this may be fun and exciting for a brief time, you and your host may tire of the living arrangements after a few days. In this case, the price of a hotel room is a small investment compared to the loss of a friendship.

Avoiding Language Mix-ups

Always remember you are a guest wherever you travel; it's always someone else's home. You may be a paying guest, but you are, none-theless, a guest.

I remember escorting one of my first travel groups to France when a fight broke out in the lobby bar between the bartender and one of our weary travelers. We'd only been in the hotel for a few minutes so I couldn't understand what had happened in such a short time to cause these two gentlemen to become so angry.

As quickly as I could, I stepped between them and convinced them to stop yelling and threatening each other. It was sort of comical because neither of them could understand a word the other was saying. The bartender spoke limited English, and our group member spoke no French. Their body language, however, was communicating loads of anger and hostility with no problem.

My traveler started the fight because he thought he was being overcharged for his scotch and water. The bartender was adamantly pointing at a sign that read $6.50 per serving. The bartender charged my client $13.00 because he ordered two servings, one of scotch and one of water.

We had just learned our first lesson in travel diplomacy; that is, "When you are away from home, you may be misunderstood or you may misunderstand, or both." The important message is to always watch the other person's reaction when you're trying to communicate while away from home. The same words may have dramatically differ-ent meanings to different people.

In the scotch and water incident, the operative word was "and." My customer ordered scotch *and* water. There would have been no misunderstanding if he had ordered scotch *with* water. By the end of our trip, my client and the bartender were best of friends and each was teaching the other about customs and values in their culture.

And the Moral of the Story Is...

Words tell us a lot about a region, a culture, or a country. Pronuncia-tion of these words add to our heritage, and travel lets us experience these differences firsthand.

For instance, do you think Texans talk funny? Not if you were born and raised in Texas. To them, folks from Maine talk funny, and if you're from Maine, the 90210 (Beverly Hills) crowd speaks a foreign language. It all depends on your perspective, and that's one of our vacation goals: to broaden our perspectives.

Here are a few examples of what you may encounter as you vacation throughout the United States.

➤ Alaskans refer to people living in the other 48 contiguous states as being from "The Lower 48."

➤ Hawaiians refer to the same group of people as living "On-the-Mainland." They get upset (and rightfully so) if the Mainland is referred to as the United States. Remember, Hawaii is also part of the United States.

➤ You'll get quizzical looks in Philadelphia if you order "pop." They refer to soft drinks as "soda."

➤ Regular coffee in New York City contains cream and sugar. If you want it without either, order it "black."

➤ A quilt and a comforter are two different coverings to keep you warm. In some parts of the United States, they mean the same thing. In others, a quilt is a two-ply covering made of different shapes and color swatches of material and a comforter is a two-ply covering of one piece of material filled with thick insulating material that is held in place by regularly placed tufts.

➤ "Rotaries" in Massachusetts are called "Circles" in the District of Columbus and "Roundabouts" in other parts of the country. (In case you're interested, they're called "circuses" in London.) If you don't know what the heck we're talking about, these are a traffic control engineer's little way of getting even with humanity. A "Rotary/Circle/Roundabout" places traffic from five or six different streets into a gigantic circle and spins it on the fast cycle until all the drivers get dizzy and exit on the wrong street. If you're ever on one, just remember that the driver on your left has the right-of-way.

➤ In Boston, pedestrians are targets. In California, they are protected with more vigor, and by more laws than is the spotted owl. If a California pedestrian steps off the curb, traffic comes to a screeching halt. If the same thing happens in Boston, drivers injure each other trying to aim for the poor soul.

All of this just goes to show you that Winston Churchill's remark about "two great nations being separated by a common language" applies to regions within the United States as well.

Different Regions, Different Values, Different Tastes

One of the great things about the United States (other than hot dogs and apple pie) is the cultural differences from region to region. In cities, these cultural differences get condensed and vary from neighborhood to neighborhood.

Some of the most enjoyable attractions of this regional and neighborhood ethnicity are the restaurant menus: Maine Lobster, Alaskan King Crab, biscuits with red-eye gravy, blackened anything-you-can-get-your-hands-on, grits, Maid-Rite's, and sushi, just to name a few.

Perfect vacation etiquette suggests you leave your cultural and food biases behind and graciously try the cuisine of the region. Sure, you may encounter a little indigestion, but more frequently, you'll discover a new taste sensation.

A Tourist's Code of Ethics

As you vacation, you have an obligation not to disturb those around you and not to ruin the experience for those who follow. The following suggestions will serve you well to this end:

➤ Always cancel reservations that you don't intend to honor. Whether it's a hotel room, a dinner reservation, a city tour, or an airline seat, the travel vendor was courteous enough to accept your request to reserve space for you, the least you can do is to let them know when you no longer need that space.

➤ If you're driving in a strange area and you're not quite sure where to go, pull to the side of the road and stop. You can read your map and determine your position much faster, safer, and with less disruption. Those behind you who know where they're going and may have to be there by a specific time will also appreciate your thoughtful gesture.

➤ Flight attendants are onboard for your safety. Periodically, they may have time to serve you a drink and a meal. If you ever need to evacuate an airplane in an emergency, you'll be glad they've been trained and are prepared to help you get out of the plane safely. Don't treat them like your personal servants-in-the-sky. They're available to help you, not to wait on you hand and foot.

➤ Every piece of carry-on luggage you bring aboard a flight takes up space that someone else may need. Don't be greedy and carry on more than your share.

➤ If you smoke, be considerate of others and don't violate no-smoking rules for planes, hotel rooms, and rental cars.

➤ Show your appreciation by tipping those people who have served you well. These may include bellmen, skycaps, waiters, maids, doormen, and the hotel concierge.

➤ If you used a travel agency, share your impressions, photographs, and comments about your vacation with them. They will then share this information with other travelers who will benefit from your experiences.

➤ Send thank-you notes to those who went out of their way to show you a good time, let you stay at their home, or took you out for a nice dinner.

➤ Use Comment Cards frequently and complete them honestly. Most companies serving the vacation traveler know they have to satisfy the needs and desires of their customers or someone else will. These companies use your comments to modify their services. They want to know what you liked and what you didn't like.

➤ If a specific individual heightened your enjoyment of your vacation, take time to find out the name of this person and their manager and write them each a short letter. Service in the travel industry is delivered one customer contact at a time. The sum total of these contacts determines how satisfying you found your vacation. If one person's efforts stand out, they deserve recognition and commendation. This lets them know you appreciate their extra efforts and encourages them to do more.

➤ Be an ecologically aware traveler. Every mile you drive and every step you take impacts our environment. A large city is just as much a campground as a National Park. You should clean up and minimize your consumption of the natural resources at both places. A sound ecological system is maintained by each one of us whether we're at home or on vacation; we all play a pivotal role in the future of our planet.

Vacationing is fun; it is supposed to be that way. Just be careful that your fun is not at the expense of someone else or our environment.

The Least You Need to Know

➤ When you vacation, open your mind to new thoughts and new experiences.

➤ Be a gracious guest. Display actions and behavior that you would want from guests in your home.

➤ Being understood is frequently a function of language, and language changes from one part of the country to another.

➤ You have a responsibility to those around you and to those that follow you.

Chapter 19

Handling the Unexpected

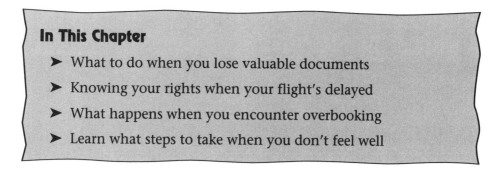

In This Chapter

➤ What to do when you lose valuable documents

➤ Knowing your rights when your flight's delayed

➤ What happens when you encounter overbooking

➤ Learn what steps to take when you don't feel well

As much as we'd like, we'll never control every aspect of a vacation. There are just too many variables involved.

Think for just a moment of the people you meet from the time you arrive at the airport until the time you board your flight. There's the skycap, ticket counter agent, gate agent, and flight attendant. Each of these people are perfect strangers, yet each plays a critical role in the success of your vacation.

From placing the correct tag on your luggage to getting you the most comfortable seat assignment, your fate rests with these strangers. For every one of these strangers that you meet face-to-face, there are at least four more behind the scenes (supervisors, baggage handlers, reservation agents, caterers, pilots, and so on) who could affect your vacation.

To predict that something will go wrong borders on the obvious. You *know* something will go wrong. What I'll do in this chapter is show you how to keep moving forward and make the most of any unexpected interruption.

Attitude Is Everything

Of all the things you can do to prepare for your vacation, the most important is to cultivate a good attitude. Feeling positive about a trip at the beginning of it is very easy; keeping that positive attitude as things begin to go wrong may take a little work.

Read the following statements until they're committed to memory and until you unequivocally believe every word:

The purpose of my vacation is to have fun.

I'm the only one who knows when I'm having fun.

I will not let anyone remove the fun from my vacation.

When things begin to go wrong, we assume they are happening only to us, and we become defensive. This makes all the people we contact defensive, and soon we have the battle lines drawn and we're off to war.

On the other hand, you can just accept the inevitable, and plan cheerfully for it. Anticipate that something will probably fall out of place, and that the "problem" might end up offering you some unique experience that you wouldn't have otherwise had. These unique experiences are often what will add fun to your vacation—and fun is what it's all about, after all.

Help! It's Lost or Stolen!

It's unfortunate; it's not fair; it's inconvenient; and I'm sorry it happened to you. Hopefully, that made you feel a little better, because regardless of what happened to your tickets, your luggage, or your credit cards, the fact is that *you no longer have them.* Our first priority is to get you back on the vacation, but we've got a little work to do first.

Lost Airline Tickets

You've lost, misplaced, or had your airline tickets stolen. It doesn't make any difference what happened or whose fault it was. The important part is that you need a ticket to board an airplane, so we're going to do two things:

1. File a Lost Ticket Application (known as an LTA in airline lingo).

2. Purchase a replacement ticket.

Lost airline tickets are like currency. If you lose a $50 bill, virtually anyone can find and spend it. The same is true with airline tickets. You are responsible for your ticket, and even if the airline gives you a replacement ticket, you will have to pay for the original ticket *and* the replacement ticket if both are used or refunded. It's amazing how many "lost tickets" get found when travelers receive the news that they may have to pay for two tickets, or in the case of a family of four, eight tickets.

Let me warn you up front, filing LTAs is not loads of fun, but it ranks way above root canals and cleaning bird cages. So let's get started.

To file an LTA, you must go to the ticket counter of the airline that issued your original ticket. Normally, this is the airline you're flying. You can go to one of the airline's City Ticket Offices (CTO) or to the airline's Airport Ticket Office (ATO). If you don't know where your airline's CTOs are located, call the airline's reservation number or your travel agent. The ATO is just a fancy acronym for the ticket counter at the airport. You'll probably find this with ease.

The type of LTA you complete depends on whether you purchased a refundable or a nonrefundable ticket. The information required to complete an LTA can be found on the itinerary that was printed when you picked up your airline tickets. If you kept a copy of your itinerary separate from your tickets, take it with you to file the LTA. If you can't locate a copy, your travel agent will be able to give you another itinerary or read you the information you'll need.

If you purchased a nonrefundable ticket with a credit card, the airline ticketing agent will ask you to complete an affidavit similar to the one shown below. By signing this affidavit, you are giving the airline authority to charge your credit card if the original ticket is used or refunded.

Front

SABRE Reference	**AMERICAN AIRLINES, INC.**
F*TKT/T325	**AFFIDAVIT**

T325 (Rev 10/93)
CPN 5686426

Ⓐ   **NON-RECEIPT OF TICKET FROM TDS**   **Ⓑ**   **LOST TICKET - FREE REPLACEMENT ISSUED**

THIS TICKET HAS NOT BEEN RECEIVED BY MYSELF OR ANYONE AUTHORIZED TO USE SAID TICKET.

I AGREE, IN RETURN FOR A FREE REPLACEMENT TICKET (NUMBER) _____ THAT SHOULD THE ORIGINAL TICKET BE REFUNDED. MY SIGNATURE ON THIS FORM IS AMERICAN'S AUTHORITY TO REBILL ME OR MY CREDIT CARD ACCOUNT FOR THE AMOUNT OF THE REFUND.

SIGNATURE: _____

DATE: _____

A NON-REFUNDABLE PROCESSING FEE HAS BEEN COLLECTED IN THE AMOUNT OF _____ MISC. RCPT. # 001 _____

(USD unless specified)
I, _____, SAY THAT ON OR ABOUT _____, I REQUESTED THAT AMERICAN AIRLINES INC. ISSUE ME A TICKET TO _____. MY TICKET WAS LOST BY ME AND IF IT IS USED OR REFUNDED AT A LATER DATE, I AGREE TO REIMBURSE AMERICAN AIRLINES. MY SIGNATURE ON THIS FORM IS AA'S AUTHORITY TO BILL ME OR CHARGE MY CREDIT CARD ACCOUNT FOR THE AMOUNT OF THE REPLACEMENT VALUE.

SIGNATURE: _____

DATE: _____

COMPLETE A OR B, AND REVERSE SIDE. ATTACH TO AUDITOR'S COUPON AND DEPOSIT IN AGENT NON-CASH DETAIL.

Back

AMERICAN AIRLINES, INC.
AFFIDAVIT

This form is used for Non-receipt of Ticket from TDS (Section A) or Lost Ticket - Free Replacement Ticket Issued (Section B).

TDS/LOST TICKET 001 _____/_____   ORIGINAL AMOUNT PAID _____
      FORM   SERIAL   (USD unless specified)
CIRCLE LOST COUPON NBRS   1   2   3   4   REPLACEMENT VALUE _____
☐ CHECK OR CASH   ☐ CREDIT CARD   CC NBR: _____   (AAdvantage only)   EXP: _____

Customer's AAdvantage # _____   Customer address _____
                                                 Street

Free replacement tkt #001 _____

Agent Die _____   City   State   Zip
Station/City code _____   Phone contact: (_____)_____
                                        Area Code

COMPLETE THIS SIDE IN FULL AND EITHER SECTION A OR B ON FRONT SIDE.
ATTACH TO AUDITOR'S COUPON AND DEPOSIT IN AGENT NON-CASH DETAIL.

Copy of American Airlines, Inc. Nonrefundable Lost Ticket Application.

If you purchased a refundable ticket, the LTA gets a little longer, the airline requires you to pay for a new ticket at the time you complete the LTA, and you have to wait 90 days before you receive a refund for your original lost ticket. The airlines use this 90-day period to check to see if anyone used or refunded your original ticket. The LTA for a refundable ticket is shown on the facing page.

```
                          AMERICAN AIRLINES
  Sabre Ref                Passenger Refunds MD-755            Agent Die:
                               P.O. Box 582880                 Location:
  F*TKT/LOST/TKT         Tulsa, Oklahoma 74158-2880            Date:
                        LOST TICKET APPLICATION
     TO BE USED WHEN A LOST TICKET IS REFUNDABLE AND/OR A REPLACEMENT TICKET IS PURCHASED BY THE CUSTOMER.
              THIS CLAIM CANNOT BE PROCESSED WITHOUT THE LOST TICKET NUMBER.
     I REQUEST A REFUND FOR AN UNUSED TICKET ISSUED BY AMERICAN AIRLINES. THIS TICKET BELONGS TO ME, BUT IT
       HAS BEEN LOST, STOLEN OR DESTROYED. TO MY KNOWLEDGE THIS TICKET HAS NOT BEEN USED.

  LOST TICKET NUMBER   0 0 1 -                       Date Purchased    /  /
                                                    TOTAL AMOUNT PAID $
```

The lost ticket number can be obtained from one of the sources below:
  If purchased from a Travel Agency, contact them for a copy of the ticket.
  If paid by check, send copies of both sides of the cancelled check.
  If paid by credit card, send copy of the billing statement.

Travel Agency Information (if applicable)

Purchaser's Name   Travel Agency Name

Address   Address

City   State   Zip   City   State   Zip

(____)____-____   (____)____-____   (____)____-____   IATA No._____
Phone   Home   Business   Phone

Passenger Name if different from purchaser
Form of Payment ☐ Check ☐ Cash ☐ Credit Card Type _____ Acct# ☐☐☐☐☐☐☐☐☐☐☐☐☐
     Government Transportation Request (GTR) Number/Other   (If Applicable)
Was any portion of the ticket used before it was lost? ☐ Yes ☐ No
If **YES**, please list used flight segments below. ◄

AIRLINE	FLIGHT#	DATE	ORIGIN	DESTINATION	Remarks

IF A REPLACEMENT TICKET WAS PURCHASED BY THE PASSENGER, PLEASE COMPLETE THIS SECTION.
Replacement Ticket Number ☐☐☐☐ - ☐☐☐☐☐☐☐☐☐
Amount Paid _____ Currency_____ (If not US Dollars)
Form of Payment ☐ Check ☐ Cash ☐ Credit Card Type _____ Acct# ☐☐☐☐☐☐☐☐☐☐☐☐☐
     Government Transportation Request (GTR) Number/Other   (If Applicable)
AA AGENT: IF REPLACEMENT TICKET IS ISSUED, DEPOSIT AUDITOR'S COUPON IN APPROPRIATE AGENT DETAIL.

A A *90 day* waiting period is required before processing.
B A refund will not be made if the lost ticket has been previously *used or refunded* to any person.
C This claim will be given consideration provided the application has been made no later than *13 months* after date of issue.
D AMERICAN AIRLINES will deduct the applicable NON-REFUNDABLE service charge of _____ for *each* ticket refunded.
E AMERICAN AIRLINES does not assume any liability for failure to identify the person using or presenting a ticket for refund as
   being the true owner of the ticket.
F If the ticket is found, return to American Airlines with a copy of Lost Ticket Application.
G If any additional information is required, American Airlines will contact you.
H Lost tickets purchased by Government Transportation Request are refundable only to the U.S. Government.
I agree to reimburse American Airlines, if after this refund is issued, the lost flight coupon(s) is used by anyone to obtain transportation or a
refund. My signature below is your authority to charge my credit card account or to bill me for the amount of refund issued.
       THIS REFUND REQUEST WILL NOT BE PROCESSED WITHOUT YOUR SIGNATURE.
              PLEASE READ THIS APPLICATION BEFORE SIGNING.

Please understand a *90 day* waiting period is required before processing.
Form C79 (Rev 2/92)
CPN 5890143   Signature of Applicant and Date

Copy of American Airlines, Inc. Refundable Lost Ticket Application.

The Lost Luggage Nightmare

Okay, your luggage is missing. Before you panic and start accusing every living soul in baggage, check around. Sometimes, luggage arrives on different flights. I recently flew from Orlando to Los Angeles and changed planes in Dallas/Ft. Worth (DFW). When we arrived at the American Airlines baggage claim area in Los Angeles, our luggage was sitting in a

The maximum liability for domestic baggage is $1,250.00 per passenger. This amount is being reviewed by the Department of Transportation, which is considering an increase to as much as $2,000. They may also create an inflation index to keep this amount current.

corner away from the baggage carousel waiting patiently—I've trained it to do that.

How did that happen, you ask? Well, our flight between Orlando and DFW arrived early. Now I know that's unusual, but it does happen—the last time I recall was 1972. Because we were early, our bags caught an early flight to Los Angeles that was not a legal connection for passengers. So the moral of this story is to always look around the edges of the baggage claim area. Sometimes, you'll find your bags waiting for you, which is a pleasant switch.

On that same trip, I watched a hysterical traveler verbally abuse an airline baggage agent because he couldn't find his suitcase, and he was sure the airline had lost it. The airline personnel asked for his flight number and then asked if he had looked around baggage claim area #4. The man stopped dead in his tracks, mumbled an apology and scampered over to area #4. He'd been waiting at area #8 for more than two hours. He'd failed to read the television monitors that tell which flights are unloaded on which carousels. He felt pretty stupid.

If your luggage was lost by the airline, you'll need to locate the airline's baggage services office and file a lost luggage claim. Most of the airlines have automated these claims so there are not any forms to complete. You will need to show the Baggage Services Agent a copy of your airline ticket, along with the baggage receipts you were given when you checked your luggage.

When you complete a lost baggage claim, you will have to declare and document the value of your bags and their contents. If you completed an inventory list while you were packing, this would be an ideal time to refer to it. Your reimbursement should arrive within 2–6 weeks. Just to prepare you, the check may not be for the full amount of the loss you claimed. The airlines have the right to adjust amounts to reflect current market value for any item.

Your airline will not reimburse you for currency, or for photographic or electronic equipment, such as cameras, stereos, VCRs, camcorders, CD players, telephones, and so on. They will also refuse to replace rare and expensive jewelry, works of art, or medication, unless you made prior arrangements and purchased excess valuation insurance before you checked your luggage.

Excess valuation insurance is available from the airline ticket counter, or you can purchase luggage insurance from your travel agent when you pay for your airline reservations.

Lost Credit Cards!

In Chapter 17, I suggested you photocopy the front and back of each of your credit cards and keep several copies in secure locations. If you followed this suggestion, you'll be able to go right down the list of credit card companies and call their toll-free number (it's usually printed on the back of each card) and report your card as lost or stolen. Some companies, such as VISA and American Express, will even ship a new card to you via an overnight delivery service.

If you didn't photocopy your credit cards (I'm now speaking from personal experience), you'll have to go through any credit card receipts you have with you and try to remember which cards you may have lost. You can find the toll-free numbers to report your cards by calling toll-free directory information at 800-555-1212. There frequently is a charge for calling toll-free directory information. There's an oxymoron lurking somewhere in there.

If you had the foresight to register your credit cards through a 24-hour service, then you can smugly make one phone call and go on with your vacation.

My Flight Is Delayed or Canceled!

It is always wise to call the airline reservation number before leaving for the airport to check on your flight's status. If the flight has been delayed or cancelled, you can save yourself hours of sitting in the airport. When you call the reservation number, just tell the agent that you have a reservation on flight number so and so, leaving this morning, from this city to that city and you would like to see if the flight is still on time. As long as you give them a real flight number and real cities, they'll give you a real answer.

If the flight is delayed, the airline has no legal responsibility to offer you any compensation. Usually, however, they're interested in keeping you as a customer, so they will make arrangements for you to fly on another airline, or they will give you a food voucher so you can spend your time waiting in an airport restaurant rather than the boarding area.

If the flight is canceled and the reason is weather or some other "Act of God," no compensation is required. If the airline cancels your flight for other reasons, they will either arrange alternative flights or they will secure and pay for hotel rooms and meals during your delay and put you on their next flight to your destination.

No one looks forward to delays, but they can be a lot of fun if you're not in a hurry. You can get some freebies and meet some new friends while you're waiting.

Sorry, We're Overbooked

Overbooking exists because a lot of people make reservations and never honor them. If airlines did not overbook they would probably have about 20 percent fewer passengers on their flights—meaning lots of seats going to waste. If hotels and car rental companies didn't overbook, they would experience similar results. Overbooking is not a practice that anyone enjoys, but it's an economic necessity because so many travelers do not honor the reservations they make.

Making the Most of Airline Overbooking

You arrive at your flight's departure gate, your flight is oversold, and you are denied boarding. You have just been "involuntarily bumped" and you are due compensation from the airline for your inconvenience.

What kind of compensation are we talking about here? According to the U.S. Department of Transportation (DOT) rules, an involuntarily bumped traveler whose arrival at his destination is delayed more than one hour but less than two on a domestic flight is entitled to $200, or 100 percent of the one-way fare, whichever is less. The airline must also honor the original ticket.

For delays longer than two hours, the compensation doubles. The airlines can offer you a travel voucher for a free domestic round-trip ticket instead of the cash, but they must give you the cash if that's what you want.

To avoid getting bumped, it's important to be at your flight's boarding gate early. If you're not there at least 15 minutes before your flight's departure, the airline can involuntarily bump you and rightfully refuse to pay you.

Airlines hate parting with cash, so when they sense an overbooked situation, they will ask for volunteers to take a later flight. For their cooperation, these volunteers receive vouchers good for discounts on future trips. There are no DOT rules covering compensation for volunteers; airlines can offer you as much or as little as it takes to get you off the plane.

If you encounter an overbooked situation and decide the travel voucher is large enough (sometimes, they'll be for a free round-trip domestic ticket) to get you to volunteer, be aware that any luggage you checked will continue with your original flight. If the alternative flight the airline offers is the next morning, you'll want to make sure your carry-on luggage is sufficiently stocked.

Most vouchers are nontransferable, so you must use them yourself, and normally, you must use them within one year.

Overbooked Car Rentals

Car rentals are not governed by DOT regulations, but they are governed by the desire to serve their customers. When you encounter an over-sold situation at the car rental counter, they will either have a reservation for you for a free car with another company, or they will upgrade you to a larger or better car at no extra charge.

Overbooked Hotels

When hotels overbook, they "walk" their confirmed guests to other hotel properties. You don't really have to walk—it's just a figure of speech. Normally, the oversold hotel picks up the tab for the night or nights spent at the other hotel. They may also upgrade you to a suite when you return.

Ugh, I Don't Feel So Good!

Getting sick at home is bad enough, but getting sick when you're traveling is absolutely the pits.

Every hotel maintains a list of local doctors who will either see you at their offices, or if you can't leave the hotel, will make a house (room) call. Don't put off calling the front desk just because you're skeptical about seeing a strange doctor. Your first priority should be getting better so you can enjoy the rest of your vacation.

Curing Jet Lag

Jet lag is caused by disrupting our body's daily biological rhythms. In plain English, the more time zones you cross in one day, the more disoriented you'll feel the next day. Here are some tips to improve your resistance to jet lag:

Don't drink alcohol, coffee, or cola when you fly. Alcohol and caffeine dehydrate your body and increase the damage caused by dry cabin air. The best drink in the air is bottled water—and lots of it. Now you know why all those flight attendants tote six-packs of Evian.

Try to alternate active periods with quiet periods while you're in-flight—just like you do at home. Get out of your seat, preferably after the flight attendants have removed the meal carts from the aisles, and take a stroll. If you know any yoga postures, practice them. This not only makes you feel better, it'll get you introduced to all kinds of great folks who will wonder what you're doing.

The Least You Need to Know

➤ Establish a "fun" attitude before you depart and prepare yourself for the unexpected.

➤ Airline tickets are like currency. If you lose yours, someone else could use it, and you'll end up buying two tickets.

➤ Volunteering to let another passenger have your seat could earn you a free ticket.

➤ When you're not feeling well, contact the hotel front-desk staff, and ask them to contact their house doctor.

Reliving Your Memories

In This Chapter

➤ Reliving your vacation through all five senses

➤ What it takes to create memorable photos

➤ The role of a travel journal

➤ How to pick a really tacky souvenir

One of the most rewarding and enjoyable aspects of a vacation is reliving the experiences of your travels while sitting in the comfort of your family room. I am sure you have all had the experience of finishing Aunt Sara's traditional boiled dinner, nervously looking at your watch, and hoping you can come up with a viable excuse to head for home before the dreaded "what we did during our 18 days in the Black Hills" slide show begins. After all, the trip took place in 1957, and you've seen the silhouettes of Aunt Sara and Uncle Harry blending with the Black Hills just one too many times. You've exhausted just about every excuse over the years and resigned yourself to another boring, three-hour travelogue.

But wait, old Sara and Harry have a new show. While you're still seated around the dinner table, the lights dim and Harry enters with two candles and commences to recite a poem created for your Aunt and Uncle by an inspired, New Age artist in Sedona, Arizona. You notice a peculiar, yet pleasant, odor wafting through the dining room and are startled to see several sticks of incense burning while your ears faintly detect the rhythmic chant of "Native American Flute Music" by R. Carlos Nakai. As the experience begins to settle in, you notice that Sara (who has difficulty boiling water, let alone boiling dinner) serves an elaborate dessert consisting of herbal tea and stone ground spiritual cakes.

Your memory of the boiled dinner has all but disappeared—thank goodness—and you've been transported to a world of Native American spirituality found only in Sedona. As Harry completes his reading, you notice a multicolored, mountain sunrise glowing on the bed-sheet-turned-projection screen, which in past years was reserved exclusively for the Black Hills boredom. The strains of music grow louder and the slides continue to evolve, shine, and dissolve as one photographic memory after another is shared by the transcended Sara and Harry.

This is what vacation memories are all about. They're an experience. They're a happening. They're an event that allows you and others to travel beyond the boundaries of your dining room to a place that elicits a glow and stimulates the five senses as though you were reliving the adventure of your perfect vacation.

Reliving the Moment

Photographs by themselves serve a purpose. Music by itself serves another purpose. And, food by itself serves yet another purpose. Now add a stick of incense as a tribute to the sense of smell, bring back the food and the music, and you've created a virtual environment for the photographs or videos of your vacation.

These are memories stimulated by what Mike Vance in his *Creative Thinking* program refers to as five-sensing. It's a technique that mixes touching, tasting, smelling, seeing, and hearing into an experience that creates three-dimensional memories. When you want to do more than just bore your neighbors with several hours of slides from Graceland

and potential Elvis sightings, and you want to make them feel like The King himself has stopped by to give a personal *TLC Tour* of Memphis, reach for your five-sensing tools and get your neighbors truly involved in experiencing your vacation.

Want to have some fun? Let's think of ten evenings that would produce outrageous, yet awesome, five-sensing vacation photographic shows. Okay Letterman, take this:

10. *White-water rafting on Idaho's Snake River*   Suggested props: Audio tapes of roaring rapids and screams of fear/delight, yellow slickers, squirt guns, industrial-strength fans, and wet wool socks.

9. *Indianola, Iowa Hot Air Balloon Classic*   Suggested props: Yanni CD, video tape from the gondola of a balloon, champagne to celebrate the perfect landing, and Dramamine for motion sickness.

8. *Snow Skiing*   Suggested props: Fire in the fireplace, hot-buttered rum, and an Andy Williams album.

7. *Anniversary Cruise*   Suggested props: Endless loop cassette of Kathy Lee singing "Ain't We Got Fun?," dessert buffet, and bon voyage streamers.

6. *Anchorage, Alaska's Winter Rendezvous*   Suggested props: Ice cubes, parkas, smoked salmon, and wildlife sounds.

5. *New England Fall Foliage*   Suggested props: Seating in rows (such as in a motorcoach), New England clam chowder, and any recording of "Autumn Leaves".

4. *New York Theater*   Suggested props: *Phantom of the Opera* CD, playbills, and deli sandwiches.

3. *County Fair*   Suggested props: Elephant ears, peanuts, corn dogs, cotton candy, and soundtrack to *County Fair.*

2. *Fourth of July in Washington, D.C.*   Suggested props: Any John Phillips Souza march; red, white, and blue bunting; "Friends of Bill's" buttons; and American flags.

1. *Hollywood and Beverly Hills*   Suggested props: Sunglasses, spot lights, tinsel, an "A" list and a "B" list, a Marilyn Monroe impersonator, and an *LA Story* video.

Pictures and Videos

Good vacation photographs and videos come in a variety of shapes, sizes, and formats. They are produced using a variety of equipment ranging in cost from a few dollars to several thousand dollars, and they are created by photographers with varying degrees of experience and talent. The important and distinguishing feature of every good vacation photograph is its capability to elicit memories. If it causes that little memory generator in our brains to click on and we begin to relive the roller coaster at Six Flags or the sunrise at the Grand Canyon, then it's not just a good photo, it's *best-of-show* quality.

Top Ten Tips for Taking Best-of-Show Vacation Photographs and Videos

10. *Include people.* Photographs without people are called scenic postcards and are available at most gift shops. You can increase the pleasure received from your vacation memories by including people in your scenery.

9. *Capture your subject's expression.* If all of your pictures and videos show the heads and feet of your subjects, you're too far away. Move closer; get that lens in someone's face.

8. *Be candid and informal.* Try to get an element of surprise into every scene. Formal poses belong in studios; you're on vacation.

7. *If your camera offers a zoom feature, use it to frame the scene.* Don't use it as a substitute for stepping closer.

6. *Ask permission.* If you think your subjects may object to having their picture taken, always ask first. Remember, you're a guest in their culture, and you should respect their beliefs and wishes.

5. *Search for scenes containing contrasts.* Whether it's old versus young or rough versus smooth, photos that expose the extremes of the moment are the most powerful.

4. *If you're using transparency film and creating slides, compose each shot using a landscape (horizontal) format.* Otherwise, the constant switching between landscape and portrait (vertical) formats will distract your viewing audience.

3. *Employ the rule of thirds when composing a scene.* This rule simply places the most important subject of each shot one-third of the way from the left side of the shot and one-third of the way from the top of the frame. This is where our eyes naturally check a photograph for meaning.

2. *Keep the sun or other major source of light behind you.* Otherwise, you'll be creating silhouettes that may have artistic merit but don't flatter the people in your vacation shots.

1. *If you're using standard, color print film, take a finished roll or two to a one-hour photo processing shop.* It's much better to discover that your camera has a problem while you're still at your destination and have a chance to take replacement pictures.

Cameras

My first camera (I still have it) was a Kodak box camera. It has no lens to clean or focus, and its shutter speed is determined not by the amount of available light, but by how fast your finger moves the lever from one side to the other. It's still a great camera, though, because it makes the photographer focus on the subject and the composition of a scene rather than the f-stops, film speeds, and lenses.

Nice equipment is a luxury, but it's not a substitute for paying attention to composition and lighting. Some of my favorite vacation photos are black and white shots I took with my box camera.

Camera Cases and Other Protection

One piece of equipment that is well worth its price tag is an x-ray-proof film container. These containers have a lead lining that protects your film from potential fogging caused by airport security systems. I've seen containers resembling stiff paper bags that are large enough to hold a small camera, and little plastic boxes that hold up to four rolls of film.

While we're talking about airport security systems, there has been controversy about placing your camera through the x-ray machine or having it hand-checked. Some maintain that the level of radiation used by the security machines is so low that it will not harm film, while others adamantly state that any level of radiation is too much. I won't contribute to this controversy other than to ask, "If there's any potential risk, why would you even consider jeopardizing your vacation memories?" Hand your camera to a security agent and ask him to inspect it manually. If he's really nice, take his picture as he moves his hand-held metal detector over your son's pockets. Great shot!

The other piece of photographic equipment that bears discussing is the camera case. If you're concerned about someone stealing your camera equipment—and if you're traveling on this planet, you should be concerned—for goodness sake, don't carry a huge bag that calls attention to your camera and its accessories. If it looks like an expensive camera bag to you, it's probably going to look even better to a thief. Carry your camera in an old backpack and keep it out of sight.

Video Cameras

The last piece of photography equipment that is a great investment is a video camera. These contraptions are not substitutes for still cameras because their output requires a viewer, and many times you just want to pull out a stack of pictures and share them with a friend or relive part of your vacation during a spontaneous moment. Setting up a VCR or your camera to play back your videos is not always spontaneous.

On the other hand, video cameras capture more than just sights; they give you motion and sound. They appeal to more of your senses, and to that extent, they contribute an important ingredient to the quality of your vacation memories. Just one question (disguised as a piece of advice), "Do you really want that little date and time stamp appearing in the lower right-hand corner of your screen forever? Wouldn't it be more attractive and accomplish the same purpose to begin each day's video by framing a tight shot of the front page of your destination's morning paper?" Just asking. If you like those little orange lights in the corner of your videos, go right ahead and ruin (oops, I mean use them in) your videos.

Dear Diary...

Photos and videos are great, but many times they fail to capture the emotion of the moment or that special feeling you can only describe in words. The perfect vacation tool to capture these magic feelings is a travel journal or diary. It doesn't have to be fancy, but it does have to be small enough to stick into your pocket or purse so it's always handy when you feel the urge to record something.

To produce the most effective and memory-stimulating journal, keep your entries brief, but brutally honest. If the ballet performance was moving and inspiring, write it down. If the breakfast buffet was disappointing and expensive, write it down. If the taxi driver told you the cutest story about the first time his mother flew aboard an airline, write it down. These little vignettes will string themselves together and provide you with countless hours of outstanding memories.

Souvenirs and Other Things That Collect Dust

My name is Scott and I am a pack rat. I keep everything; not just piles of it, but entire rooms of it. I've tried the 12-step cure and the 101-way antidote. Nothing seems to help.

I share this rather personal character flaw with you just so you know that I'm not the best person to give you advice about buying souvenirs. My impulse is to buy them all and keep them forever. The only good I can squeeze from my affliction is that my estate sale will be an awesome world-class flea market. All those tacky things you've ever seen at a souvenir stand and asked yourself, "Now, who would ever buy something like this?" will be available once again.

With that confession as background, here is my list of Top Ten Tacky, Must-Have Vacation Souvenirs:

10. *Matches*   They're free, and since so many people have stopped smoking, they're plentiful.

9. *Menus*   Please don't steal them; remember that you're a guest. Many times, if you ask nicely, the restaurant will give you a special copy of their menu. I especially like menus that include a history of the restaurant and the family that founded it.

8. *Golf balls*   Most resort golf courses have their logo imprinted on golf balls. These make for an interesting family room display, and if you buy the white ones, you don't have to dust them very often.

7. *T-shirts*   Like fine wine, you can never have too many T-shirts.

6. *Flyers and brochures*   These come in all shapes and sizes and cover everything from the destination's history to a description of a special event or attraction. These are not only great for reliving your vacation memories, they are outstanding tools for planning your activities for your next vacation.

235

5. *Postcards*   Send yourself a bunch of cards with little descriptions of your impressions of your destination. Not only will you have another memory-jogging device when you arrive home, you'll have some pleasant items in that pile of mail waiting for you to counter all those bills.

4. *Anything with your destination's name painted on it*   There's nothing better than a bottle opener that screams Niagara Falls in day-glo orange. These make great gifts, too.

3. *Books*   It doesn't have to be about your destination; it can be a book written by a local resident.

2. *Baggage tags*   On a recent trip we saw a coffee table with an epoxy top that had about 15 baggage tags embedded in it. It was a great conversation piece, which was fortunate because its owners were pretty boring.

1. *Pieces of art*   Again, like books, a piece of art doesn't have to depict the destination as long as it evokes memories of the destination. A piece of quarry tile from Avalon, a hand-carved seal from Alaska, and a ceramic bear from Big Bear Lake are a few of my most favorite treasures.

The Least You Need to Know

➤ Don't bore folks with yet another dry slide show of your last vacation; recreate the destination experience using props that appeal to all five senses.

➤ Ensure that you're getting great vacation photos by having some processed before you return home.

➤ The most important piece of photographic equipment you can buy is a lead-lined bag to protect your film from radiation.

➤ Buy souvenirs that elicit memories and give you a lifetime of dusting pleasure.

Chapter 21

Planning Your Next Perfect Vacation

In This Chapter

➤ Learning from past vacation experiences

➤ Creating a filing system to capture new vacation ideas

➤ How to keep up with current travel opportunities

Some count him unhappy that never traveled—a kind of prisoner, and pity his case that, from his cradle to his old age, he beholds the same still, still,—still the same, the same.

—Burton

Travel, especially vacation travel, is a wonderful teacher. It allows us to learn, and it allows us to grow, stretch, and change. It teaches us that most of our differences are superficial and that our abundant similarities give us a new understanding of each other's needs. This understanding fosters new friendships, which are among the greatest joys of traveling.

Vacation travel, like most activities, improves with practice and experience. The adage that says, "The more you know about travel, the more you know how little you really know about travel," is true. Our goal is not to learn all we can about travel, but rather to learn about what we like and dislike about our vacations. Although this chapter concludes our discussion about planning the perfect vacation, it is just the beginning of your planning for your future vacations.

Analyzing Your Recent Vacation

After you've returned home and had an opportunity to swap your vacation routine for your working routine, take a few minutes and create a Vacation Assessment File. This can be an 89¢ notepad from your local drug store or a manila file folder for your home filing system. In this case, the media is *not* the message; your thoughts and impressions are.

Find a time when you won't be interrupted and gather all your vacation participants to review and discuss all the things that worked and all the things that didn't work on your vacation. Make detailed notes about such things as your hotel, campsite, or other accommodations; the meals you shared; your rental car; the amount of activity; the amount of free time; and the various sights you saw.

Discuss not only what you did or didn't do, but tell each other how you now feel about each aspect of your vacation. Be honest, but be realistic. If it rained every day of your vacation and you found that to be a really negative experience, don't let that taint every other part of your vacation. Always try to balance the bad parts with positive elements. This balance is important and allows you to better plan your next adventure.

Updating Your Vacation Profile

Over time, your vacation needs, wants, goals, and desires will change. You may want more adventure or more relaxation. It doesn't matter. What is important is your ability to monitor and recognize these changes. Refer to Chapters 2 and 3 and create a new vacation profile.

I've encountered many vacationers who begin our conversation by saying, "Well, I guess it's time to buy our tickets to Naples again." When I tell them it sounds like they're a little tired of Naples, they agree. They also say that there's not much they can do to get out of going because everyone expects them to be there.

I suggest that if you fall into the "Naples Again" vacation syndrome that you reassess your vacation profile and break out of that rut. Ask yourself what you would do if Naples were closed this year. Just pretend someone put a big sign on it that said, "Closed for Repairs, See Y'All Next Year." You may be very surprised and, better yet, excited by your answer. You may even do it.

By the way, I love Naples and I'm certainly not suggesting that it is a boring vacation spot. I'm not even suggesting that you shouldn't travel there multiple times. It's a grand Floridian beach community that has lots of class and many very nice residents. I'm just suggesting that like too much chocolate gives you a stomachache, headache, and acne, too much of any one vacation destination gives you boredom, apathy, and dullness.

So, if you break free of your old patterns, stop eating so much chocolate, and plan to visit a new destination on your next vacation, you'll start feeling much better—and you won't get acne. (Although I once played a doctor in a school play, I am not a medical professional and the preceding is not medical advice. Okay?)

Keeping Up with the Changes

Staying informed about new and exciting vacation ideas is easy and one of the best ways to break out of your old habits and vacation routines. The popularity and massive scope of vacation travel makes it a natural theme for numerous magazines, newsletters, and on-line information services. If you stop by any bookstore or newsstand, you'll find numerous publications that will fill your vacation-idea larder to capacity. If you tap into any of the online services mentioned in Chapter 15, you'll fill megabytes of computer hard disk space. Finding vacation ideas is not a problem; storing and retrieving these ideas is another matter.

If you really want to be prepared and make your next vacation as perfect as possible, develop a little filing system. Computer freaks call these things Information Retrieval Systems, but that's too formal for us. We'll just call this system, "A Place Where We Can Easily Put Vacation Ideas and Stuff and Quickly Find Them Later."

All you'll need is a "Place" and some "Stuff." I like those plastic file folder holders with a hinged lid, two clasps, and a handle. Mine holds about 30 hanging file folders and came from one of those big discount stores with a "mart" in its name. They hold enough information to be valuable, yet their handle makes them portable. This lets you take your vacation ideas out on the back porch and start dreaming and planning—unless it's February and you live in Minneapolis, in which case a nice rug in front of the fireplace will provide a more comfortable spot.

Rearranging Chaos

Let me warn you up front, getting organization tips from me is about as bizarre as getting a root canal from a stand-up comic—about as funny, too. Anyway, if I can just find my notes about vacation filing systems... bear with me, please... I know they're here... I just saw them Thursday. Oh wow, here's that phone number I needed yesterday. Ah ha, here they are, my notes about constructing a simple file system so you can easily store vacation ideas and quickly retrieve them.

Five Steps to a Vacation Filing System

1. Choose a container to house your files. A drawer, portable file box, or just an abandoned cardboard box work just fine. The important part of this step is to locate this container where it is dead solid handy. You want to be able to read a newspaper article, tear it out, and drop it in one of your files.

2. Select three or four major vacation categories that you currently find interesting. If you have more than four, that's fine, you've probably always been an overachiever. You'll find your categories will grow as you become more aware of the travel opportunities that appeal to you. Your categories may be Cruises, Theme Parks, and Bicycling Tours, or you may choose Hawaii, Alaska, and Rome. If you're really undecided, your categories may be United States, Europe, and Everywhere Else.

3. Develop a habit of gathering every interesting piece of vacation literature and bringing it back to your file container. If you do this correctly, you'll resemble a squirrel gathering and storing nuts for the winter, only probably not as cute.

4. Create an index folder. Although this sounds ominous and highly technical, it's as simple as writing "Index" on a file folder label and putting a blank sheet of paper inside. As you add clippings to your files, just make a note on this sheet of paper saying what you found and where you stored it. Sort of like this: "Hyatt announces Internet site—Hotels," or "Antonio's in Parma, Ohio, announces two-for-one pizza—Restaurants," or "PGA West offers golf package—Shopping." If you're a little confused about the last one, it has to do with the fine art of compromise. You know, like, "I'm sure you wouldn't mind if I played golf while you went shopping in Palm Springs for five hours."

5. Finding stuff you want and discarding the rest constitutes the last step. Periodically, like during the summer and winter solstices, you need to systematically rummage through your files and make notes about the clippings that interest you and discard the articles that seemed like a good idea at the time, but have since lost their luster. Think of your vacation filing system as a winery where you store a gaggle of good ideas and let them ferment and age so you can stop by to sip and taste frequently.

Bon Voyage

I hope you've had half as much fun flipping through these pages as I've had translating my thoughts into words, and every once in awhile a complete sentence. As you've probably sensed, I have a passion for travel and I love sharing that with you. It's a great affliction. Hopefully, someday our travel paths will cross and we'll make an acquaintance, share a few travel stories, and continue to reduce the number of strangers in our lives.

Bon voyage and safe passage.

The Least You Need to Know

➤ Start planning your future vacations right now. Start a simple filing system to collect all the interesting clippings and notes you discover during the coming months. Even if your next vacation isn't scheduled for many months, it's time to get started.

➤ If you organize your vacation thoughts, experiences, and desires, you'll have much better control over your future vacations.

➤ Start now expanding your web to collect travel and vacation suggestions. Find a travel agent that complements your style of vacation travel. Subscribe to travel magazines, and subscribe to an online service and monitor the travel discussions.

➤ Create a vacation filing system and make frequent deposits and withdrawals.

May the road rise to meet your feet,
the wind be always at your back,
the sun shine warm upon your face,
the rains fall soft upon your fields,
and until we meet again, may God
hold you in the palm of His hand.

—Irish Blessing

Index

Uplifting Experience.

Dollar would like to lend you a hand when renting for your next vacation. Reserve an economy or compact size car, ask for the "**Uplifting Experience**" and you will receive a complimentary upgrade to the next car class at no extra charge by mail.

Dollar makes it easy for you to enjoy your next vacation. We provide great service from a smiling sales agent, and quality Chrysler products. It is no wonder that Dollar is tops with the "idiots" of the world.

So call to receive your upgrade certificate by mail and make your next vacation an uplifting experience!

Dollar features quality Chrysler products like the Dodge Neon, and the Plymouth Acclaim.

Worldwide Reservations, Call
1-800-800-4000.

DOLLAR® RENT A CAR

NO-BRAINER SAVINGS FROM BUDGET.

$25 Off
weekly rental

Five or more days. Intermediate through luxury size car.
Promo Code: TTT (MTTC144 effective 4/1/95)

Looking for an easy way to save? Rent from Budget and rest assured you're getting the perfect deal on the perfect car for the perfect vacation. For reservations, contact your travel consultant or call Budget at **800-527-0700**.

THE SMART MONEY IS ON BUDGET.

We feature Lincoln-Mercury and other fine cars.

HERE ARE SOME DETAILS YOU SHOULD KNOW: Just mention promotion code TTT (MTTC144 effective 4/1/95) when you reserve an intermediate through luxury size car, and receive $25 off your weekly rental. Five-day minimum rental necessary to qualify for discount. This offer is valid at participating Budget locations through March 31, 1996, and is subject to vehicle availability. Car must be returned to renting location, except in some metro areas where intra-area drop-offs are permitted. Local rental and age requirements apply. Discount applies to time and mileage only and is not available in conjunction with any other discount, promotional offer, CorpRate®, government, or tour/wholesale rate. Refueling services, taxes and other optional items are extra. Additional driver, underage driver and other surcharges are extra. Blackout dates may apply.

Experience The Perfect Vacation...
Plus $100 Savings!

Save $100 when you purchase a Hyatt Vacations®
package. Hyatt Vacations® offers
outstanding values on hotel accommodations,
taxes, airport transfers or car rental, and optional
airfare. You'll enjoy Hyatt hotels and resorts in
Hawaii, the Caribbean, the Continental
United States and Mexico, with your $100 savings
from Hyatt Vacations®.

**Reservations are required, so call your
Travel Planner or Hyatt Vacations®
at 1-800-772-0011.**

Terms and Conditions:
•Specify "Idiots Guide to Travel" Offer
•Only available on Hyatt Vacations® packages - minimum
of three consecutive night stay
•Total of $100 off a Hyatt Vacations® package
•Travel must be completed by 12/16/95
•Offer subject to Hyatt Vacations® terms and conditions

Where the Perfect Vacation Begins.

PLUG YOURSELF INTO...

The Macmillan Information SuperLibrary™

Free information and vast computer resources from the world's leading computer book publisher—online!

FIND THE BOOKS THAT ARE RIGHT FOR YOU!

A complete online catalog, plus sample chapters and tables of contents give you an in-depth look at *all* of our books, including hard-to-find titles. It's the best way to find the books you need!

- **STAY INFORMED** with the latest computer industry news through our online newsletter, press releases, and customized Information SuperLibrary Reports.

- **GET FAST ANSWERS** to your questions about MCP books and software.

- **VISIT** our online bookstore for the latest information and editions!

- **COMMUNICATE** with our expert authors through e-mail and conferences.

- **DOWNLOAD SOFTWARE** from the immense MCP library:
    - Source code and files from MCP books
    - The best shareware, freeware, and demos

- **DISCOVER HOT SPOTS** on other parts of the Internet.

- **WIN BOOKS** in ongoing contests and giveaways!

TO PLUG INTO MCP: ➜   **WORLD WIDE WEB: http://www.mcp.com**

GOPHER: gopher.mcp.com

FTP: ftp.mcp.com

Windows® 10 For Seniors

3rd Edition

by Peter Weverka

Windows® 10 For Seniors For Dummies®, 3rd Edition

Published by: **John Wiley & Sons, Inc.,** 111 River Street, Hoboken, NJ 07030-5774, www.wiley.com

Copyright © 2018 by John Wiley & Sons, Inc., Hoboken, New Jersey

Published simultaneously in Canada

For general information on our other products and services, please contact our Customer Care Department within the U.S. at 877-762-2974, outside the U.S. at 317-572-3993, or fax 317-572-4002. For technical support, please visit https://hub.wiley.com/community/support/dummies.

Wiley publishes in a variety of print and electronic formats and by print-on-demand. Some material included with standard print versions of this book may not be included in e-books or in print-on-demand. If this book refers to media such as a CD or DVD that is not included in the version you purchased, you may download this material at http://booksupport.wiley.com. For more information about Wiley products, visit www.wiley.com.

Library of Congress Control Number: 2018938747

ISBN 978-1-119-46985-8; ISBN 978-1-119-46988-9 (ebk); ISBN ePDF 978-1-119-46992-6 (ebk)

Manufactured in the United States of America

C10017580_021320

Table of Contents

Introduction

Windows 10, Spring 2018 Creators Update, is the latest generation of Microsoft's operating system, the master program that makes a computer useful and provides support to other programs, including word processors, photo viewers, and web browsers. Much as an education equips you to read a novel or play a game, Windows 10 equips your computer to perform a wide range of activities. You can use Windows 10 and other software (or *apps*) to read or write a novel, play games or music, and stay in touch with friends and family around the world.

As Windows has evolved over the past 30 years, so have computers — the *hardware.* Today, you can buy a computer as small as a paperback book, and even such a little computer is unimaginably more powerful than (and a fraction of the cost of) computers just 10 years ago. The hardware consists of the screen, as well as optional components such as a keyboard and a mouse.

You don't need much time with a computer to conclude that there has to be an easier way to do things. At times, computers seem overly complex and inscrutable. Have you used a cellphone lately? Or a TV remote control? Why are the controls on every microwave oven different? Why does every new tool offer countless options you don't want that obscure the ones you do want? Well, I don't have the answers to those questions, but I do have step-by-step instructions for many tasks you want to perform using Windows 10.

After many years of working with computers, I find that they reward patience, curiosity, and a little methodical exploration. Seniors, in particular, know that learning never really stops and that learning new things keeps one young, at least figuratively. By the end of this book, you may be a multitasking computerist performing virtual gymnastics with Windows 10. On the other hand, if this book helps you do only one thing — use email, browse the web, or enjoy photos or music — that one useful thing may be all you need.

About This Book

Age is just a number. This book is intended for anyone getting started with Windows 10 who wants step-by-step instructions without a lot of discussion. Numerous figures with notes show you the computer screen as you progress through the steps. Reading this book is like having an experienced friend stand behind you as you use Windows 10 . . . someone who never takes control of the computer away from you.

Windows 10 is a work in progress. Microsoft updates the Windows 10 operating system from time to time to make it more secure and agreeable to the people who use it. (Chapter 3 explains how to check for updates to Windows 10.) Because the operating system is continuously updated, the screen shots you see in this book may not exactly match what you see on your screen.

Conventions Used in This Book

This book uses certain conventions to highlight important information and help you find your way around:

» **Different methods for performing steps:** In general, you can complete a step in three ways. I list the choices as follows:

- **Mouse:** If you have a mouse, follow these instructions.
- **Touchscreen:** You may be able to touch your screen to perform tasks.
- **Keyboard:** Keyboard shortcuts are often the fastest way to do something.

When you have a choice between these methods, experiment to determine which is easiest for you.

TIP

» **Tip icons:** Point out helpful suggestions related to tasks in the step lists.

» **Bold:** I use bold for figure references as well as for when you have to type something onscreen using the keyboard.

Many figures have notes or other markings to draw your attention to a specific part of the figure. The text tells you what to look for; the figure notes help you find it.

» **Website addresses:** If you bought an e-book, website address are live links. In the text, website addresses look like this: www.dummies.com. See Chapter 6 for information on browsing the web.

» **Options and buttons:** Although Windows 10 often uses lower-case in options and on buttons, I capitalize the text for emphasis. That way, you can find a button labeled Save Now, even though onscreen it appears as *Save now*.

How to Read This Book

You can work through this book from beginning to end or simply look at the table of contents or index to find the instructions you need to solve a problem or learn a new skill whenever you need it. The steps in each task get you where you want to go quickly, without a lot of technical explanation. In no time, you'll start picking up the skills you need to become a confident Windows 10 user.

Technology always comes with its own terms and concepts, but you don't need to learn another language to use a computer. You don't need any prior experience with computers or Windows. Step-by-step instructions guide you through specific tasks, such as accessing the news or playing a game. These steps provide just the information you need for the task at hand.

Foolish Assumptions

I assume that you have a computer and want clear, brief, step-by-step instructions on getting things done with Windows 10. I assume also that you want to know just what you need to know, just when you need to know it. This isn't Computers 101. This is Practical Windows 10. As an old friend of mine said, "I don't want to make a watch; I just want to know what time it is."

How This Book Is Organized

This book is divided into four parts to help you find what you need. You can read from cover to cover or just jump to the page that interests you.

» **Part 1: Getting Started with Windows 10:** In Chapter 1, you turn on the computer and get comfortable with essential parts of Windows 10, such as the Start screen, as well as how to use a mouse, touchscreen, or keyboard. Explore features of Windows 10 apps in Chapter 2. To customize Windows 10 to work better for you, turn to Chapter 3. In Chapter 4, you create and modify user account settings, such as passwords. Discover the desktop, how to manage windows, and how to customize the desktop in Chapter 5.

» **Part 2: Windows 10 and the Web:** Use the web to stay current and keep in touch. Turn to Chapter 6 to use Edge to browse the web. Send and receive email in Chapter 7. Turn to Chapter 8 to explore a handful of apps that can help you stay in touch with friends and get to know the outside world better.

» **Part 3: Having Fun with Windows 10:** If you haven't been having any fun until now, I've failed you. Expand your tools and toys in Chapter 9 by connecting to Microsoft Store to install new apps. In Chapter 10, you enjoy photos on Windows 10 and put your own photos on the computer. If you want to listen to music and watch a video, see Chapter 11.

» **Part 4: Beyond the Basics:** In Chapter 12, you learn about the care and feeding of Windows 10, which requires a little maintenance now and then. Find out how to connect a printer and other hardware, such as a mouse and a second screen, in Chapter 13. Do you appreciate the saying "a place for everything and everything in its place"? Chapter 14 is where you organize your documents. You back up your files to insure against loss and refresh Windows 10 when it gets cranky, all in Chapter 15.

Beyond the Book

In addition to what you're reading right now, this book comes with a free access-anywhere Cheat Sheet that helps you choose the Windows 10 default application for opening files, manipulate app windows, open a second desktop window, and handle notifications. To get this Cheat Sheet, simply go to www.dummies.com and search for "Windows 10 For Seniors For Dummies Cheat Sheet" by using the Search box.

1
Getting Started with Windows 10

Chapter **1**

Getting Acquainted with Windows 10

Windows 10 is an *operating system* (the master program for any computer). You can use Windows 10 on a wide range of devices, from a smartphone to a big-screen TV/entertainment system: One size fits most. You can not only use the same programs with a range of hardware but also access the documents you create (such as photos and email — files and data, to nerds) from any Windows-based computer, giving you extraordinary freedom of choice and mobility.

Although countless companies create programs you may use, Micro-soft attempts to make similar functions consistent across different programs. For example, opening a document or emailing a photo to a friend involves the same steps regardless of the programs you use. You don't have to learn a different way of doing common tasks in each program. This consistency will serve you well when using Windows 10 and other new programs.

In this chapter, you start your computer and work with the *Start screen*, the dashboard for Windows 10. You explore options for using the Start screen with your *hardware* (the computer and related devices). Then you exit Windows 10 and go right back in for more.

The easiest way to get Windows 10 is preinstalled on a new computer. If your current computer runs an older version of (Windows 7, Windows 8, or Windows 8.1), you can upgrade to Windows 10, although older machines may lack newer functions, such as a touchscreen.

Tell Your Computer What to Do

How do you get Windows 10 to do what you want it to do? You can command a computer in many ways, depending on your equipment (hardware). For example, a desktop computer has different options from a handheld phone. You may have any or all of these choices:

>> Mouse

>> Touchscreen

>> Keyboard

Another device for controlling Windows is a touchpad, which is commonly found on a laptop keyboard. You move your finger on the touchpad to move the pointer on the screen.

If you have a computer with more than one of these devices, you might use one device exclusively or, more likely, vary your choice according to the task. Use whichever technique is easiest for you, but don't be afraid to experiment. In the next few sections, you discover the ins and outs of using all these methods of controlling Windows 10. Then you're ready to turn on your computer and use these methods.

In the steps throughout this book, *choose* or *select* refers to using a mouse, the touchscreen, or a physical keyboard. *Drag* refers to using a mouse or a finger.

Move the Mouse

A *mouse* is a soap-bar-sized device that you move across a desk with your hand. Move the mouse and note how the arrow called a *mouse pointer* moves across the computer screen. A mouse has two or more buttons; some also have a scroll wheel between the buttons.

The following terms describe methods for using a mouse with Windows 10. In each, move the mouse first to position the pointer over a specified item before proceeding:

» **Click:** Move the onscreen arrow-shaped mouse pointer over a specified item and press and release the left mouse button: That's a click (sometimes called a left-click to distinguish it from a right-click).

» **Right-click:** Press and release the right mouse button to display available functions. Note that the word *click* by itself means use the left mouse button.

» **Drag:** Press and hold down the left mouse button, and then move the mouse pointer across the screen. When you want to move an object, you drag it. Release the mouse button to release the object.

TIP

Watch for the word *click* to indicate using a mouse button and *roll* to indicate using the mouse wheel.

Touch the Screen

A *touchscreen*, as the name says, enables you to touch the screen to tell your computer what to do. You typically use one finger or two, although touchscreens may allow you to use all ten digits. In some cases, you can also use a special pen called a *stylus* instead of your finger. Tablet computers and some smartphones have touchscreens. Touchscreens are less common on desktop or laptop computers, but that situation is changing. Not sure what type of screen you have?

When you have Windows 10 running, give the screen a gentle poke with your index finger to see what happens.

The following terms refer to ways you interact with a touchscreen:

» **Tap:** Briefly touch the screen. You *select* an object, such as a button, by tapping it.

» **Drag:** Touch and hold your finger on the screen, then move your finger across the screen. You *move* an object, such as an onscreen playing card, by dragging it.

» **Swipe:** Touch and move your finger more quickly than with drag. You can swipe your finger across the screen from any of the four sides of the screen to display options and commands. You swipe pages to move forward or back. You may see the word *flick* instead of *swipe.* Some people insist that a flick is faster or shorter than a swipe, but let's not get caught up in that.

» **Pinch and unpinch:** Touch a finger and thumb or two fingers on the screen. Move your fingers closer to each other to *pinch* and away from each other to *unpinch.* Generally, a pinch reduces the size of something on the screen or shows more content on the screen. An unpinch (an ugly word) *zooms in,* increasing the size of something onscreen to show more detail.

TIP
Watch for the words *tap, swipe,* or *pinch* to indicate using your finger. Touch actions are often called *gestures.*

TIP
See the upcoming section "View the Touch Keyboard" if your computer doesn't have a physical keyboard, as is often the case with a touchscreen.

Use a Keyboard

A typewriter–like keyboard is a traditional device for controlling a computer and is especially useful when you must enter a lot of text. Special key combinations, called *shortcut keys*, are often the quickest way to do anything (though they require some memorization).

The following keys are particularly noteworthy. No offense intended to fans of keys not noted here. Although you won't use all these keys immediately, you'll find it helpful to locate each one on your keyboard.

Press indicates that you use the keyboard (physical or virtual) for the specified key or sequence of keys (just as *click* indicates a mouse action and *tap* indicates touch). Combinations of keys are not pressed simultaneously. Instead, press and hold the first key in the specified sequence, press the second key, and then release both. (I explain exceptions to this method as necessary.)

» 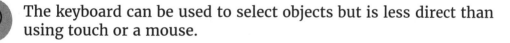: Called the Windows key, this key is usually located on either side of the spacebar, which is the largest key. ▦ works by itself, as you'll soon see, and also in combination with many other keys. Throughout the book, I specify these combinations where you might use them. There will be a quiz later. (Kidding! No quizzes.)

» **Tab:** Press the Tab key to highlight an item. Press Tab repeatedly to skip items you don't intend to select.

The keyboard can be used to select objects but is less direct than using touch or a mouse.

» **Arrow keys:** Press the arrow keys to move the cursor or selection of an object in the direction the keys point (left, right, up, or down). In some contexts, Tab and the right arrow do the same thing. Sorry to be vague, but context matters at times.

» **Enter:** In most cases, the Enter key on the keyboard chooses a selection, much as clicking or tapping does. However, you may need to use the Tab key or an arrow key to select an item before pressing the Enter key.

» **Ctrl, Alt,** and **Shift keys:** These keys are used with other keys for commands. For example, press Ctrl+C to copy selected text or an object. (That is, while pressing and holding down the Ctrl key, press the C key — no need to press Shift for an uppercase C. Then release both keys.) The Shift key is used with another key for uppercase.

» **Backspace:** As you enter text, each press of Backspace erases the character to the left of the cursor.

» **Delete:** As you enter text, each press of the Delete key erases the character to the right of the cursor. On some keyboards, this key is labeled Del.

» **Function keys:** All keys function, but Function keys are labeled F1 through F12. You don't use these much in this book, but you should locate them. Laptops often have a separate Function Lock key to turn these keys on or off.

» **Page keys:** Locate the Home, End, Page Up, and Page Down keys for future reference. Use these to move the screen, a page, or the cursor. (On some keyboards, the Home, End, Page Up, and Page Down keys work as numbers when the Num Lock key is activated.)

View the Touch Keyboard

Windows 10 can display a touch keyboard onscreen. This feature is vital for devices that have a touchscreen and no physical keyboard. With a touchscreen, the touch keyboard appears automatically when the *cursor* (a blinking vertical bar) indicates that you can enter text in a box. If the touch keyboard doesn't appear automatically, you may also see a separate box floating above or below the text box. Tap that floating box to display the keyboard. To type using the keyboard, simply tap or click a letter, number, or symbol key.

TIP

Here are the different types of touch keyboards:

» The *standard layout* (also called QWERTY) appears automatically (see **Figure 1-1**). The Enter key changes depending on the context.

» The *uppercase layout,* shown in **Figure 1-2,** appears when you tap the Shift key on the standard layout.

» The *numbers and symbols layout,* shown in **Figure 1-3,** appears when you tap the &123 key on the standard layout. Tap the &123 key again to return to the standard layout.

Tap (or press Esc) to close the touch keyboard

FIGURE 1-1

FIGURE 1-2

FIGURE 1-3

» The control keys overlay (see **Figure 1-4**) appears on five keys on the standard layout when you tap the Ctrl key. The Ctrl keys are used in common tasks, such as copying (Ctrl+C) or moving (Ctrl+X) selected text. The overlay disappears automatically after you tap one of the control keys (A, Z, X, C, or V).

» The *emoji layout,* shown in **Figure 1-5,** appears when you tap the Smiley Face key. Tap the Smiley Face key again to return to the standard layout. (Emojis are also called *emoticons* or *smileys.*)

FIGURE 1-4

FIGURE 1-5

TIP

To quickly enter an emoji without opening the touch keyboard, press ■+period (.). The emoji panel appears. Click or tap an emoji to enter it onscreen.

But wait! There's more. Tap the keyboard key, which is in the upper-left corner of any layout, to display the four options shown in **Figure 1-6.**

» Tap the Standard button (refer to **Figure 1-6**) to return to the standard layout from one of the other layouts.

» Tap the Split button to view the *split keyboard layout,* shown in **Figure 1-7.** This layout is handy for typing with your thumbs while holding two sides of a tablet.

» Tap the Narrow button to see a narrow keyboard suitable for thumb typing.

» Tap the Handwriting button to view the *handwriting layout,* shown in **Figure 1-8.** This layout enables you to write with a finger or a stylus (a special pen). Windows converts your scribbles to block text (if it can make sense of your scribbles).

» Tap the Expanded button to view a keyboard with keys such as Tab, Caps, and Shift that appear on a conventional keyboard.

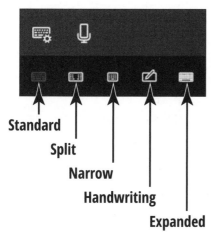

FIGURE 1-6

FIGURE 1-7

FIGURE 1-8

If your touchscreen doesn't come with a stylus, you can buy one and use it instead of your finger for improved precision.

TIP

Turn On Your Computer

1. Push the power button briefly and release it. Every computer has a power button. (When we can no longer turn them off, the machines win.) If you have a desktop computer tower, the power button is probably on the front of the tower. Otherwise, you might have to feel around the front and sides of the screen or near the hinges of a laptop. Typically, your computer will beep, some buttons will light, and the screen may flash a logo or a message that disappears before you can read it. (Just let that go.) Soon, you will see the Windows 10 Lock screen.

2. Turn on any separate hardware (such as a monitor, speakers, or a printer), if necessary.

3. Enter your password and press Enter (or select the Submit button, the button on the right side of the password textbox). Soon the Windows 10 desktop screen appears, as shown in **Figure 1-9.**

TIP

If you don't see the Password text box, jiggle the mouse or press a key on the keyboard to wake up Windows 10.

TIP

The first time you turn on a new computer, a series of Windows Setup screens appears. Accept the defaults or change them appropriately and then select the button labeled Next.

TIP

If your computer doesn't have a keyboard, as is the case with many tablet computers, see the preceding section, "View the Touch Keyboard," for information on how to type onscreen.

TIP

If this is the first time that Windows 10 has started on your computer, you must create a user account, even if no one else will use the machine. See Chapter 4 for details on creating and changing user accounts.

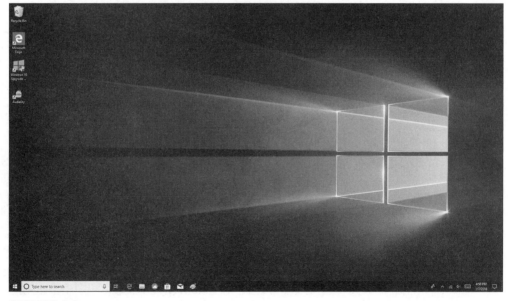

FIGURE 1-9

Check Out the Start Screen

1. Start your computer — if it isn't started already — and sign in to your user account. You'll see the Windows desktop screen (refer to **Figure 1-9**).

2. Open the Start screen, as shown in **Figure 1-10.** Use one of these methods to open the Start screen:

- **Mouse:** Click the Start button (you'll find it in the lower-left corner of the screen).

- **Touchscreen:** Tap the Start button.

- **Keyboard:** Press the key.

FIGURE 1-10

3. Examine the Start screen and note the colorful rectangular icons called *tiles.* These tiles represent available *apps* (short for application programs, an older term for programs or software). By clicking or tapping an app tile, you can open an app. After you start to use the app tiles, they may display changing information, such as the current weather. (See Chapter 2 for information on using individual apps.)

4. Scroll down the names of apps on the left side of the Start screen. You see an alphabetical list of all the apps that are installed on your computer, as shown in **Figure 1-11, left.** By clicking or tapping an app in this list, you can open an app. Scroll on the Start screen when you want to open an application but can't find its tile.

Under "Most Used," the Start screen lists apps you recently opened. You can click or tap an app name on the Most Used list to open an app.

While the Start screen is open, you can type the name of an app to open it. For example, to open the Weather app, type **weather.** A panel opens with the names of apps that include the word *weather* (you also see apps from the Microsoft Store and web pages with the word *weather*). Select the Weather app listing in the panel to open the Weather app.

5. Scroll through the alphabetical apps list to Windows Administrative Tools, and then click or tap the down-arrow to the right of the name *Windows Administrative Tools*. As shown in **Figure 1-11, middle,** a list of apps appears under the Windows Administrative Tools heading.

In the alphabetical apps list, some names are really headings, not apps. The down arrows tell you where the headings are. Click or tap a down arrow to see the list of apps under a heading.

Rather than scroll through the alphabetical list to find an app, you can select a letter in the list and then select a letter in the pop-up list of letters that appears (refer to **Figure 1-11, right**). For example, to quickly get to the Weather app, select any letter and then select the W on the pop-up list.

6. Notice the buttons in the lower-left corner of the Start screen. From top to bottom, these buttons are your image, Settings, and Power, as shown in **Figure 1-12.**

Rather than buttons, you can see button names on the Start screen (see **Figure 1-12**) by selecting the menu button in the upper-left corner of the Start screen.

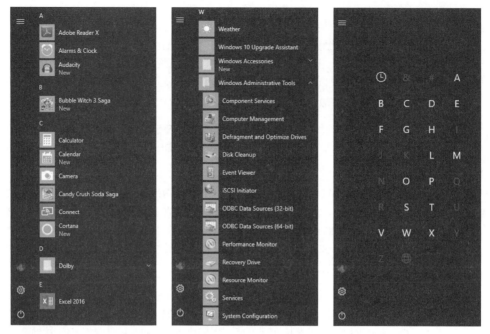

FIGURE 1-11

FIGURE 1-12

7. Click or tap your image (or image and name) on the Start screen. As shown in **Figure 1-13,** you see a drop-down menu with commands for changing account settings (see Chapter 3), locking your screen (see "Start Again on the Lock Screen," later in this chapter), and signing out in a favor of another person who shares your computer (see Chapter 4). Who would think that clicking your name would open a drop-down menu?

FIGURE 1-13

8. Click or tap the Power on the Start menu. As shown in **Figure 1-14,** you see a pop-up menu with commands for putting your computer to sleep, shutting down your computer, and restarting your computer. Later in this chapter, "Shut Down Your Computer" looks into the options on this pop-up menu.

9. Click or tap the Start button, or press the ⊞ key. Doing any of these actions when the Start screen is open closes the Start screen. You can also close the Start screen by clicking anywhere on the desktop when the Start screen is open.

Sleep

Shut down

Restart

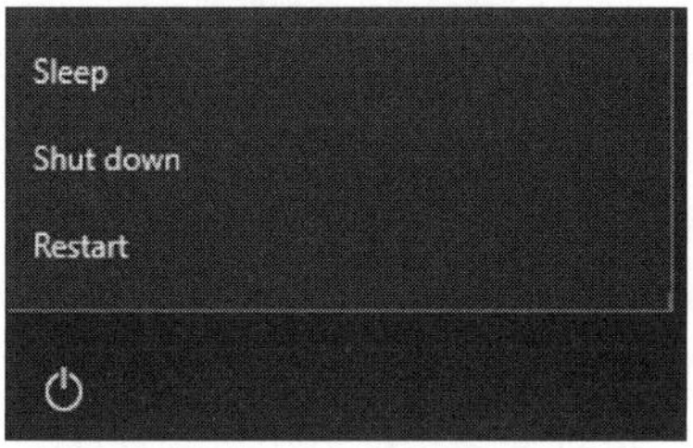

FIGURE 1-14

Shut Down Your Computer

1. When you have finished using your computer for a while, you may want to shut down Windows 10. Begin by displaying the Start screen:

   - **Mouse:** Click the Start button.
   - **Touchscreen:** Tap the Start button.
   - **Keyboard:** Press the ■ key.

2. Click or tap Power on the Start menu (refer to **Figure 1-14**).

3. Available options appear in a pop-up box. Some or all of the following options appear:

   - **Sleep:** This option reduces the computer's power consumption without exiting Windows 10 or closing apps (some computers don't offer this option). As a result, when you wake the computer by moving the mouse or touching the screen or the keyboard, everything is exactly as you left it: Apps and documents are open, if they were open before Sleep.

   - **Shut Down:** This option exits Windows 10 and saves power by turning the computer off. In exiting Windows 10, Shut Down closes any apps that are currently running.

   - **Hibernate:** This option combines Sleep and Shut Down. Hibernate records which apps are running but also completely shuts down the computer. When you start the computer, Windows 10 opens all programs you were using, just as Sleep does.

   Hibernate and Shut Down are equally green options — they save the same amount of power. Sleep is a little less green but saves time if you are returning to the middle of a task.

   - **Restart:** Temporarily shuts down Windows 10 and turns it on again. Use Restart when Windows 10 asks you to or when Windows 10 is misbehaving.

   You can also shut down your computer by using the Start button. Move the pointer over the Start button and right-click. A pop-up menu appears. Select Shut Down or Sign Out on the pop-up menu, and then select an option (Sleep, Shut Down, Hibernate, or Restart).

4. Choose Shut Down to turn off the computer.

TIP

On most computers, pressing the power switch also shuts down the computer. On a laptop, closing the lid may shut down the laptop or put it in sleep or hibernation mode.

TIP

For a desktop computer, consider using a power strip to plug in the computer, the monitor, and the printer. After you shut down or hibernate the computer, turn off the power strip to save power.

Start Again on the Lock Screen

1. Turn on your computer. Every time you turn on your computer, the Lock screen appears. As shown in **Figure 1-15,** the Lock screen displays the time, day, and date along with a photo. (You discover how to change this photo in Chapter 3.)

2. Dismiss the Lock screen with one of these methods:

- **Mouse:** Click anywhere, roll the wheel toward you, or drag the entire screen up.

- **Touchscreen:** Drag the entire screen up.

- **Keyboard:** Press any key.

FIGURE 1-15

3. If you don't use a password, wait briefly for the Start screen to appear. If you use a password, enter it with a physical or touch keyboard. Then press Enter or select the arrow next to the password box to display the Windows desktop screen.

4. Take a break before reading Chapter 2.

TIP

When you take a long break from your PC, it automatically goes to sleep. Windows 10 puts your computer to sleep to save battery life. To decide for yourself how much time passes before your computer goes to sleep, select the Settings button and choose Personalization on the Windows Settings screen. Then, on the Personalization screen, choose Lock Screen. Scroll down the screen to the Screen Timeout Settings link and select this link. You come to the Power & Sleep screen. Choose a setting from the Sleep menu. For example, choose 15 minutes to put your computer to sleep after 15 minutes of inactivity.

Chapter **2**
Using the Start Screen and Apps

The Windows 10 *Start screen* appears when you select the Start button in the lower-left corner of the screen or you press the ⊞ key. It provides access to just about everything you do with Windows 10.

The Start screen is home to numerous programs, or *apps* (short for applications). An app performs a function or displays information. For example, the Weather app offers weather reports (surprise!) and the Maps app helps you map a route between two places. Apps can be simple or complex.

Apps appear on the Start screen as *tiles.* A tile, which may be square or rectangular, displays the app's name and symbol or icon. A tile that displays changing information is called a *live tile.* An open app typically covers the screen, hiding other apps that are open. However, some apps can be displayed side-by-side with a function called *snap*.

Two categories of apps are available:

» *Windows 10 apps* are modern looking and rich with information. They are designed to work with touchscreens as well as with a mouse. Weather and Edge are the first two such apps you use in this chapter. (The Maps and Calendar apps function similarly to the Weather app, each with a unique focus.)

» *Desktop apps* always open with the desktop behind them. Most desktop apps don't have the look or consistent functions of Windows 10 apps. Desktop apps may not respond to touch as reliably as Windows 10 apps.

You select an app to use in one of two ways:

» **Mouse:** Move the mouse pointer over an app tile. Click the left mouse button to select the tile and open the app.

» **Touchscreen:** Tap the app tile with one of your fingers.

In this chapter, you open, close, and use some of the apps that come with Windows 10. You also switch between apps and the Start screen, and switch directly between two apps. You find out how to search for apps not shown on the Start screen. You discover how to organize the Start screen by rearranging tiles into groups. Finally, you can try out Cortana, the robotic Windows digital assistant.

See Chapter 9 for information on getting new apps from the Microsoft Store.

Although some steps are specific to one app, most of the steps you follow in this chapter can be repeated in any app.

Open Windows 10 Apps

1. Select the Start button, as shown in **Figure 2-1.** Selecting this button opens the Start screen, also shown in **Figure 2-1.**

   You can also open the Start screen by pressing the ■ key.

Weather tile

FIGURE 2-1

2. Use the mouse or a finger to select the Weather tile. (If you've used Weather before, the tile shows a temperature reading in a certain location.) The Weather app opens to the Forecast screen, as shown in **Figure 2-2.** It shows the current temperature and weather forecast for your default location. Select the Show Options button (see **Figure 2-2**). As do most apps, Weather has a Show Options button in the upper-left corner. Select this button to expand the app bar and see the names of options on the app bar. Select the button again to collapse options on the app bar.

TIP

The first time you open the Weather app, a Welcome screen appears. It asks whether you want to show temperatures in Fahrenheit or Celsius and what your location is. By location, the Weather app wants to know where you live, or, if you're a vagabond, where you spend the majority of your time. Choose Detect My Location or enter a city or town name in the Search box, and from the menu that appears as you type, select the name of the town or city that you call home. You can always change these settings by selecting the Settings button in the app bar and choosing options on the Settings screen. (See "Change App Settings," later in this chapter.)

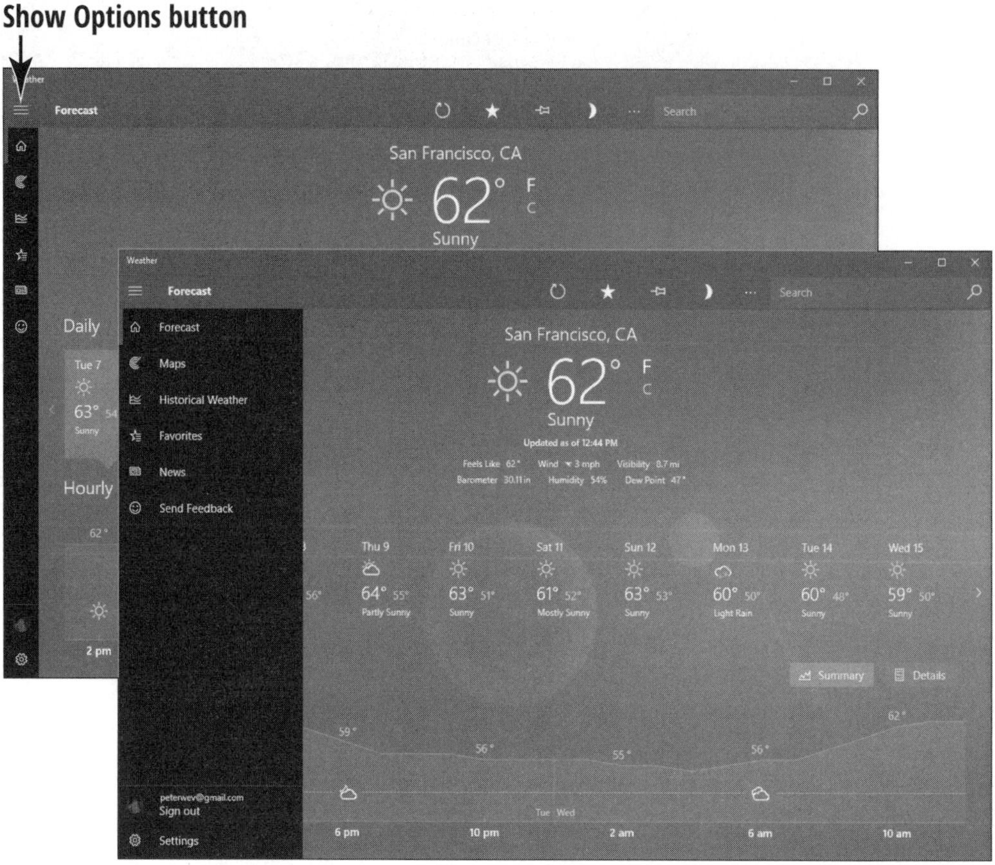

Show Options button

FIGURE 2-2

3. Switch back to the Start screen using one of these methods:

- Tap or click the Start button.

- Press the ⊞ key.

Focus on the method you think is easiest. However, keep in mind that alternative methods of controlling your computer are always available.

4. On the Start screen, check to see whether the Weather tile displays current weather information, as in **Figure 2-3.** The Weather app has a *live tile,* meaning that its tile on the Start screen displays changing information.

Weather has a live tile

FIGURE 2-3

5. Switch back to the Weather app by selecting its tile with the mouse or your finger. The Weather app reappears.

6. Switch back to the Start screen.

7. Select the Microsoft Edge tile (look for a blue icon). The Edge screen appears, as shown in **Figure 2-4.**

TIP

If the Edge tile doesn't appear on your Start screen, scroll in the alphabetical list of apps to the Edge app tile and select it.

TIP

Edge is a browser, which is an Internet application for exploring the web. Chapter 6 covers Edge in detail.

8. Scroll downward to see all that is on the web page you are visiting. Use these techniques to scroll:

   - **Mouse:** Drag the scroll box on the right side of the screen up or down. If your mouse has a wheel, you can also turn the mouse wheel to scroll.

   - **Touchscreen:** Swipe the screen up or down.

9. Switch to the Start screen by selecting the Windows button or pressing the ⊞ key.

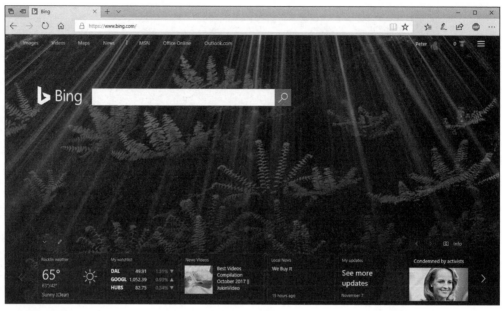

FIGURE 2-4

10. On the Start screen, select the Weather tile. Switch back and forth between the Weather app and the Start screen a few times to get comfortable with switching between an app and the Start screen.

Switch among Open Apps

1. Open the Weather app, as in the preceding section.

2. Switch to the Start screen and open the Edge app.

3. Switch to Task view, as shown in **Figure 2-5.** In Task view, thumbnail versions of all open apps appear on the screen. You can switch to Task view with one of these methods:

- **Mouse:** Click the Task View button on the taskbar (refer to **Figure 2-5**).

- **Touchscreen:** Swipe from the left edge of the screen or tap the Task View button.

- **Keyboard:** Press ⊞+Tab.

Drag to open apps and files you opened in the past

Select a thumbnail to switch apps

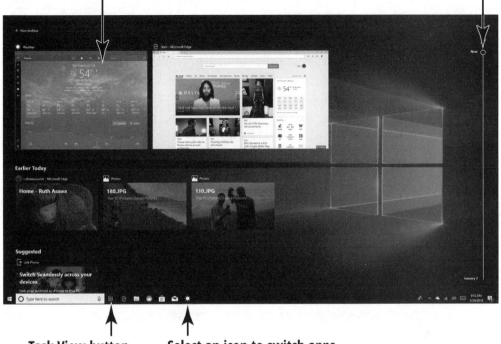

Task View button   **Select an icon to switch apps**

FIGURE 2-5

4. Select the Weather app to switch to it. Task view offers one way of switching between apps. Use the Task View method to switch between apps when many apps are open onscreen. Seeing tiles for all open apps makes switching from one app to another easy.

TIP

Besides offering thumbnail versions of open apps in Task View, Windows 10 also gives you the opportunity to backtrack and open apps you used in days past. Scroll down the screen or drag the slider to see thumbnail pictures of your past activities. Selecting a thumbnail picture opens the app you were using in the past.

TIP

Chapter 5 explains how you can open a second desktop on the screen and in so doing keep some of your open apps on one screen and some of your open apps on another. When you're running many apps, opening a second desktop is a great way to be able to switch quickly from one app to another.

5. Select the Edge app icon on the taskbar to switch to the Edge app (refer to **Figure 2-5**). The taskbar is located along the bottom of the screen. Whenever you open an app, Windows 10 places its icon on the taskbar. You can select an icon on the taskbar to switch to an open app.

Some icons appear permanently on the taskbar. For example, the File Explorer icon is always on the taskbar regardless of whether File Explorer is running. Chapter 5 explains how you can pin your favorite apps to the taskbar. Pinning an app to the taskbar places an icon there so that you can open an app quickly.

6. Press Alt+Tab and continue to hold down the Alt key after you press Tab. A window showing thumbnails of all open apps appears onscreen, as shown in **Figure 2-6**. While holding down the Alt key, press the left- or right-arrow key to select the Weather thumbnail, and then release the Alt key. The Weather app appears onscreen. Pressing Alt+Tab is yet another way to switch between open applications.

FIGURE 2-6

Chapter 5 demonstrates techniques for moving windows onscreen, changing the size of windows, and snapping windows to the side of the screen.

Close Windows 10 Apps

1. On the Start screen, select the Weather app if the Weather app isn't already open.

2. Close the Weather app (or any open app) with one of these methods:

   - **Mouse:** Click the Close button (the X) in the upper-right corner of the screen.

   - **Touchscreen:** Tap the Close button (the X) in the upper-right corner of the screen.

   - **Keyboard:** Press Alt+F4.

   You don't have to close apps. However, having unneeded apps open makes switching between apps more of a challenge because of unneeded thumbnails in the app switcher.

3. On the Start screen again, select the Weather app tile to reopen the Weather app. Notice the Weather app icon on the taskbar along the bottom of the screen.

4. Display the context menu on the Weather app icon and choose Close Window on the context menu, as shown in **Figure 2-7.** Use one of these techniques to display the context menu on a taskbar icon:

   - **Mouse:** Right-click the icon.

   - **Touchscreen:** Touch and hold the icon until a rectangle appears around the icon, and then release your finger.

You can close an app from the taskbar

FIGURE 2-7

TIP

To close an app that is frozen (an app that is unresponsive), press Ctrl+Shift+Esc. The Task Manager opens. It lists all apps that are currently running. Select the app you want to close and then select the End Task button.

Use the App Bar

1. From the Start screen, open the Weather app if it isn't already open.

2. The *app bar* contains functions specific to the current app. Display the app bar by selecting the Show Options button. **Figure 2-8** shows the app bar in the Weather app.

Show Options button

App bar

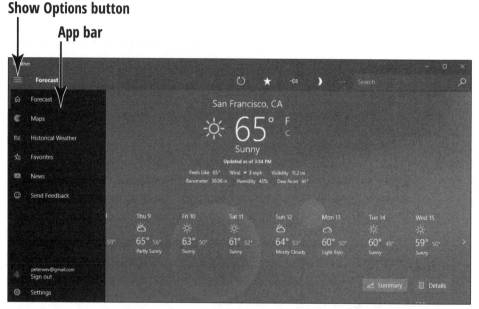

FIGURE 2-8

TIP

The app bar may appear across the top of the screen, the left side of the screen, or in both locations.

3. In the Weather app, the app bar leads you to different functions. Select Maps, for example, to see a weather map of the area where you live.

4. Display the app bar in Weather again. Then select News. A screen appears with news stories about weather in the country where you live.

5. Display the app bar again and take notice of the Home icon. Wherever you travel in an app, you can return to the app *home screen* by selecting this icon.

In most apps, you can select the Back button (a left-pointing arrow) to return to the previous screen you viewed. The Back button is found in the upper-left corner of most screens.

Add a Location in Weather

1. From the Start screen, open the Weather app if it isn't already open. With the Weather app on the screen, select the Show Options button to expand the app bar and see the option names (refer to **Figure 2-8**).

2. Select the Favorites button on the app bar. The Favorites screen appears, as shown in **Figure 2-9.** Your screen will show a different live tile.

3. Select the Add to Favorites tile, which looks like a plus in a square. The Add to Favorites screen appears.

4. Type a location name, such as a city, in the box under Add to Favorites, as shown in **Figure 2-10.** As you type, matching location names appear below the box. If you see the location you want, select that name to add a tile for that location to the Places screen. No need to click the Add button, unless your location does not appear automatically.

You can add other locations by repeating Steps 3 and 4.

5. Select the tile for the location you added. The Weather app displays full information for the location you selected.

You can switch among multiple locations by using the Favorites button on the app bar.

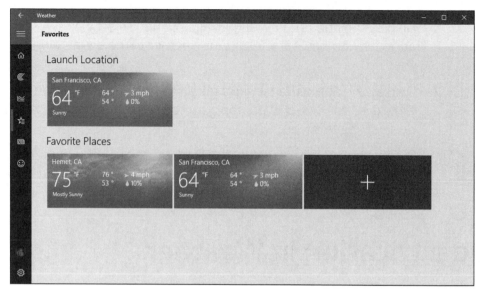

FIGURE 2-9

Type in the box

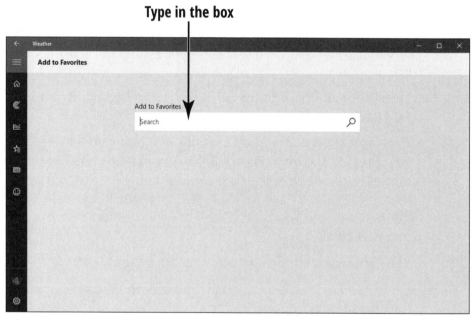

FIGURE 2-10

6. Return to the Start screen. Your new favorite location does not appear on the Weather tile — yet. Select the Weather tile on the taskbar to return to the Weather app. Notice that, in addition to the app bar on the left side of the screen, an app bar for the selected location appears along the top of the screen.

7. Select the Pin button on the app bar at the top of the screen, as shown in **Figure 2-11.** On the confirmation message box, select Yes. Selecting the Pin button adds a tile for the current location to the Start screen. (If you don't see the Pin button, repeat Steps 2–5 to add a favorite location.)

Pin this location to the Weather app tile on the Start screen

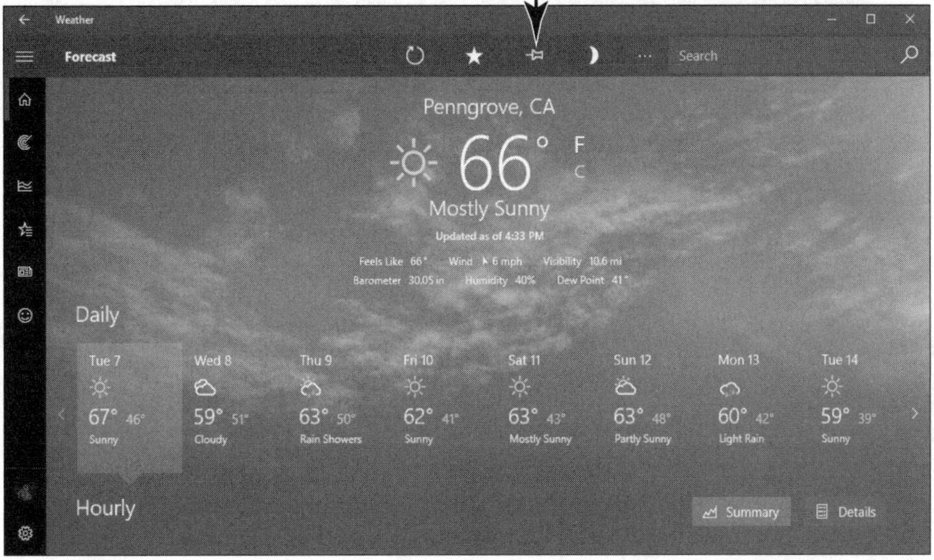

FIGURE 2-11

8. Return to the Start screen. The original Weather tile appears, as well as the new tile. You may have to scroll downward to see the new Weather tile.

9. Select the new Weather tile to open the app with that location.

10. Display the app bar for Weather, which is shown in **Figure 2-12.** Select the Unpin button at the top of the screen to remove the tile for the current location from the Start screen. If the Unpin button doesn't appear, repeat Step 7.

Select Unpin

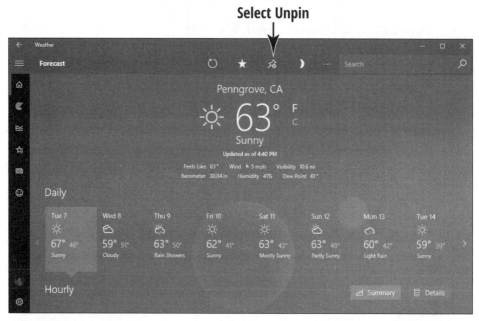

FIGURE 2-12

Return to the Start screen. The location you unpinned no longer appears.

TIP

Add locations for friends, family, and travel destinations and pin these new locations to the Start screen. See "Arrange and Group Apps on the Start Screen," later in this chapter, if you want to group these tiles.

Change App Settings

1. On the Start screen, select the Weather tile if the Weather app isn't open already.

2. In the Weather app, select the Settings button on the app bar. The Settings screen appears, as shown in **Figure 2-13.** Settings is the bottommost option on the app bar. If you have trouble locating it, select the Show Options button, the topmost button on the app bar, to see the buttons on the app bar.

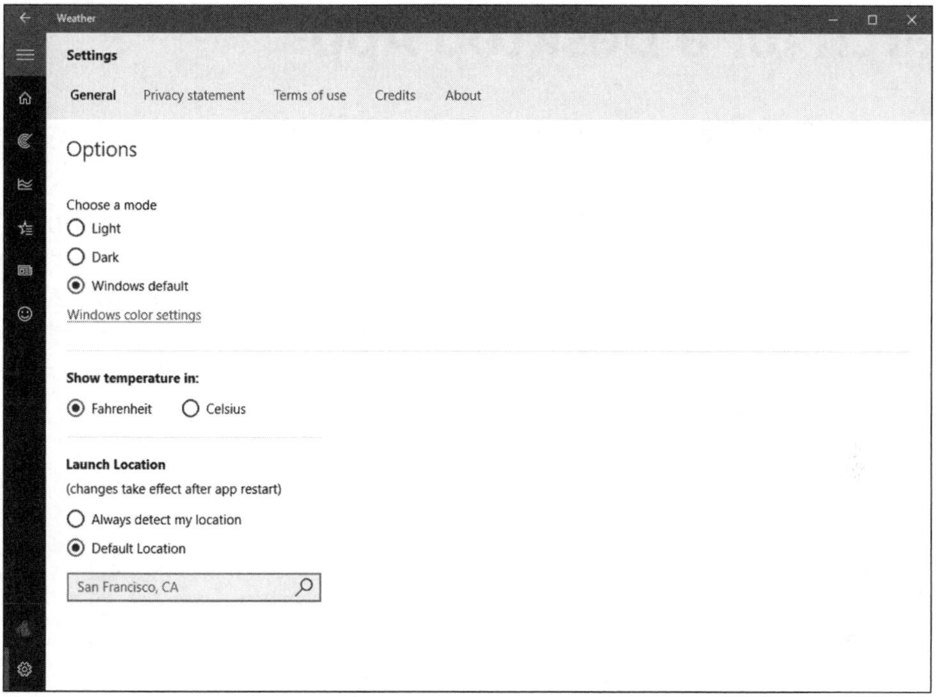

![Weather app Settings screen showing Options with mode selection (Light, Dark, Windows default), temperature units (Fahrenheit/Celsius), and Launch Location settings with San Francisco, CA as default]

FIGURE 2-13

TIP

It may be hard to remember whether you need the Settings panel or the app bar to do something. In general, functions on the app bar are used more frequently than those on the Settings panel. When in doubt, guess — that's how discoveries are made.

3. Choose whether to show air temperatures in Fahrenheit or Celsius.

4. Choose a Launch Location option. The Always Detect My Location option tells the Weather app to note by way of your Internet connection where you are currently and give the weather report for that place. Select Default Location and enter the name of the place where you live if you want to receive weather forecasts for that place.

TIP

Select Privacy Statement in the Settings window if you're interested in how Microsoft collects data about you when you use Weather and other apps made by Microsoft. You see a page clotted with legalese and other obfuscations.

TIP

Changes to settings take effect immediately. You don't have to save or activate your changes.

Search for a Desktop App

1. Open the Start screen: Click the Windows button in the lower-left corner of the desktop or press ⊞.

2. In the Search box (you find it to the right of the Windows button), type **calc** (the first four letters of the word *calculator*). The Search panel appears on the left side of the screen, as shown in **Figure 2-14.** To begin with, the Search panel lists what it thinks are the best matches for the term you entered. You can search for just about anything from the Search box.

Redirect your search

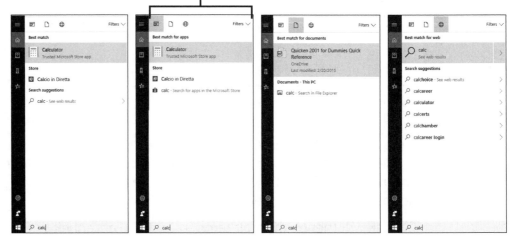

FIGURE 2-14

TIP

Select an icon at the top of the Search panel (refer to **Figure 2-14**) to redirect your search. For example, select the Documents icon to search for files on your computer; select the Web icon to search the web. You can select the Filters icon to open a drop-down menu and search for any number of things, including music files, folders, and videos.

3. Type **ulator** to finish typing the word *calculator.* The Search panel lists only items with the complete word *calculator* in them, including the Calculator app.

4. Select the Calculator app to open it on the desktop, as shown in **Figure 2-15.** To perform a calculation, select the buttons on the screen or use a keyboard.

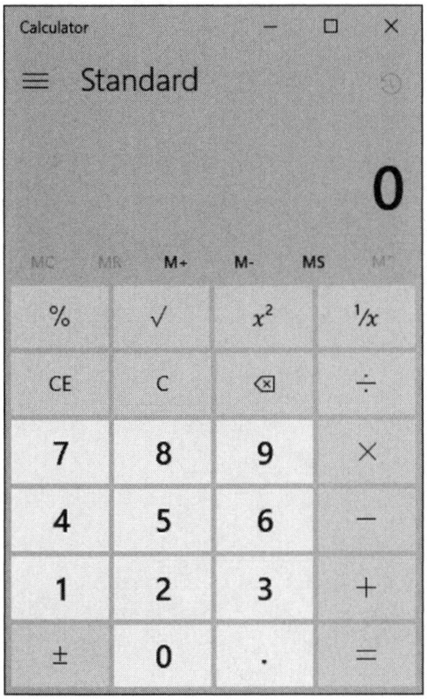

FIGURE 2-15

5. Return to the Start screen: Click the Windows button in the lower-left corner of the desktop or press ⊞.

6. Type **calculator** again in the Search box. Again, the Search panel appears, and the Calculator app appears at the top of the Search panel (refer to **Figure 2-14**).

7. Display the context menu on the Calculator app and choose Pin to Start on the context menu, as shown in **Figure 2-16.** (If Unpin from Start appears on the context menu, the Calculator tile is already on the Start screen; disregard this step.) Use one of these techniques to display the context menu:

- **Mouse:** Right-click Calculator in the Search panel.

- **Touchscreen:** Touch and hold Calculator in the Search panel until the context menu appears, and then release your finger.

Best match

Calculator
Trusted Microsoft Store

Pin to Start

Pin to taskbar

Search suggestions

Rate and review

calculator - See web resul

Share

Store (1)

calculator

FIGURE 2-16

8. Open the Start screen and note where the Calculator tile appears. You can open the Calculator by selecting this tile.

TIP

To remove a tile from the Start screen, display its context menu and select Unpin from Start.

Arrange and Group Apps on the Start Screen

1. You can rearrange tiles on the Start screen by dragging them to different places. On the Start screen, drag the Calculator tile to a different location. As you move the tile, other tiles move out of the way, like a game of Dodge Tile.

2. To start with, the Start screen places tiles in one of two groups: Life at a Glance and Play and Explore. You can find these group names at the top of the start screen. Tap or click the words *Play and Explore* to change the name of the Play and Explore group. A text box appears, as shown in **Figure 2-17.** Enter a new name here (or keep the old name) and press Enter.

Click or tap to change a group name

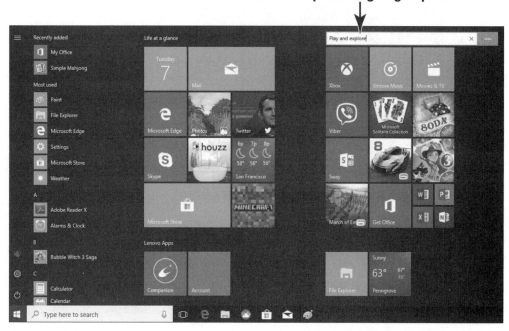

FIGURE 2-17

3. Create a new group for Calculator by dragging the Calculator tile to the lower-right corner of the Start screen so that it's separate from other tiles. Then gently drag the pointer above the Calculator tile. The words *Name group* and two horizontal lines appear after you stop dragging, as shown in **Figure 2-18, top.**

4. Tap or click after you see the two vertical lines. A text box appears, as shown in **Figure 2-18, middle.** You just created a new group with Calculator as the tile.

5. Type a name for the group into the text box, as shown in **Figure 2-18, bottom.** You can change the name at any time by repeating Steps 3 and 4. To remove the name, select the X to the right of the text box. Create groups to organize app tiles on the Start screen.

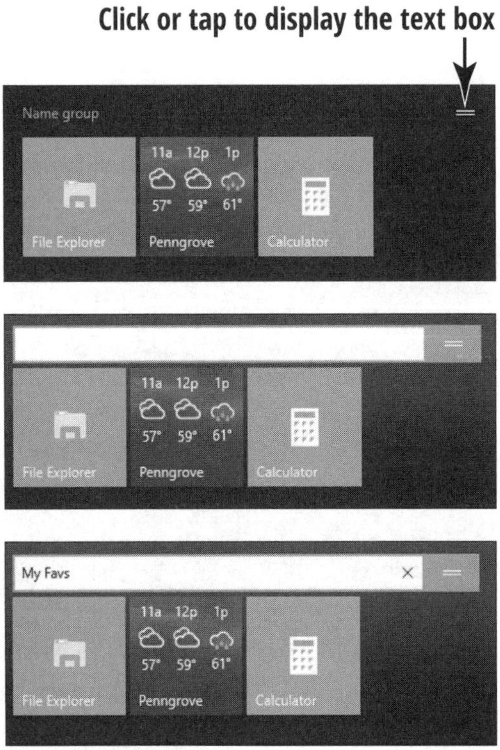

Click or tap to display the text box

FIGURE 2-18

6. Use one of the following methods to open the context menu on the Calculator tile:

- **Mouse:** Position the pointer over the tile and right-click. (A left click would open the app.)

- **Touchscreen:** Swipe slightly down or up on the tile. (A direct tap would open the app.)

Change the size of the Calculator tile. On the context menu, select Resize and then select the Wide option on the submenu, as shown in **Figure 2-19.** (The options you see on a touchscreen are the same, but are arranged differently on the context menu.) As well as the Wide, Medium, and Small options, Windows 10 provides a Large option for some tiles.

TIP

Choose the Large or Wide resize option for apps you use often. The larger the tile, the easier it is to find on the Start screen.

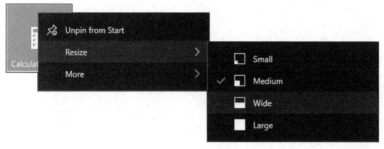

FIGURE 2-19

7. Locate a tile on the Start screen that doesn't need to be there. Then select the tile and select Unpin from Start on the context menu to remove the tile from the Start screen. (See Step 6 if you need instructions for displaying the context menu.)

TIP

The Start screen becomes more useful and personal when you eliminate tiles that you don't need and arrange tiles to suit your sense of order.

Ask Questions of Cortana

1. Click or tap in the Type Here to Search box (looks like a circle) on the left side of the taskbar. As soon as you click or tap, a "digital assistant" called Cortana springs to life, as shown in **Figure 2-20, left.** Cortana can respond to questions you ask with your voice.

TIP

To use Cortana, your computer's microphone must be up and running. Turn to Chapter 13 if the microphone on your computer isn't connected or working properly.

2. Select the Microphone icon and say aloud, "Tell me a joke." As you say these words, they appear in the text box, and if all goes right, Cortana recites a joke. As well, the words of the joke appear on the screen, as shown in **Figure 2-20, right.**

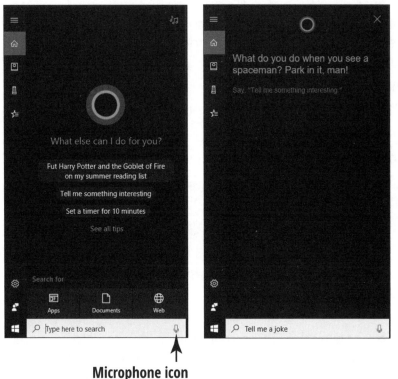

Microphone icon

FIGURE 2-20

3. Select the Microphone icon, say the words "Hey, Cortana," and ask, "What is the weather in Chicago, Illinois?" Cortana gives you the weather in Chicago.

TIP

Ask questions of Cortana while the word *Listening* appears in the box. Seeing this word tells you that Cortana is prepared to field a question.

4. Select the Microphone icon and ask aloud, "What should I name my cat?" In this instance, Cortana can't answer, so your browser opens to the Bing search engine, as shown in **Figure 2-21.** The question "What should I name my cat?" has been entered in the Search box, and the results of the search point to information about cat names. Regardless of whether Cortana can answer a question, you can always select the See More Results on Bing.com link in Cortana to open your browser to the Bing website and conduct a search there.

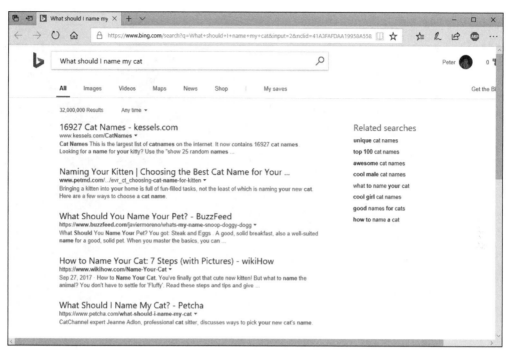

FIGURE 2-21

5. Cortana can remind you to attend events and appointments. Select the Microphone icon and then say, "Remind me." Cortana replies, "Sure thing, what should I remind you about?" or "What do you want to remember?" Meantime, you see a Cortana panel like the one in **Figure 2-22, left.** Next, say "Walk the dog." Cortana asks when you want to be reminded and you see a screen like the one in in **Figure 2-22, middle.** Reply, "In five minutes," and answer "yes" when Cortana asks you to confirm that you want to be reminded. As long as you begin by saying "Remind me," Cortana can record reminders like this.

6. On the Cortana App bar, select the Notebook button and then select the Reminders button (the light bulb). You go to the Reminders screen, as shown in **Figure 2-22, right.** You see the reminder to walk the dog.

Say "Remind me" to record a reminder

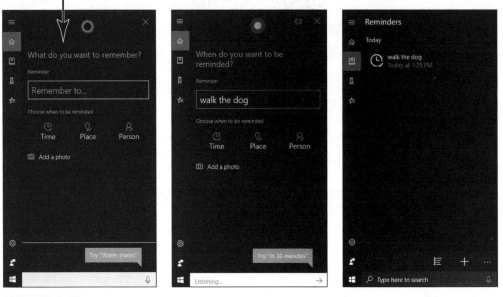

FIGURE 2-22

Chapter **3**
Adjusting Windows 10 Settings

O ut of the box, Windows 10 is showy and colorful. If you don't like that look, however, you can change the photos and colors you see on the screen. Adjusting Windows 10 settings can also make Windows 10 easier and more fun to use. When you're ready, you can dive in and make Windows 10 yours.

In this chapter, you personalize the Lock screen. You see this screen many times a day, so it should please you. You also choose a picture to identify your account on the Start menu. This chapter also explains how to make your screen easier to see and enable features such as Narrator, which reads aloud content from the screen. Finally, you discover how to customize the Start menu and decide which notifications pop up in the lower-right corner of your screen.

Many people leave Windows 10 largely as they found it. Some love to tweak, tinker, and tune. How far you go in personalizing Windows 10 is up to you — it's your computer, after all.

See Chapter 4 for information on changing passwords and other User settings.

TIP

Access the Settings Screen

1. Starting on the desktop, click or tap the Start button (or press the ⊞ key).

2. Choose Settings on the Start menu, as shown in **Figure 3-1** (your Start menu may look different).

Turn to Chapter 1 if you need help opening an app on the Start menu.

TIP

Click or tap to enlarge the Start menu

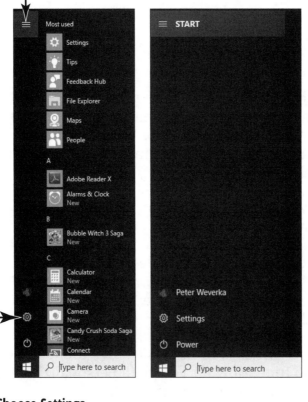

Choose Settings

FIGURE 3-1

TIP

As shown in Figure 3-1, you can click or tap the Options button at the top of the Start menu to enlarge the menu and make it easier to read.

3. The Settings screen appears, as shown in **Figure 3-2.** The Settings screen is the starting point for changing the settings here, there, and everywhere on your computer.

4. One at a time, select each icon in the Settings screen, starting with System, to see the options available. Select the Back button (the square with the left-pointing arrow, located in the upper-left corner of the screen) to return to the Settings screen.

5. On the Settings screen, enter the word **printer** in the Find a Setting box (located at the top of the screen; refer to **Figure 3-2**). As soon as you enter the word, the Settings screen shows you a list of settings that pertain to printers. You can select a setting on the list to open the dialog box where the setting is located.

Search for a setting

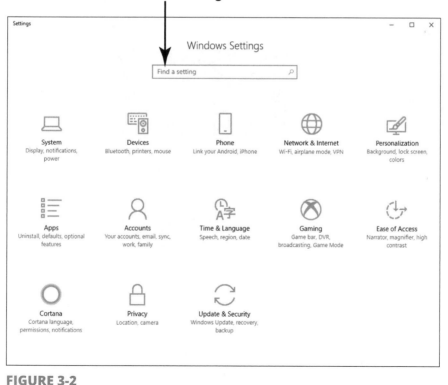

FIGURE 3-2

TIP

Windows 10 offers many different settings. Locating them can be a chore. Often the easiest way to find a setting is to enter its name in the Find a Setting box on the Settings screen.

Personalize the Lock Screen

1. On the Settings screen, select Personalization.

2. On the Personalization screen, select Lock Screen. The Lock Screen Preview screen opens, as shown in **Figure 3-3.** On the Background drop-down menu, choose Picture (if it isn't already chosen), as shown in **Figure 3-3.**

See a picture on the Lock screen

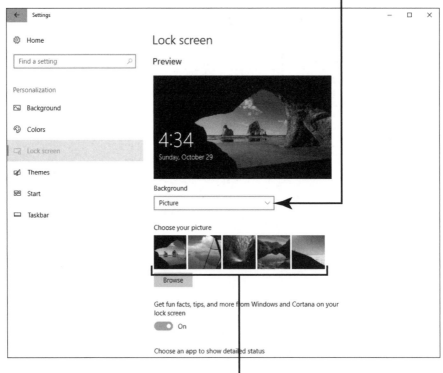

Choose a picture thumbnail

FIGURE 3-3

TIP

The Lock screen is the first screen you see when you start Windows 10.

3. Just above the Browse button, select each thumbnail photo, one at a time. The larger preview photo changes to show the thumbnail you selected. Select a photo that's different from the one you started with. (You can always change it later.)

TIP

You can use the Browse button to select one of your own photos from the Pictures folder. See Chapter 10 for information on adding photos to this folder and its subfolders.

TIP

Rather than see one image on the start screen, you can see a slide show of images in your Pictures folder. On the Background menu, choose Slideshow.

4. Return to the Start screen. Select your account picture (the topmost of the four icons on the left side of the Start screen). The menu shown in **Figure 3-4** appears. Select Lock on the menu to display the Lock screen.

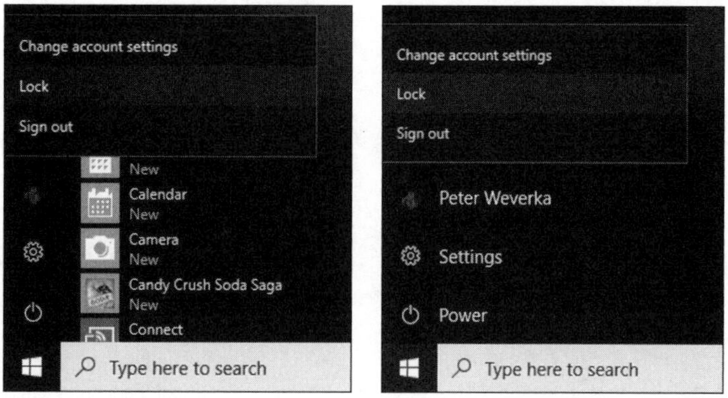

FIGURE 3-4

TIP

You can lock your computer anytime by pressing ⊞+L.

5. The photo you selected in Step 3 appears on the Lock screen. Display the Password screen as follows:

- **Mouse:** Click anywhere.
- **Touchscreen:** Swipe up.
- **Keyboard:** Press any key on the keyboard.

6. Enter your password, if you have one. The Windows desktop screen appears.

Choose an Account Picture

1. On the Settings screen, select Accounts. See "Access the Settings Screen," earlier in this chapter, if you need help opening the Settings screen. Your current Account picture appears in the Your Info screen, as shown in **Figure 3-5.** (If you haven't selected a picture yet, your picture may just be an outline.)

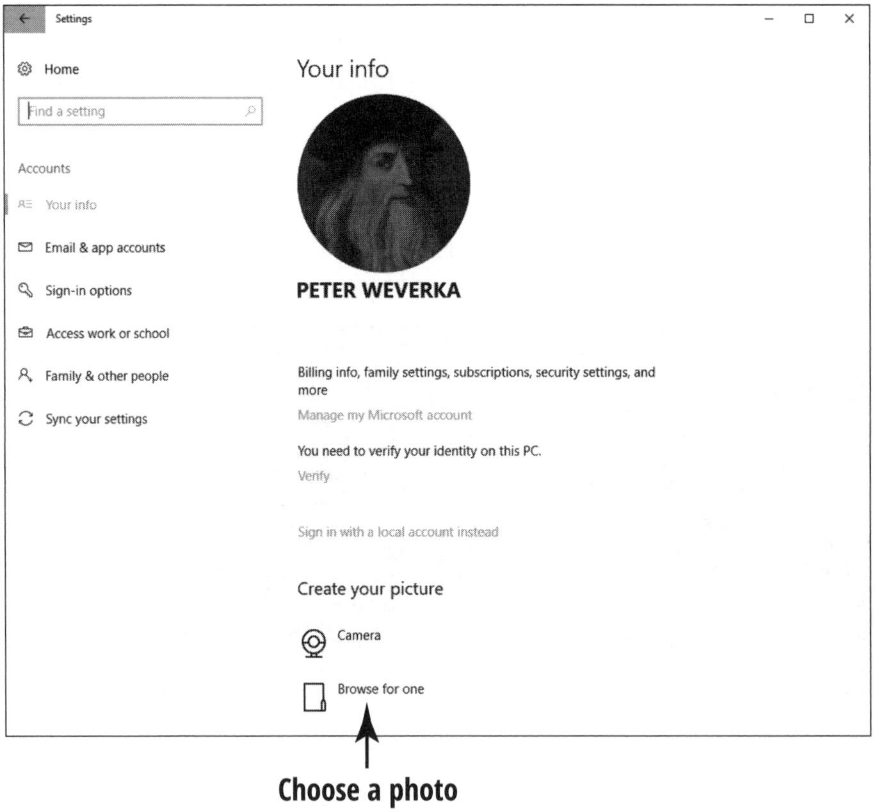

← Settings		— □ ×
⚙ Home	**Your info**	
Find a setting		
Accounts		
A≡ Your info		
✉ Email & app accounts	**PETER WEVERKA**	
🔍 Sign-in options		
💼 Access work or school	Billing info, family settings, subscriptions, security settings, and more	
🧑 Family & other people	Manage my Microsoft account	
🔄 Sync your settings	You need to verify your identity on this PC.	
	Verify	
	Sign in with a local account instead	
	Create your picture	
	📷 Camera	
	🗋 Browse for one	

↑
Choose a photo

FIGURE 3-5

TIP

Your account picture appears on the password screen and the Start screen.

2. To choose one of your photos, select the Browse for One button. The contents of your Pictures folder appears in the Open dialog box. From here, you can select the Up button to access any folder on your

computer or select a subfolder to open. When you find the picture you want, select it and then select the Choose Picture button. Or select Cancel to return to the previous screen without changing your account picture.

See Chapter 10 for information about adding photos to your Pictures folder.

3. If you have a built-in or attached camera (called a *webcam*), select the Camera app under Create Your Picture. The Camera app opens with a preview of what your camera sees. See Chapter 10 for information on taking pictures with a webcam.

You may be able to use another app to select or create a picture. Select the app under Create Your Picture.

4. Return to the Start screen to see your new account picture. To return to the Start screen, click or tap the Start button or press ⊞ on your keyboard.

The easiest way to access the Accounts screen and change your account picture is through your account name. On the Start screen, select your name and then select Change Account Settings, as shown in **Figure 3-6.** Voilà! The Accounts screen appears, with Your Info selected.

FIGURE 3-6

Check for Important Updates

1. To check for updates to Windows 10, select Update & Security on the Settings screen. See "Access the Settings Screen," earlier in this chapter, if you need help getting to the PC Settings screen.

2. On the Update & Security screen, select Windows Update. The Windows Update screen appears, as shown in **Figure 3-7.**

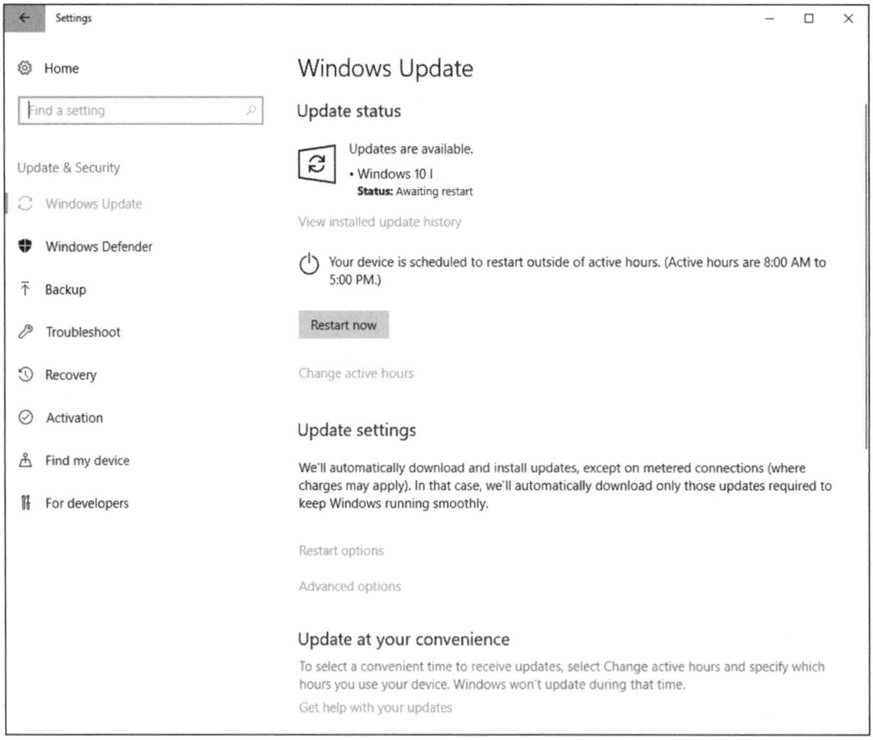

FIGURE 3-7

3. The Windows Update screen informs you when Windows 10 last checked for updates and whether any were found. Select the Check for Updates button to find out whether any updates are available and update Windows 10 on your computer.

4. For some updates to be installed, your computer has to shut down and restart. In cases like this, you see the Restart Now button on the Windows Update screen. You can select the Restart Now button to

install the updates right away or just wait until next time you shut down and restart on your own to install the updates.

Another way to handle updates is to simply leave your computer on overnight. Windows 10 performs the update as you sleep.

TIP

5. You may see a message that one or more updates will be downloaded and installed automatically. You do not have to do anything to install these updates — the update process is automatic. Return to the desktop to let Windows 10 manage updates automatically.

You can select the Advanced Options link on the Windows Update screen to choose how Windows 10 installs updates. Select the View Installed Update History button and get a history of updates that Windows 10 has made to your computer.

TIP

Installing an update seldom takes more than a few minutes. You can use your system during the update process.

TIP

For information on other updates and maintaining Windows 10, see Chapter 12.

TIP

Make Windows 10 Easier to Use

1. On the Settings screen, select Ease of Access, as shown in **Figure 3-8.** (See "Access the Settings Screen" for help.) The Ease of Access screen offers many settings to make your computer, mouse, and monitor easier to use. These settings are organized into three categories: Vision, Hearing, and Interaction.

Here's a quick way to open the Ease of Access screen: Press ⊞+U (for *usability*).

TIP

2. Under Vision, choose the Display settings (refer to **Figure 3-8**). These settings make the screen easier to view and read. You find settings here for making text larger and brighter.

3. Also under Vision, choose the Cursor & Pointer Size settings to change the size and color of the mouse pointer. As shown in **Figure 3-9,** Windows 10 offers mouse pointers of different sizes and colors. Choose the combination that tickles your fancy.

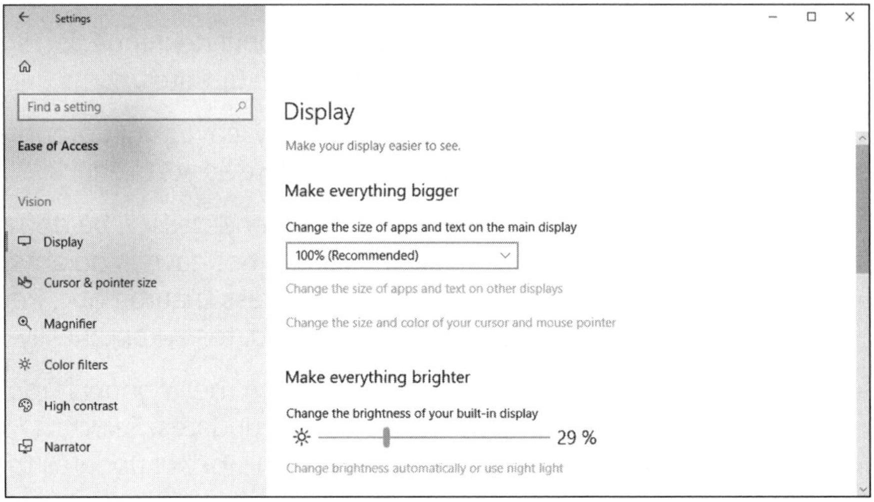

FIGURE 3-8

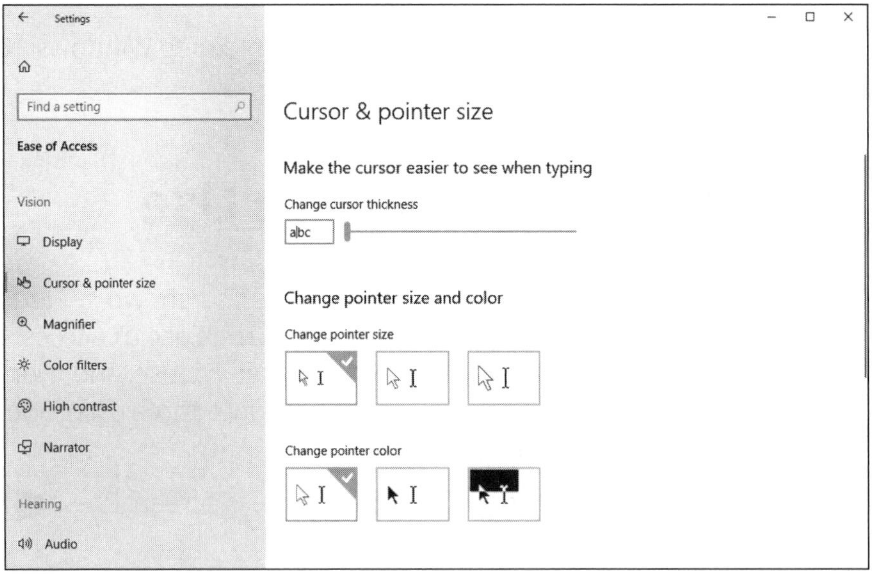

FIGURE 3-9

4. Again under Vision, choose Magnifier settings to enlarge what is on your computer screen. These settings are for people who have difficulty seeing. When Magnifier is turned on, the Magnifier toolbar appears onscreen, as shown in **Figure 3-10.** (Click or tap the magnifying glass icon on the taskbar to see this toolbar, if necessary.) Click or tap the plus sign on the Magnifier toolbar to zoom a portion of the screen for easier viewing. Click or tap the minus sign to see the screen at normal size.

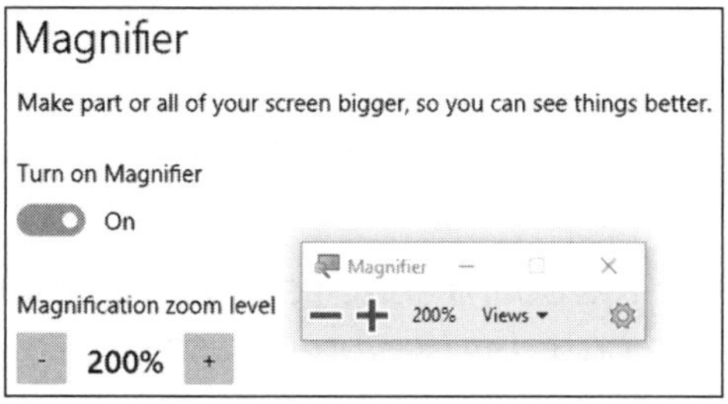

Magnifier

Make part or all of your screen bigger, so you can see things better.

Turn on Magnifier

On

Magnification zoom level

- 200% +

Magnifier — □ ×

— + 200% Views ▾ ⚙

FIGURE 3-10

TIP

Without turning the Magnifier switch on, you can magnify the screen. Press ⊞ +plus key to zoom in using Magnifier. Press ⊞ +minus key to zoom out using Magnifier.

5. Under Vision, choose a Color Filters setting if you are color blind. If you know which type of colorblindness you have — deuteranopia, protanopia, tritanopia — you can choose its name on the Color Filters menu to make seeing items on screen easier.

6. Under Vision, choose High Contrast settings to alter the screen in a way that might make seeing text easier. These settings are also for people who have difficulty seeing. After you choose a theme, you can choose a color for text, hyperlinks, disabled text, selected text, button text, and backgrounds. Click Apply after you make your choices. Choose None and click Apply if you want to return to the default Windows 10 contrast settings.

7. Under Vision, choose Narrator settings to have content on the screen read aloud. These settings are for people who have difficulty reading. After turning on the Narrator switch, you choose voice, speed, and pitch settings to determine what the narrator's voice sounds like.

8. Under Hearing, choose Audio Settings to increase the default volume and control whether you hear stereo or mono sound on your computer. If you have a poor-quality speakers, turning the Mono Audio option to On can improve the sound.

9. Also under Hearing, choose Closed Captions settings to control how subtitles appear in audio and video presentations. Choose Font settings to describe what you want the text in the captions to look like. Choose Background and Window settings to describe what the box where the captions appear looks like. The Preview box shows what your choices mean in real terms.

10. Under Interaction, choose Speech settings to dictate text instead of typing it, control how Cortana works, and control your computer and device with voice commands.

11. Also under Interaction, choose Keyboard settings to type without using a physical keyboard. This onscreen keyboard uses the layout of a conventional keyboard. However, most people find that the standard Windows 10 virtual keyboard is more flexible. See Chapter 1 for information on the virtual keyboard layouts.

12. Again under Interaction, choose Mouse settings if for some strange reason you want to control the mouse with the keys on the numeric keypad.

TIP

More Ease of Access settings are available through the Ease of Access Center in the Control Panel, as shown in **Figure 3-11.** To open the Control Panel to the Ease of Access Center, type **ease of access** in the Type Here to Search box and choose Ease of Access Center in the search results.

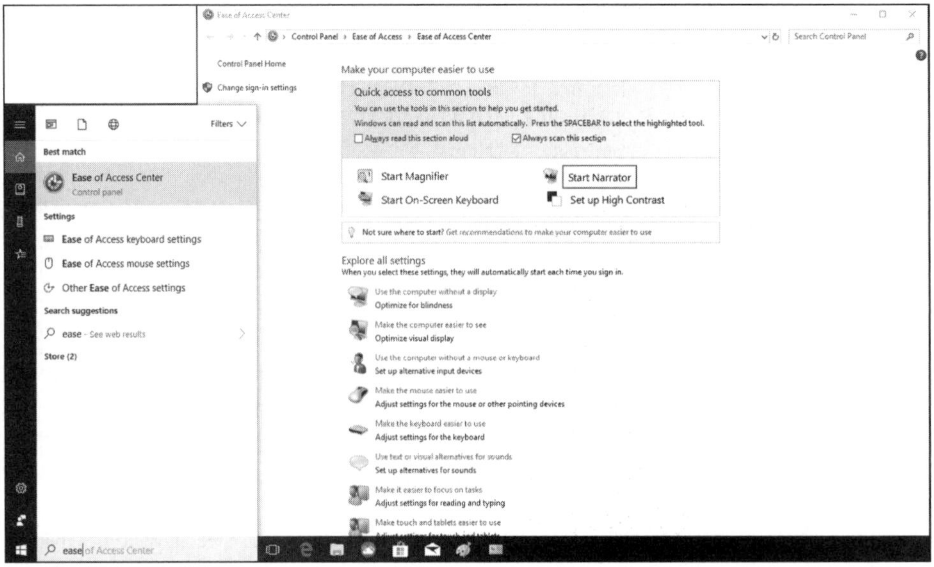

FIGURE 3-11

Customize the Start Menu

1. On the Settings screen, select Personalization. See "Access the Settings Screen," earlier in this chapter, if you need help opening the Settings screen.

2. On the Personalization screen, select Start. The Start screen opens, as shown in **Figure 3-12.** This screen offers ways to customize the Start menu and the Start screen.

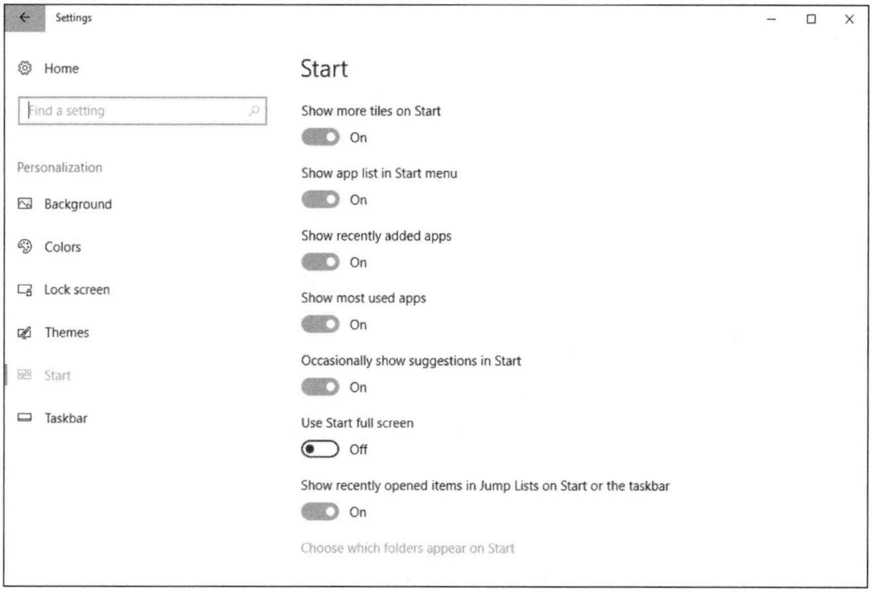

FIGURE 3-12

3. Under Start, drag the sliders to On or Off to choose what you want Windows 10 to display on the Start screen and Start menu:

- **Show More Tiles:** Enlarges the Windows 10 Start screen. Choose this option if your Start screen is crowded with app tiles.

- **Show App List in Start Menu:** Places a list of apps installed on your computer on the Start menu. The apps are listed in alphabetical order.

- **Show Recently Added Apps:** Places the names of apps you recently acquired on the Start menu. The names of these apps appear under the "Recently Added" heading.

- **Show Most Used Apps:** Places the names of programs you use most often on the Start menu. The names of these programs appear under the "Most Used" heading.

- **Occasionally Show Suggestions in Start:** Places the names of apps and files on the Start screen that Windows 10 believes you want to see there.

- **Use Start Full Screen:** Makes the Start screen cover the entire desktop, rather than a portion of the desktop.

- **Show Recently Opened Items in Jump Lists on Start or the Taskbar:** Allows you to quickly open folders, files, and windows from the Start menu and taskbar. When you move the pointer over an app or program on the Start menu, an arrow appears; select the arrow to see a menu of items you can open. When you move the pointer over an icon on the taskbar, thumbnail windows appear so that you can choose which window to open.

TIP

You can list the apps you like best at the bottom of the Start menu next to the Power and Settings commands. On the Start screen (refer to **Figure 3-12**), select the Choose Which Folders Appear on Start button. A new screen with a list of popular apps appears. Select the apps whose names you want to appear on the Start menu.

Handling Notifications

1. *Notifications* are the sometimes pesky little message boxes that appear in the lower-right corner of the screen when you least expect them. You can decide for yourself whether notifications appear and which notifications you want to see. On the Settings screen, select System. See "Access the Settings Screen," earlier in this chapter, if you need help opening the Settings screen.

2. Select Notifications & Actions to see the screen shown in **Figure 3-13.** The top of this screen is for customizing the Quick Actions panel. Scroll past Quick Actions options to see the options for customizing how and when notifications appear.

FIGURE 3-13

3. Under Notifications in the Notification & Actions screen, turn options on or off to tell Windows whether you want notifications to appear on your screen.

4. Scroll down the Notification & Actions screen to the area called Show Notifications from These Senders. You see an alphabetical list of apps that can deliver notifications. Drag the On/Off sliders to tell Windows 10 which applications you want to deliver notifications.

5. Select the Close button (the X) to close the Settings window.

Chapter 4

Working with User Accounts

Windows 10 seeks an Internet connection automatically from the moment you start it. More often than not, you connect to the Internet using a wireless or *Wi-Fi* connection. For this reason, if you start a laptop or tablet in a coffee shop or library, you may see a notification that one or more network connections are available. That's convenient.

A computer without an Internet connection is an island, if not a paperweight. Connecting to a network, however, opens a door to your computer — and malefactors try to push through that door to access your computer. Windows 10 has a *firewall* that monitors and restricts traffic in and out. Don't be afraid of connecting to the Internet, but be aware of the risks and be careful to connect to a network that seems trustworthy. In Chapter 1, you create a local user account. You need a Microsoft Account to take full advantage of Windows 10 features such as the Microsoft Store for apps (see Chapter 9), OneDrive for online storage (see Chapter 15), and synchronized settings between computers. In this chapter, you create a Microsoft Account and choose a secure method for logging in to your account. You also discover how to switch to Airplane mode, create a local account, and switch from a local account to a Microsoft Account. To control access to your computer, you find out how to use a password, to unlock your computer.

TIP

If other people use your computer, you may want to create more than one local account. When each person who uses your computer has a separate account, you can keep data, apps, and settings tidy and private. I recommend having only one administrator account for each computer.

Even if you're the only one using your computer, you may want more than one account. For example, if you create a local account, you can experiment with the new account — changing the look and function of Windows 10 — without affecting your first account.

TIP

Many of the steps in this chapter involve entering text, such as your name. If you don't have a physical keyboard, use the virtual keyboard, which is covered in Chapter 1.

Connect to the Internet

1. On the Windows desktop, look to the Network icon to see whether your computer is connected to the Internet. This icon is located to the left of the time and date readings in the lower-right corner of the screen, as shown in **Figure 4-1.**

TIP

Select or choose options by moving the mouse pointer and left-clicking or by tapping a touchscreen with your finger.

2. Select the Network icon. The Networks panel appears on the right side of your screen, as shown in **Figure 4-2,** and lists all available network connections. There may be no connections or dozens.

TIP

If you see *Not connected* and *No connections available,* you may be out of luck. Check your computer documentation to see whether your PC has wireless capability and whether you need to turn on a mechanical switch.

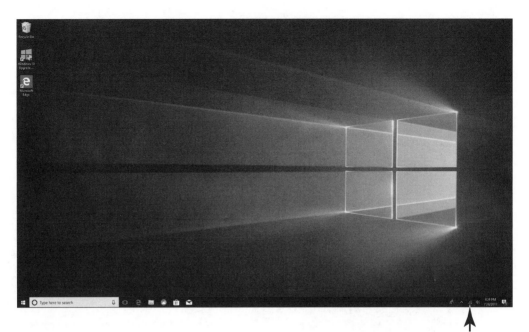

Network connection icon

FIGURE 4-1

TIP

If your computer is near a router (DSL or cable) and you don't have wireless capability, connect your PC and the router using an Ethernet cable, which is thicker than a phone line, with wider connections.

3. Select a connection. Note that not all displayed connections are accessible or desirable.

TIP

If you're not sure that you can trust a connection, you might want to forego a connection — better safe than sorry. (Unsafe wireless connections can be used to eavesdrop on your activities, though that scenario is rare.) However, if an available connection sports the name of the establishment you're in or near, such as a restaurant or a coffee shop, the connection may be safe. The same is true of connections at libraries, airports, and many other public spaces.

4. After you select a connection, the selected tile expands and displays the Connect Automatically check box, as shown in **Figure 4-3.** If you trust the connection and might want to use it again, select the check box. Otherwise, deselect the check box. To continue, select the Connect button.

Available wireless connections

Connect automatically next time

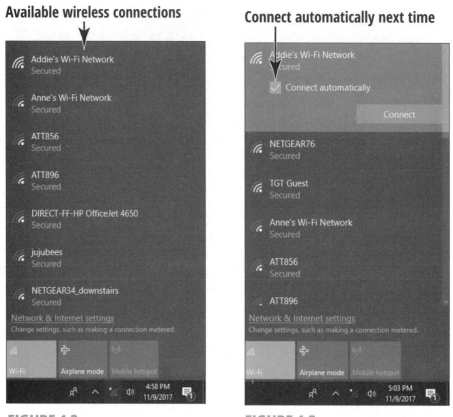

FIGURE 4-2

FIGURE 4-3

5. You may be prompted to enter a network security key (a series of characters), which limits access to those who know the key. See **Figure 4-4.** The key protects that network and its users. If you're using a hotel's connection, you can obtain the key from the front desk. If you don't know the key, select Cancel. Otherwise, enter the key (dots appear as you type) and select Next.

A secure network requires a key

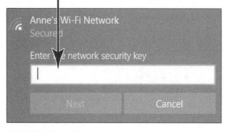

FIGURE 4-4

TIP

If the connection is public and open, you won't be prompted for a key. Open connections are common in libraries, coffee shops, and other places many people come and go.

6. If you entered the correct key or none was required, you may see this message: *Do you want to turn on sharing between PCs and connect to devices on this network?* The term *sharing* refers to allowing computers access to your files or to a device, such as a printer. You should share at home but not in a public location. Choose one of the following:

- **No:** This option prevents you from connecting directly with other computers and protects your computer from networks in public places. You'll still have Internet access.

- **Yes:** This option enables you to share documents and devices between your computers on a home or office network.

TIP

If you're not sure about which option to choose, go with No.

7. When a Wi-Fi connection is established, *Connected* appears next to the network name in the Networks panel, as shown in **Figure 4-5.** The connection name and signal strength appear as well. The connection strength (but not the name) appears next to the time and date in the notification area in the lower-right corner of the screen (see **Figure 4-5**).

TIP

If you selected the Connect Automatically check box (in Step 4), the connection will be used anytime it is available. If you move your computer to another location out of range of this network (usually a few hundred yards), you will have to repeat these steps to connect to another network.

Disconnect (or Switch to Airplane Mode)

1. When you shut down your computer or move your computer far enough away from the connection, your computer disconnects from the Internet automatically. Suppose you want to disconnect on your own? To disconnect your computer from the Internet, display the Networks panel again (refer to **Figure 4-5**).

Connection status

Select to disconnect

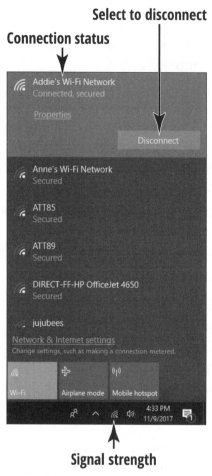

Signal strength

FIGURE 4-5

2. Select the Disconnect button. (If you disconnect your computer, reconnect before continuing to Step 3.)

3. For safety's sake, airlines don't want passengers to send or receive wireless data signals while the airplane is in flight; these signals can interfere with the airplane's communications systems. This is why the captain gives the order to "turn off all electrical devices." Rather than turn off your computer, however, you can switch to Airplane mode. To do so, open the Networks panel and select the Airplane Mode button. This button is located at the bottom of the Networks panel.

4. In Airplane mode, an airplane icon appears to the left of the time and date readings in the lower-right corner of the screen, as shown in **Figure 4-6.** Your computer doesn't send wireless data signals in Airplane mode. To switch out of Airplane mode and reconnect to the Internet, select the airplane icon to display the Network panel. Then select the Airplane Mode button (refer to **Figure 4-6**).

Airplane icon

Select to leave Airplane mode

FIGURE 4-6

Switching to Airplane mode is much more convenient than turning off your computer's network connection and turning it back on again. It takes but a second or two.

TIP

Create a New Microsoft Account

1. On the Start screen, select your picture on the left side of the screen. In the pop-up menu that appears, choose Change Account Settings, as shown in **Figure 4-7.** The Settings app opens to the Accounts screen. Your account information appears with the words *Local Account* under your name, as shown in **Figure 4-8.**

If you see don't see *Local Account*, you already have a Microsoft Account and don't need to follow these steps.

TIP

Select for fast access to the Accounts screen

FIGURE 4-7

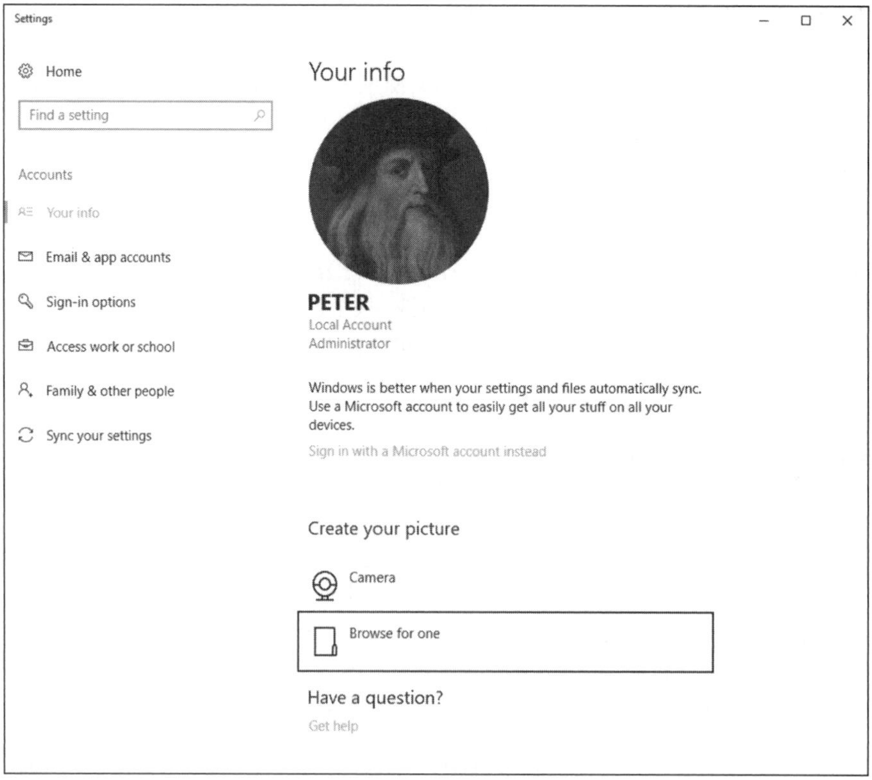

FIGURE 4-8

2. Select the Sign In with a Microsoft Account Instead link. The Make It Yours screen appears. To create a new account, select the Create One! link.

3. On the Let's Create Your Account screen (see **Figure 4-9**), type the email address you want to use for this account in the Email Address box. Microsoft will send notices about your Microsoft Account to the address you enter.

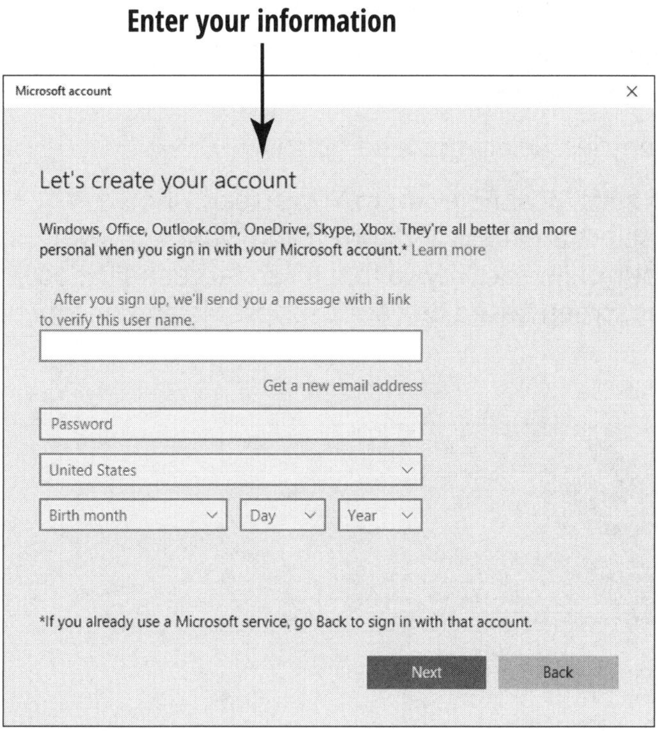

Enter your information

FIGURE 4-9

4. In the Password box, type a password. Dots appear instead of what you type. Use at least eight characters, including at least two uppercase letters, two lowercase letters, two numbers, or two symbols. No spaces are allowed.

TIP

Your password should be easy enough for you to remember and type, but not easy for someone else to guess. Don't use the names of any family members (including pets). A good password can be difficult to create, so try this trick: Think of a memorable phrase or lyric. Next, use the first letter from each word, capitalizing some of those letters. Then substitute some letters with numbers (for example, 3 for the letter *E* or the number 0 for the letter *O*). Don't put your password on a sticky note near your screen.

5. If your country or region is not preselected, select your country.

6. Select the month, day, and year of your birth. (You can lie, but be sure to remember your response.)

7. Review your entries. Select the Next button.

8. On the See What's Most Relevant to You screen, shown in **Figure 4-10,** select the first check box if you want to allow Microsoft to monitor your online activity so that it can target online advertisements to your screen based on your user profile and history of surfing the web.

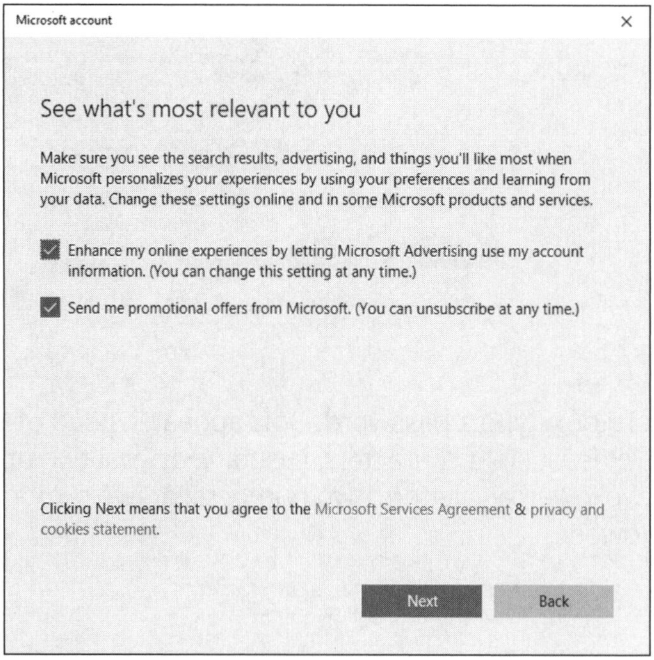

Microsoft account   ✕

See what's most relevant to you

Make sure you see the search results, advertising, and things you'll like most when Microsoft personalizes your experiences by using your preferences and learning from your data. Change these settings online and in some Microsoft products and services.

☑ Enhance my online experiences by letting Microsoft Advertising use my account information. (You can change this setting at any time.)

☑ Send me promotional offers from Microsoft. (You can unsubscribe at any time.)

Clicking Next means that you agree to the Microsoft Services Agreement & privacy and cookies statement.

| Next | Back |

FIGURE 4-10

9. If you don't want to receive promotional offers and surveys, select the check box to remove the check mark from the second check box.

10. Select the Next button. The Sign In to This Device Using Your Microsoft Account screen appears. Enter the password to your local account, if you had a password. Then click Next. Congratulations! You just created a Microsoft Account.

Create a Local Account

1. "Local account" is Microsoft's name for your ability to start your computer without signing in to Microsoft. Before you create or sign in with a local account, save your work. Then select the Start button, select your picture on the Start menu, and in the pop-up menu that appears (refer to **Figure 4-7**), choose Change Account Settings. You see the Accounts screen. If you see the words *local account* on this screen, you're already signed in with a local account.

You can't download and install apps from the Microsoft Store without signing in with a Microsoft Account. Nor can you upload files to OneDrive. So why have a local account? If you're concerned about privacy and security, if you don't want Microsoft to peer over your shoulder and track your every move when you use your computer, consider creating a local account. You can always switch to your Microsoft Account when you want to install apps from the Microsoft Store, use OneDrive, or use Skype (see "Switch from a Local to an Existing Microsoft Account," later in this chapter).

To create a local account for someone else to use your computer, see "Create a Local Account for Someone in Your Household," later in this chapter.

2. Choose the Sign In with a Local Account Instead link. You see the screen shown in **Figure 4-11.** Enter the password of your Microsoft Account and select Next.

3. In the next screen, shown in **Figure 4-12,** enter a user name, a password (twice), and a word or two to jar your memory if you forget your password; then select Next.

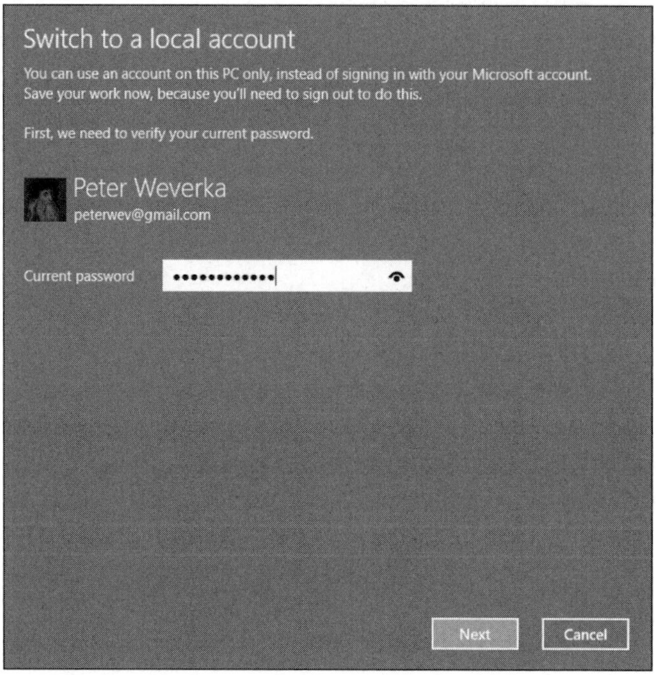

Switch to a local account

You can use an account on this PC only, instead of signing in with your Microsoft account. Save your work now, because you'll need to sign out to do this.

First, we need to verify your current password.

Peter Weverka
peterwev@gmail.com

Current password ··············· 👁

[Next] [Cancel]

FIGURE 4-11

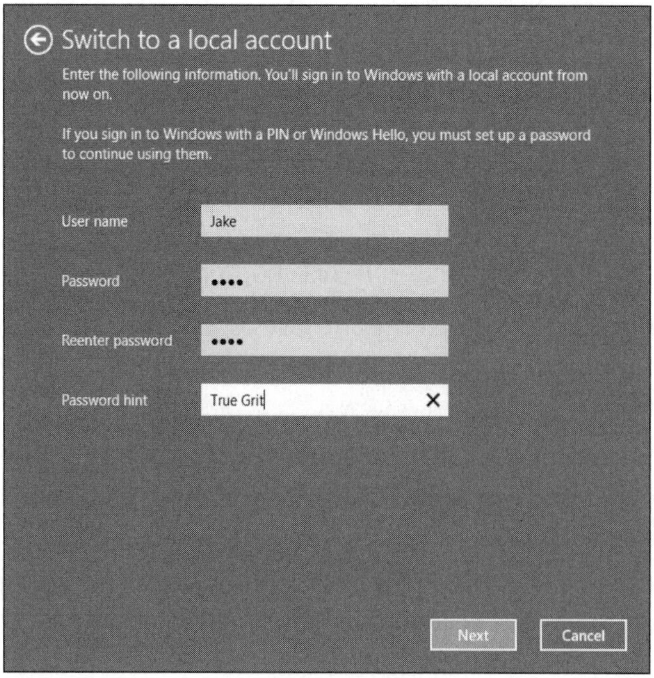

⊖ Switch to a local account

Enter the following information. You'll sign in to Windows with a local account from now on.

If you sign in to Windows with a PIN or Windows Hello, you must set up a password to continue using them.

User name	Jake
Password	····
Reenter password	····
Password hint	True Grit ✕

[Next] [Cancel]

FIGURE 4-12

TIP

Passwords are case sensitive. In other words, your computer recognizes uppercase letters and lowercase letters when you create and enter a password. Remember which letters in your password are upper- and lowercase.

TIP

If you want to sign in to your local account without having to enter a password, leave the Password, Reenter Password, and Password Hint text boxes blank. Later in this chapter, the sections "Create a Password for a Local Account" and "Change or Remove a Local Account Password" explain the ins and outs of local account passwords.

4. Select the Sign Out and Finish button. Your Microsoft Account closes, Windows restarts, and you see the Windows 10 screen.

5. Enter the password you created in Step 3. When you start your computer, Windows 10 assumes that you want to sign in with the account you were using when you last shut down your computer. If you shut down when signed in with your local account, you are asked to provide the password for your local account the next time you start your computer.

TIP

When you start a computer with more than one account, account names appear in the lower-left corner of the Windows 10 screen. Select an account name in the lower-left corner to tell Windows which account to open.

Switch from a Local to an Existing Microsoft Account

1. Follow these steps to sign in with your Microsoft Account when you are currently signed in with your local account. On the Start screen, select your name in the upper-left corner of the screen and then choose Change Account Settings from the pop-up menu that appears (refer to **Figure 4-7**). The Accounts screen opens. Your account information appears with *Local Account* under your name (refer to **Figure 4-8**).

TIP

If you don't have a Microsoft Account already, see "Create a New Microsoft Account," earlier in this chapter.

TIP

If you don't see *Local Account* under your user account name, you're already signed in with your Microsoft Account.

2. Select the Sign In with a Microsoft Account Instead link. The screen shown in **Figure 4-13** appears. Type the email address of your Microsoft Account (or the phone number associated with the account) and select the Next button.

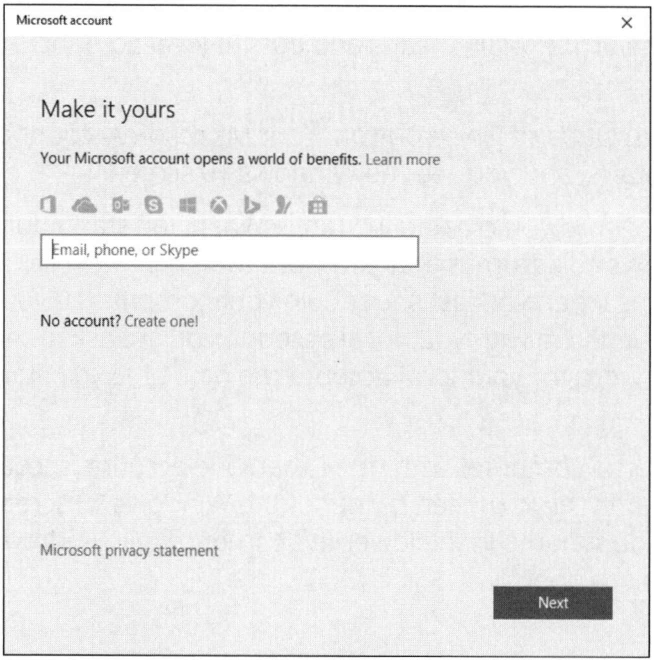

Microsoft account   ×

Make it yours

Your Microsoft account opens a world of benefits. Learn more

Email, phone, or Skype

No account? Create one!

Microsoft privacy statement

Next

FIGURE 4-13

3. Enter the password of your Microsoft Account and select the Sign In button.

4. In the Current Windows Password text box, enter the password of your local account, as shown in **Figure 4-14.** The Accounts screen opens, where you see the user name and email address of your Microsoft account.

Enter your local account password

FIGURE 4-14

Create a Local Account for Someone in Your Household

1. Consider creating a local account for each person who uses your computer. A local account is more than just a way to sign in. Each local account preserves the user's settings and Internet browsing history. When you set up a local account, Windows 10 creates separate folders called Documents, Pictures, Videos, and Music for the account holder. Only the account holder can open and edit files in these special folders. To create a local account, select your name on the Start screen and choose Change Account Settings on the menu that appears (refer to **Figure 4-7**). The Settings app opens to the Accounts screen.

To create a local account, you must be your computer's administrator. To see whether you're the administer, look for the word *Administrator* below your name on the Your Info page of the Settings screen.

TIP

2. On the left, select Family & Other People. On the right, select Add Someone Else to This PC. The How Will This Person Sign In screen appears.

3. At the bottom of the How Will This Person Sign In screen, select the link called I Don't Have This Person's Sign-In Information.

TIP

If you know you want a Microsoft Account instead of a local account, jump to "Create a New Microsoft Account" or "Switch from a Local to an Existing Microsoft Account," earlier in this chapter.

4. On the next screen (it's called Create an Account for This PC), enter the user name in the first box, as shown in **Figure 4-15.** Use the person's first name, last name, first and last name, initials, or nickname — something easy to remember and type.

Only the user name is required for a local account

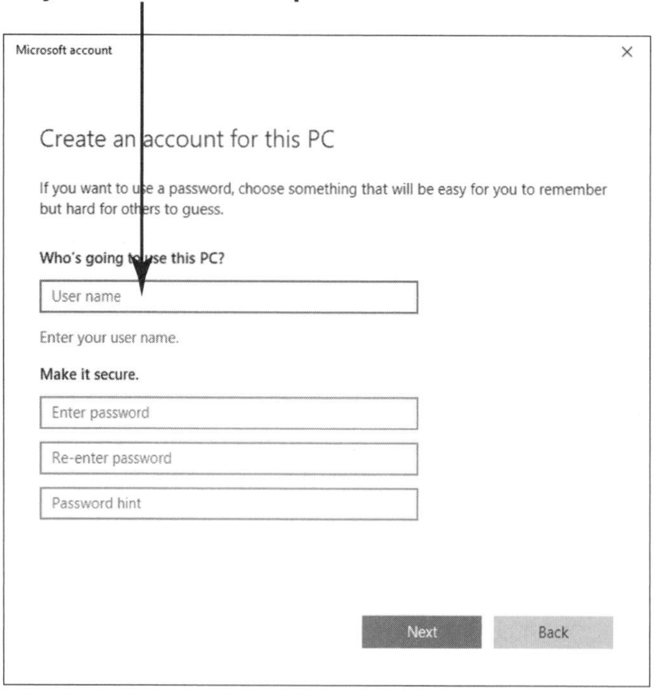

FIGURE 4-15

TIP

You are not required to use a password with a local account, which makes signing in easy. However, without a password, anyone can use the computer and access information that you might want to protect.

5. In the Password box, enter a password (or skip to Step 8 if you don't care to create a password for your account). A dot will appear for each character you type.

TIP

For suggestions on creating a good password, see the tip in Step 4 in the section, "Create a New Microsoft Account," earlier in this chapter.

6. In the Reenter Password box, type the same password exactly.

7. In the Password Hint box, type a reminder that only you will understand.

TIP

For laptops or other portable devices, consider using your phone number with area code as the hint (if you're sure you don't need a real hint). The hint appears when someone tries and fails to enter login information. By including your phone number, you might help an honest person return your lost, stolen, or misplaced device to you.

8. After completing all the available boxes, choose the Next button. In the Accounts screen, the new user name appears under Other People, as shown in **Figure 4-16.**

9. Return to the Start screen and select your user name. Notice that the new user name appears on the drop-down menu. You can switch between accounts by selecting a user name on the drop-down menu. To sign out of an account, choose Sign Out.

10. In the drop-down menu, select the new user name to switch to that account.

11. A screen appears with the new user name. If you used a password on the new user account, type that password in the box and select the onscreen right arrow or press Enter. If you didn't use a password, select the Sign In button.

TIP

The first time you sign in as a new user, you have to wait a moment while apps are installed for the new user. Soon the generic Start screen appears. (Any settings you changed in your account do not transfer to other accounts.)

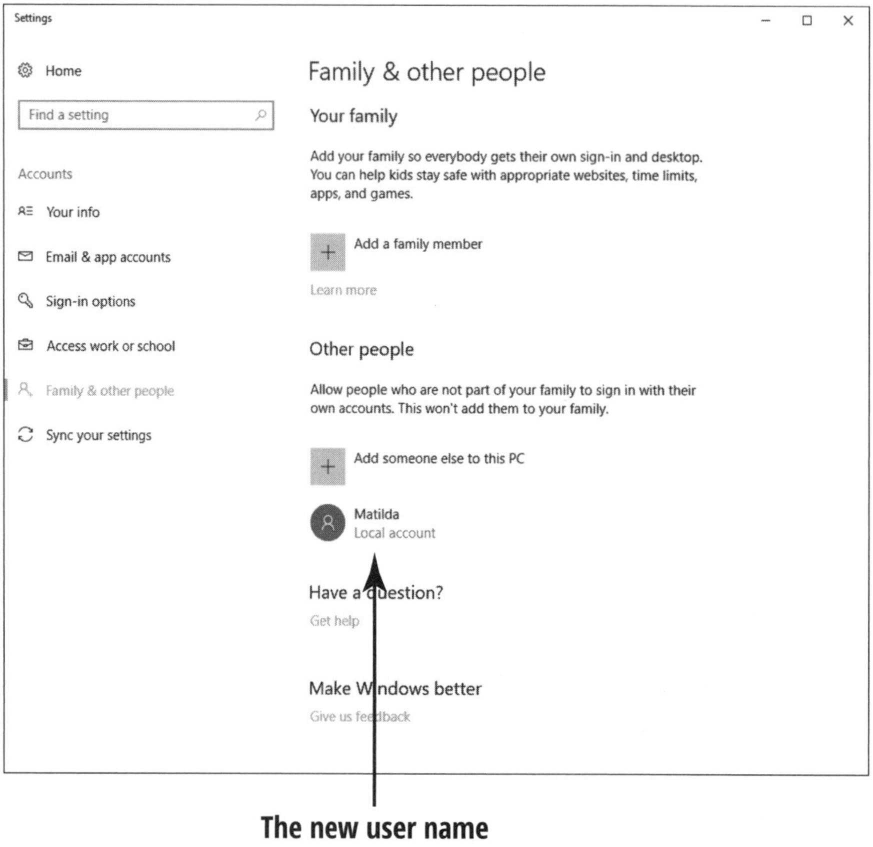

![Settings window showing Family & other people screen]

Settings — □ ✕

⚙ Home

Find a setting 🔍

Accounts

A≡ Your info

✉ Email & app accounts

🔍 Sign-in options

💼 Access work or school

👤 Family & other people

🔄 Sync your settings

Family & other people

Your family

Add your family so everybody gets their own sign-in and desktop. You can help kids stay safe with appropriate websites, time limits, apps, and games.

➕ Add a family member

Learn more

Other people

Allow people who are not part of your family to sign in with their own accounts. This won't add them to your family.

➕ Add someone else to this PC

👤 Matilda
Local account

Have a question?

Get help

Make Windows better

Give us feedback

The new user name

FIGURE 4-16

TIP

When you start a computer for which you've created more than one user account, the users' names appear in the lower-left corner of the Windows 10 screen. To tell Windows which user to sign in with, select a user name on the Windows 10 screen before signing in.

Create a Password for a Local Account

1. On the Start screen, select your name. From the drop-down menu that appears, choose Change Account Settings (refer to **Figure 4-7**). The Settings app opens to the Accounts screen.

TIP

If you already have a password, see the "Change or Remove Your Password," later in this chapter.

2. On the left, select Sign-in Options.

3. If you don't have a password but want one, select the Add button under Password.

TIP

The buttons available under Sign-in Options depend on your current setup. You may see buttons that enable you to create, change, or remove a particular setting.

4. In the Create a Password screen, shown in **Figure 4-17,** enter a password in the New Password box.

TIP

For a local account, the password can be any length. See Step 4 in the "Create a New Microsoft Account" section for suggestions about creating a good password.

5. In the Reenter Password box, enter the password again.

6. Enter a hint to remind yourself — and no one else — about your password.

7. Select Finish. If any error messages appear, correct the entries and select Next again.

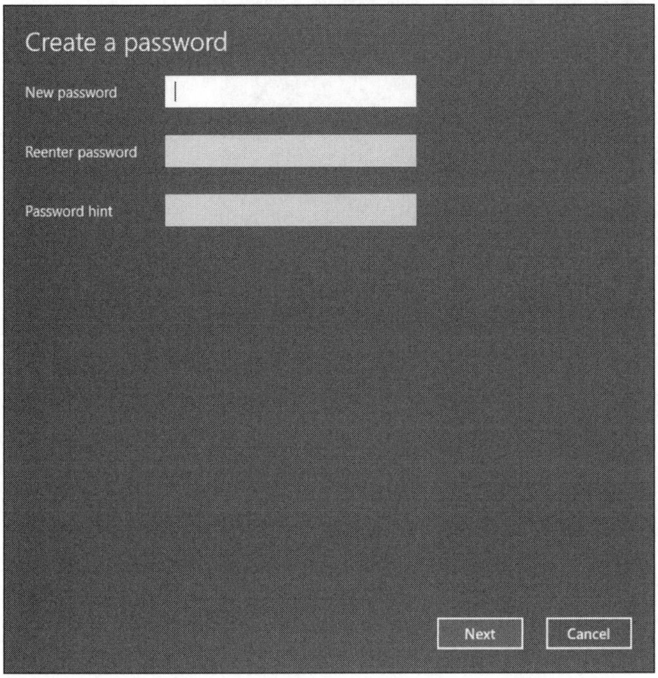

Create a password

New password

Reenter password

Password hint

Next Cancel

FIGURE 4-17

Change or Remove a Local Account Password

1. On the Start screen, select your name, and then choose Change Account Settings. On the left side of the Accounts screen, select Sign-in Options.

2. Select the Change button.

If you don't have a password but want one, see the preceding "Create a Password for a Local Account" section.

3. On the Change Your Password screen, enter your current password and then select the Next button.

4. On the next Change Your Password screen (see **Figure 4-18**), enter the new password. (If you don't care to have a password, select Next and skip to Step 7.)

If you don't want a password, leave these boxes blank

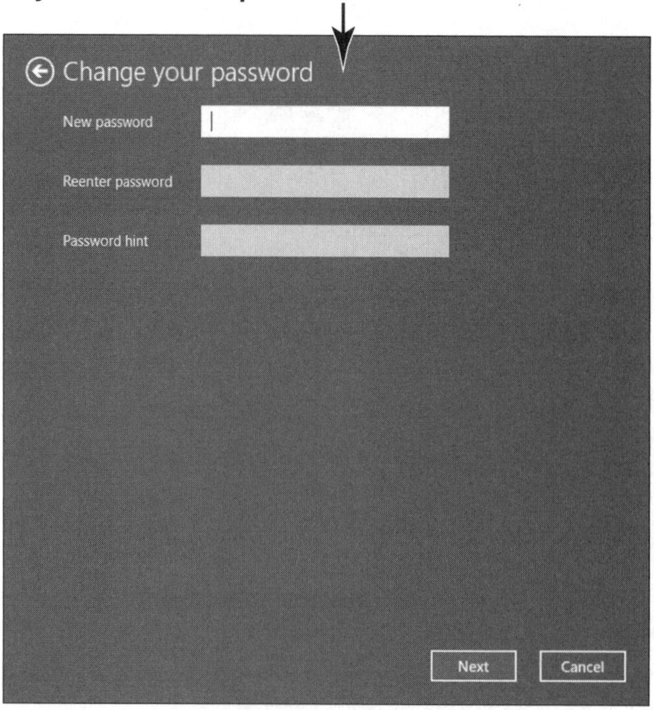

FIGURE 4-18

TIP

To remove your current password and use no password, leave all boxes blank. However, especially if you have a laptop that you carry with you, going without a password isn't recommended. Without a password to safeguard it, anyone can get into your laptop.

5. In the Reenter Password box, enter the password again.

6. Enter a hint to remind yourself — and no one else — about your password. Then select Next. If any error messages appear, correct the entries and select Next again.

7. The final screen indicates that you must use your new password the next time you sign in. (This message appears even if you left the password blank, in which case you won't need any password.) Select Finish.

Change a Microsoft Account Password

1. On the Start screen, select your name and choose Change Account Settings to open the Accounts screen. Then select Sign-in Options.

2. Select the Change button.

3. On the Please Reenter Your Password screen, enter your current password and then select the Sign In button.

4. On the Help Us Protect Your Info screen, choose how you want to receive the security code that Microsoft sends to change a password. (In Step 5, you enter this security code.) When you created your Microsoft Account, you gave Microsoft your email address and perhaps phone numbers for receiving calls and texts. Choose how you want to receive the code — by email, telephone, or text. Select the Next button when you are ready to proceed.

5. Retrieve the security code that Microsoft sent to you by email, phone, or text, and enter it in the Code text box, as shown in **Figure 4-19.** Then click or tap the Next button.

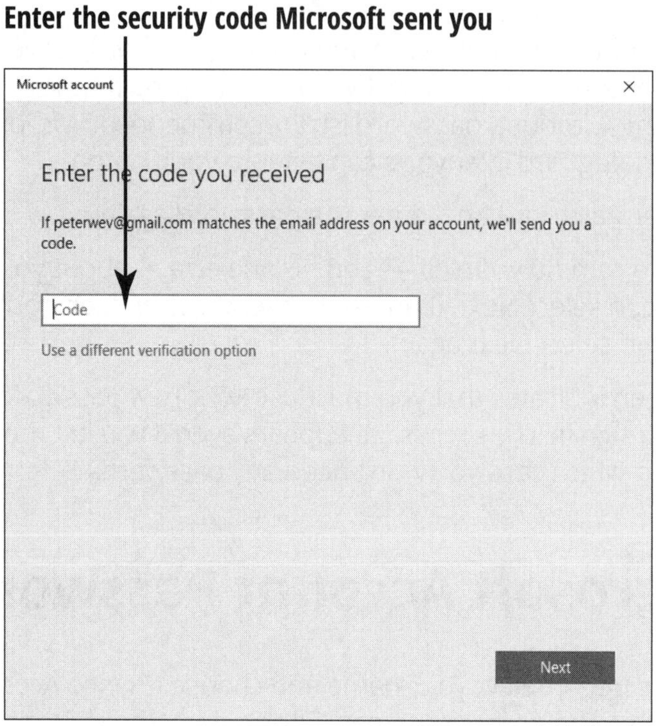

Enter the security code Microsoft sent you

Microsoft account   ✕

Enter the code you received

If peterwev@gmail.com matches the email address on your account, we'll send you a
code.

| Code |

Use a different verification option

Next

FIGURE 4-19

6. In the Change Your Password screen, as shown in **Figure 4-20,**
enter your old password and your new password twice; then select
Next.

TIP

If I said you should choose a password that is easy to remember but
difficult for others to detect, would you think my advice was gratu-
itous and unnecessary? Maybe. But I'm telling you anyway.

7. The next screen boldly announces, "You've successfully changed your
password!" Select the Finish button. As a security measure, Microsoft
sends you a notice — by email, phone, or text — telling you that your
password was changed.

FIGURE 4-20

Delete a Local Account

1. Before you delete a local account, make sure that the user of that account is signed out. Moreover, you must be signed in to a Microsoft Account to delete a local account.

2. Select your name on the Start screen and choose Change Account Settings. You land in the Your Info page of the Settings screen. Does it say "administrator" under your name? I hope so, because you must be your computer's administrator to delete a local account. On the Accounts screen, select Family & Other People.

3. Select the account you want to delete and then select the Remove button, as shown in **Figure 4-21.**

4. In the Delete Account and Data window, select the Delete Account and Data button.

Take heed of the onscreen warning. Deleting a user account removes the user's data, including all documents, music, and other files. If you're not sure which option is best, choose Cancel.

FIGURE 4-21

Chapter 5
Getting Comfortable with the Desktop

The *desktop* is Grand Central Station as far as Windows 10 is concerned. Sure, you can open applications from the Start screen (Chapter 2 explains how), but with a few simple modifications, you can open applications from the desktop as well. When you're running more than one application, you can go to the desktop and quickly switch from one application to another. In fact, in Windows 10, you can create a second "virtual" desktop for one set of open applications (applications that pertain to leisure, let's say), and when the boss isn't looking, you can switch to the second desktop to play games or chat with friends.

One key feature of the desktop is the *taskbar*, a strip along the bottom of the screen that shows icons for desktop programs. The taskbar can be used to run and switch between desktop programs. Most programs on the desktop run in windows, as opposed to the full-screen nature of Windows 10 apps.

In this chapter, you get acquainted with the desktop, the taskbar, and windowed apps. You change the date, time, and time zone, as needed. You resize and reposition windowed apps, and discover how to "add a desktop" for a second set of open applications. You select a background for the desktop and make some desktop apps more convenient to use by pinning them to the taskbar. Finally, you work with the Task Manager, which lets you end any app — desktop or Windows 10.

The desktop originated when using the mouse was the most common method for selecting objects (touchscreens were non-existent). Therefore, on the desktop, a few tasks are easier to do with the mouse than with touch or a keyboard.

This chapter is an introduction to the desktop. See Part 4 to dive a little deeper into desktop functions, such as organizing documents.

Check Out the Desktop

1. Go to the desktop (if you aren't already there) by using one of these techniques:

   - On the Start screen, select the Desktop tile.

   - With the Start screen open, display the desktop simply by clicking or tapping the Windows button (it's located in the lower-left corner of your computer screen).

   - Press ⊞+D.

   - Right-click the Windows button and choose Desktop on the pop-up menu that appears.

2. Your desktop has a picture in the background. Examine your desktop for *icons* — small pictures that represent either programs, which perform functions, or documents, such as letters and photos. You select an icon to run a program or open a document. The Windows 10 desktop displays an icon for the Recycle Bin, where deleted documents go. The Recycle Bin may be the only icon on your desktop, or you may see others. See Chapter 14 for information on using the Recycle Bin.

3. The area at the bottom of the screen is the *taskbar,* shown in **Figure 5-1.** From left to right, the taskbar offers these amenities:

- **Windows button:** Selecting this button opens the Start screen. (Click or tap the button a second time to close the Start screen.)

- **Search box:** You can enter a search term here to look for Windows settings, applications, files on your computer, and information on the Internet. See Chapter 2 for information about using this part of the taskbar to ask questions of Cortana, the talking digital assistant.

- **Task View button:** Selecting this button brings up thumbnail images of applications currently running on your computer. You can select an application thumbnail to switch to an application. You can also select New Desktop to open a second desktop (see "Open a Second Desktop," later in this chapter, for more information).

- **Icons:** Some icons appear on the taskbar automatically. Very likely, your taskbar has icons for File Explorer and Edge. You can select these icons to open File Explorer and Edge. When you open an application, Windows 10 places its icon on the taskbar.

- **Icon tray:** The *icon tray* displays icons for programs that run automatically when your computer starts. The date and time are to the right of the icon tray. On the right side of the icon tray is the Notification icon.

TIP

You can use the taskbar to switch among programs by selecting the icon for the program you want to use.

4. Select an icon on the taskbar to open the associated program. (Refer to **Figure 5-1** if you aren't sure where the taskbar is located.)

TIP

You select items on the desktop or in the taskbar by clicking with the mouse or tapping the touchscreen. To some extent, you can use the Tab and arrow keys, but that's an awkward method.

TIP

If you have a touchscreen, note the taskbar icon for the virtual keyboard. See Chapter 1 for information about using the keyboard.

5. Right-click over an icon or tap and hold until a small box appears, and then release. A *context menu* appears with options specific to the icon you selected, as shown in **Figure 5-2.** Select anywhere else on the desktop to dismiss this menu. Repeat this on a few different areas of the screen to see how the context menu changes.

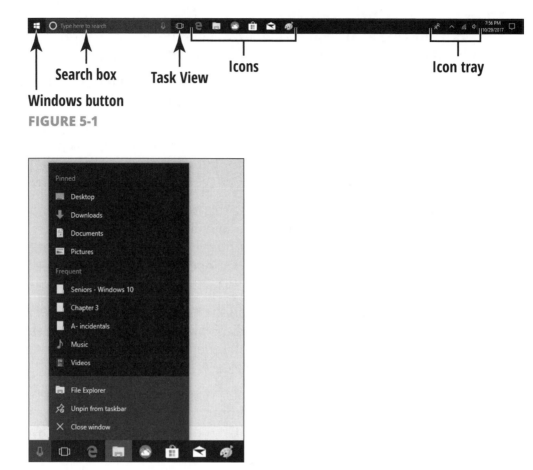

Search box **Task View** **Icons** **Icon tray**

Windows button

FIGURE 5-1

FIGURE 5-2

Change the Date or Time

1. Select the date and time displayed in the taskbar. A calendar and clock pop up, as shown in **Figure 5-3.**

TIP
Selecting the date and time on the taskbar also brings up an agenda list from the Calendar. Chapter 8 describes the Calendar in tedious detail. You can click or tap the Hide Agenda button to hide the agenda list.

2. If the date or time is incorrect for your location, select the Windows button and then select the Settings button on the left side of the Start screen. The Settings screen opens. Select Time & Language. You see the Date & Time window, shown in **Figure 5-4, left.**

FIGURE 5-3

3. Windows 10 determines the correct time and date from the Internet, and your computer should show the right time and date, but if it doesn't, turn off the Set Time Automatically option and select the Change button. You see the Change Date and Time screen (see **Figure 5-4**). Select the correct date and time in this screen. Change the time by using the little triangles that point up (later) or down (earlier) or by entering the specific hours and minutes. Select Change to keep your change or Cancel to ignore your change.

4. Back in the Date and Time window, select your Time Zone from the drop-down list, if necessary. Turn the Adjust for Daylight Saving Time option on or off as appropriate.

5. To change the format with which the time and date are displayed in the lower-right corner of the screen, select the Change Date and Time Formats link in the Date and Time window. Then, in the Change Date and Time Formats window (see **Figure 5-5**), choose how you want the date and time to be displayed on your computer screen.

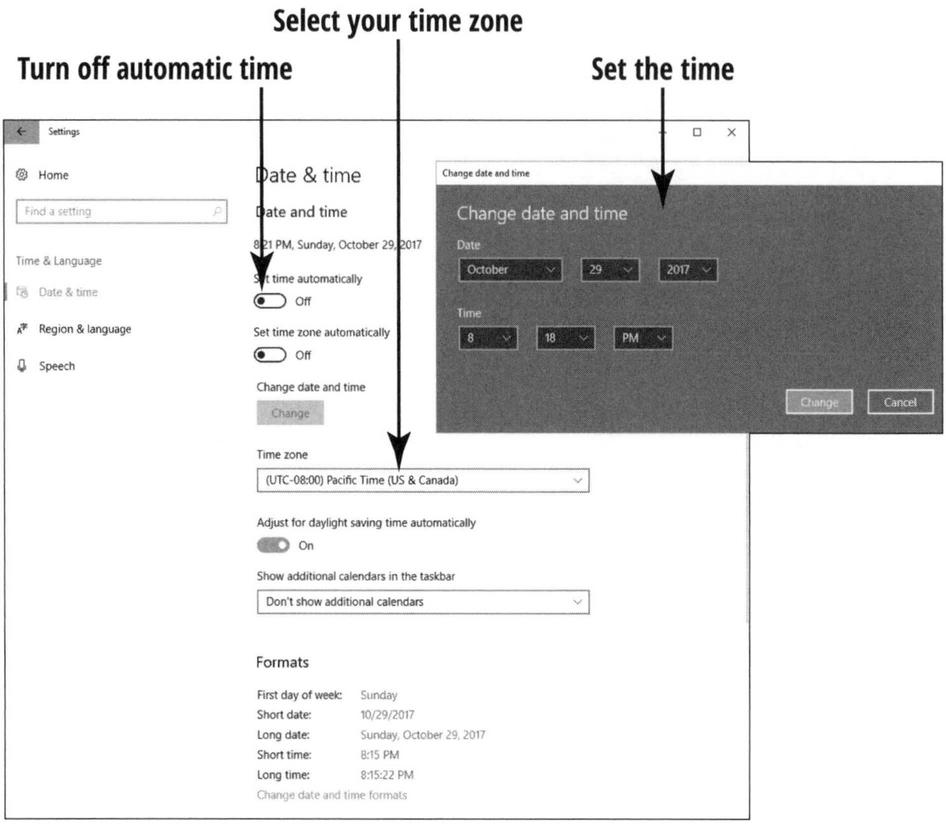

Select your time zone

Turn off automatic time

Set the time

FIGURE 5-4

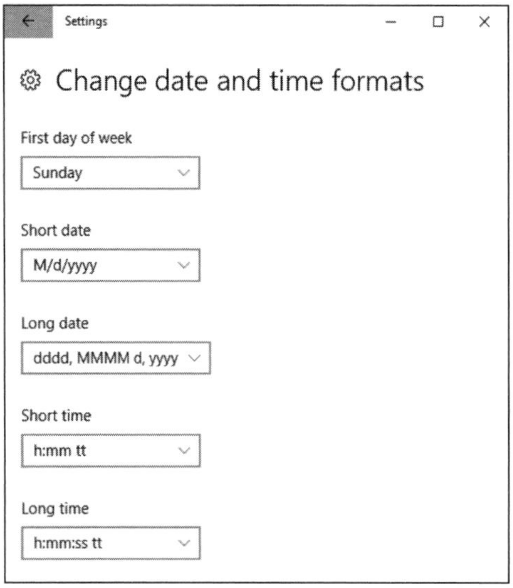

FIGURE 5-5

Explore the Parts of a Window

1. In the taskbar, select the File Explorer icon (it looks like a folder). File Explorer opens, as shown in **Figure 5-6.**

TIP

File Explorer enables you to view your computer storage, such as hard drives, and folders, which are used to organize your documents. See Chapter 14 for information on using File Explorer.

2. Explore the example window in **Figure 5-6,** starting at the top left:

   - **Quick Access toolbar:** The *Quick Access toolbar* gives you fast access to common operations, such as creating a new folder. This toolbar is not present in all windows and may feature different functions, depending on the window.

   - **Title bar:** The *title bar,* which is the top line of the window, lists the name of the file or folder that is currently open.

   The title of the window in **Figure 5-6** is This PC, the location File Explorer is focused on when you open File Explorer.

TIP

   - **Minimize:** The *Minimize button,* located in the upper-right corner of the window, shrinks or hides the window's contents. The program that the window contains is still running and open, but the window is out of sight. You'll still see the program's icon in the taskbar. Select the Minimize button when you want to ignore a particular window but aren't actually done with it. To restore the window, select its icon in the taskbar.

   - **Maximize/Restore:** The *Maximize button* (the button with a single square in the upper-right corner of the window) fills the screen with the contents of the window. Select the Maximize button to hide the desktop and other open windows, to concentrate on one window, and to see as much of the window's contents as you can. The *Restore button* (the button with two squares in the upper-right corner) is the name of the button that appears after you select the Maximize button; it replaces the Maximize button. Select the Restore button to return the window to its previous size, which is between maximized and minimized. (Press ▓+up-arrow key to maximize, and ▓+down-arrow key to restore or minimize.)

- **Close:** The *Close button* is the button with the X in the upper-right corner of the window. Select the Close button when you are done with the window. Close is also called Quit and Exit. (Press Alt+F4 to close the current window or the desktop itself. This keyboard shortcut works for Windows 10 apps, as well.)

- **Ribbon:** The *Ribbon* is a toolbar that provides access to many functions organized as groups within tabs. The tabs appear across the top of the Ribbon. The first time you run File Explorer, the Ribbon is hidden (collapsed). Display the Ribbon by selecting the caret symbol (^) on the far right, next to Help (the question mark). Select the caret again to hide the Ribbon. You can also press Ctrl+F1 to toggle the Ribbon on and off. (Leave the Ribbon visible for this chapter.) The tabs remain in view and function the same. Although Ribbons vary between programs, most Ribbons have File and View tabs. To use a tab, select its name to display its functions, and then select the item you want to use.

TIP

The Ribbon can help you discover new functions.

- **Contents:** The bulk of the window contains the program or document you're using. File Explorer displays locations on the left and objects in that location on the right.

- **Status bar:** Along the bottom edge of the window, some programs display information about the window or its contents in a single-line *status bar.* File Explorer lists how many files are in the currently open folder and how many files (if any) have been selected.

TIP

Scan the edges of windows. Often, important information and functions are pushed to these edges around the main content area.

3. Select the Close button (the X) to close File Explorer.

TIP

Although the Quick Access toolbar and the Close button work on a touchscreen, they are small targets. You may find a stylus more accurate when dealing with smaller elements.

TIP

See Chapter 2 for information on finding other desktop programs, such as the Calculator.

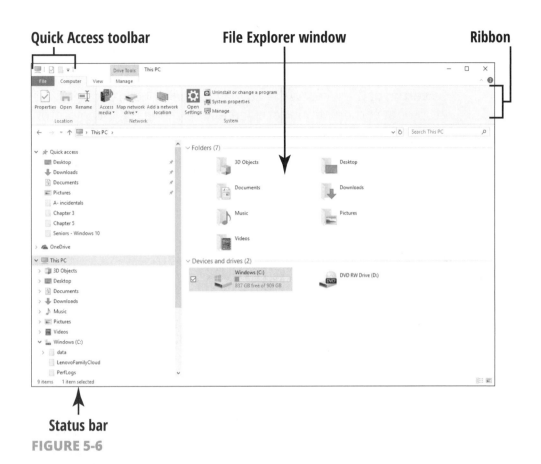

Quick Access toolbar   **File Explorer window**   **Ribbon**

Status bar

FIGURE 5-6

Resize a Window

1. To resize a window, open File Explorer by selecting the folder icon in the taskbar. (Refer to **Figure 5-6.**)

2. If the window is maximized (fills the screen), select the Restore button to make the window smaller.

3. Use one of these methods to resize the window:

   - **Mouse:** Move the mouse pointer to the right edge of the window until the pointer changes to a double-headed arrow, called the *resize pointer*. Click and drag the edge of the window, using the resize pointer. (To drag, click and hold down the mouse button while you move the mouse.)

   - **Touchscreen:** Drag the right edge of the window.

Drag left to shrink the window and right to expand it.

4. Resize the window's width and height at the same time by dragging a corner of the window. If you want a challenge, try resizing the top-right corner without accidentally selecting the Close button.

5. Resize the window's width *or* height by dragging any of the four sides.

You may want to resize a window to show only what you need to see, nothing more. Practice resizing from any side or corner.

6. Leave the window open as you go on to the next task.

Arrange Some Windows

1. On the desktop, select and open the Recycle Bin by double-clicking or double-tapping its icon. The Recycle Bin contains deleted files and folders. It appears in another File Explorer window. See **Figure 5-7.**

Double-click by clicking the left mouse button twice, without a pause. Double-tap by tapping twice in quick succession.

2. If File Explorer isn't still open from the preceding section, open it by selecting the folder icon in the taskbar. You now see two overlapping windows on the desktop (refer to **Figure 5-7**), one titled *This PC* and the other titled *Recycle Bin.*

The window in front of the others is called the *active* window. All other windows are *inactive.* Note that the title bar of the active window is a different color from the title bar in any inactive window. Selecting anywhere in an inactive window makes it active and moves it to the front of the others.

3. Drag the Recycle Bin title bar (avoiding the buttons on the left and right ends) to move that window a little.

4. Drag the This PC title bar (again, avoiding the buttons on both ends). The This PC window moves in front of the Recycle Bin as you move it. Move both windows so that you can see a little of each (refer to **Figure 5-7**).

5. Practice moving both windows. Arranging windows helps you see and do more than one thing at a time. Use the techniques from the preceding section, "Resize a Window," to see as much as you can of both windows at one time.

If you can't see the title bar of the window you want to move, move the other window to uncover the hidden title bar.

TIP

6. Leave both windows open for the following task.

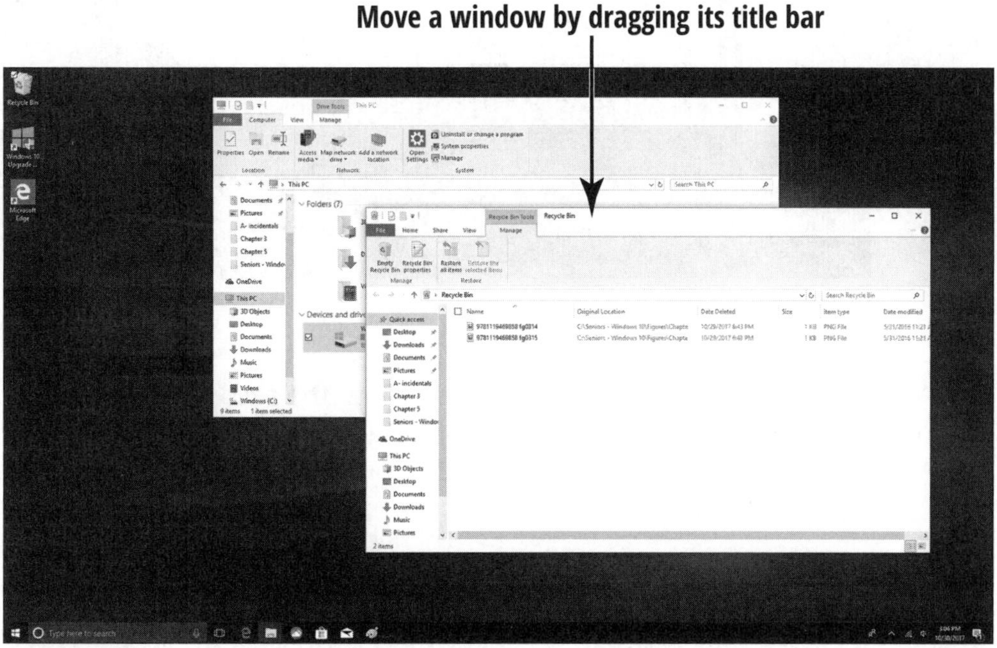

Move a window by dragging its title bar

FIGURE 5-7

Snap a Window

1. Drag one of the windows you worked with in the preceding section to the left edge of the screen. When the mouse pointer or your finger reaches the left edge of the screen, you see an outline on the screen, as shown in **Figure 5-8.** When you release the mouse or your finger, the window resizes automatically to fill the left half of the screen, as shown in **Figure 5-9.** This procedure is called *snap*. (To snap a window using the keyboard, press ⊞+left arrow to snap a window to the left; press ⊞+right arrow to snap a window to the right.)

Drag the window to the far left   **Note the outline**

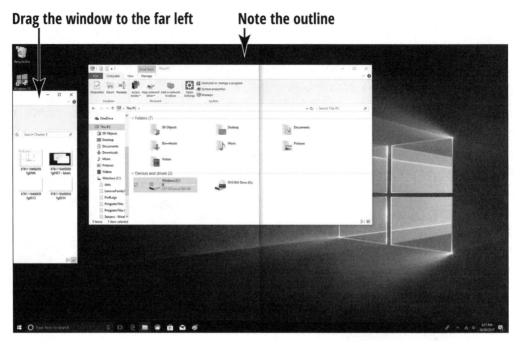

FIGURE 5-8

2. After you snap the first open window, the second open window appears in thumbnail form (see **Figure 5-9**). Tap or click this second window thumbnail to make it fill, or snap to, the right side of the window.

TIP

When two or more windows are displayed side by side like this, they are called *tiled* windows.

3. Drag either window by the title bar away from the edge of the screen. The window returns to its previous size.

4. Drag the window you moved in Step 3 to the upper-right corner of the window. When the mouse pointer or your finger touches the corner of the screen, you see an outline on the screen, but this time the outline occupies the upper-right corner of the screen. And guess what? When you release the mouse pointer or your finger, the window snaps to the upper-right quadrant of the screen. In this way, by snapping windows to the corner of the screen, you can tile four windows on your screen, not two windows.

Tap or click to snap the other window

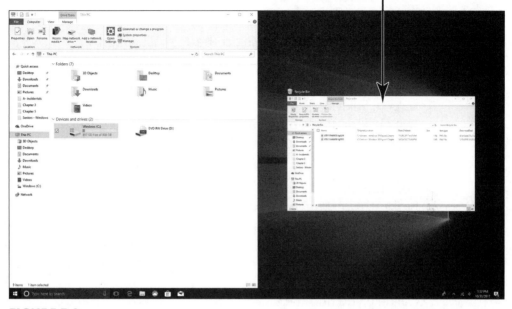

FIGURE 5-9

TIP

You can maximize a window by dragging it to the top edge of the screen. Dragging a window to the top is the equivalent of selecting the Maximize button (see the section "Explore the Parts of a Window," earlier in this chapter).

5. Drag the title bar of each open window away from the side of the screen so that neither window is "snapped." You'll need these open windows if you want to move on to "Open a Second Desktop," the next topic in this chapter.

Open a Second Desktop

1. If File Explorer and Recycle Bin aren't open on your desktop (because you didn't follow the previous exercise in this chapter), open those programs now.

2. Select the Task View button on the taskbar. As Chapter 2 explains, you can use this button to switch between open application windows. After you select the Task View button, thumbnail versions of open windows appear on the desktop. At this point, you can select a thumbnail to go to a different application, but don't do that just yet.

You can press ⊞+Tab to select the Task View button.

3. Notice the New Desktop button that appears after you select the Task View button. This button is located in the upper-left corner of the screen. Select the New Desktop button now. As shown in **Figure 5-10**, two desktop tiles appear at the top of the screen. The desktop tiles are labeled "Desktop 1" and "Desktop 2."

4. Select Desktop 2. You see a brand-new, pristine desktop. Congratulations; you are now in Desktop 2. Create a second (or third or fourth) desktop when you want to keep the first desktop from getting crowded with too many applications or to better organize your work. For example, if you are using applications for your work and using other applications for leisure purposes, put the work applications on one desktop and the leisure applications on another. This will help you find the application you want to work with.

Go to a different desktop

New Desktop button

FIGURE 5-10

5. While you are on Desktop 2, open the Photos app. Having just one application on the desktop makes working with that application a little easier.

6. Select the Task View button again. You can see, on the Desktop 2 tile, the Photos app.

7. Move the pointer or your finger onto the Desktop 2 tile, and when the Close button appears, click or tap the Close button to close Desktop 2. The Photos app that you opened on Desktop 2 now appears on Desktop 1, the only open desktop. When you close a desktop, all its open applications move to the desktop that is still open.

Choose a Desktop Background

1. Select the Windows button to open the Start menu. Then, on the Start menu, choose Settings to open the Settings window.

2. Select Personalization. Then, in the Personalization window, select Background (if it isn't already selected). The Background screen, shown in **Figure 5-11,** is the place to go to choose a background for the Windows desktop.

TIP
You can use the Personalization window to customize many aspects of the desktop. The more time you spend on the desktop, the more worthwhile this personalization may be.

3. In the Personalization window, select Picture on the Background menu (see **Figure 5-11**).

4. Select any photo to make that photo the desktop background. The background changes immediately. To see the entire desktop, minimize the Settings window. Restore the Settings window by selecting its icon in the taskbar or by repeating the preceding steps.

TIP
To use a photo of your own as the desktop background, select the Browse button and choose a photo in the Open dialog box.

5. On the Background menu, choose Solid Color to experiment with making a solid color the desktop background. After you choose Solid Color, a color palette appears in the Personalization screen (see **Figure 5-11**). Select a color in the color palette. The background

changes immediately. What do you think of having a color background? You can minimize the Settings window to get a good look at your new desktop background.

6. Choose the background you like best — a picture or a color — on the Personalization screen and then close the Settings window.

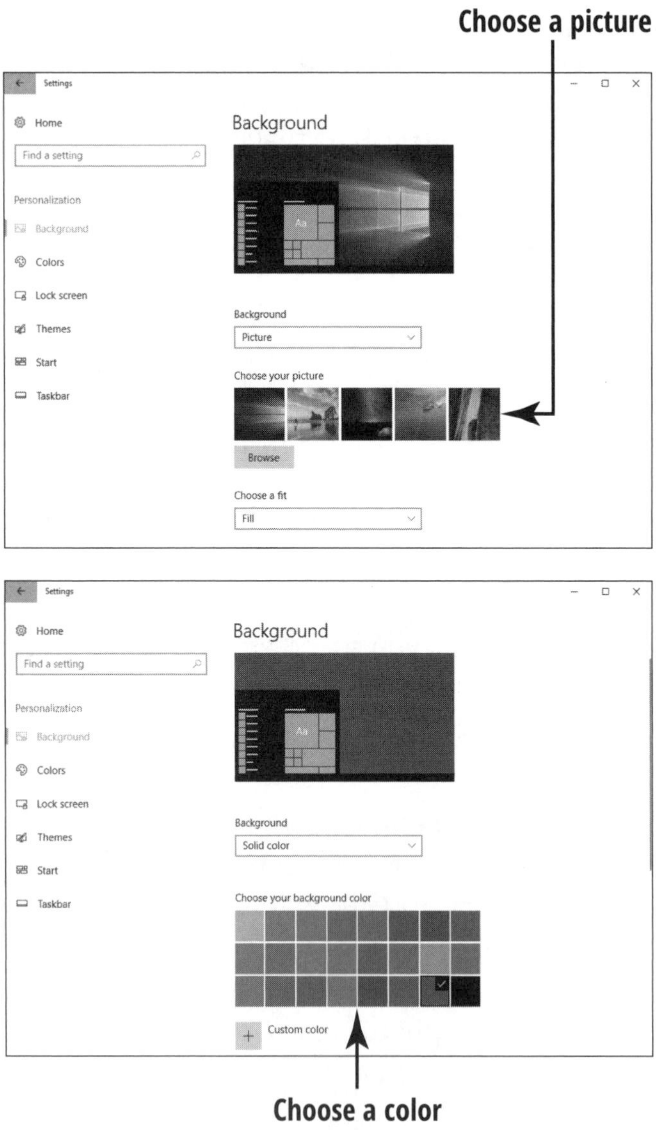

Choose a picture

Choose a color

FIGURE 5-11

Pin Icons to the Taskbar

1. On the Start screen, scroll to the Calculator tile, as shown in **Figure 5-12.**

2. Use one of these methods to display the shortcut menu on the Calculator tile:

    - **Mouse:** Right-click the Calculator tile.

    - **Touchscreen:** Swipe the Calculator tile down or up slightly.

3. Select More on the shortcut menu. A submenu with more options appears (see **Figure 5-12**).

4. Select Pin to Taskbar on the submenu. Doing so places the icon for Calculator in the desktop taskbar for easy access. The Calculator icon appears in the taskbar, as shown in **Figure 5-13.**

    Press ⊞+D to go directly to the desktop at any time.

5. Repeat Steps 1 and 3 and then select Unpin from Taskbar.

TIP

Place an application icon on the taskbar

FIGURE 5-12

TIP

A fast way to remove an icon from the taskbar is to right-click it and choose Unpin from Taskbar on the shortcut menu.

6. Switch to the desktop. The Calculator icon is gone.

TIP

Pinned icons have a killer feature: *jumplists,* which are short menus of tasks and documents specific to the pinned app. To see the jumplist of a pinned app, right-click its icon in the taskbar or tap and hold on the icon until a small box appears. Try that with the File Explorer icon in the taskbar. Not all desktop apps have jumplists.

Calculator is pinned

FIGURE 5-13

Stop Apps with the Task Manager

1. On the desktop, select Task Manager from the taskbar context menu (shown in **Figure 5-14**) using one of these methods:

- **Mouse:** Right-click over an empty area of the taskbar and select Task Manager from the context menu.

- **Touchscreen:** Tap and hold an empty area of the taskbar until a small box appears; then release. Select Task Manager from the context menu.

- **Keyboard:** Press Ctrl+Shift+Esc to display the Task Manager directly.

2. The Task Manager lists any running apps — both desktop apps and Windows 10 apps. Select an app, also referred to as a *task.* Note that the End Task button is now available, as shown in **Figure 5-15, left.** You don't have to end this task, but you could. Any of the tasks in the Task Manager window can be ended without consequences.

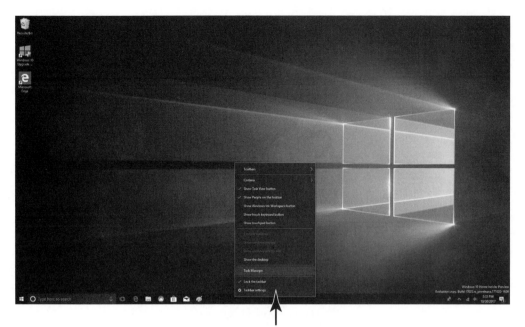

Taskbar context menu

FIGURE 5-14

Select a task

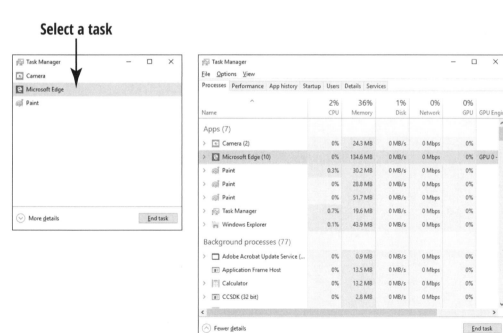

FIGURE 5-15

TIP

Be careful about ending an app used to create something (for example, a word-processing app) because you could lose data you haven't saved before ending the task. Use the Task Manager to end tasks that you can't end otherwise, such as a frozen or locked app or one that seems to slow down everything.

3. Select the More Details option. The Task Manager expands and displays detailed information about every process running on the computer (refer to **Figure 5-15, right**). There's more to Task Manager, although you may not need all its capabilities. Select Fewer Details to return to the simpler version.

4. Close the Task Manager.

2

Windows 10 and the Web

Chapter **6**

Finding What You Need on the Web

The World Wide Web — or, simply, the web — provides quick access to information and entertainment worldwide. One part library, one part marketplace, and one part soapbox, the web makes everything equidistant. From down the block to halfway around the world — even out into space — everything is a few clicks or taps away. News, shopping, and the electronic equivalent of the town square await you.

You explore the web using a *web browser*, a program designed to make browsing the web easy, enjoyable, and safe. In this chapter, I show how you can use the Edge browser to step beyond your computer into the global village.

You browse *web pages*, which are published by governments, businesses, and individuals — anyone can create web pages. Each web page may consist of a few words or thousands of words and pictures. A web page is part of a larger collection called a *website*, which consists of a group of related web pages published on a topic by an organization or individual. Companies and individuals create websites to organize their related pages.

Pages and sites on the web have some common characteristics:

» **Unique addresses,** which are formally called *URLs* (URL stands for Uniform Resource Locator, in case you're ever on *Jeopardy!*).

» **Connecting links** that move you from page to page when you select them. These *links* (also called *hypertext links* or *hyperlinks*) often appear underlined and blue. Pictures and other graphic images can also be links to other pages. You can tell when a picture or image is a link by moving the pointer over it. The pointer changes from an arrow to a hand when it is over a hyperlink picture or image. Exploring the web using links is easier than typing URLs.

In this chapter, you use Edge to browse the web. To get the most out of browsing, you juggle multiple sites simultaneously and find out how to bookmark your favorite websites. You also find out how to search for almost anything and make use of some nice features in Edge. Finally, this chapter shows how to view web pages without seeing pesky advertisements.

TIP

Edge is by no means the only browser. Microsoft invented Edge to coincide with the release of Windows 10. You are hereby encouraged to test-drive other, more established browsers, namely Mozilla Firefox (www.mozilla.org) and Chrome (www.google.com/chrome/browser).

Browse the Web with Edge

1. Open Edge by selecting its tile on the Start screen or its icon on the taskbar. Edge opens to the *start page,* as shown in **Figure 6-1.** This page presents websites and news stories that Microsoft thinks are of interest to you based on your browsing history. If you haven't used Edge yet or haven't used it very often, you don't have a browsing history to speak of, and the websites and news stories you see here probably look quite tepid. (Later in this chapter, "Explore Edge Features" explains how to choose what web pages you see when you start Edge.)

Address bar

FIGURE 6-1

TIP

When you start Edge, you may see an error message if you're not connected to the Internet. If so, see Chapter 4 for information on connecting. See "Bookmark and Revisit Your Favorite Websites," later in this chapter, for instructions about choosing a home page.

2. Note the *address bar* at the top of the Edge screen (refer to **Figure 6-1**). In the address bar, type **www.dummies.com.** As you type, search suggestions appear in a drop-down menu. Either select www.dummies.com in the search suggestions or press Enter. The web page for the Dummies Press appears, as shown in **Figure 6-2.**

TIP

If you have trouble finding the address bar, try clicking with the mouse or tapping with your finger near the top of the screen, to the right of the four buttons (Back, Forward, Refresh, and Home). This will make the address bar appear.

3. Select a link on the page with a click or a tap. Where are the links? Just about everywhere. When you move the pointer over a link, it changes from an arrow to a hand — that's how you can tell where the links are.

4. Select the Back button (or press Alt+left arrow) to return to the preceding page. This button (an arrow) is located in the upper-left corner of the screen (refer to **Figure 6-2**). Select the Back button to backtrack and revisit pages.

Back button

Forward button   **Add to Favorites or Reading List button**

FIGURE 6-2

5. Select the Forward button (or press Alt+right arrow) to move forward to the page you visited in Step 3. The Forward button is next to the Back button (refer to **Figure 6-2**). Edge remembers the pages you visit to make it easy to go forward and back.

TIP

To zoom in and make a web page look bigger, press Ctrl+plus sign. To zoom out, press Ctrl+minus sign.

6. Select the Add to Favorites or Reading List button on the right side of the screen (or press Ctrl+D). After you select this button, a panel appears, as shown in **Figure 6-3.** Select the Save button to add Dummies.com to your Favorites list. Later in this chapter, "Bookmark and Revisit Your Favorite Websites" explains how to go to your favorite websites by selecting sites on the Favorites list.

TIP

You can change the text in the Favorites panel before you select the Add button. However, there's usually no need to change the text unless it's overly long or unclear.

Browsing the web consists of entering addresses, following links, going forward and back, and revisiting your favorite websites. Relatively simple activities can absorb hours.

TIP

7. Keep Edge open if you want to go on to the next topic in this chapter.

FIGURE 6-3

Open Multiple Pages in Separate Tabs

1. Open Edge if it isn't already open.

2. Go to the Google website at www.google.com. You can get there by typing **www.google.com** in the address bar and pressing Enter.

3. Select the New Tab button (or press Ctrl+T). This button is located to the right of the rightmost tab, as shown in **Figure 6-4, top.** The Where to Next? web page appears, as shown in **Figure 6-4, middle.** What's more, a new tab (not coincidentally called New Tab) appears at the top of the screen.

4. On the new tab, enter **www.dummies.com** in the address bar and press Enter. You open the Dummies website on the second tab, as shown in **Figure 6-4, bottom.** Now two websites are open in Edge. Google.com is open on the first tab; Dummies.com is open on the second. Notice the web page names on the tabs.

   To close a tab, select its Close button (the X) or make sure that you are looking at the page you want to close and press Ctrl+W.

   TIP

5. Select the first tab, the one with the name Google. You return to the Google website.

Browsing in multiple tabs allows you to keep one page open while visiting another, perhaps to compare information or to follow a different thought.

TIP

The keyboard shortcut for switching between tabs is Ctrl+Tab.

6. Select the Show Tab Previews button. This button is located to the right of the New Tab button (refer to **Figure 6-4, top**). Selecting the New Tab Previews button displays thumbnail images of websites that are open so that you can tell which website is which. Select the Hide Tab Previews button to close the thumbnail images (the button is where the Show Tab Previews button used to be).

New Tab button

Show Tab Previews button

New tab   **Switch between tabs**

FIGURE 6-4

7. Select the Close button (the X) on the Dummies.com tab to close that particular tab. Close tabs when you want to reduce clutter and simplify switching among open tabs.

TIP

The keyboard shortcut for closing the current tab is Ctrl+W. (*W?* Long story.)

Search for Anything

1. With Edge open, go to the address bar and type **travel.** A list of websites with the word *travel* appears, as Edge attempts to match what you type with a page that you have browsed. (Ignore this list for this exercise, but take advantage of it later.) Select Bing Search on the right side of the address bar to open the Bing website.

TIP

You can search the Internet from the Start screen without opening Edge. Type a search term in the Web Search box. The Search panel lists items pertaining to the search term you entered, including ideas for web searches. Select a web-related item to search with Edge.

2. A search results page appears, as shown in **Figure 6-5.** The results come from www.bing.com, which is the default search engine for Edge. A *search engine* is simply a website that provides links to web pages that match your search. (That definition, however, ignores the complex process going on behind the scenes.)

3. Scroll down the page of search results. Select any link you want to follow. If you get to the bottom of the page, select the Next button to see more search results.

TIP

Some of the "search results" are advertisements. In Bing searches, the results at the top of the page and the right side of the page are paid for. Be careful of these advertisements, which are designed to sell you something, not to provide information. If you prefer not to see advertisements on web pages, see "Block Ads on Web Pages," later in this chapter.

4. Return to the previous screen by selecting the Back button (or pressing Alt+left arrow).

Search results (and advertisements)

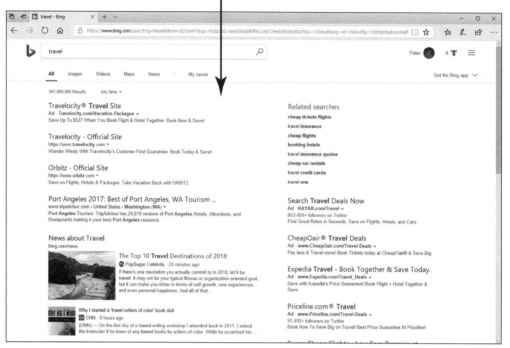

FIGURE 6-5

5. Select the address bar and type **travel new mexico** (no capitals needed). As you type, potential matches for your terms appear in the drop-down list. If you see an item matching the search you want, select it in the list. Otherwise, press Enter.

TIP

Different search engines turn up different results. Other search engines include Google (www.google.com), Ask (www.ask.com), and Yahoo (www.yahoo.com). To use one of these search engines when exploring the web, enter its address in the address bar.

6. Note the tabs at the top of the Bing page, below the Search box. The first tab is All, which contains the results you see by default. Additional tabs vary with the search. Select each of the tabs, which may include any of the following:

- **Images** displays pictures matching your terms.

- **Videos** displays clips and snippets related to your search terms.

- **Maps** will help you get there.

- **News** displays search results from recent news, instead of all the results of the broader web.

7. Leave Edge open if you want to move on to the next topic.

Bookmark and Revisit Your Favorite Websites

1. Open Edge, if it isn't already open, and go to your favorite website on the Internet (or if you don't have a personal favorite, go to mine: www.google.com/advanced_search). If you've spent any time on the Internet, you soon find websites that you want to visit again and again. Rather than memorize the addresses of these websites, you can add them to your Favorites list to make revisiting them quite easy.

2. Select the Add to Favorites or Reading List button (located on the right side of the address bar; it's shaped like a star). The Favorites panel opens, as shown in **Figure 6-6.** Use this panel to describe the websites you want to revisit, and store their names in the Favorites panel (you'll take a look at the Favorites panel in Step 4).

3. Before selecting the Add button to add your favorite website to the Favorites list, consider doing the following:

- Enter a shorter, more concise, more descriptive name in the Name text box.

- Open the Save In menu and select a folder name to store the website in a folder. (Step 8 explains how to create folders of your own.)

4. To verify that the website you are currently visiting has been added to the Favorites list, select the Hub button, select the Favorites button in the Hub panel (if it isn't already selected), and look for your website in the Favorites panel, as shown in **Figure 6-7.**

5. Select the Back button to go to the website you visited previously. This button is located in the upper-left corner of the screen. Next, select the Hub button and, in the list of bookmarked websites, select the website you bookmarked in Step 3 (see **Figure 6-7**). Your favorite website opens on the screen.

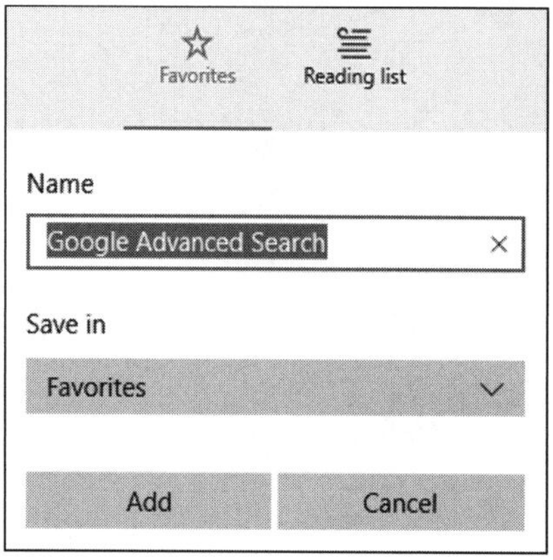

FIGURE 6-6

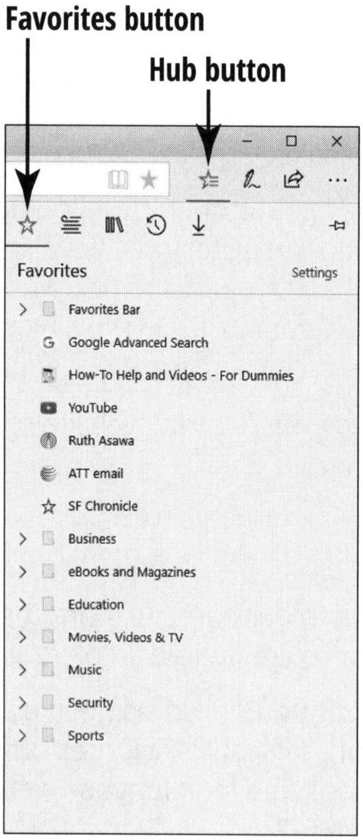

Favorites button

Hub button

FIGURE 6-7

TIP

Don't hesitate to bookmark a website that you expect to revisit. Unless you bookmark it and add it to your Favorites list, you might not be able to find it again.

TIP

To remove a website from the Favorites list, display the Favorites list, move your finger or the pointer over the website's name, display the context menu, and select Delete.

6. You can make the Favorites bar appear below the address bar, as shown in **Figure 6-8.** Merely by clicking or tapping a website name on the Favorites bar, you can go straight to a favorite website without having to open the Favorites panel. To display the Favorites bar, open the Favorites panel and select Settings (refer to **Figure 6-8**). In the Settings panel, choose Show the Favorites Bar (refer to **Figure 6-8**). Any website you really, really like is a candidate for the Favorites bar.

7. Select the Hub button and then select Favorites to open the Favorites panel (refer to **Figure 6-7**). From here, you can manage websites that you have deemed your favorites:

- **Reorder the websites and folders:** Drag a website or folder up or down in the Favorites panel until it lands in the right place.

- **Remove a website (or folder):** Display the folder or website's context menu (right-click or touch it with your finger). Then choose Delete.

- **Create a folder:** Display the context menu by right-clicking or touching a part of the panel. Then choose Create New Folder on the context menu, scroll to the bottom of the Favorites panel, and type the folder's name.

- **Rename a website (or folder):** Display the context menu, choose Rename, and enter a new name.

TIP

Folders can be a big help in organizing and finding bookmarks in the Favorites panel. If you're the type who likes to bookmark websites, give some thought to creating folders to store your bookmarks.

8. Leave Edge open if you want to move on to the next topic.

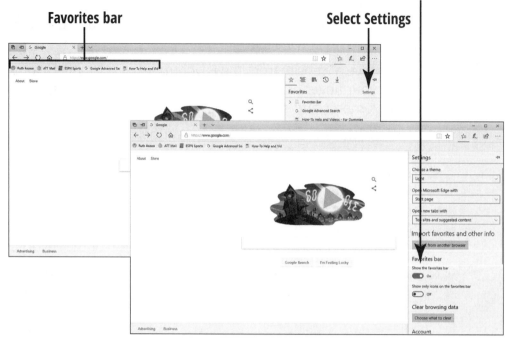

Favorites bar

Choose Show the Favorites bar

Select Settings

FIGURE 6-8

Explore Edge Features

1. Go to your absolute favorite web page so that you can pin this web page to the Start screen. Select the More Actions button (it's located in the upper-right corner of the screen). Then choose Pin to This Page to Start on the drop-down menu and select Yes in the confirmation dialog box that asks whether you really want to pin this web page to the Start menu.

2. Close Edge and then go to the Start screen and select your favorite web page's tile. By selecting this tile, you do two things at one time — you start Edge and open it to your favorite website. Isn't that convenient?

3. Select the Hub button, and in the panel, select the History button. As shown in **Figure 6-9,** the History panel opens. This panel offers the means to backtrack to websites you visited in the past hour, the past day, or the previous week.

History button   Clear history

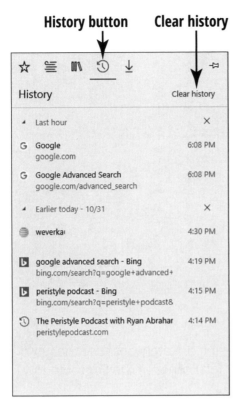

FIGURE 6-9

4. Scroll to the bottom of the History panel to delve into ancient history and see websites you visited some time ago. Select a website to open it in Edge.

TIP

To erase your browsing history and remove all web page names from the History panel, select the Clear History link (shown in **Figure 6-9**).

5. Steps 3 and 4 demonstrate how Edge keeps track of web pages you visited, but what if you resent this kind of snooping? You can browse the web without letting Edge keep a historical record of the websites you visited. To browse in private, select the Settings and More button (it shows three dots and is located in the upper-right corner of the screen) and choose New InPrivate Window in the drop-down menu. Edge opens a second, "InPrivate" window, as shown in **Figure 6-10.** Websites you visit privately are not recorded in the History panel. Close the InPrivate window for now (or browse a while and then close it).

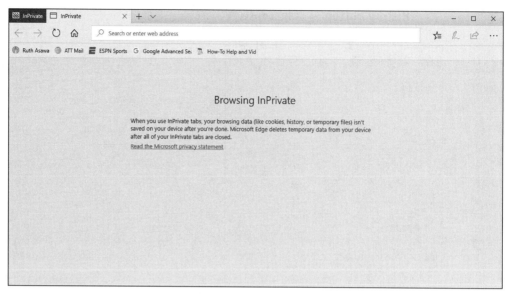

FIGURE 6-10

TIP

You can tell when you're browsing privately because the word *InPrivate* appears in the upper-left corner of the Edge window (see **Figure 6-10**).

6. When you start Edge, you see the start page, which offers websites and news stories that Microsoft thinks you will like (refer to **Figure 6-1**). You can, however, decide for yourself what you want to see when Edge starts. Select the Hub button, select the Favorites button to go to the Favorites tab, and choose Settings. The Settings panel opens, as shown in **Figure 6-11.** Under Microsoft Open Edge With, tell Edge what you want to see first thing:

- **Start page:** Contains websites and news stories that Microsoft thinks you will like based on your browsing history (refer to **Figure 6-1**).

- **New tab page:** You see the Where to Next? page with an address bar and links to popular websites (refer to **Figure 6-4, middle**).

- **Previous pages:** You can see web pages that you were reviewing the last time you closed Edge.

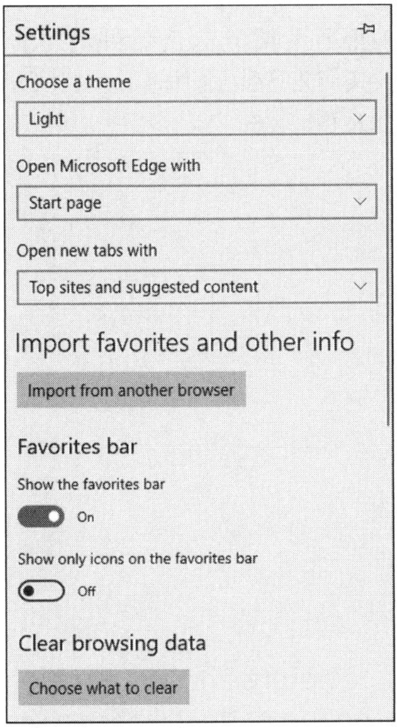

FIGURE 6-11

- **A specific page or pages:** After you choose this option, enter the address of the web page you want to see and select the Save button. You can enter more than one web page to open more than one when you start Edge.

7. Close Edge or keep reading if you're inclined to find out how to turn off the ads on web pages.

Block Ads on Web Pages

1. As you soon find out if you spend any time on the web, web pages are full of cumbersome advertisements. They often get in the way. How would you like to strip the ads from the web pages you visit? You can do that by installing an app from the Microsoft Store called Adblock Plus. Chapter 9 explains how to install an app from the Microsoft Store. Close Edge, go to the Microsoft Store, and install Adblock Plus now (and visit Chapter 9, if necessary). Installing takes only half a minute. I'll wait for you here.

2. The first time you open Edge after Adblock Plus is installed, you see the message screen shown in **Figure 6-12.** Select the Turn It On button. Then go to a web page of your choice.

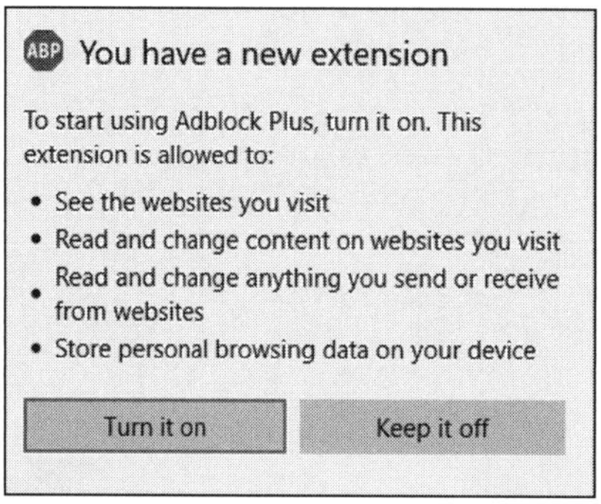

FIGURE 6-12

3. **Figure 6-13** shows the same web page before and after Adblock Plus was installed. Notice the large ad at the top of the first Edge screen. This ad is absent from the same screen on the bottom of the figure. After you install Adblock Plus, the Adblock Plus button (with the letters ABP) appears in the upper-right corner of the screen (refer to **Figure 6-13**). A number next to the button tells you how many ads were blocked on the web page you're visiting.

4. Click the ABP button. You see the drop-down menu shown in **Figure 6-14.** It also tells you how many ads were blocked. If for some reason you want to see ads on a web page, open the drop-down menu and select Enabled on This Site to disable Adblock Plus. You have to select the Refresh button in Edge (it's located next to the Home button) to see the ads.

5. Click or tap anywhere on the web page to close the Adblock Plus drop-down menu.

Advertisement   **Adblock Plus (ABP) button**

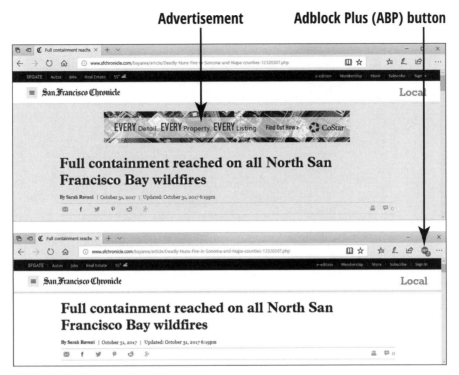

FIGURE 6-13

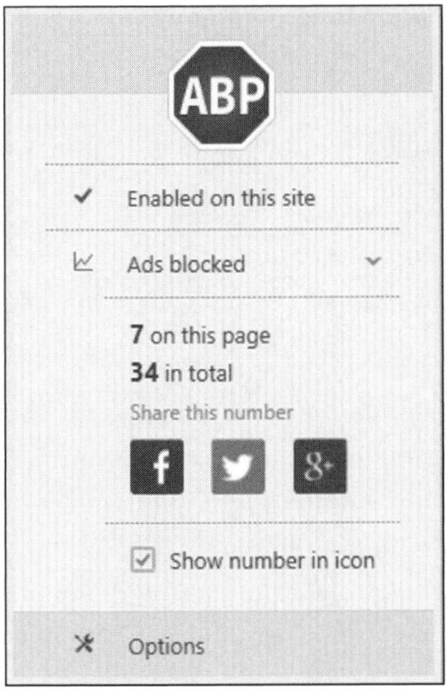

FIGURE 6-14

Chapter 7
Emailing Family and Friends

E very day, billions of email messages circle the globe, conveying greetings, news, jokes, even condolences.

Email also provides a way to send and receive *attachments*, such as documents or photos. Who needs faxes or postcards?

The Mail app gives you access to email using your Microsoft Account. Your Microsoft Account can be associated with an email address from any email service provider, including Microsoft's own Hotmail (`www.hotmail.com`), Live (`www.live.com`), Outlook (`www.outlook.com`), or Xbox (`www.xbox.com`). You can also use email services such as Yahoo (`www.yahoo.com`) and Gmail (`www.gmail.com`) without having a Micro-soft Account. However, you have to access non–Microsoft Account email using a web browser or an app other than Microsoft's Mail app. See Chapter 6 for information on browsing the web.

In this chapter, you use the Mail app for email. You compose, format, and send email, files, and pictures. You also discover how to respond to incoming email.

TIP

If you don't have a physical keyboard, see Chapter 1 for information on using the virtual keyboard.

Use the Mail App

1. For email on Windows 10, select the Mail tile on the Start screen or the Mail icon on the taskbar. The Mail app opens. If you're currently signed in to your Microsoft Account, the Mail app knows your email address. (You gave it to Microsoft when you created the account.) This address is listed on the Mail screen, and you're ready to go. If you're not currently signed in using a Microsoft Account, enter your email address and password on the Sign In screen that appears and then select Sign In. (See Chapter 4 for information on creating a Microsoft Account.)

TIP

The first time you use the Mail app, you are invited to "add an account." In other words, Windows 10 offers its help linking an email account you have to the Mail app. Select the Add Account button and follow the onscreen instructions for making an email account available to the Mail app. See "Add an Email Account to Mail," later in this chapter, for more information.

2. When you start the Mail app, you land in the Inbox folder. If you haven't used your Microsoft Account for email, you probably don't have any messages in your Inbox folder. Who would have written you already? You may, however, see a message or two from Microsoft.

3. On the Inbox screen, select the Expand/Collapse button, as shown in **Figure 7-1.** The Folders panel expands and you can see the names of all your folders in the Folders panel. In the Mail app, email is kept in folders.

TIP

The number beside each folder name tells you how many unread email messages are in each folder.

4. Select any of the following folders in the Folders panel and then select the Expand/Collapse button to return to the Mail panel (you have to select More in the Folders panel to see some of these folders):

- **Inbox:** Email you have received but not moved elsewhere appears here, including both read and unread email.

- **Archive:** The Mail app provides this folder for email that you want to keep on hand for archival purposes.

- **Drafts:** As you compose email (next section), you can save your message as a draft until you are ready to send it.

- **Junk:** Messages are moved here — either automatically or by you — instead of the Inbox, if they are suspected of being, well, *junk*. The more common term for unwanted email is *spam*. (It's a long story.) You may want to check this folder occasionally to see whether a message was misfiled here.

- **Sent:** Copies of the email you send are stored here, appropriately enough.

- **Trash:** Self-explanatory? You can move deleted messages out of the Trash folder if you change your mind about deleting them.

Select the Expand/Collapse button to expand the Folders panel

Select to conduct a search

New Mail button

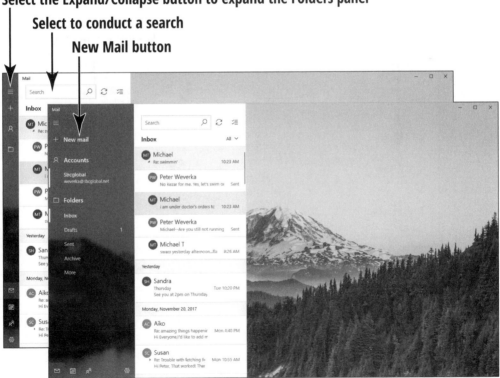

FIGURE 7-1

TIP

You may see other folders in the Folders panel besides the folders described here. If you linked the Mail app to an email account with other folders, those folders are also listed in the Folders panel.

5. Proceed to the next section, "Write an Email Message."

TIP

To search for stray email messages, go to the Search box, and enter the content you're searching for. For example, enter a subject, sender, or something in the message.

Write an Email Message

1. To compose an email message in the Mail app, select the New Mail button (it looks like a plus sign) in the upper-left corner of the screen (refer to **Figure 7-1**). (It doesn't matter which folder you're in when you select this button.) The Compose screen appears, as shown in **Figure 7-2.**

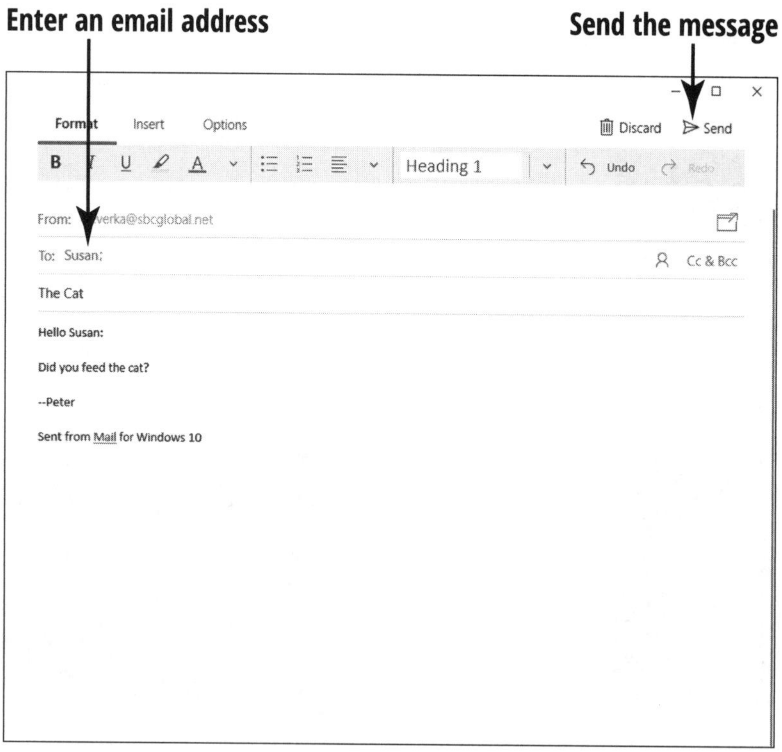

Enter an email address   **Send the message**

FIGURE 7-2

2. In the To box, type an email address. If the Mail app recognizes the address because you've sent email to or received email from the person to whom you're addressing your message, a pop-up box appears so that you can select the person's address without having to type it. Press the Tab key, touch the screen, or use the mouse to move to the next option.

To send email to more than one person at one time, select the Cc & Bcc button (located to the right of the address line). Then type a recipient's address in the Cc box (and the Bcc box as well, if you want to send a blind copy without revealing you've done so). (Once upon a time, *CC* stood for *carbon copy,* and then it became *courtesy copy.*) Technically, it makes no difference whether you use additional To addresses or the CC.

3. Enter a few words in the Subject box describing your message's content or purpose.

4. Select below the Subject line. Type your message. Avoid all caps — purists consider caps to be SHOUTING! No need to press Enter as you approach the end of the line — this isn't a typewriter.

Some people start a message with a salutation, such as *Hi Peter*, but many people do not. Some people sign email using their initials. Email can be as formal or casual as you choose to make it.

Words underlined with a red squiggle aren't recognized by Windows 10 and may be misspelled. Right-click or tap and hold to see a pop-up menu, and choose Proofing on the menu. You see a list of suggested spellings. Choose the correct spelling if it is on the list. You can also go to the Options tab and select the Spelling button there.

5. When you're ready to send the message, select the Send button (you'll find it in the upper-right corner of the Compose window; refer to **Figure 7-2**). If you decide not to send the message, select the Discard button.

Email you compose but haven't sent yet is kept in the Drafts folder. You can postpone writing a message and finish it later by going to the Drafts folder and opening your message there. To go the Drafts folder, select the Expand/Collapse button (if necessary) and then select Drafts in the All Folders panel.

6. If you select the Send button, your message is sent and you return to the folder you were in at the beginning of Step 1.

7. Repeat from Step 1 as needed.

TIP

Mail puts a signature at the bottom of email messages: "Sent from Mail for Windows 10." If you don't like this signature or want to put your own signature at the bottom of all the emails you send, select the Settings button on the bottom of the Folders panel. The Settings panel opens. Select Signature and either turn off signatures or enter a signature of your own.

Format Email

1. If you want to add bold, italics, or other formats to email, select the text you want to fancy up in the Compose window, as shown in **Figure 7-3.** If no text is selected, your formatting will apply to the word in which the *cursor* (the blinking vertical line in the content) is located.

   - **Mouse:** Click and drag the mouse pointer over the text you want to select.

   - **Touchscreen:** Tap and drag over the text you want to select.

   - **Keyboard:** With the cursor at the beginning of the text you want to select, hold down the Shift key as you press the right or down arrow to select text. Release the Shift key only after you have completed your selection.

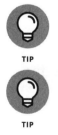
TIP

TIP

To apply formatting to one word, double-click or double-tap that word to select it and display the app bar in one step.

The keyboard shortcut to select all text is Ctrl+A. No mouse or touchscreen method is quite so complete.

2. Using the commands on the Format tab, select from the following formatting options:

   - **Bold:** Bold is used for emphasis to make text stand out.

   - **Italic:** Although italic can also be used for emphasis, it may be harder to read than normal or bold text.

   - **Underline:** Because links are usually underlined automatically, you may want to avoid underlining text that isn't a link.

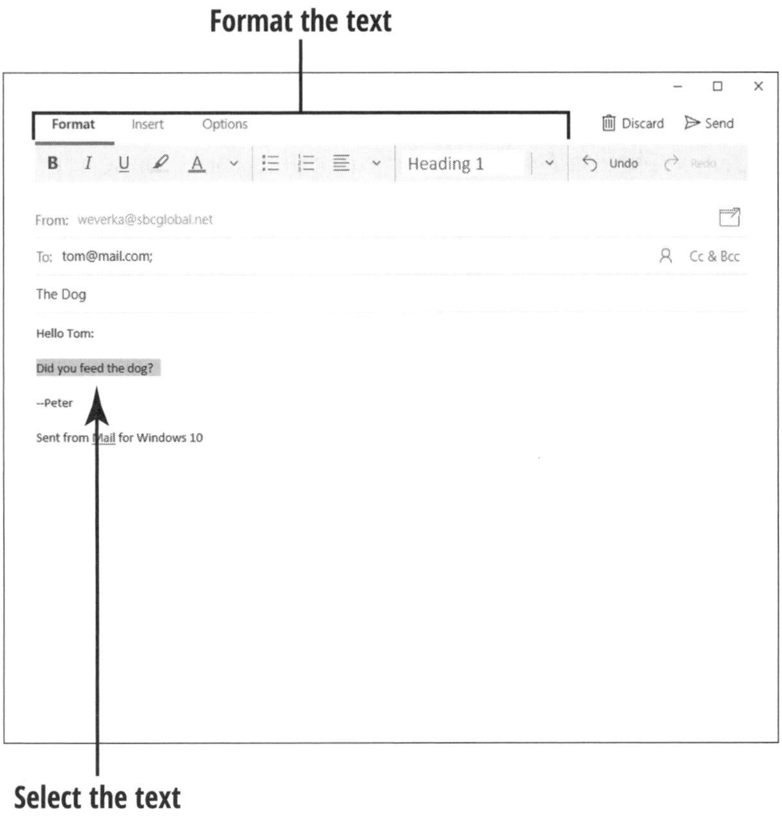

Format the text

Select the text

FIGURE 7-3

- **Bulleted list:** Select the Bullets button and enter items for the list. As you enter items, Mail attaches a bullet point to the start of each line.

- **Numbered list:** Select the Numbering button and type the list. As you type, Mail assigns a number to each line.

- **Styles:** Choose a style from the drop-down menu. A style applies many formats simultaneously. Heading 1, for example, enlarges the text and turns it blue.

See Chapter 1 for information on using the virtual keyboard's emoticons.

To create a hyperlink, go to the Insert tab and select the Link button. Then enter the address destination of the hyperlink in the address bar that appears. See Chapter 6 for more information about hyperlinks.

3. When you finish formatting the text, select the Send button.

Send Files and Pictures

1. To send a file or picture with your email message, go to the Insert tab. As shown in **Figure 7-4,** the Insert tab offers tools for sending files and pictures.

2. Select the Files button to send a file. The Open dialog box appears. Locate and select the file you want to send and then select the Open button in the dialog box. You can send more than one file with an email message. In the Compose window, files you want to send appear as thumbnails under the heading "Attachments" (see **Figure 7-4**). Click the X button on a file if you change your mind about sending it.

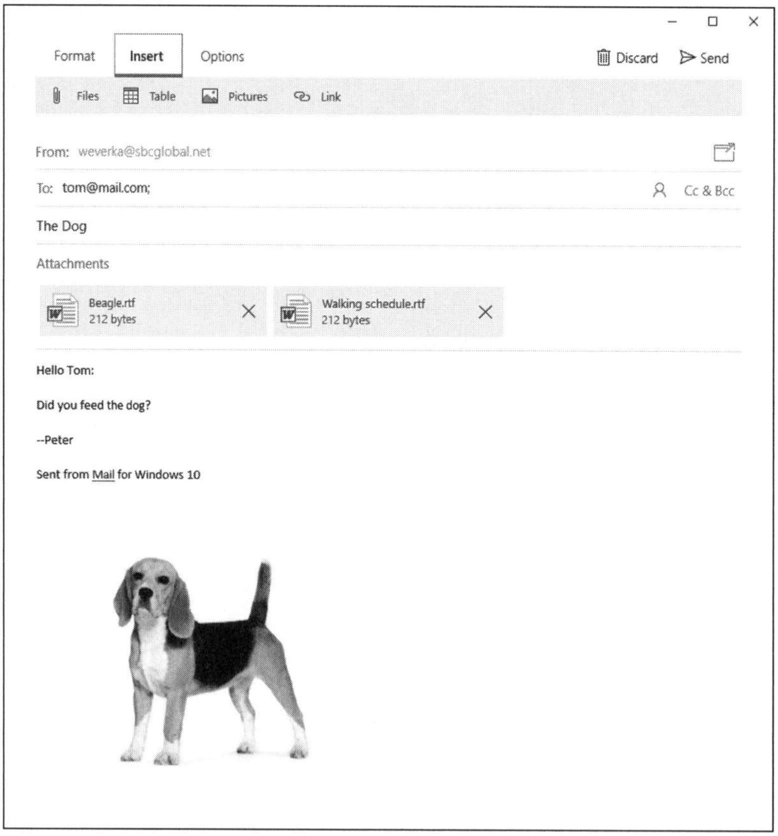

FIGURE 7-4

3. To send a picture with an email message, place the cursor where you want the picture to be. Then select the Pictures button on the Insert tab. The Open dialog box appears. Select the picture and then click or tap the Insert button.

TIP

You can format pictures before sending them. Click or tap a picture to select it in the Compose window. The Picture tab appears. Using the tools on this tab, you can rotate, crop, and resize pictures.

4. When you have finished attaching your files and pictures, select the Send button to send them on their merry way.

TIP

Chapter 10 explains how you can use the Photos app to send photos to others.

Read and Respond to Incoming Email

1. On the Start screen, select the Mail tile. The Mail app opens to the Inbox folder.

2. Select a message under the Inbox heading. The content of the message appears to the right, as shown in **Figure 7-5.**

TIP

In email terminology, bouncing messages back and forth with someone about the same subject is called a *conversation.* When you select an email message that is part of a conversation, the other messages in the conversation appear as well so that you can select and reread them (refer to **Figure 7-5**).

3. After you read the message, you can respond to or forward it if you want. Select the Reply or Reply All button to reply; select the Forward button to forward the message. Selecting any of these buttons starts a new message (refer to **Figure 7-2**) that includes the text of the original message. The subject line is automatically *RE: [the original subject]* (in the case of replies) or *FW: [the original subject]* (in the case of forwarded messages). Complete your message and select the Send button.

TIP

Reply All sends your response to all the other recipients, if a message is addressed to more than one person. The Reply option sends your response only to the sender. Select Forward to send the selected message to someone else. You can add your own text or remove portions of the forwarded message in the process.

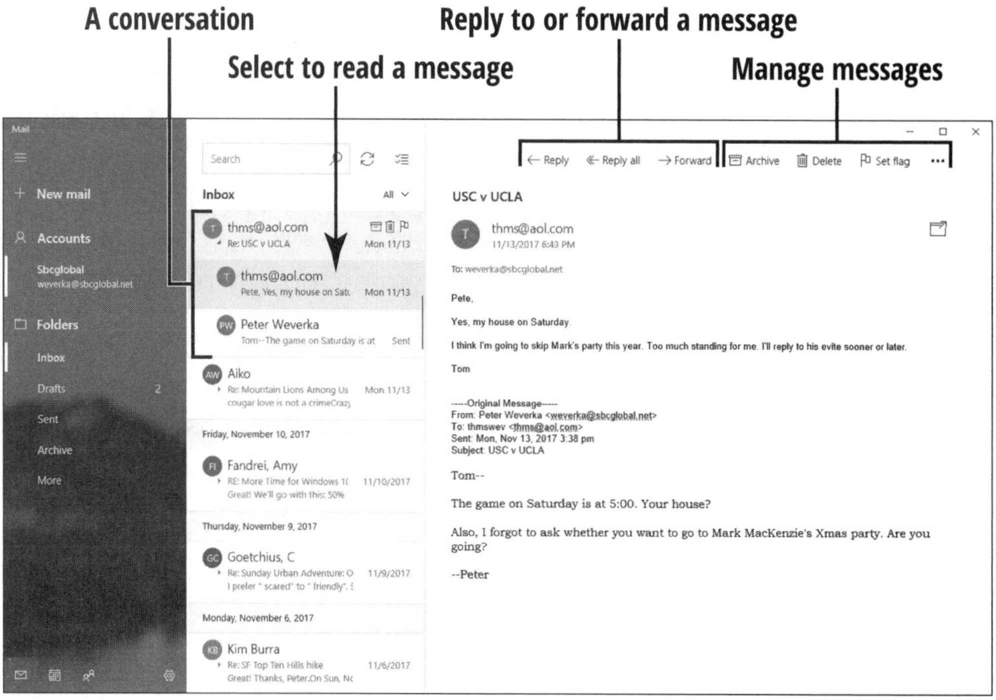

A conversation　　　　Reply to or forward a message

Select to read a message　　　　Manage messages

FIGURE 7-5

TIP

See the sections "Write an Email Message" and "Format Email," earlier in this chapter, for more information on composing an email message.

4. Select any message in the Inbox category. Note the following options for managing messages (to take advantage of some of these options, select the More button in the upper-right corner of the screen):

- **Delete:** Use this option to delete the message.

- **Set Flag:** Use this option to place a flag icon next to the message in the Inbox so that you remember to deal with the message later on. You can swipe right to flag a message.

- **Mark Unread/Read:** Use this option if you want the message to appear unread (marked with a horizontal blue line in the Inbox). Some people do this with messages they want to deal with later.

- **Move:** Use this option to move the selected email from one folder to another. To access the Move option, select the More button, the three dots on the right side of the toolbar. After you select Move on the More drop-down menu, select a folder in the Move To panel to move your email.

TIP

If you add email accounts from providers such as Gmail, you may see additional categories or options. See the section "Add an Email Account to Mail" at the end of the chapter.

Change Mail Settings

1. In Mail, display the Settings panel, shown in **Figure 7-6.** To display the Settings panel, display the Folder panel and select the Settings button (you'll find it in the lower-right corner of the Folder panel). The Settings panel appears on the right side of the Mail screen.

Settings

Manage Accounts

Personalization

Quick Actions

Automatic Replies

Reading

Signature

Notifications

Email security

What's new

Help

Trust Center

Feedback

About

FIGURE 7-6

2. On the Accounts panel, select Manage Accounts, and then select the email account with settings that need a change. The Account Settings dialog box appears (see **Figure 7-7, left**).

3. Negotiate the Account Settings dialog box and select the Save button:

- **Account Name:** The name of the email service provider. You can change this, if you want. I might use *Peter's email.*

- **Change Mailbox Sync Settings:** Click or tap here to open the Sync Settings dialog box (see **Figure 7-7, right**) and change how and when the Mail app collects email. Skip to Step 5 if you choose this option.

- **Delete Account:** Deletes the email account. The Mail app is no longer associated with the account after you delete it.

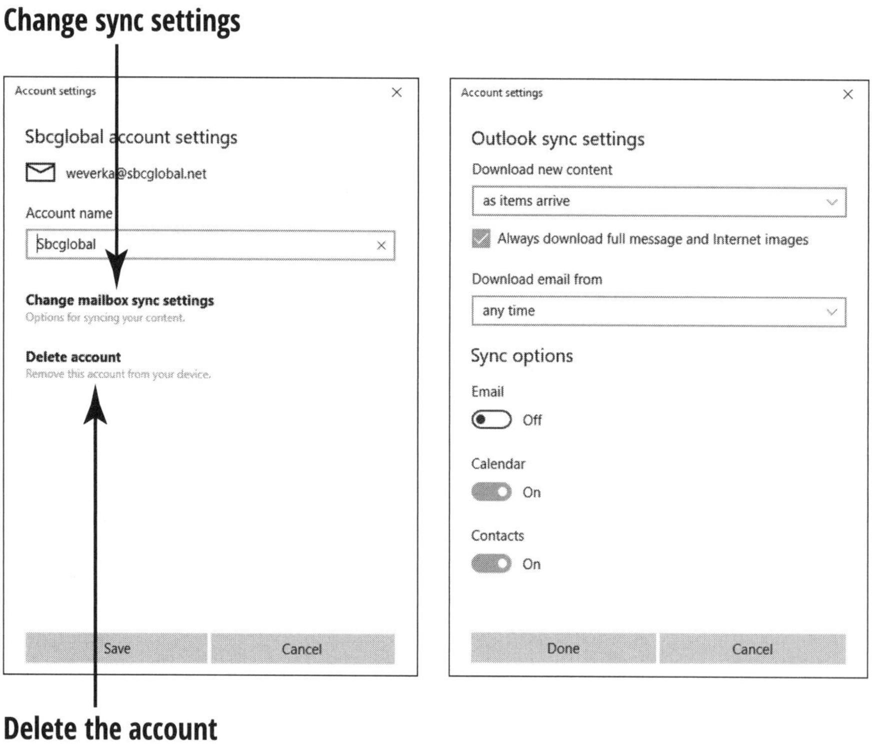

Change sync settings

Delete the account

FIGURE 7-7

4. In the Sync Settings dialog box (refer to **Figure 7-7, right**), choose settings and select the Done button:

- **Download New Content:** If you don't want email constantly streaming into your Inbox, you can change this setting to every

15 or 30 minutes, Hourly, or only when you select the Sync This View button (which is located next to the Search button).

- **Always Download Full Message and Internet Images:** Select this option if pictures aren't appearing in your incoming email messages.

- **Download Email From:** You can limit how far back to download messages to your computer. This setting isn't relevant in a new email account.

- **Sync Options:** Turn the Email setting to Off only if you don't want the Mail app to receive email from the account. Turn the other two settings, Calendar and Contact, to Off if you don't want the Mail app to retrieve information from the Calendar app or People app.

Add an Email Account to Mail

1. If you have another email address, you can add it to Mail. Adding an account has definite advantages. Instead of going hither and yon to collect your email from different accounts, you can collect all your mail in one place — the Mail app. The following steps explain how to add an existing Gmail account to Mail. In Mail, display the Settings panel (refer to **Figure 7-6**) and then select Manage Accounts.

2. In the Manage Accounts panel, select Add Account.

TIP

Many people have more than one email address. Your Internet service provider probably gave you an email account, and you may have another through work or school. However, this feature isn't for everyone.

3. In the Choose an Account dialog box, select the service with which you have an email account. If your service doesn't appear here, select Other Account. If you have a Gmail address (or you just want to see what's next), select Google.

4. On the Connecting to a Service screen, enter your Gmail address, select Next, and enter your password in the appropriate box. Then select Next. Select the Back button if you don't want to continue.

5. The next screen informs you how your Gmail account will connect with the Mail app. Scroll to the bottom of this screen and select the Allow button.

6. In the dialog box that says you've added an account, select Go to Inbox.

7. Return to the Manage Accounts folder (select the Settings button and choose Manage Accounts in the Settings panel). As shown in **Figure 7-8,** the Manage Accounts panel shows you the names of your accounts. You can switch to a different account by selecting its name in the Manage Accounts panel.

TIP

See the preceding section, "Change Mail Settings," for the steps to review or change settings for your newly added account.

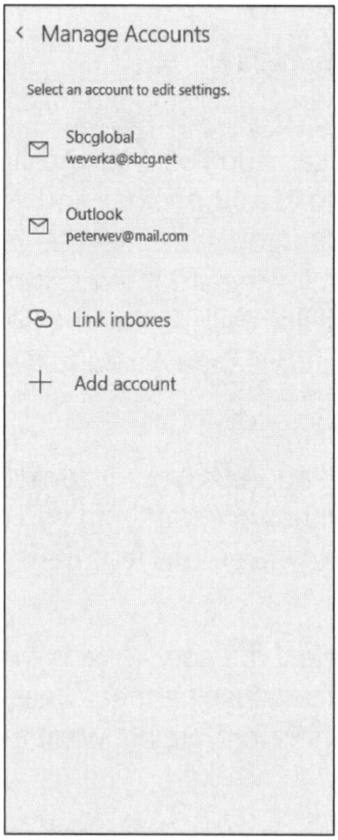

‹ Manage Accounts

Select an account to edit settings.

✉ Sbcglobal
weverka@sbcg.net

✉ Outlook
peterwev@mail.com

⊟ Link inboxes

+ Add account

FIGURE 7-8

Chapter **8**

Exploring Apps for Your Daily Life

This chapter describes a handful of apps that the average Joe or Jane might use every day. It shows how to store contact information — names, email addresses, phone numbers, and the like — in the People app so that you can find this information quickly. You also use the Calendar app to keep track of birthdays, anniversaries, appointments, and other events.

This chapter delves into the Maps app, showing you how to use it to get directions and to look up hotels and restaurants when you're on the go. You see how two Windows 10 apps, Sticky Notes and Alarms & Clock, can help you complete tasks on time, and how WordPad can help you with your word processing chores.

Finally, this chapter demonstrates how to make the Lock screen indicate whether you've received email and how to chat face-to-face with family and friends over the Internet with Skype.

Add Contacts to the People App

TIP

1. On the Start screen, select the People app.

   You need a Microsoft Account to use Mail, Calendar, and People. When you sign in to one, you're signed in to all three apps. See Chapter 4 for information on creating a Microsoft Account.

2. If you haven't signed in already using your Microsoft Account, the Sign In screen appears. Enter your Microsoft Account email address and password, and then select Sign In.

3. What you see first in People depends on whether the app found contact information associated with your Microsoft Account. You may see familiar names or an invitation to connect to other services. For now, add a new contact manually. (You connect to other services later.) Display the New Contact screen by selecting the New Contact button, as shown in **Figure 8-1.**

TIP

   The first time you run the People app, you are greeted with a Welcome screen. Select the Get Started button on this screen. If you manage your email through the Mail app (a subject covered in Chapter 7), you can load contact information from the Mail app into the People App. On the Let's Get Started screen, select the Get Ready button.

4. Much of the information on the New Contact screen (shown in **Figure 8-1**) is optional. Enter the information that you want access to throughout Windows 10, not just in the People app. (For example, think about what you want to access in Mail.) You can enter any person's name and information you want, but let me suggest the following:

   - **Save To:** Ultimately, you may link multiple accounts using the People app. Which account do you want this new contact associated with? For now, only one option may be available.

   - **Name:** Enter the contact's full name.

   - **Mobile Phone:** Select Mobile Phone and note the many categories of phone numbers — Home, Work Company, and so on — on the pop-up list.

   - **Personal Email:** Select Personal Email and notice the three email categories — Personal, Work, and Other — on the pop-up list. Choose a category and enter the contact's email address.

New Contact button

Enter contact info

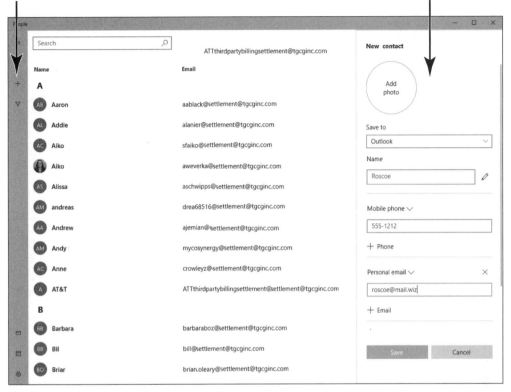

FIGURE 8-1

5. Note the following buttons with plus signs. Select each in turn to see the available options. Add data as you please:

   • **Email:** Add up to two more email addresses.

   • **Phone:** Add up to seven more phone numbers!

   • **Address:** Add up to three mailing addresses.

   • **Other:** Options include Job Title, Significant Other, Website, and Notes, a box for free-form notes.

6. When you're done, select Save to add this contact (or select Cancel to throw away the new contact). The added contact appears on your list of contacts. Select the person's name to see his or her contact information, as shown in **Figure 8-2.**

TIP

Select the Edit button (look for the pencil) to edit a contact's information. After you select the Edit button, the Contact screen appears so that you can edit away.

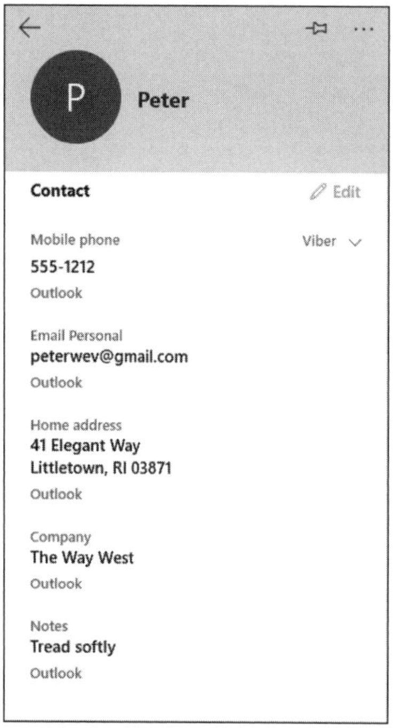

FIGURE 8-2

TIP

You can pin a contact to the taskbar. Select the person's name, display the context menu (by clicking or tapping), and choose Pin to Taskbar.

Delete a Contact

1. Open the People app if the People app isn't already open.

2. In the Contacts list on the left side of the screen, select the name of the contact you want to delete. Especially if your list of contacts is a lengthy one, it pays to go through the list from time to time and delete the names of people you are no longer associated with.

TIP

On the People screen, enter a letter or type a name in the Search box. Entering a letter produces a drop-down list of names that start with the letter you entered. Typing a name produces a list of names. Select a name on the list to go to the name.

3. Select the More button, shown in **Figure 8-3.** Selecting this button opens a drop-down list.

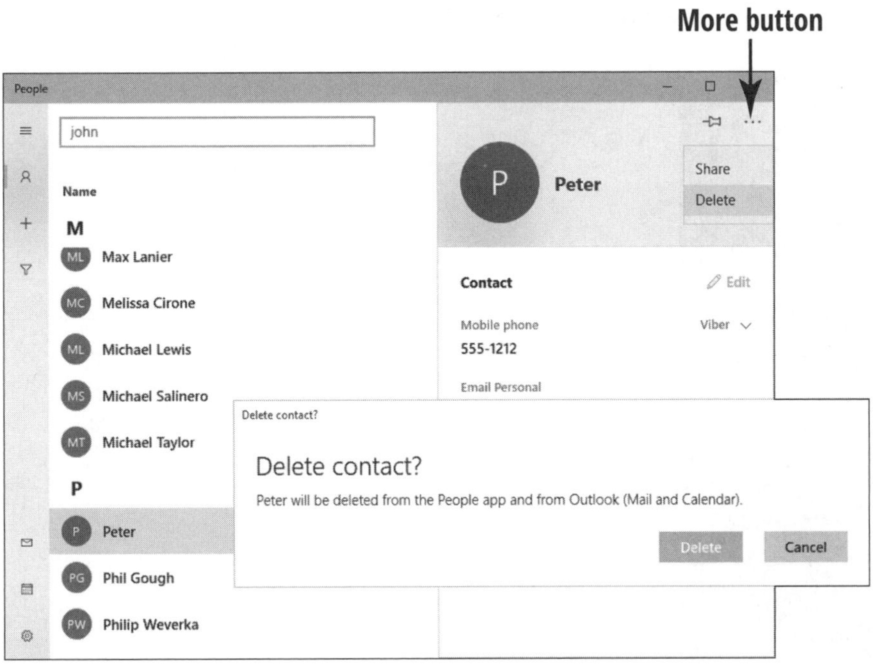

FIGURE 8-3

4. Select Delete on the drop-down list.

5. In the dialog box that asks whether you really want to do it, select the Delete button (refer to **Figure 8-3**).

Add a Birthday or Anniversary to the Calendar

1. To see the calendar and add events, open the Calendar app from the Start screen, as shown in **Figure 8-4.** You may see events and appointments from services you connected to in People or Mail.

2. On the Calendar app bar located along the top of the screen (refer to **Figure 8-4**), select each of the following formats:

   • **Day:** This format displays a single day with a box for each hour. Select arrows near the top of the screen to scroll back or forward one day at a time. Scroll up and down to see more hours in the day.

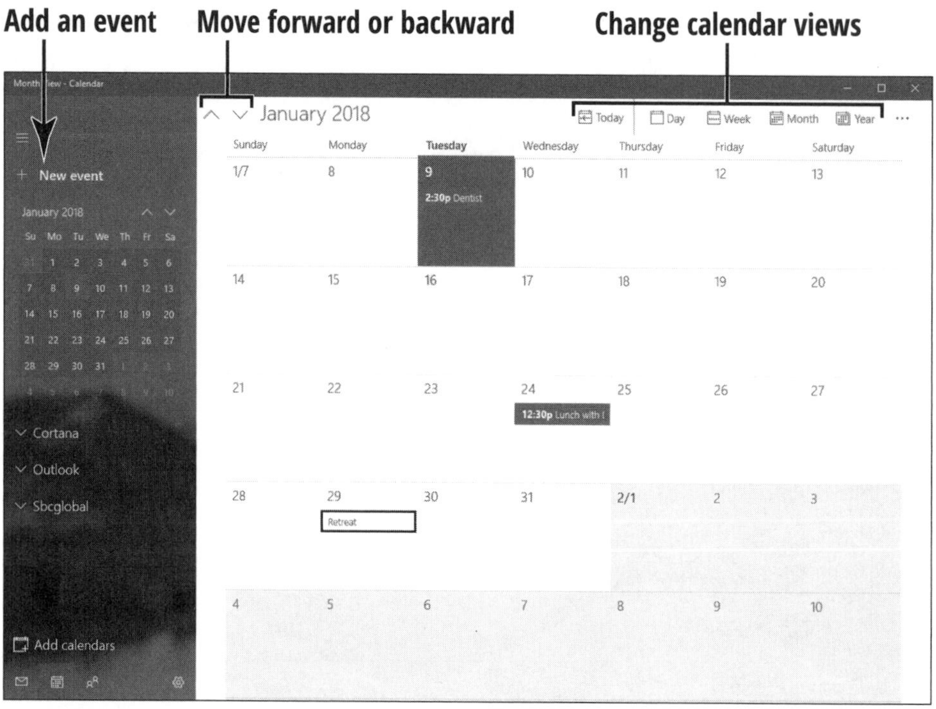

Add an event   **Move forward or backward**   **Change calendar views**

FIGURE 8-4

- **Week:** The current week appears. Scroll or use the arrows to go from hour to hour or week to week.

Open the drop-down menu on the Week button and choose Work Week to see the current workweek (Monday through Friday).

TIP

- **Month:** The current month appears in the classic month layout. (Depending on the size of your screen, you may have to scroll to see this format.) Today is highlighted with a different color. Use arrows near the top to move forward and back a month at a time.

- **Year:** The months of the year appear. You can select a month to open a month in Month view.

Select the Today button on the Calendar app bar to go immediately to today's date on the Calendar.

TIP

3. The Calendar offers two ways to add an event, the short-but-cursory way and the slow-but-thorough way:

- **Short but cursory:** Click or tap the day on which the event is to occur (in the Month format) or the hour and date on which it is to occur (in the Day or Week formats). You see the pop-up window shown in **Figure 8-5.** With luck, this little window is all you need to describe the event. Type the event's name, and if it isn't an all-day event, deselect the All Day check box (if necessary) and use the start time and end time menus to describe when the event starts and ends. You can also type the event's location. Select the Done button when you finish describing the event (or select the More Details link to open the Details screen and go to Step 4).

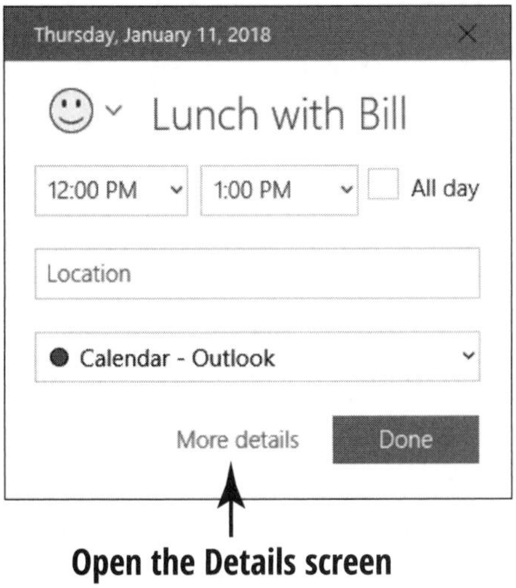

Open the Details screen

FIGURE 8-5

- **Slow but thorough:** Select the New Event button (refer to **Figure 8-4**). The Details screen appears, as shown in **Figure 8-6.** Move on to Step 4.

4. Under Details, enter or (or change) any of the following data for the event:

- **Event Name:** Describe the event in one to three words. The description you enter will appear on your calendar.

- **Location:** If listing the location will help you get to the event on time, by all means list it. The location, like the event name, appears on the calendar.

- **Start and End:** Select the calendar icon, and on the pop-up menu that appears, choose the day on which the event begins and then the day on which it ends.

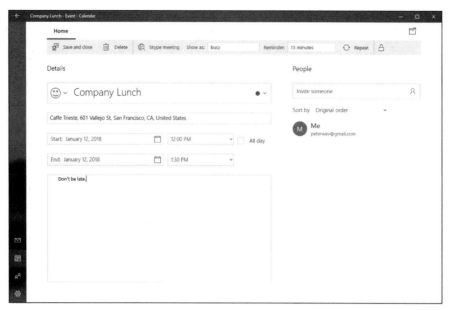

FIGURE 8-6

TIP

- **Hours/All Day:** If this isn't an all-day event, deselect the All Day check box, if necessary. Then use the drop-down menus to describe when the event will occur.

  If the event is one that recurs, you can schedule it on a weekly, monthly, or yearly basis on the calendar. Weekly staff meetings, birthdays, and anniversaries are examples of recurring events. Select the Repeat button on the app bar along the top of the screen to schedule a recurring event. Then, using the Repeat options that appear in the Details screen, describe how often the event occurs, when it occurs, and when it will cease occurring.

- **Event Description:** Describe the event in detail if you think it's necessary. Should you wear the tux or zoot suit? The ball gown or the formal dress? This is the place to record your thoughts on the matter.

5. Optionally, use the commands on the app bar at the top of the screen to further describe the event:

   - **Show As:** Choose an option on this menu if you share your calendar with someone, such as a receptionist, who may schedule you for other events. You can declare yourself free, tentative, busy, or out of the office.

- **Reminder:** How far in advance of the event do you want Calendar to display a notification? Choose None, 5 Minutes, 15 Minutes, 30 Minutes, 1 Hour, 1 12 Hours, 1 Day, or 1 Week.

- **Private:** Select this option (look for the lock symbol) to prevent this event from appearing on a shared or public calendar. The event remains visible on your own screen.

6. When you're done, select the Save and Close button. (Select the Delete button if you don't want to create an event.)

7. On the calendar, your event appears on the specified date and time.

8. To edit an event, select it on the calendar. The Details screen opens. Add or change any detail.

TIP

To delete an event, open it in the Details screen and select the Delete button select the Delete button (a trash can).

TIP

If your Microsoft Account is connected to a third-party service such as Gmail, events from that service appear on your calendar. To load third-party service information into the Calendar app, select the Settings button (in the lower-left corner of the screen) and select Manage Accounts in the Settings panel. You see a list of accounts. Select the account, and in the Account Settings screen, select Change Mailbox Sync Settings. Then, on the Sync Settings screen, choose whether to sync the calendar on the third-party service with the calendar you see in the Calendar screen.

Search and Explore with the Maps App

1. Select the Maps app on the Start menu to open the Maps app. Use this app to locate places and to get driving or walking directions.

2. Click or tap in the Search box. A drop-down list appears. It lists items you already searched for, if you searched already. You can select an item on the list to revisit it.

3. Type **1 california st, san francisco** (you don't need to enter capital letters) in the Search box. As you type, options appear in the Search panel. Select the address you entered, not the names of businesses located at the address. As shown in **Figure 8-7**, the Maps app shows

you where the address is located; it also provides a photo. As well as typing addresses in the Search box, you can enter the names of places and landmarks.

4. Select the Zoom Out button (or press Ctrl+minus sign) on the app bar in the map. Then select the Zoom In button (or press Ctrl+plus sign). The tools on the app bar can help you read the map better (refer to **Figure 8-7**).

Enter an address or search term

Directions button

Zoom in and out

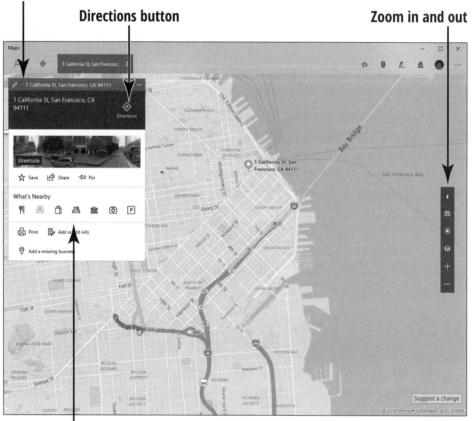

Find restaurants, hotels, and other goodies

FIGURE 8-7

5. Select the Directions button (refer to **Figure 8-7**), which is the button in the upper-left corner near the Search box (or press Ctrl+D). Tools appear to help you get from place to place. Click or tap in the Starting Point box (Box A), and when the drop-down menu appears, choose **1 California St** the address you already entered. In the Destination box (Box B), enter **1501 haight st** and choose the 1051 Haight St address in San Francisco in the drop-down menu that appears.

6. Select the **Get Directions** link. As shown in **Figure 8-8,** the Maps app gives you several sets of driving directions between the two addresses and tells you how long each drive will take. Select a drive in the list to get specific instructions for driving between the two addresses. After you select a drive, you can click or tap the Print icon to print the instructions.

Select a route

Select a tab to return to a previous screen

FIGURE 8-8

7. Are you walking, not driving? In that case, select the Walking icon at the top of the Search panel to get directions for walking between the two locations. You can also select the Transit icon to get directions for getting there by public transportation.

8. Select the Search button (the magnifying glass in the upper-left corner of the screen) and then select **1501 Haight St., San Francisco** in the drop-down menu. You get a detailed look at the streets surrounding this address. Select the Restaurants icon under What's Nearby (refer to **Figure 8-7**) to see restaurants on the map. You can select the name of a restaurant to find out more about it. The What's Nearby icons also provide the means to find attractions, parking, hotels, and other goodies.

9. The Maps app keeps tabs on your travels. Select a tab along the top of the screen to retrace your steps and revisit a map you saw earlier.

Remind Yourself to Do Tasks with Alarms & Clock

1. Select the Alarms & Clock app on the Start menu to open the Alarms & Clock app. Use this convenient little app to remind yourself when something needs doing, find out what time it is in other parts of the world, or time an activity.

2. To make your computer remind you when a task needs completing, select Alarm (if it isn't already selected) on the app bar along the top of the screen. Then select the Add New Alarm button (the plus sign in the lower-right corner). You see the New Alarm screen, shown in **Figure 8-9, left.**

3. Set the alarm to ring in two minutes. Note the time on the clock on your computer and use the scroll arrows on the screen to set the time to two minutes from now. To set the time, click or tap the arrows above and below the hour, minute, and AM/PM settings until you see "In 2 Minutes" on the screen.

4. Click or tap the generic name Alarm (1) and enter a descriptive name in its place. Then select the Save button.

5. In two minutes, the alarm goes off and a notice appears in the lower-right corner of your computer screen (refer to **Figure 8-9, right**). It tells you the task that needs doing. Select Dismiss (or Snooze if you want the alarm to go off one more time in 5 minutes or the Snooze amount you set).

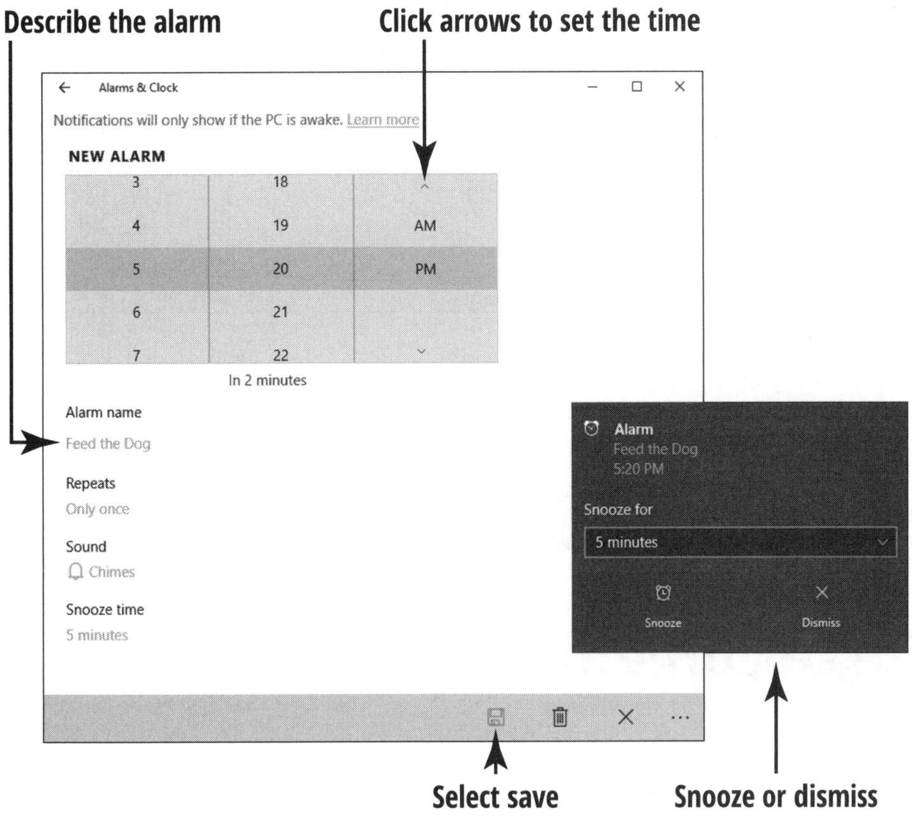

Describe the alarm   **Click arrows to set the time**

Select save   **Snooze or dismiss**

FIGURE 8-9

6. Click or tap the Back button (in the upper-left corner of the Alarms & Clock window) to backtrack. Then select World Clock on the app bar. From the World Clock screen, you can see what time it is in different cities and find out how many hours ahead or behind they are, as shown in **Figure 8-10.** To enter a city on the world map, select the Add New Clock button and enter the city's name in the Enter a Location box.

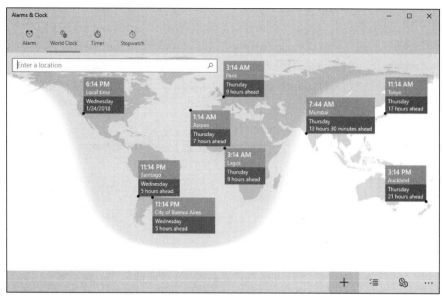

FIGURE 8-10

7. Select Stopwatch on the app bar along the top of the screen. The next time you want to see how long it takes you to complete a task, go to the Stopwatch screen and select the Start button. When the task is complete, return and select Pause.

Write Documents with WordPad

1. Windows 10 comes with a word processing app called WordPad. Word processors are applications that you can use to write letters, reports, and other documents. WordPad isn't as sophisticated as its cousin Microsoft Word, the world's most famous word processor, but it's pretty darn good. And it doesn't cost anything. Moreover, you can open documents created in Word in WordPad. Word can read WordPad documents, too. To start WordPad, type **WordPad** in the Search box in the lower-left corner of the Windows screen and choose WordPad on the pop-up menu. WordPad opens, as shown in **Figure 8-11.**

The following UI text appears in the figure:

Document - WordPad

File   Home   View

Cut   Calibri   36   A⁺ A⁻   Find
Copy   B I U abc x₂ x² A ▾ ✎ ▾   Picture Paint Date and Insert   Replace
Paste   drawing time object   Select all
Clipboard   Font   Paragraph   Insert   Editing

The quick brown

fox

jumped over |

the

lazy dog.

100%

FIGURE 8-11

TIP

For reasons I don't understand, WordPad isn't available on the alphabetical list of app names on the Start screen. The only way to start WordPad is to type its name in the Search box, pin WordPad to the Start menu, or pin it to the taskbar and start it from there. Chapter 5 explains pinning apps to the Start menu and taskbar.

2. Type a few words and then select the words by dragging over them. You can tell when words are selected because they are highlighted. After you select words, you can reformat them. Open the Font Family menu on the toolbar and choose your favorite font. Then open the Font Size menu and choose a font size. By changing fonts and font sizes, you can change the words' appearance.

3. Click or tap the Bold button (the B) on the Home tab (or press Ctrl+B). The words are boldfaced. Boldfacing, italicizing (select the Italic button), and underlining (select the Underline button) are other ways to change the appearance of words.

4. Select the Linespace button and choose an option — 1.0, 1.15, 1.5, or 2 — on the drop-down list that appears. In this way you can change the amount of space between lines. For example, choosing 2 double-spaces the text you selected.

TIP

You can choose formatting commands *before* you start typing. The commands you choose are applied to the words you write next. It isn't necessary to write the words first and then select them to make formatting changes.

5. Drag the Zoom slider in the lower-right corner of the screen to the right (or click or tap the Zoom In button on the right side of the slider). Zooming in increases the size of text on the screen so that you can see it better. Drag the slider to the left (or click or tap the Zoom Out button) to make the text look smaller.

6. Press Ctrl+S or select the Save button (located in the upper-left corner of the screen) to save your document. You see the Save As dialog box. WordPad documents are saved in the RTF format (RTF stands for *rich text format*). As I mention earlier, Microsoft Word can read and display RTF files. Enter a name for your document and select the Save button.

TIP

Chapter 14 explains how to open, save, and otherwise manage files.

Write a Sticky Note to Yourself

1. Select Sticky Notes on the Start menu to open the Sticky Notes app. A sticky note — like the ones in **Figure 8-12** — appears on the screen. Sticky notes are the digital equivalents of the yellow stick-'em tabs that people attach to their computers and desks. Use sticky notes to remind yourself to do something or be somewhere.

2. Type the note. Then move the pointer over the stripe at the top of the note and drag the note to a corner of the screen.

TIP

You can change the size of a sticky note. Move the pointer over the lower-right corner of the note. When the pointer changes to double arrows, start dragging.

3. Click or tap the Add Note button (refer to **Figure 8-12**). Another sticky note appears. Write a second note and drag it to a corner of the screen.

4. Click or tap the Delete Note button on one of your notes (refer to **Figure 8-12**). A message box asks whether you want to delete the note. Select Delete.

Write a new note   Delete a note

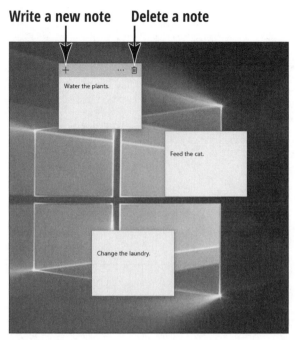

FIGURE 8-12

Tweak Quick Status Settings

TIP

1. Quick Status settings appear on the Lock screen to show you what's what. To change these settings, open the Start screen and select Settings. On the Settings screen, select Personalization. On the Personalization screen, select Lock Screen.

   See Chapter 3 for information about the Lock Screen settings.

2. Scroll to the bottom of the Lock Screen settings to the Choose Apps to Show Quick Status item, as shown in **Figure 8-13.**

3. Some apps can display quick status information on the Lock screen. For example, Mail displays the number of unread messages in the Mail app. To add an app to the Lock screen, select one of the plus signs and choose an app name on the pop-up menu.

4. To change one of the current apps, select its icon and then choose a different app on the pop-up menu.

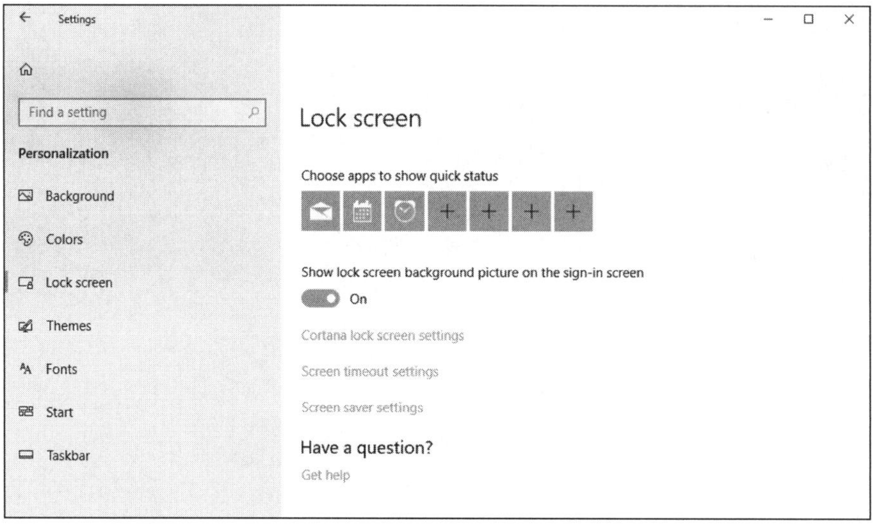

FIGURE 8-13

5. To remove an app from the Lock screen, select it and choose None on the pop-up menu.

6. Return to the Start screen.

Chat Face-to-Face with Skype

1. On the Start screen, select the Skype app. You can use this app to video chat with others. To use Skype, your computer must have audio and video capability. You can also use Skype if a webcam is connected to your computer.

You need to sign in to your Microsoft Account before you use Skype. See Chapter 4 for information about creating a Microsoft Account.

The easiest way to make calls through Skype is to enter the names of the people you want to call on your Contacts list in the People app. See "Add Contacts to the People App," earlier in this chapter.

2. The first time you use the Skype app, the screen asks whether it can access your camera, microphone, and Contacts. Select Yes on all counts.

3. The Skype screen lists the names of people on your Contacts list (from the People app) and people you have called before using Skype. You can select one of these people to call them now. If the person you want to call isn't listed, enter his or her name in the Search Skype box and select the Search button (which looks like a magnifying glass). The Skype directory opens, as shown in **Figure 8-14.** Scroll to find the person you want to call, using the person's photo ID and geographical information as your guide.

FIGURE 8-14

4. When you see the name of the person you want to call, select the name. Then, on the call screen, select the Video Call button (refer to **Figure 8-14**). You hear a ring tone as the call is made, and you see the person's face if he or she answers, as shown in **Figure 8-15.** Your face appears in the lower-right corner of the screen so you can see what your face looks like to the caller. Start talking. Smile. Trade the latest news. Have a ball.

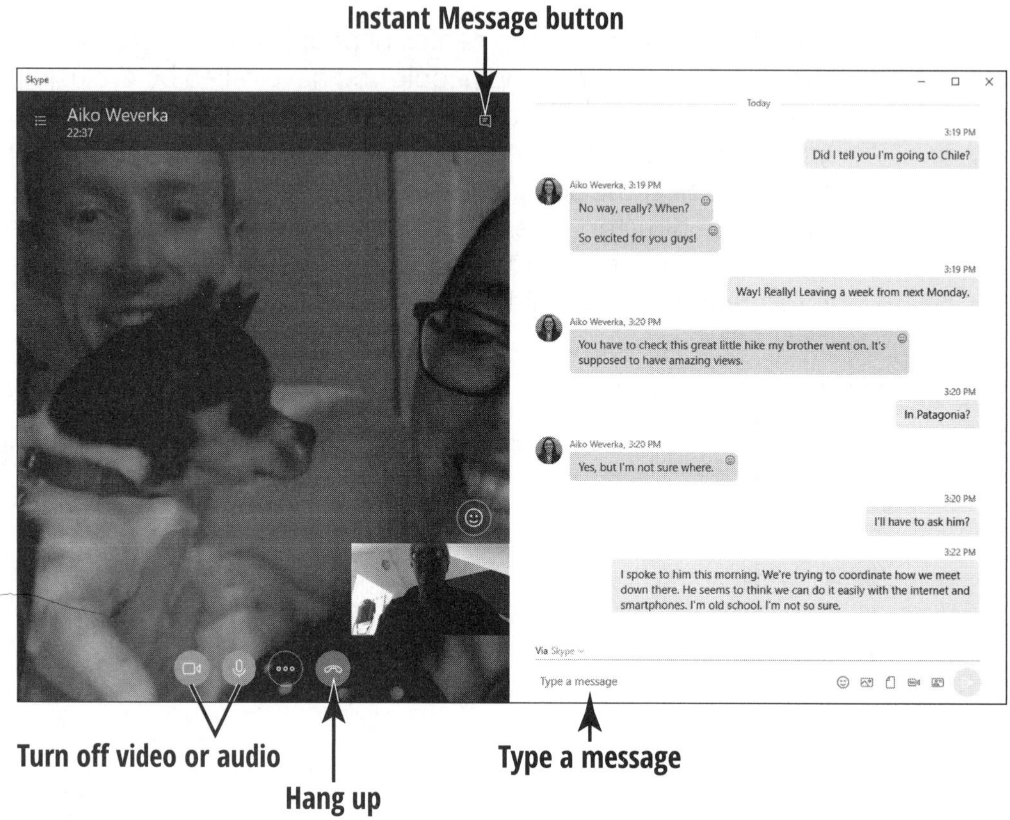

Instant Message button

[Figure 8-15 screenshot of Skype window showing a video call with Aiko Weverka and an instant message conversation panel]

Skype

Aiko Weverka
22:37

Today

3:19 PM
Did I tell you I'm going to Chile?

Aiko Weverka, 3:19 PM
No way, really? When?
So excited for you guys!

3:19 PM
Way! Really! Leaving a week from next Monday.

Aiko Weverka, 3:20 PM
You have to check this great little hike my brother went on. It's supposed to have amazing views.

3:20 PM
In Patagonia?

Aiko Weverka, 3:20 PM
Yes, but I'm not sure where.

3:20 PM
I'll have to ask him?

3:22 PM
I spoke to him this morning. We're trying to coordinate how we meet down there. He seems to think we can do it easily with the internet and smartphones. I'm old school. I'm not so sure.

Via Skype

Type a message

Turn off video or audio

Hang up

Type a message

FIGURE 8-15

TIP

Select the Video and Microphone buttons when you need a little privacy (refer to **Figure 8-15**). Select the Video button to turn off your video (the other caller can't see you); select the Microphone button to turn off your audio (the other caller can't hear you).

TIP

Select the Instant Message button (in the upper-right corner of the screen) to send an instant message to the other caller (refer to **Figure 8-15**). The message panel appears. In the bottom of the message panel (refer to **Figure 8-15**), type your message and select Send (or press Enter). Sending text messages is a useful way to communicate when you have technical difficulties or the other caller isn't answering. Select the Instant Message button again to close the Instant Message panel.

5. Select the red Hang Up button to complete your call.

6. When someone calls you, the Incoming Call panel appears, as shown in **Figure 8-16.** Select Video (at the bottom of the panel) to initiate the call.

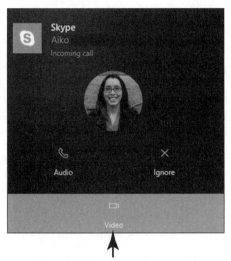

Select Video to receive a call

FIGURE 8-16

3
Having Fun with Windows 10

IN THIS PART . . .

Find and purchase apps at the Microsoft Store.

Take and edit photos and videos.

Play music and watch videos.

Chapter 9
Exploring the Microsoft Store

Y̲ou can do many things with Windows 10, such as send email, browse the web, play games, and look at photos and videos. You can read the news and chat with family and friends. All these functions and more involve computer programs. Back in the day, such programs were called *applications.* Now, we call them *apps.*

Windows 10 comes with a few apps installed, such as the Weather and Maps apps. (See Chapter 2 for information on using these two apps and apps in general.) To obtain other apps — free or otherwise — you use the Microsoft Store.

To install an app from the Microsoft Store, you need a Microsoft Account. See Chapter 4 for information on setting up a Microsoft Account.

Microsoft tests and approves all apps in the Microsoft Store. For quality and security purposes, you can install Windows 10 apps only from the Microsoft Store.

In this chapter, you peruse the apps and games in the Microsoft Store, including those already installed on a new machine. You install a new game, discover how to manage the apps and games you own, and see how to rate and review an app or game. Finally, you find out how to make sure that the Microsoft Store can receive payments in case you want to buy an app or game.

Explore Apps and Games by Category

1. On the Start screen, select the Store tile.

2. Look over the Store home screen, as shown in **Figure 9-1.** The home screen shows top-rated apps and games, as well as apps, movies, TV shows, and books that Microsoft thinks you will be interested in based on your previous purchases, if you made any. Notice the navigation bar along the top of the screen (see **Figure 9-1**). It offers six choices: Home, Apps, Games, Music, Movies & TV, and Books. Wherever your travels take you in the Store, the navigation bar appears along the top of the screen so that you can return to the home screen or redirect your search for apps, games, music, movies and TV shows, or books.

TIP

You can also navigate in the Store by selecting the Back button in the upper-left corner of the screen. Selecting this button returns you to the previous screen you were looking at.

3. Select Apps on the navigation bar to go to the Apps screen, and then scroll toward the bottom of the screen. As you scroll downward, you see the familiar categories — apps that Microsoft recommends for you, top paid apps, top free apps, best-rated apps, and so on. If the apps in a category interest you, you can select the category's Show All button to investigate the apps in the category.

4. At the bottom of the Apps screen, you see the categories shown in **Figure 9-2.** Now you're getting somewhere. These categories are very useful for finding apps that are worth installing on your computer. Using the scroll bar as necessary, take a moment to look over the app categories:

- **Books & Reference:** Read and research.

- **Business:** Analyze business data.

- **Developer Tools:** Make your software work better.

Navigation bar

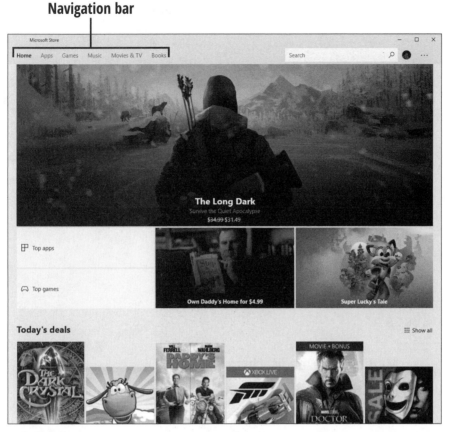

FIGURE 9-1

- **Education:** Study the stars, languages, or piano, or prep for the SAT.

- **Entertainment:** Check out apps that don't fit the other categories, such as those for drawing.

- **Food & Dining:** Locate eateries, as well as rate and review restaurants.

- **Government & Politics:** Learn more about the government and its workings.

- **Health & Fitness:** Want to get in shape? There's an app for that.

- **Kids & Family:** Discover family-activity apps and apps for children.

- **Lifestyle:** If you think entertainment is a vaguely defined category, check out lifestyle.

Select a category to start browsing

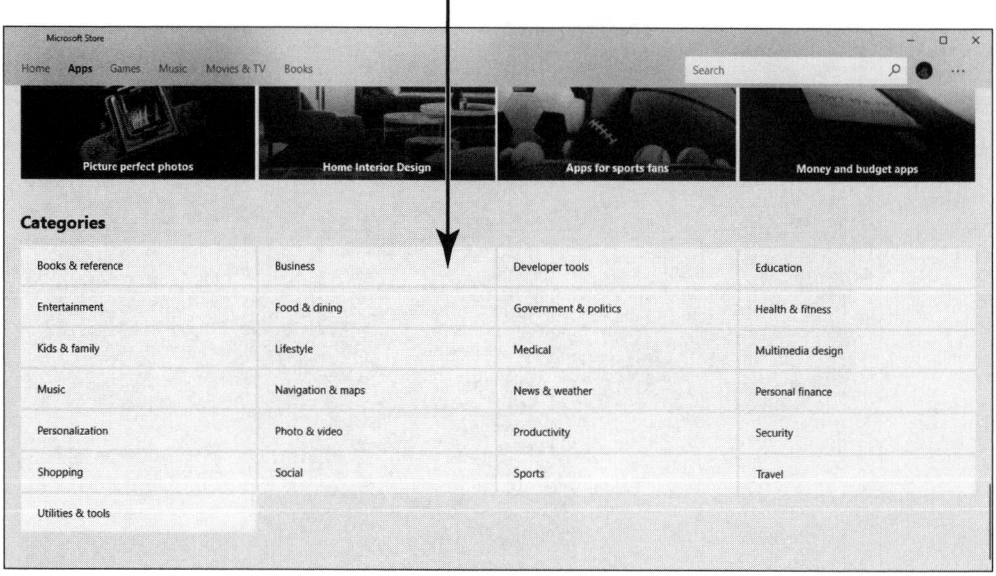

FIGURE 9-2

- **Medical:** Get medical information.
- **Multimedia Design:** Be creative with photos and video.
- **Music:** Listen to, make, and mix music.
- **Navigation & Maps:** Get there faster.
- **News & Weather:** Keep current.
- **Personal Finance:** Track your spending and investing.
- **Personalization:** A catchall category if ever there was one.
- **Photo & Video:** View, edit, and share photos and videos.
- **Productivity:** Send email and create schedules.
- **Security:** Keep your computer and data safe.
- **Shopping:** Put the world's catalogues at your fingertips.
- **Social:** Connect to friends and family.
- **Sports:** Follow your favorite sport or team. (Yeah, cricket!)
- **Travel:** Get there and back.
- **Utilities & Tools:** Check out apps for your computer.

You may see other categories, as well.

TIP

Is the app you want educational or entertainment? Will it make you productive or is it a tool? The category to which an app is assigned is determined by the app developer. In some cases, it's not clear why an app is in one category and not another. So it goes.

5. Select the Education category. In the Chart drop-down menu on the left side of the screen, select Top Free to see apps that you can install for free (see **Figure 9-3**). On the Type drop-down menu, select Games to see educational games. Use the Chart and Type menus to refine your searches. They are available wherever you travel in the Store app.

6. Select Games on the navigation bar and scroll to the bottom of the Games screen. You pass the familiar Top Free and Best-Rated categories. On the bottom of the screen are categories you can select to browse by category. The Games screen works just like the App screen.

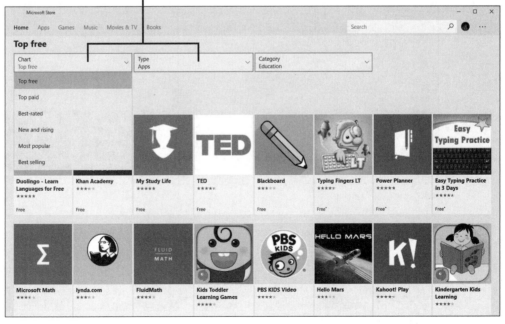

FIGURE 9-3

7. Return to the Store home screen using one of these methods:

- **Back button:** Click or tap the Back button (or press the Backspace key) as many times as necessary to return to the home screen. This button is located in the upper-left corner of the screen.

- **Navigation bar:** Select Home on the navigation bar (refer to **Figure 9-1**).

TIP

Did you see an app you want to acquire as you completed these steps? If so, skip to "Install a New App or Game," later in this chapter.

Search for an App or Game by Name

1. On any Store screen, click in the Search box. This box is in the upper-right corner of the screen, as shown in **Figure 9-4.**

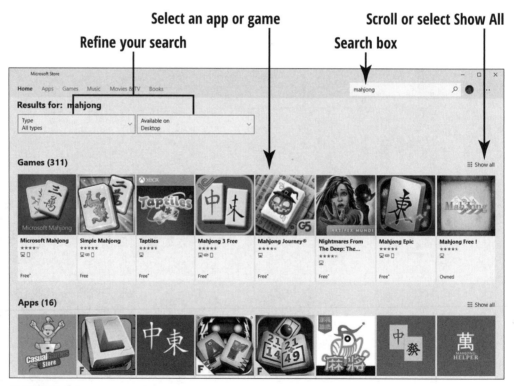

FIGURE 9-4

2. Type **mahjong** in the Search box and press Enter. As shown in **Figure 9-4,** apps and games with the word *mahjong* in their names appear in the Results window. The Results screen tells you how many apps and games match your search. After this initial search, you can turn the search in different directions:

- **Refine the search:** Select Games in the Type drop-down menu to narrow the search results to games. As well, you can open the Available drop-down menu and choose Desktop, Xbox, or another option that describes the platform where you prefer to play games.

- **Show all apps or games:** Select a Show All link to see only apps or games on the screen.

3. Select Games in the Type drop-down menu to see games with *mahjong* in their titles, as shown in **Figure 9-5.** Notice that the refine options have changed. Now you can select a category in the Available On drop-down menu to narrow the search results to games in a particular category.

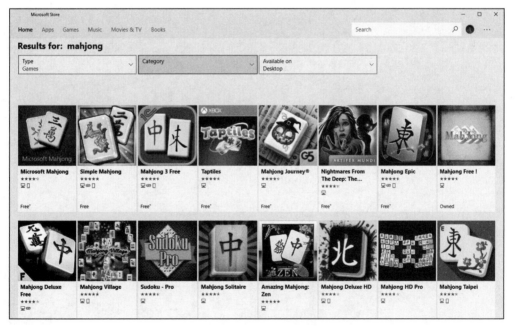

FIGURE 9-5

4. Scroll to Simple Mahjong in the search results.

5. Proceed to the next section, "Install a New App or Game," or return to the home screen.

Install a New App or Game

1. In the Store, search for the Simple Mahjong game. (See the section "Search for an App or Game by Name" for details.) Then select this game on the Results screen.

2. The screen shown in **Figure 9-6** appears. This (and any) game or app screen has lots of information.

Installation notice   **Rating**

FIGURE 9-6

TIP

The Back button (left-pointing arrow) next to the game's name takes you back to the previously viewed screen.

3. On the top half of the screen, note the following:

- The Get/Price button (don't click it just yet). This button is called Get if the game is free; otherwise, the button lists the cost of the app or game.

- The average rating in stars (five stars is the best).

- A description of the app or game.

TIP

For more details about the app or game, select the More link below the description.

- Screenshots that show what the app or game looks like onscreen.

- System requirements that describe what type of computer and operating system are needed to play the game.

4. To read reviews by users, scroll down. You see the reviews that Microsoft deems most useful.

5. Select the Get button to download and install Simple Mahjong. Because the game costs nothing, the button reads "Get."

6. If you're not already signed in, enter your Microsoft Account email address and password on the screen that pops up. Then select Sign In.

TIP

Many apps are free. Before you buy an app, see the section "Add Billing Information to Microsoft Store."

TIP

If you purchase an app, you are buying a license to install that app on up to five machines using the same Microsoft Account. The Microsoft Store will track how many times and on which machine the app is installed.

7. The download indicator appears in the upper-right corner of the screen and a progress bar shows the game being downloaded and installed. When the installation is complete, the words *This product is installed* appear below the game's name (refer to **Figure 9-6**). What's more, the message *Simple Mahjong was just installed. Check it out* appears in a pop-up message in the lower-right corner of the computer screen.

TIP

Installing an app may take a few seconds or a few minutes. You can do anything while an app installs — except use the app.

TIP

If you don't see *This product is installed,* the app may still be installing. If after a few minutes you still don't see this message, select the Get button again.

8. To play Simple Mahjong or to use any game or app after you install it, select the Start button. You may see the recently installed app on the Start menu under Recently Added, as shown in **Figure 9-7.** If you don't see it there, start your game or app the conventional way — by looking for the game or app in the alphabetical list (refer to **Figure 9-7**). If you haven't used an app yet, the word New appears below its name, as shown in the figure. Select the game or app's tile on the Start menu to open the game or app.

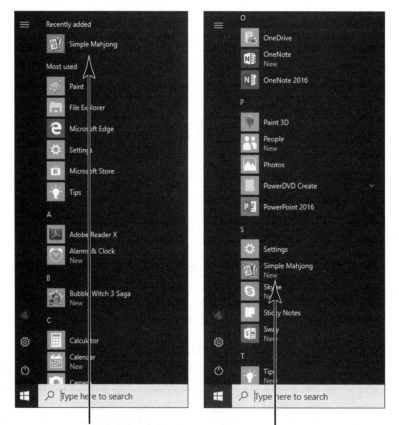

Look for recently installed apps here

The word New appears under recently installed apps

FIGURE 9-7

TIP

You can move the Simple Mahjong tile to the Start screen. See Chapter 3 for information on rearranging tiles on the Start screen.

Examine Your Apps and Games

1. To see which apps and games you have, select the See More button. This button (look for the three dots) is located to the right of the Search box, as shown in **Figure 9-8.** A drop-down menu appears after you select the See More button. This drop-down menu is the place to start when examining, updating, rating, and uninstalling apps and games.

See More button

FIGURE 9-8

2. Choose My Library on the See More drop-down menu (refer to **Figure 9-8**). The My Library screen appears, as shown in **Figure 9-9.**

3. Scroll to see which apps you have or select a Show All link to open a window that lists only your apps or your games. For each game or app, you see an icon and the name of the game or app. Last, a downward-pointing arrow indicates whether the app or game has been successfully installed. If you don't see this arrow, the app or game isn't installed on your computer.

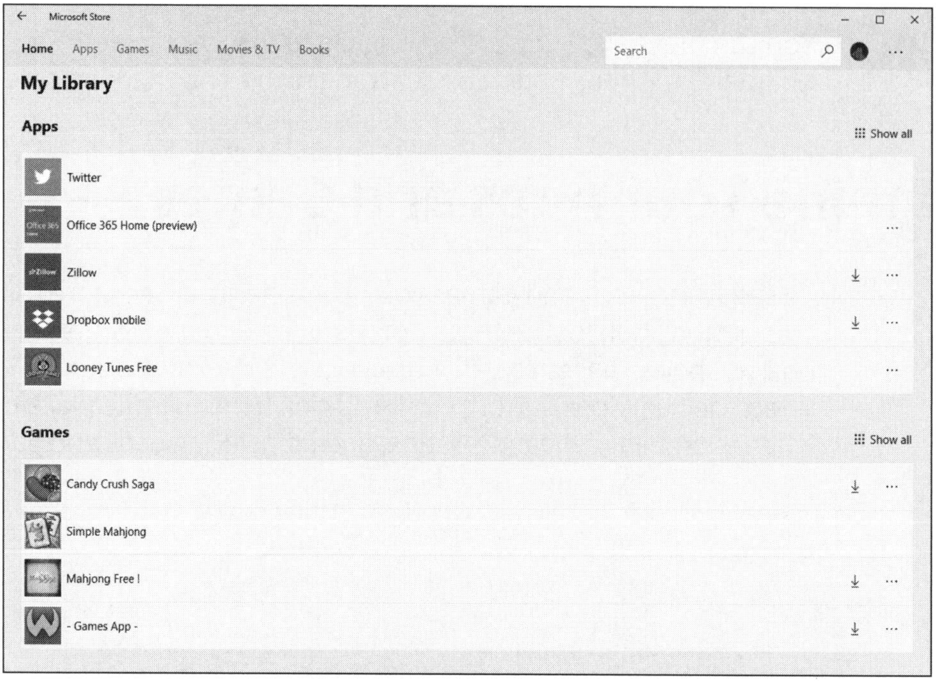

The following figure shows the Microsoft Store window with the My Library screen.

Microsoft Store

Home   Apps   Games   Music   Movies & TV   Books   Search

My Library

Apps   ⠿ Show all

Twitter

Office 365 Home (preview)

Zillow

Dropbox mobile

Looney Tunes Free

Games   ⠿ Show all

Candy Crush Saga

Simple Mahjong

Mahjong Free !

- Games App -

FIGURE 9-9

How can you have an app or game you haven't installed? If you sign into more than one computer using your Microsoft Account, you might install an app or game on one machine but not another.

TIP

Rate and Review an App or Game

1. On the My Library screen (refer to **Figure 9-9**), select the Simple Mahjong app. If you don't have this app, see the section "Install a New App or Game," earlier in this chapter, or substitute any app you have installed.

2. As shown in **Figure 9-10,** scroll to the Ratings and Reviews section of the Mahjong Free window and select the Rate and Review button. The review screen appears (refer to **Figure 9-10**). Every app and game has a Rate and Review button.

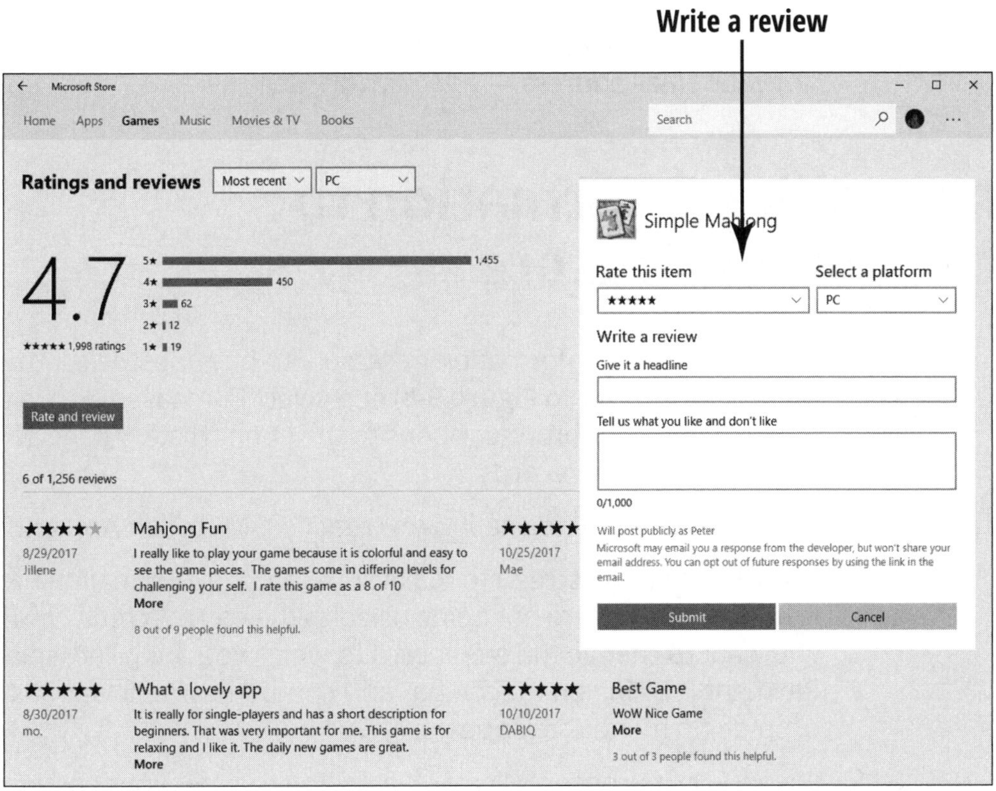

Write a review

FIGURE 9-10

TIP

You can rate or review only apps and games that you've installed, and you must be signed in with your Microsoft Account. To rate or review a preinstalled app or game, install the app or game to associate the app with your Microsoft Account.

3. In the Rate This Item menu, choose the number of stars you want to give this game. (Select one star for the lowest rating; select five for the highest rating.) In the Headline box, type a summary or overview of your comments, such as *Great app* or *Needs work*.

4. In the Tell Us box, say what you will, up to 500 characters, including spaces and punctuation. Be helpful, if possible. Select the Submit button when you're done with your review (or Cancel to abandon your review).

TIP

Your comments may help another person decide whether to install an app. In addition, the app's developer may use customer feedback to fix problems or add features.

TIP

Your Microsoft Account name and picture, if you have one — but not your email address — appear with your review.

Add Billing Information to the Microsoft Store

1. To add the billing information necessary to buy apps, select the See More button (refer to **Figure 9-8**) and select Purchased on the drop-down menu. Your browser opens to the Order History page of your Microsoft Account records.

TIP

See Chapter 4 for information on creating a Microsoft Account.

2. Scroll through the screen to make sure that the information here is accurate. If you are not being billed to the correct credit card or you want to change the credit card to which you are billed, select Payment & Billing on the toolbar and choose Payment Options on the drop-down menu that appears.

3. For security purposes, Microsoft asks you to enter your password on the next screen. Enter your password and select the Sign In button.

TIP

You may be asked on the next screen to verify who you are by submitting a security code. Provide the necessary information for Microsoft to contact you and select the Send Code button. After the code arrives by email or in a text message, enter it in the screen that asks for a security code.

4. Select a payment method (or select Edit Info if Microsoft already has credit card information on you) and do the following:

   - Select your credit card type.

     You must fill out all parts of this form except for Address Line 2.

TIP

   - Enter your credit card number in the box provided. Don't enter dashes or spaces.

   - Under Expiration Date, select the month (MM) and year (YYYY) your card expires.

   - Enter your name as it appears on your credit card.

- Under CVV, enter the three- or four-digit verification code from your credit card. (Select What's This? for an illustration of the location of this code on your card.)

5. In the Billing Address section, do the following:

   - Enter your street address, city, state, and ZIP Code.

   - Select your Country/region.

   - Under Phone Number, enter your area code in the first box and the remainder of your number in the second box.

6. When you're ready to continue, select Next.

7. If any of your data is incomplete or invalid, the form remains onscreen. Look for indications of a problem. Review each entry before selecting Submit.

8. If your information was accepted, you return to the Your Account screen. Under Payment and billing info, note your credit card type, the last four digits of your number, and the expiration date.

Chapter **10**

Taking Photos and More

Windows 10 makes enjoying digital photos easy. You can pick and choose photos to look at or display a group of photos in a slide show. You set a favorite photo to be your Lock screen background so that you see it every time you start Windows 10.

If you have a printer, you can print photos for yourself or to send to someone. Even black-and-white prints of color photos may be nice. If you have a scanner, you can even scan photos to make digital copies of photographs that as yet exist only in paper form.

Of course, if you want to take your own photos, nothing beats having a digital camera. Copy photos from your camera to your Pictures folder for viewing and sharing. Or use the Camera app with the built-in camera found in many laptops and tablets.

In this chapter, you use the tools that come with Windows 10 for working with, printing, scanning, and editing photos.

Take Photos (and Videos) with Your Computer

1. Select the Camera app on the Start screen. If you don't have a web-cam, the app screen displays *Please connect a camera.* If you don't have a built-in webcam, or the resolution of the one you have is too low, you can easily add a webcam. Simply plug the camera into your computer — it's that easy.

TIP You can choose from many good webcam models. Generally, get the highest video resolution you can afford, because you'll probably use the camera for video chats. Consider the size of the camera, its attachment to your computer, and whether it has a microphone (you definitely need a microphone).

TIP For instructions about opening apps such as the Camera app, visit Chapter 2.

2. The first time you use the Camera app, the screen displays *Let Windows camera access your location?* Select Yes to continue. (If you don't want to continue, don't choose No unless you never expect to use this app. Instead, simply switch back to the Windows desktop.)

3. The Camera app opens, and there's a good chance you recognize the face staring back at you. Very likely the face isn't wearing a hat and dark glasses like the debonair guy in **Figure 10-1.** To take a photo, smile and then click or tap the Camera button (it's on the right side of the screen). You may hear a shutter click. Your photo is placed automatically in a folder called Camera Roll in the Pictures folder.

4. If you see a Change Camera option, select that option. Some tab-lets and laptops have two cameras, one that faces you and one that points in the opposite direction. Switch to the camera away from you when you want to use your computer for something other than a self-portrait. Take another picture — they're free. Select Change Camera again to switch back to see yourself.

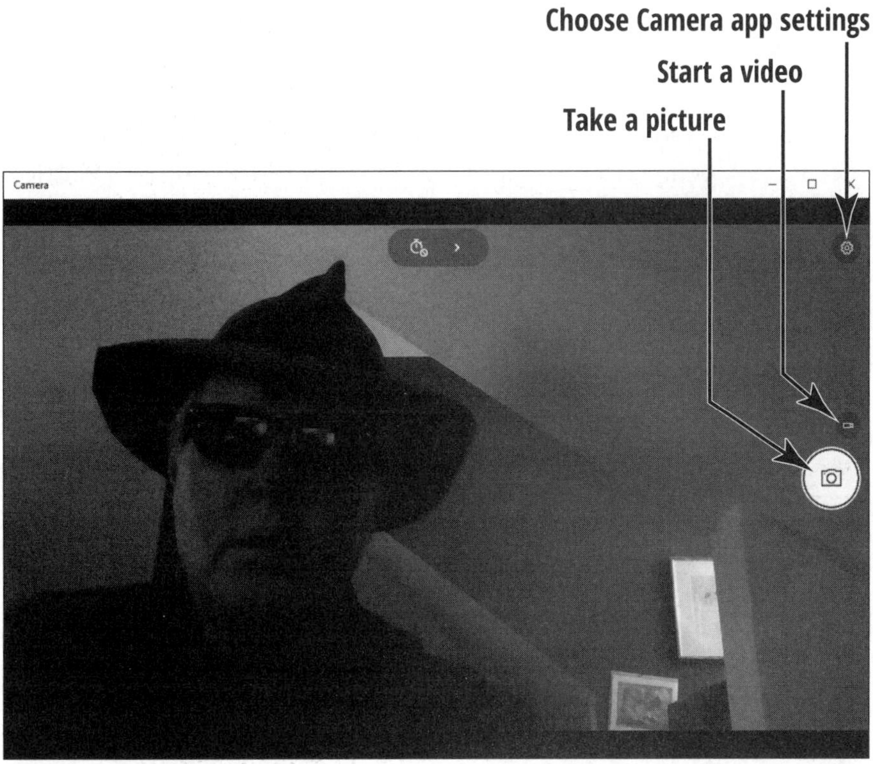

Choose Camera app settings

Start a video

Take a picture

FIGURE 10-1

5. Select the Video button (shown in **Figure 10-1**). Nothing happens until you click or tap the Video button a second time, at which point you're in moving pictures. A counter indicates the length of the video. Short is sweet in video. You can speak, too. Click or tap the Video button to stop the video. As with photos you take with the Camera app, videos are saved initially in the Camera Roll subfolder of the Pictures folder. Select the Camera button to turn off the video function and return to taking still photos (with the next click or tap).

Leave the Camera app open to explore the Camera settings, which I explain next.

Choose Camera Settings

1. If the Camera app isn't open, open it now. Then select the Settings button located in the upper-right corner of the Camera window (refer to **Figure 10-1**). The Settings panel opens, as shown in **Figure 10-2.** From here, you can tell the Camera app how to take photos and videos.

SETTINGS

Press and hold camera button

| Disabled |

Photos

Aspect ratio

| 16:9 |

Framing grid

| Off |

Time lapse
When the timer is on, keep taking photos until I press the camera button again.

Off

Videos

Video recording

| 1280x720p/30 fps |

Flicker reduction

| 50 Hz |

Related settings

Change where photos and videos are saved

Choose whether camera can use location info

Change privacy settings

FIGURE 10-2

2. Under Press and Hold Camera Button, choose what happens when you hold down the Camera button rather than click or tap it. The Video option creates a video; the Photo Burst option creates a series of snapshots; the Disabled option turns this feature off.

3. Under Photos, decide how you want to take photos:

- **Aspect ratio:** These options determine whether you shoot narrow (the 4:3 option) or widescreen (the 16:9 option) photos.

- **Framing grid:** These options help you aim the camera. For example, the Crosshairs option places crossing lines in the center of the screen so that you know where the center of your photos will be.

4. Under Videos, decide how you want to take videos:

- **Video recording:** These options determine how many pixels appear in your videos across the screen horizontally and vertically. A *pixel* is one point of color. Suffice it to say, the more pixels in the setting, the larger the video screen is.

- **Flicker reduction:** These options reduce the flickering that can occur when video is taken under fluorescent light. Consider choosing an option other than Disabled if you are filming indoors. The 50 Hz (hertz) setting applies to the U.S. and Canada, where the AC (alternating electrical current) runs at 50 Hz; the 60 Hz setting applies to rest of the world.

5. Return to the Camera app by clicking or tapping the Camera app screen.

6. Return to the Start screen. See the section "View Photos with the Photos App" to see and maybe edit the photos you just took.

Copy Photos from Your Camera

1. If your digital camera came with a cable, connect that cable to the camera, connect the other end of the cable to a USB port on your computer, and turn your camera on. If your laptop or tablet has a built-in card slot, you can take the memory card out of the camera and insert it in that slot.

TIP

2. If your computer doesn't have a built-in card slot, consider buying a small memory card reader that plugs into your computer and works with your camera's memory card. You don't need a multicard reader, just a reader with a single slot the size of your camera card. I consider a card reader more convenient than using a cable.

TIP

The techniques described here for importing photos from a camera also apply to videos. Follow these steps as well to copy videos from your digital camera to your computer.

3. Windows 10 detects your camera and may briefly display a notification indicating *Select to choose what happens with this device.* If you're quick enough to tap or click this notification, Windows 10 displays your choices, as shown in **Figure 10-3.** Select Open Device to View Files, if that option is available, to open File Explorer to the photos on your camera, as shown in **Figure 10-4 (top).** Then skip to Step 4. If you didn't catch the notification in time or you didn't see the notification, continue to Step 4 to import photos another way.

Canon PowerShot ELPH 100...

Choose what to do with this device.

Import photos and videos
Photos

Import photos and videos
OneDrive

Open device to view files
File Explorer

Take no action

FIGURE 10-3

TIP

See Chapter 3 for information on increasing the time a notification remains onscreen.

4. Select the File Explorer icon on the taskbar to start File Explorer. Then look for and select your camera in the Folders panel on the left side of the screen (refer to **Figure 10-4, top**). Your camera is located under *This PC* in the Folder pane.

TIP

See Chapter 14 for detailed information about using File Explorer.

5. In File Explorer, select the photos you want to copy from your camera to your computer. Depending on your camera setup, the photos may be in a subfolder (refer to **Figure 10-4, top**). Use these techniques to select the photos:

Select your camera (or one of its subfolders)

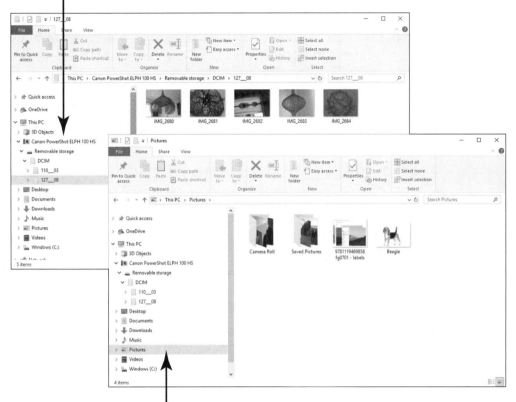

Copy to the Pictures folder (or one of its subfolders)

FIGURE 10-4

- Hold down the Ctrl button and click or tap photos to select them individually.

- Press Ctrl+A to select all the photos in a folder.

6. Copy the photos you selected so that you can paste them into a folder on your computer. Use one of these techniques to copy the photos:

- Press Ctrl+C.

- On the Home tab in File Explorer, select the Copy button.

7. In File Explorer, select the folder where you want to copy your photos.

TIP

If you want to be able to view and edit your photos with the Photos app, select the Pictures folder or one of its subfolders, as shown in **Figure 10-4 (bottom)**, and copy the photos there.

TIP

Organizing photos can be a challenge. If you dump more than a few dozen photos into the Pictures folder without using folders, finding a specific photo later will be difficult. Using folders with unintelligible names doesn't help, either. Most of my folder names are based on the year and month (such as 2018–06) or the subject, such as Luke the Lovehound.

8. Paste the photos into the folder you selected in Step 7. Use one of these techniques:

- Press Ctrl+V.

- On the Home tab in File Explorer, select the Paste button.

TIP

If you often import photos from a digital camera or memory card, you can speed the process by telling Windows to open File Explorer immediately when you attach your camera or memory card to your computer. On the Start menu, choose Settings and type **autoplay** in the Find a Setting box. In the Search Results panel, select AutoPlay Settings. The AutoPlay window opens, as shown in **Figure 10-5.** In the Memory Card and Camera sections, choose Open Folder (or Open Device) to View Files (File Explorer).

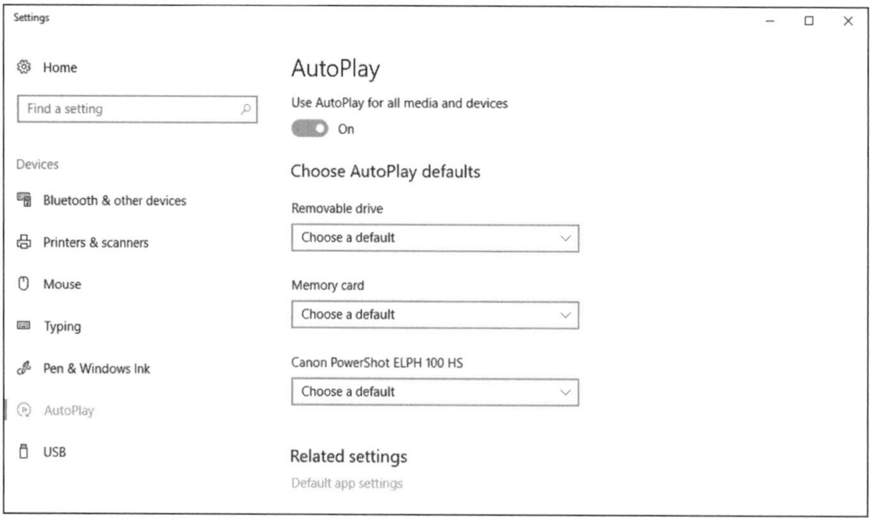

FIGURE 10-5

View Photos with the Photos App

1. To see photos on your computer, select the Photos app on the Start screen. The Photos screen opens to the Collection window, as shown in **Figure 10-6.** It shows the contents of the Pictures folder (and its subfolders) on your computer. Your screen will look different.

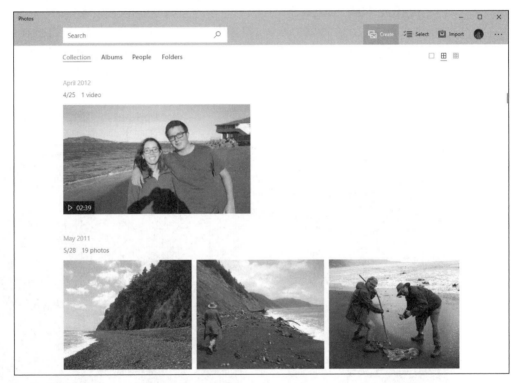

FIGURE 10-6

2. If you don't see any pictures, skip to one of the following sections:

   - If you have a digital camera, see "Copy Photos from Your Camera."

   - If your computer has a built-in camera or a webcam, see "Take Photos (and Videos) with Your Computer."

3. If you see pictures, scroll down to see more photos. Photos are presented by the dates on which they were taken.

You can take a screenshot — a picture of the current screen — by pressing ⊞+Print Screen. (A touchscreen or mouse equivalent is not available.) The screen dims slightly to indicate the capture, which is stored automatically in the Screenshots folder in your Pictures folder. Use this technique to create your own documentation of problems or something you want to see again later.

4. Select any photo to display it in the Photos app window, as shown in **Figure 10-7.** Scroll through the photos by selecting an arrow on the left side (to go back) or right side (to go forward) of the screen or by clicking or tapping the right edge or left edge of the screen. You can also press the PageDown key (forward) or PageUp key (back).

Return to tile view   **App bar**   **Display more options**

Select to move back

Select to move forward

FIGURE 10-7

5. Click or tap anywhere on your photo to display the app bar (see **Figure 10-7**). Select the More button (the three dots on the right side of the App bar) and select Slide Show on the menu that appears. The photos appear in succession. Stop the slide show by clicking or tapping a photo.

Select the More button on the right side of the app bar to display some new commands — Open With, Copy, Set As, and File Info, to name a few. By selecting File Info, you can see each photo's name, when it was taken, and its file size.

6. Zoom in and out on a photo using one of these methods (repeat to zoom in or out more):

   - **Mouse:** Click the Zoom button at the top of the screen. A slider appears. Drag the slider to the left to shrink the photo; drag the slider to the right to enlarge the photo.

   - **Touchscreen:** Touch two fingers on the screen. Move your fingers apart to zoom in. Pinch your fingers closer together to zoom out.

   - **Keyboard:** Press Ctrl+plus sign (actually, press the equals sign — no need to press the Shift key) to zoom in. Press Ctrl+minus sign to zoom out.

Zoom in to see part of a photo made larger.

Use the Delete button in the app bar to delete a photo. See Chapter 14 for information on undeleting files.

7. Select the arrow on the left side of the app bar to return to tile view. In this view, you can see more than one photo.

The Photos app offers many options for editing photos. See the section "Edit Photos Using the Photos App," next in this chapter.

Edit Photos Using the Photos App

1. You can use the Photos app to change a photo, including making it smaller. In the Photos app, click or tap the photo you want to edit so that it fills the screen, select the Edit & Create button, and choose Edit on the drop-down menu. The right side of the app bar offers tools for editing photos: Crop and Rotate, Enhance, Edit, and Adjust.

2. Select the Edit & Create button on the app bar and then choose Edit on the drop-down menu (or simply press Ctrl+E). The Editing window opens, as shown in **Figure 10-8.** This window offers many tools for touching up photos. To edit a photo, select a retouching method on the right side of the screen (Crop and Rotate, Enhance, or Adjust) and then choose editing options.

3. Using the Enhance method, you can take advantage of preset edits to photographs. After you select Enhance, filter presets appear on the right side of the screen (refer to **Figure 10-8, top**). They offer the chance to change the light and color of a photograph in one fell swoop. Drag the slider at the bottom of the screen to further change the look of a photograph.

If you make mincemeat of a photograph and you want the original version back, select the Undo All button. Selecting this button restores a photograph to its original, pristine state.

4. Choose the Adjust method to alter the brightness and color of your photograph (refer to **Figure 10-8, bottom**). Drag the Light and Color sliders to adjust the brightness and contrast.

5. Many photos can be improved by *cropping,* which involves cutting out distracting elements and keeping just part of the photo. You might crop a photo to concentrate on its most important part. To crop, make sure that the Crop & Rotate method is selected on the right side of the screen. Then either select an aspect ratio or choose the Custom aspect ratio and drag the size or corners of the picture box until the photo is to your liking. The box tells you which parts will remain after cropping, as shown in **Figure 10-9.** As well, you can drag the photo itself to adjust the photo's placement. Select the Done button when you finish cropping your photograph.

Sometimes when you import photos from a digital camera or scanner, they arrive askew because the photographer turned the camera the wrong way when shooting. You can correct this error by selecting Crop & Rotate and then selecting the Rotate button until the photo turns right-side-up.

6. Select Save when you finish doctoring your photograph.

You can select the Save a Copy button to keep the original photograph as well as the edited version.

Choose an editing method

Save your edits

FIGURE 10-8

Choose an aspect ratio

Adjust the size of the box

FIGURE 10-9

Print Photos Using the Photos App

1. If necessary, connect the cable from your printer to the USB port on your computer and make sure that your printer is turned on.

2. In the Photos app, select the photo you want to print using a click or tap to display the photo at full screen.

3. Select the Print button on the right side of the app bar (refer to **Figure 10-7**). The Print window appears, as shown in **Figure 10-10**. If you don't see the Print button, move the pointer to the top of the screen to display the app bar. Select your printer.

TIP

Here's a handy keyboard shortcut that works in any app: Press Ctrl+P to open the Print window straightaway.

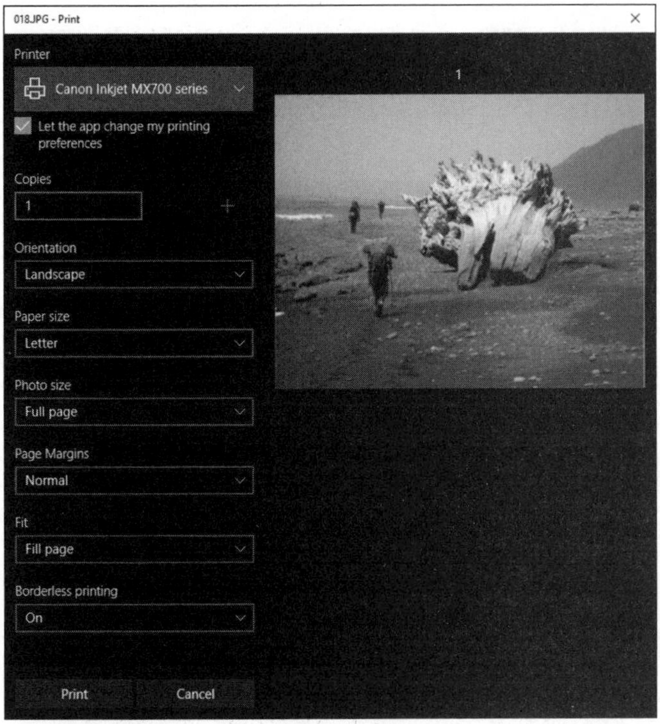

FIGURE 10-10

4. Select a printer. Note the preview. Select the Print button.

Chapter 13 explains printing in detail.

TIP

Scan Photos and Documents

1. Scan photos and documents to preserve them in digital form. Old family photos and heirloom documents such as birth certificates are candidates for scanning. *Scanning* means to render a paper photograph or document as a computer file so that you can post it on the Internet or send it by email. To scan photos and documents, you must have a scanner or a printer that is capable of scanning (most printers have a scanning capability). To start, connect the cable from your scanner or printer to the USB port on your computer. Make sure that your scanner or printer is turned on. If you're using a printer, put it in Scan mode (which probably means pressing the Scan button).

2. Put the item you want to scan in your scanner or printer.

3. Enter the word **scan** in the Search box on the left side of the taskbar. On the pop-up menu that appears, select Windows Fax and Scan. The Windows Fax and Scan application opens, as shown in **Figure 10-11.**

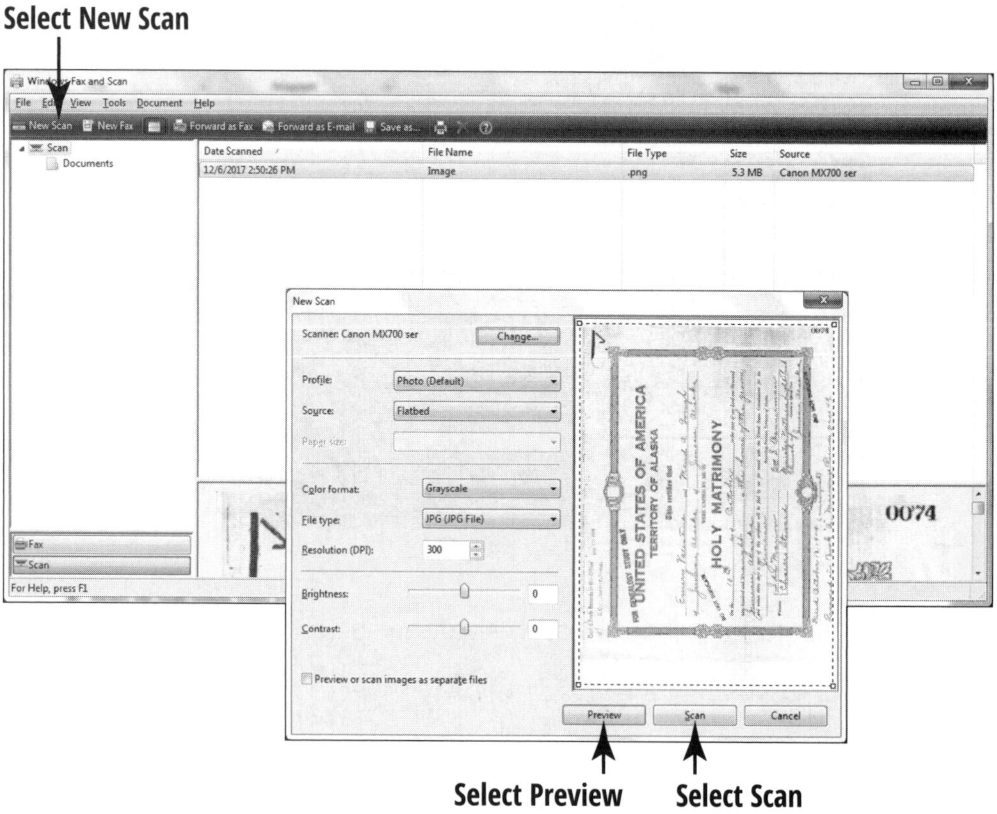

Select New Scan

FIGURE 10-11

Select Preview   Select Scan

4. In the navigation window, select Scan and then select the New Scan button. The New Scan dialog box appears (refer to **Figure 10-11**). Starting here, you can tell Windows whether you want a high-quality or low-quality scan. On the Color Format menu, for example, choose Grayscale or Black and White instead of Color if you're scanning a black-and-white document. Choose a Resolution (DPI) higher than 300 to render your photo or document in greater detail.

Unless you're scanning more than one item, deselect the Preview or Scan Images as Separate Files option. This option creates a separate digital file for each item in your scanner.

TIP

5. Select the Preview button. The preview window shows what your photo or document will look like when it is scanned. If you don't like what you see, play with the settings in the New Scan dialog and select the Preview button again.

6. Select the Scan button when you're ready to scan your document. Your scanned photo or document appears in the Windows Fax and Scan window with the generic filename "Image."

7. Select your newly scanned image and then select the Save As button. The Save As dialog box appears. Enter a descriptive name for the item, choose a folder to store it in, and select the Save button.

TIP

Chapter 14 explains how to save files.

Chapter **11**
Enjoying Music and Videos

The term *media* on computers refers to something other than text. Audio and video are examples of media. *Audio* is a catchall term for music and other sound files, such as books on CD. *Video* includes files that you can shoot with your digital camera as well as Hollywood blockbusters.

The delivery of music has come a long way from Edison's wax cylinder or even vinyl LPs. Nowadays, music is entirely digital. The Groove Music app lets you play your music collection and makes it easy to explore new music. Use Windows Media Player to play audio CDs, to copy audio files to your computer, and to burn songs onto a CD.

The Movies & TV app is similar to the Groove Music app, but it's for video instead of music. You can use it to play your homemade videos.

In this chapter, you play a music CD, copy CDs to your computer for easier access, and burn a CD. You also explore the Groove Music and Movies & TV apps. Finally, you discover how to make a voice recording.

TIP You'll need a different app to play DVDs. Search Microsoft Store for Media Center or for a DVD player app. See Chapter 9 for more information on Microsoft Store.

TIP Popular alternatives for music or videos include Hulu, iTunes, Netflix, and YouTube. All of these are accessible through the web browser. Search Microsoft Store for related apps.

Play and Copy Music from a CD

1. If you have a CD or DVD disc drive or slot on your computer, insert a music CD, label side up for horizontal drives. (Vertical drives are less predictable.)

2. Windows 10 detects your CD and may briefly display this notification: *Select to choose what happens with audio CDs.* If you're quick enough to tap or click the first notification, Windows 10 displays your choices, as shown in **Figure 11-1.** Select Windows Media Player and then skip to Step 5.

FIGURE 11-1

TIP See Chapter 3 for information on increasing the time a notification remains onscreen.

3. If you missed the notification, go to the desktop and select the File Explorer icon (which looks like a folder) in the taskbar.

4. In the panel on the left side of File Explorer, select your CD drive or DVD drive. You may see the words *Audio CD* or *DVD Drive* in the panel.

5. On the Ribbon, select the Manage tab under Drive Tools. Then select AutoPlay. As shown in **Figure 11-1,** the notification from Step 1 reappears (and stays onscreen until you select something). Select Windows Media Player.

6. If you see the Welcome to Windows Media Player screen, select Recommended Settings and then select Finish. The Windows Media Player plays your music.

7. For access to more options, select Switch to Library, the small button under the X in Windows Media Player, as shown in **Figure 11-2.**

FIGURE 11-2

8. Note the following controls at the bottom of the Windows Media Player, as shown in **Figure 11-3:**

   - **Shuffle:** Select this button to turn on *shuffle,* which randomly mixes the tracks you play. Select again to turn off shuffle, and the tracks play in the order in which they appear onscreen.

   - **Repeat:** Select this button to play all the tracks again after all have played. Select again to turn off the repeat function.

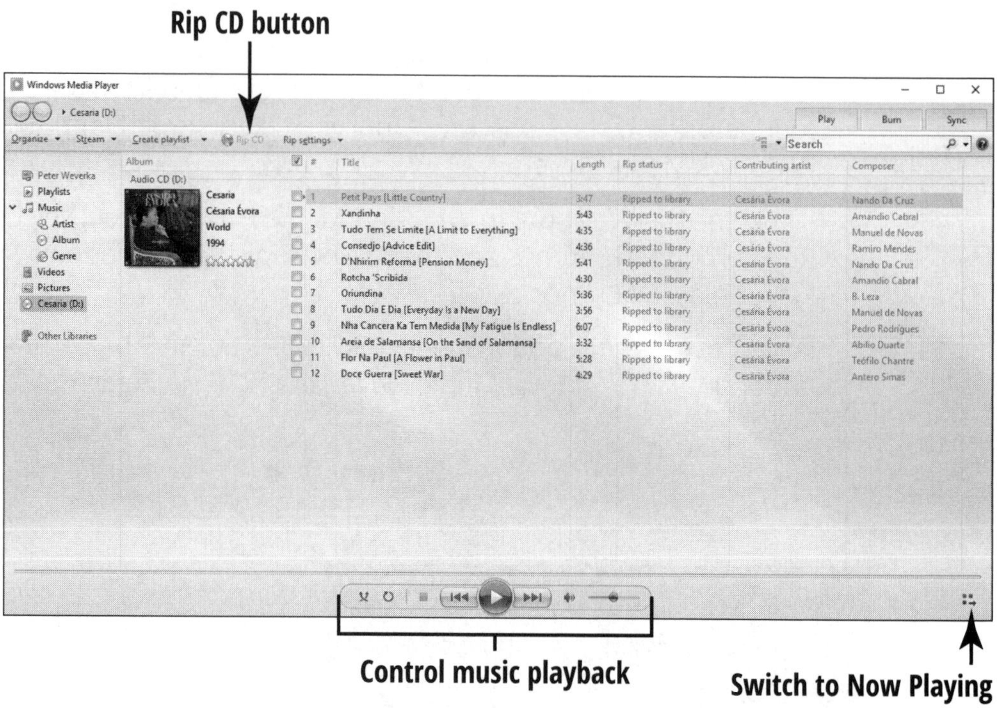

Rip CD button

Control music playback   Switch to Now Playing

FIGURE 11-3

- **Stop:** Select to stop playing.

- **Previous:** Select this button to skip to the previous track. Select and hold to rewind to an earlier point in the track.

- **Play/Pause:** Select the button with two vertical lines to pause play mid-track. Select the same button (now with a triangle pointing to the right) to resume playing from the point you paused.

- **Next:** Select this button to skip to the next track. Select and hold to fast-forward through the track.

- **Mute/Unmute:** Select this button to silence the player. Although the track continues to play, you won't hear it. When Mute is on, a red circle with a slash appears next to the speaker icon. Select the button again to hear the track.

- **Volume:** Drag the slider to the left to decrease or to the right to increase the volume of the track. Your speakers may also have a manual volume control. Windows 10 has a separate volume control in the taskbar, as well.

- **Now Playing:** You select this button, which is located far to the right of the toolbar, to reduce the player to a small size (refer to **Figure 11-2**).

9. To copy the CD tracks to your Music library, select Rip CD. This button is located on the toolbar along the top of the screen (refer to **Figure 11-2**). Ripping a song on a CD takes about a minute. As each song is ripped, the words *Ripped to Library* appear in the Rip Status column of the Windows Media Player.

Be sure to refer to this as *ripping a CD* around your younger friends. But not the youngest, because they think that CDs are way passé and MP3s rule. (MP3 is an audio file format common to portable digital music players and music downloads.)

If you plan to rip a lot of CDs, select Rip Settings ⇨ Rip CD Automatically and Rip Settings ⇨ Eject CD After Ripping. Just inserting the CD will copy files to your Music library as it plays the CD. Audiophiles should choose Rip Settings ⇨ Audio Quality ⇨ 192 Kbps (Best Quality).

10. When the copying process finishes, remove your CD. To play this music in the future, start Windows Media Player, choose Artist, Album, or Genre under Music, select the CD you ripped, select a song title, and select the Play button.

Songs you rip from a CD are kept on your computer in a subfolder of the Music folder. To copy or move music that you ripped from a CD, open the Music folder, open the subfolder named after the CD you ripped, and copy or move the files.

You can play anything in the Music library by using the Groove Music app. See the next section, "Listen to the Groove Music App."

Pin the Windows Media Player to the taskbar for easy access: Click the right mouse button over the icon in the taskbar, or tap and hold until a box appears and then release. On the menu that pops up, select Pin to Taskbar. You can also search for Windows Media Player on the Start screen. See Chapter 2 for information on pinning apps to the Start screen.

TIP

If your music CD doesn't play automatically the next time you insert one, you can tell Windows 10 how to handle audio CDs. On the Start screen, click or tap Settings and then type **autoplay** on the Settings screen. In the search results, select AutoPlay Settings. The Settings screen opens to the AutoPlay settings. Turn on the Use AutoPlay for All Media and Devices option to make CDs play automatically.

Listen to the Groove Music App

1. Select the Groove Music app on the Start screen. The Groove Music app home screen appears, as shown in **Figure 11-4.** The Groove Music app enables you to play songs that you ripped (copied) from CDs, songs that you purchased from iTunes and other music purveyors, and playlists that you created from songs you own.

TIP

If you see *Can't sign in,* you're not connected through a Microsoft Account. You'll still be able to do the steps in this section, though. You need to sign in only to buy music.

2. Initially, the Groove Music app recognizes music files kept in these folders on your computer: C:\Users\Your Name\OneDrive\Music and C:\Users*Your Name*\Music. Maybe you keep your music files in other folders. To tell the Groove Music app where your music files are, tap or click the Settings button (refer to **Figure 11-4**). In the Settings screen, select the *Choose Where We Look for Music* link. The Build Your Collection dialog box appears, as shown in **Figure 11-5.** Select the Add Folder button, choose a folder in the Select Folder dialog box, and tap or click the Add This Folder to Music button. Then select Done. Repeat these instructions to add all the folders where you store music files.

3. To find the song you want to hear, choose an option in the navigation pane and get to it:

- **Search:** Type the name of an artist, album, or song in the Search box. As you type, suggested matches appear below the Search box. For now, ignore these suggestions (but take advantage of them in the future to save typing). Instead, select the magnifying glass or press Enter. Search results appear.

Locate songs   **Settings button**

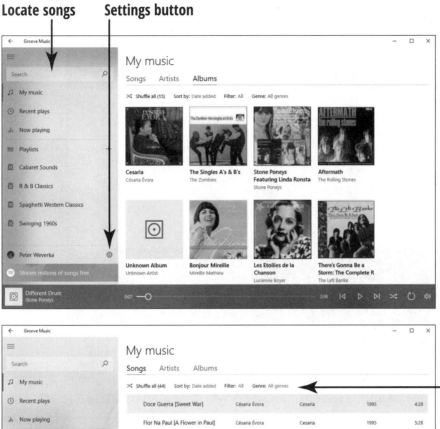

Play songs

Filter and sort results

FIGURE 11-4

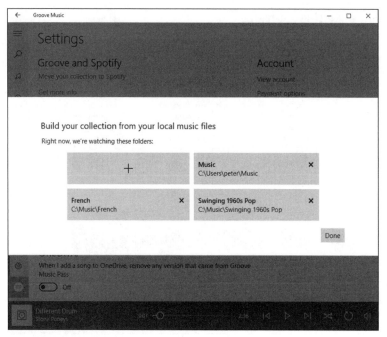

FIGURE 11-5

- **My Music:** After you make this choice, select Songs, Artists, or Albums (refer to **Figure 11-4**) to search from a song list, a list of artists, or a list of albums.

- **Recent Plays:** A list of albums you played recently appears. Scroll to find an album.

TIP

If the search results list is a long one, you can narrow your search with the Filter and Sort options (refer to **Figure 11-4**). Filtering narrows the search results to songs on your computer, songs on OneDrive, and other criteria. Sorting arranges the results in alphabetical order, date-added order, or by artist, or by album.

4. Select a song or album in the search results. Note the following options (not all of which may appear on the current screen):

- **Play:** Plays the song. Notice the controls at the bottom of the screen for pausing the song and controlling the volume (refer to **Figure 11-4**).

- **Play All:** Plays the songs on the album, starting with song 1.

- **Add To:** Opens a pop-up menu with playlists, and you can add the song to one of those playlists (see "Create and Manage Playlists," the next topic in this chapter).

- **Show Artist:** Opens a screen with other songs you own by the same artist. Click the back arrow to return to the Results screen.

TIP

You can listen to music as you conduct a search. To return to the song or album that is currently playing, select the Now Playing button.

5. To control the volume level on your speakers, use either the volume controls in Groove Music or the Windows 10 volume controls. Select the Speakers icon in the lower-right corner of the Groove Music screen or the Windows 10 screen. A volume slider appears, as shown in **Figure 11-6** (the figure shows the Windows 10 volume controls). Slide the control to adjust the volume. Select the speaker icon on the right side of the slider to mute or unmute all sounds.

FIGURE 11-6

6. Switch back to the Start screen. The Groove Music app continues to play. The Groove Music tile on the Start screen displays the album art and title of the current song. Select the Music tile to return to the app.

7. Leave the Groove Music app open if you care to discover how to create a playlist, the next topic in this chapter.

Create and Manage Playlists

1. Create a playlist with the Groove Music app to play your favorite songs — songs from different artists — one after the other. After you create the list, you select it in the Groove Music app to play it. To create a playlist in the Groove Music app, select the Create New Playlist button (a plus sign). You see the Name This Playlist dialog box, shown in **Figure 11-7.** Select the words *Name This Playlist,* enter a descriptive name for your playlist, and select Create Playlist.

2. The Groove Music App has buttons to add songs to a playlist. Next time you're listening to a song or album and you think, "I like that song; it should be on a playlist," do one of the following to add the song to a playlist, as shown in **Figure 11-8:**

   - **Add a song:** Select a song's Add To button and select a playlist on the pop-up menu that appears.

   - **Add all the songs on an album:** Select the Add To button on the album name and select a playlist on the pop-up menu.

   See "Listen to the Groove Music App," earlier in this chapter, if you need help finding and listening to music on your computer.

3. To play the songs on a playlist, select the name of the playlist on the left side of the screen. The playlist opens, as shown in **Figure 11-9.** Select the Play All button to play the songs in order from first to last. Of course, you can select any song on the list and select its Play button to play it.

4. To change the order of songs on a playlist or remove a song, follow these instructions:

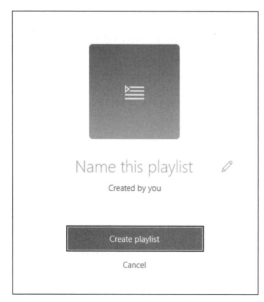

FIGURE 11-7

Add an album

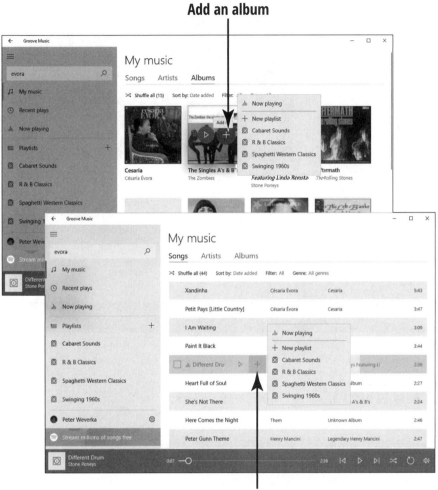

Add a song

FIGURE 11-8

- **Change the order of songs:** Drag a song higher or lower on the list with your mouse or finger.

- **Remove a song:** Display the song's context menu and choose Delete from Playlist. To display the context menu, right-click its name with your mouse or hold your finger on the name.

TIP

To delete a playlist, open it. Then select the Delete button. (Depending on the size of your screen, you may have to select the More Options button to see the Delete button.)

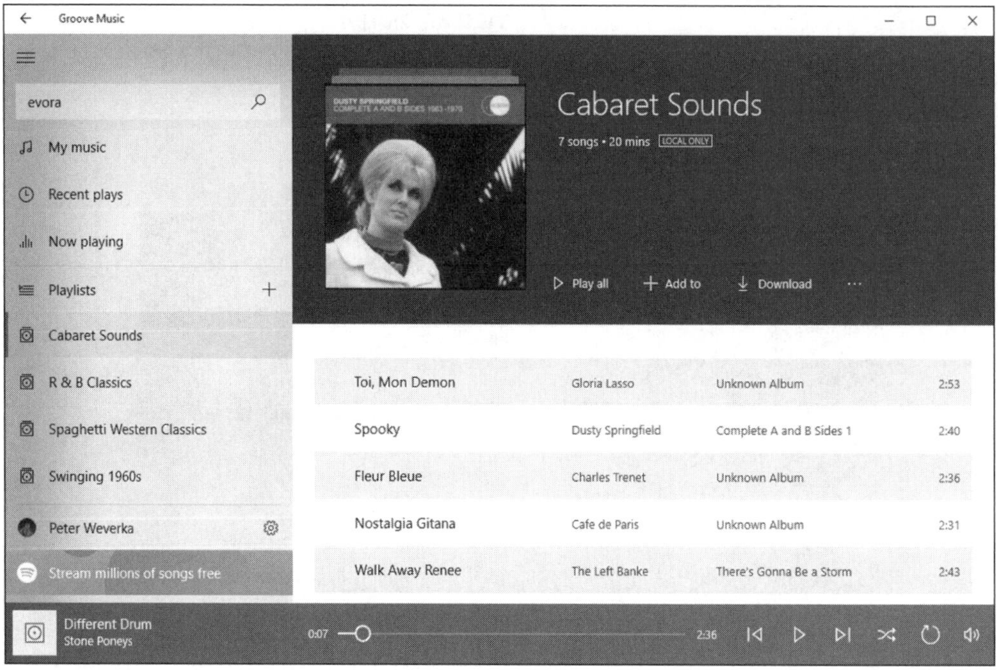

FIGURE 11-9

Watch Videos

1. Select the Movies & TV app on the Start screen. Microsoft designed this app for watching movies from the Microsoft Store and for watching homemade videos. To watch homemade videos, select the Personal tab on the menu bar. The Videos screen appears, as shown in **Figure 11-10.** Use the Video screen to watch videos.

2. Unless you store your videos in the `C:\Users\Your Name\Videos` folder, you don't see any videos. To tell the Video app where you store your videos, select the Add Folders button. You come to the Build Your Collection screen. Select the Add button (the plus sign), and in the Folder Suggestions dialog box, select the folder where videos are stored and then select the Add Folders button. Repeat these instructions to add all the folders where you store videos.

3. To play a video, select it on the Home screen. It appears in the video player screen, as shown in **Figure 11-11.** Along the bottom of this screen are controls for pausing, playing, and changing the volume level. Drag the slider below the video screen to rewind and fast-forward.

Go to the Personal tab

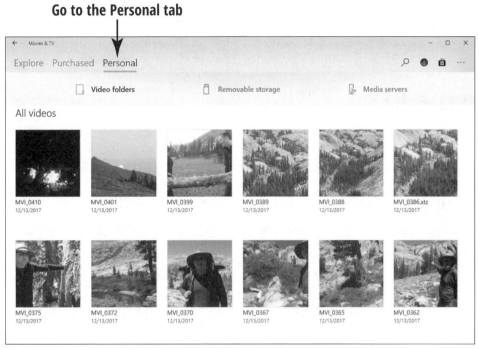

FIGURE 11-10

Video controls

Drag to rewind or fast-forward
FIGURE 11-11

4. Select the Back button (located in the upper-left corner of the screen) to return to the Movies & TV home screen.

Burn a CD

1. *Burning a CD* means to copy songs from a computer to a CD. Burn a CD so that you can play the songs on your car's CD player or pass along your favorite songs to a friend. To burn a CD, start by opening Windows Media Player, as shown in **Figure 11-12.**

TIP

Earlier in this chapter, "Play and Copy Music from a CD" explains Windows Media Player in detail.

2. Create a playlist so that Windows Media Player knows which songs to burn to the CD. To create a playlist, select the Create Playlist button and enter a name for the playlist where the words *Untitled Playlist* appear. The name you enter then appears under Playlists on the left side of the screen.

3. Locate songs for your playlist and drag and drop their titles one by one onto your playlist name. The words *Add to [Playlist Name]* appear when you drag a song title onto your list. Use these techniques to locate songs so you can drag them in the playlist:

   - **Browse for songs:** Under Music, select Artist, Album, or Genre on the left side of the screen (refer to **Figure 11-12**). A list of artists, albums, or genres appears.

   - **Change views:** Open the Change Views drop-down menu and choose Icon, Title, or Details to make finding a song title easier.

   - **Search for songs:** Enter a search term in the Search box.

4. Select your playlist on the left side of the screen. The songs you selected for the list appear, as shown in **Figure 11-13.** To listen to the songs on a playlist, select its name and click or tap the Play button at the bottom of the screen.

TIP

You can edit a playlist. While the list is playing, place more songs on the list (follow Step 3) or remove songs from the list by right-clicking and choosing Remove from List.

Drag titles over the playlist name

Create the playlist

FIGURE 11-12

5. After you create a playlist, you can burn it to a CD. With Windows Media Player open, insert a blank CD in your computer's CD or DVD drive. Then select the Burn tab (refer to **Figure 11-13**) and drag a playlist from the left side of the screen to Burn List on the right.

You can change the order of the songs before you burn them onto a CD. Drag song titles up or down the list to change the song order.

TIP

6. Note the Audio CD bar on the right side of the screen. It tells you whether there is enough disc space to burn all the songs on the list. If there is enough space, select the Start Burn button. It can take a few minutes to burn a CD. When the job is complete, your computer ejects the CD. I suggest playing it to see whether the songs copied correctly to the CD. While you're at it, label the CD by writing on it with a felt-tip (not a ballpoint) pen. Label the top of the CD, not the bottom.

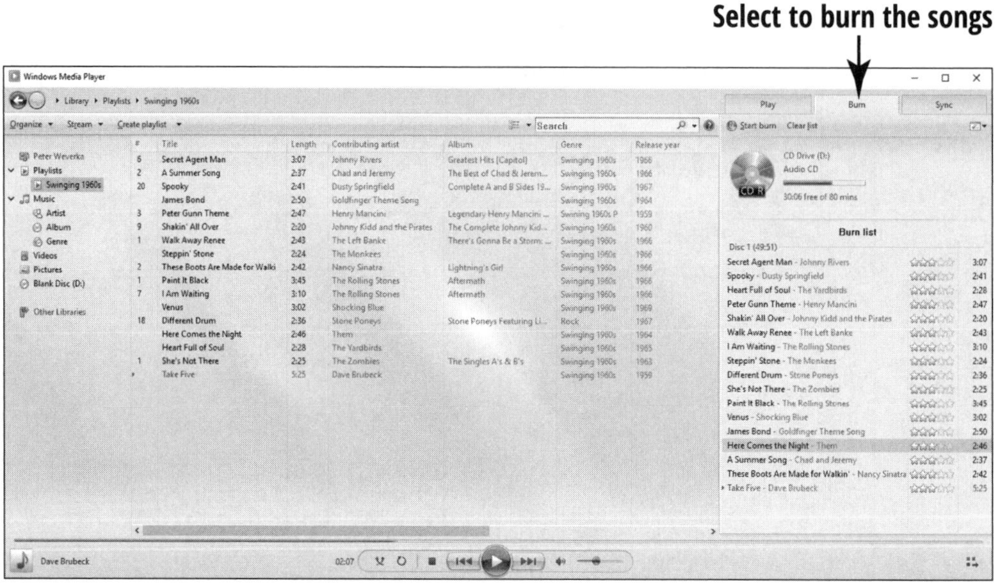

Select to burn the songs

(Screenshot of Windows Media Player showing a playlist "Swinging 1960s" with columns Title, Length, Contributing artist, Album, Genre, Release year, and a Burn list on the right side.)

FIGURE 11-13

Make a Voice Recording

1. Open the Voice Recorder app to record your voice. As shown in **Figure 11-14,** Voice Recorder lists recordings you already made (if you made any recordings).

TIP It goes without saying, but your computer needs a built-in microphone or microphone jack for plugging in a microphone if you want to make voice recordings.

TIP The first time you run Voice Recorder, a dialog box asks, "Let Windows Voice Recorder access your microphone?" Select Yes. To change this later, go to the Settings app.

2. Select the Record button (or press Ctrl+R) to begin a recording. A timer tells you how long your recording is. You can select the Pause/Resume button to temporarily stop a recording. Select the Pause/Resume button again to continue recording.

3. Select the Stop Recording button (located in the middle of the screen) to end a recording. The name of your recording appears in the list under the generic name *Recording*. To give it a more descriptive name, right-click or tap to display the recording's context menu (refer to **Figure 11-14**), choose Rename, enter a name, and select the Rename button.

Select a recording and select Play

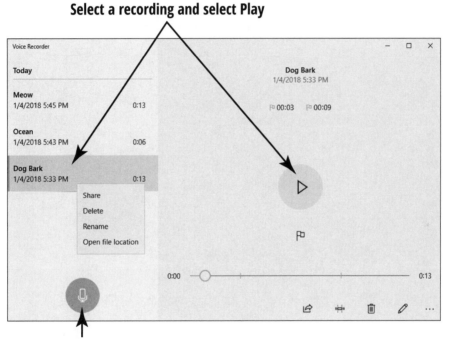

Start a recording

FIGURE 11-14

TIP

To delete a recording, display its context menu and choose Delete.

TIP

To access a Sound Recorder file, perhaps to copy or move it, display its context menu (refer to **Figure 11-14**) and choose Open File Location. The Sound Recordings folder opens. From here, you can copy or move the file. See Chapter 14 if you need instructions for handling files.

Beyond the Basics

4

Chapter **12**
Maintaining Windows 10

Windows 10 is a bit like a car. To make it run well, you have to maintain it.

Windows 10 uses the Security and Maintenance screen to keep you informed of issues that pertain to your computer's health. The screen divides issues into Security and Maintenance sections. The Reliability Monitor can help you pinpoint problems with hardware and software.

Machines such as toaster ovens aren't getting any smarter. Your computer, however, can be programmed to do something it's never done before. To make your computer capable of doing new things, you install new programs. On the other hand, your computer may have some programs that you'll never use and wouldn't miss. You don't have to get rid of them, but doing so is easy enough and frees a little space on your computer.

In this chapter, you work with the Security and Maintenance screen to check your computer's health status. You also install a program on the desktop and, optionally, uninstall one. This chapter also shows how to make your computer work faster by controlling the startup apps, defragmenting your hard drive, and deleting unnecessary system files. Finally, you discover how Windows Defender can protect your computer against spyware, viruses, and other foreign invaders.

Install a New Program on the Desktop

1. You can install software that you download from the web or from a CD or DVD for use on the desktop. (Windows 10 apps must be installed through the Microsoft Store.) In this set of steps, you install Audacity, a free program for editing audio files. To install Audacity, open your browser and enter **audacityteam.org/download** in the address bar. You land on the web page for downloading Audacity. (See Chapter 6 for information on using the Edge browser.)

TIP

If a website offers to install a program automatically, look at that suggestion with suspicion. It may be legitimate or it may be malevolent. Decline downloads from sources that you don't know and trust already.

2. Select the Audacity for Windows link.

3. Select the Audacity Installer link. In the dialog box that asks you whether to save the file, select Save.

4. Your browser displays a message at the bottom of the browser window, as shown in **Figure 12-1.** Select the Run button. If the User Account Control dialog box appears, select the Yes button to tell Windows you want to download and install the program. In the Select Setup Language dialog box, choose English and select OK.

TIP

Generally, if the installer for a program offers Express or Custom installation options, choose the Express option to let the installer set up the program without further input from you. The Custom or Advanced Settings option allows you to specify where to install the program and, perhaps, which parts of the program to install.

5. In the Setup – Audacity dialog boxes that appear, click Next until you come to the dialog box that asks whether you want to install the program. Select the Install button. In the Information dialog box shown in **Figure 12-2, top,** select the Next button. Last but not least, select the Finish button in the dialog box that tells you that Audacity has finished installing, as shown in **Figure 12-2, bottom.** The Audacity program opens on your screen.

TIP

Many programs try to connect to the Internet for updates during installation or when you run the installed program. The first time you run a program, you may be asked whether you want to register the program or configure some aspect of the program. Go with the default (assumed) responses, if you're not sure.

6. Close Audacity. You can do that by selecting the Close button (the X) in the upper-right corner of the screen.

7. Select the Start button to open the Start screen. Audacity appears twice on the apps list, once at the top under "Recently Added" and again under the letter *A*. Moreover, the word *New* appears under the name Audacity in the alphabetical list to indicate that you installed the program recently.

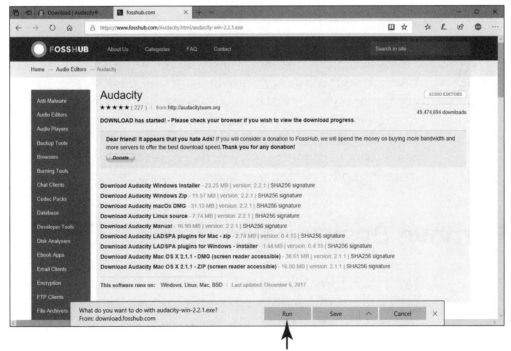

Select Run

FIGURE 12-1

FIGURE 12-2

TIP

To install a program that comes on a CD or DVD, insert the program disc into your computer's disc drive or tray, label side up (or, if your computer has a vertical disc slot, insert the disc with the label side facing left). The AutoPlay dialog box appears. Select the option to run Install or Setup. User Account Control may ask whether you really want to run this program. (Windows 10 tries to keep you from installing software unintentionally by asking for confirmation.)

Remove Desktop Programs

1. Unlike Windows 10 apps from the Microsoft Store, desktop programs are installed and uninstalled directly through the desktop itself. To see which desktop programs are installed, open the Control Panel. Type **control panel** in the Search box (which is located on the left side of the taskbar) and select Control Panel in the Search panel.

TIP

Many of the functions covered in this chapter are part of the Control Panel, which presents many functions for tweaking your computer setup.

2. In the Control Panel window (shown in **Figure 12-3**), under Programs, select Uninstall a Program. (You don't have to uninstall anything; you can simply see what the option offers.) You see the Programs and Features window.

3. The Programs and Features window lists desktop programs, not Windows 10 apps. Initially, these programs are sorted by name. You may want to see the date you last used each program because a program you haven't used in ages may be a candidate for removal. (Otherwise, skip to Step 5.) Use one of the following techniques to display the date last used:

   • **Mouse:** Move the mouse pointer over any column heading, such as Name. Click the right mouse button.

   • **Touchscreen:** Tap and hold down on any column heading, such as Name. When a box appears around your fingertip, lift your finger.

4. On the context menu that appears, select More. In the Choose Details window (shown in **Figure 12-4**), select Last Used On and then select the OK button. The Last Used On column appears to the right of all the other columns.

Uninstall a desktop program or just look

FIGURE 12-3

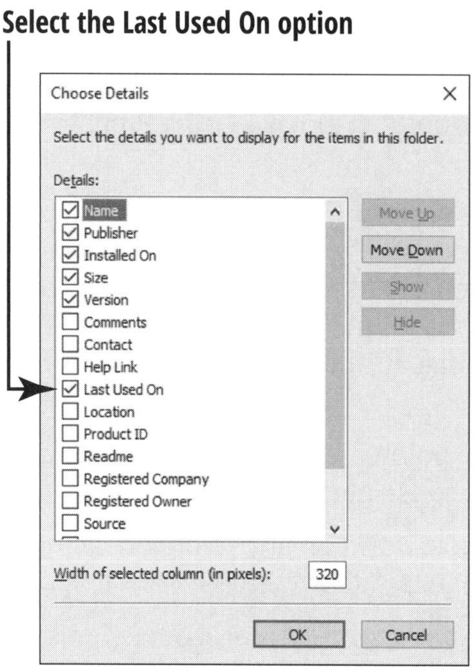

Select the Last Used On option

Choose Details   ✕

Select the details you want to display for the items in this folder.

De_t_ails:

☑ Name
☑ Publisher
☑ Installed On
☑ Size
☑ Version
☐ Comments
☐ Contact
☐ Help Link
☑ Last Used On
☐ Location
☐ Product ID
☐ Readme
☐ Registered Company
☐ Registered Owner
☐ Source

Move _U_p
Move _D_own
_S_how
_Hi_de

_W_idth of selected column (in pixels):   320

OK   Cancel

FIGURE 12-4

TIP

Before you uninstall a program that you may want to reinstall later, make sure that you have a copy of it on a CD or DVD (or that you know where to download it from the web again). You have no undo option when you uninstall a program.

5. To uninstall a program, select it. For this example, select Audacity, as shown in **Figure 12-5.** You don't have to uninstall Audacity, but if you do, you can follow the steps in the preceding section to reinstall it.

6. Select the Uninstall button (located above the list of program names). Some programs offer the Change and Repair options as well as Uninstall. Repair or Change may be useful for a desktop program that you want to keep but isn't running as expected. When Windows 10 asks whether you really to uninstall, select Yes or No.

7. If you uninstalled Audacity or another program, it will no longer appear in the Programs and Features window or on the Start screen.

TIP

Just because you can uninstall a program doesn't mean you should. You can simply ignore programs you don't use. Look at a program's name, publisher, and date installed to determine whether you actually use a program. You may recognize a program you installed recently, as opposed to one installed before you got your computer. If you find that it's more productive to remove large programs than small ones, repeat Steps 3 and 4 to group by size.

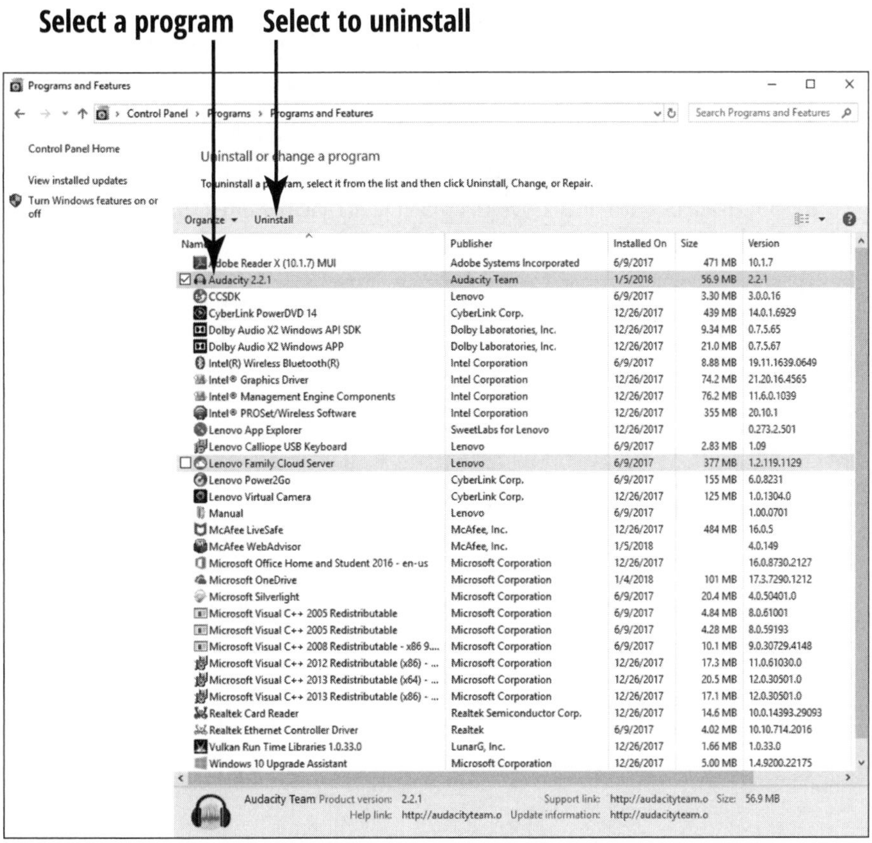

Select a program   **Select to uninstall**

FIGURE 12-5

Control Startup Apps

1. Startup apps are applications that start running when you turn on your computer. You might be surprised by how many startup apps run in the background without your knowing it. Occasionally you install new software or download a program from the Internet and discover that it runs automatically whether you like it or not. Sometimes the number of startup apps slows the computer down.

To see which apps start running automatically when you turn on your computer, start the Task Manager with one of these techniques:

- **Keyboard:** Press Ctrl+Alt+Del and select Task Manager on the blue screen.
- **Desktop:** On the Desktop, enter **task** in the Search box and then select the Task Manager tile on the menu that appears.

2. Select More Details (if necessary) in the Task Manager window and then select the Startup tab, as shown in **Figure 12-6.** This is the list of applications that start when your computer starts.

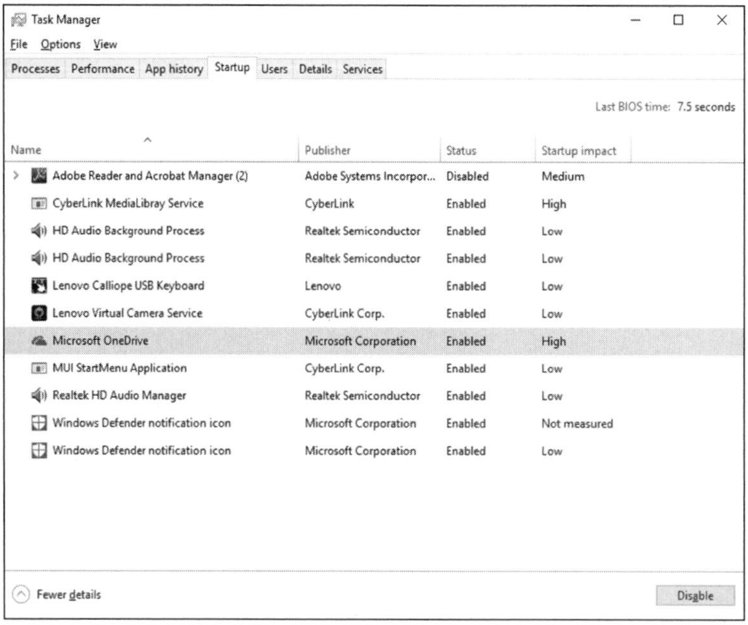

Task Manager
File Options View
Processes Performance App history Startup Users Details Services
Last BIOS time: 7.5 seconds
Name Publisher Status Startup impact
Adobe Reader and Acrobat Manager (2) Adobe Systems Incorpor... Disabled Medium
CyberLink MediaLibray Service CyberLink Enabled High
HD Audio Background Process Realtek Semiconductor Enabled Low
HD Audio Background Process Realtek Semiconductor Enabled Low
Lenovo Calliope USB Keyboard Lenovo Enabled Low
Lenovo Virtual Camera Service CyberLink Corp. Enabled Low
Microsoft OneDrive Microsoft Corporation Enabled High
MUI StartMenu Application CyberLink Corp. Enabled Low
Realtek HD Audio Manager Realtek Semiconductor Enabled Low
Windows Defender notification icon Microsoft Corporation Enabled Not measured
Windows Defender notification icon Microsoft Corporation Enabled Low
Fewer details
Disable

FIGURE 12-6

3. Use one of these techniques to open your browser, go on the Internet, and find out what one of these startup applications does:

- **Mouse:** Right-click an application and choose Search Online.
- **Touchscreen:** Tap and hold down the name of an application. When a box appears around your fingertip, select Search Online.

4. Notice the Startup Impact column in the Task Manager. Applications with a high impact such as Microsoft OneDrive may be slowing

down your computer. If you decide that one of these applications is unwanted or is slowing you down, disable it. (Don't worry, you can enable it later on very easily, as I explain shortly.) To disable an application, select its name in the list and then select the Disable button.

TIP

To enable a startup application in the Task Manager (refer to **Figure 12-6**), select its name and then select the Enable button. The Status column in the Task Manager tells you whether a startup application has been disabled.

Explore System Information

1. On the desktop, type **control panel** in the Search box. This box is located on the left side of the taskbar. The Search panel appears.

2. Select Control Panel in the Search panel. In the Control Panel, select System and Security.

3. In the System and Security window, select System. The System window shown in **Figure 12-7** appears. This screen is chock-full of information and functions. Note each of the following areas onscreen:

   - **Windows edition:** Of course, you have Windows 10. However, Windows 10 comes in two primary editions: the Home edition, which you are likely to have, and the Pro edition, for computer professionals. You may find information here about so-called Service Packs, which are large collections of updates to Windows 10.

   - **System:** This section displays details about your hardware, including the processor, the amount of installed memory (RAM), and other details.

   - **Computer name, domain, and workgroup settings:** This information pertains to your network, if you have one. If a computer can't connect to a network, the problem is often related to the name of the Workgroup (a network). The Change Settings function lets you change the Workgroup name to match other computers on the same network.

TIP

   Windows 10 gives your computer a nondescript, generic name to begin with. To give your computer a more descriptive name, select Change Settings in the Computer Name, Domain, and

Workgroup Settings section of the System window (refer to **Figure 12-7**). The System Properties dialog box appears. Select the Change button and enter a new name in the Computer Name/Domain Changes dialog box.

- **Windows activation:** In an effort to control software piracy involving bootlegged copies of Windows 10, each copy of Windows 10 must be activated. Odds are that you activated your copy the first time you started your computer. If you don't see *Windows is activated* in this section, select the adjacent link.

TIP

Don't be alarmed by the System information and options. If all goes well, you don't have to use most of what you find here. Some familiarity with this screen will be useful, however, if all doesn't go well later.

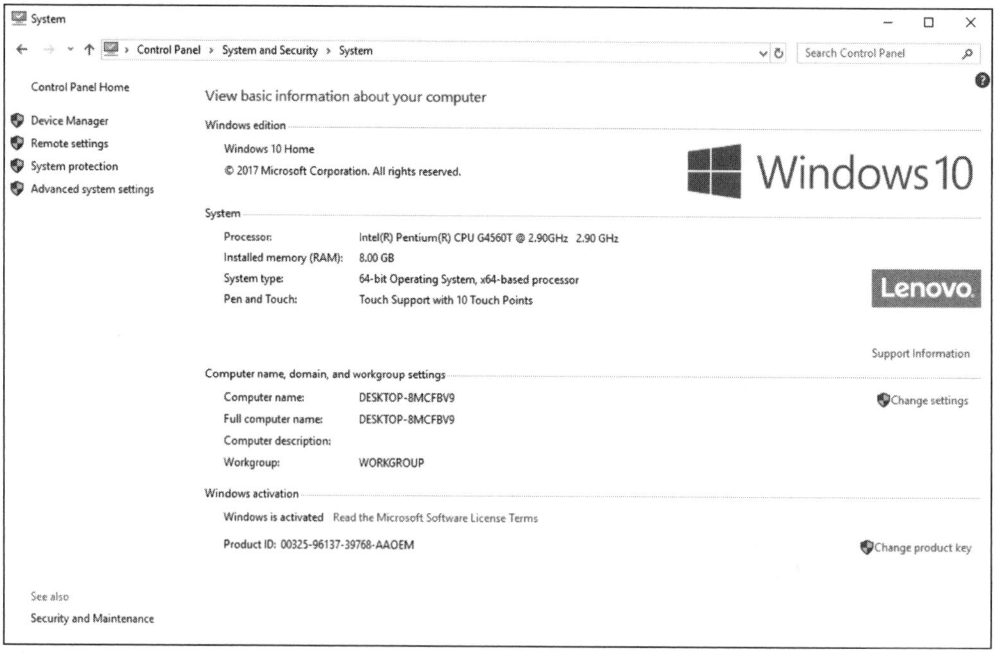

FIGURE 12-7

Check Your Security and Maintenance Status

1. In the System window (refer to **Figure 12-7**), select Security and Maintenance in the lower-left corner. The Security and Maintenance window appears, as shown in **Figure 12-8.**

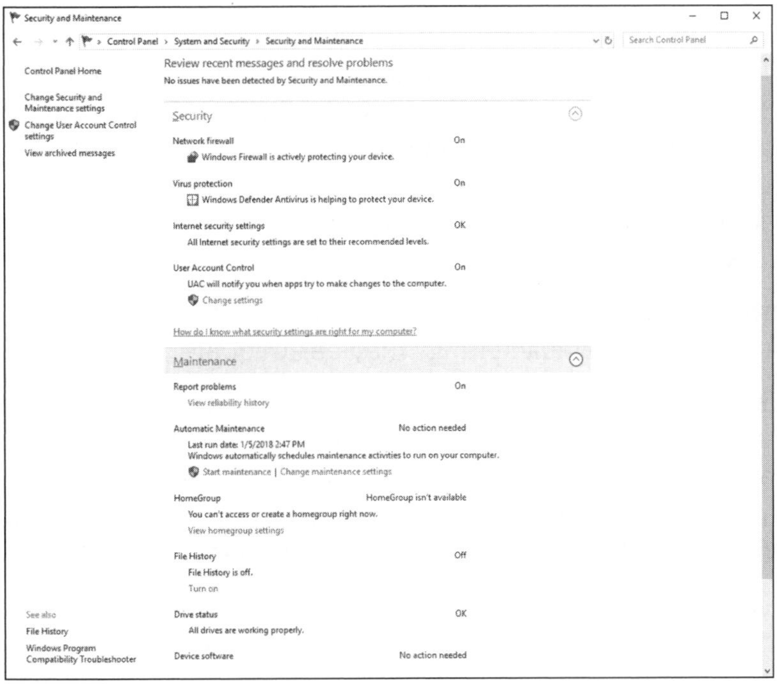

FIGURE 12-8

TIP

Another way to open the Security and Maintenance window is to type **Security and Maintenance** in the Search box on the Windows taskbar.

2. Note any message displayed under Review Recent Messages and Resolve Problems. Ideally, you see *No issues have been detected by Security and Maintenance.* If you see a message concerning a specific problem, select that message for more information.

3. Select the Security heading in the Security and Maintenance window. That section expands to detail security functions. Every option should display *On* or *OK.* Here's a brief description of each item under Security:

- **Network Firewall:** The firewall scans Internet traffic and blocks activity from programs that don't have explicit permission to use Internet access. When you install a program that uses the Internet, you may be asked to approve the connection the first time. The safest practice is to reject online connections that you don't initiate or recognize.

- **Virus Protection:** Having virus protection for your computer is essential. Windows Defender, an antivirus protection program, comes with Windows 10, although you can install another antivirus program if you want. Later in this chapter, "Protect Your Computer with Windows Defender" explains how the Windows Defender works.

- **Internet Security Settings:** These settings pertain to your browser. The default settings may be adequate.

- **User Account Control:** This function notifies you of programs that try to make changes to your system and requires that you confirm any such changes. In particular, UAC lets you know when a program tries to run or install software that may be malicious. When in doubt, say No or Cancel to UAC messages.

4. Select the Maintenance heading to see what that section includes. Functions under Maintenance consist of the following:

- **Report problems:** This setting is on, allowing Windows 10 to regularly check for solutions to problems it uncovers. (In Step 5, you run the Reliability History report from this part of the screen.)

- **Automatic Maintenance:** Your computer automatically performs critical updates, security scans, and diagnostics each day.

TIP

If your computer is in a guest room or bedroom, you may want to change the Automatic Maintenance setting to run maintenance tasks at some time other than the default 3:00 a.m. Your computer may actually wake up at that hour for maintenance (although, if your computer is connected to a power strip, you can turn off the power strip and prevent your computer from turning on automatically in the middle of the night). If the computer can't run maintenance at the appointed hour, it will do so at the next opportunity.

- **HomeGroup:** A *homegroup* is a network that allows you to share files and printers between two or more computers.

- **File History:** See Chapter 15 for information on using the File History option, which is off by default.

- **Drive status:** *Drives* are hard disks inside or attached to your computer. Your documents, photos, and Windows 10 itself are stored on one or more drives. Ideally, the drive status is *All drives are working properly*. See Chapter 15 for information on backing up and restoring files.

- **Device software:** If a device on your computer needs a driver or other type of software to run properly, you are alerted here. Select Install Device Software to install the software.

TIP

The Security and Maintenance window is a troubleshooting tool, so you should check it if you have problems running Windows 10.

5. Under Report Problems, select View Reliability History. As shown in **Figure 12-9,** the Reliability Monitor screen graphs your computer's stability and indicates hardware and software problems, including those you may not be aware of. On this screen, red circles indicate critical events such as computer crashes; blue circles are information about software installation and updates; and yellow triangles indicate warnings about noncritical events (something that didn't crash the computer). Select a day in the graph to display details in the lower portion of the screen.

TIP

Reviewing the Reliability Monitor screen helps you distinguish between a one-time glitch and a recurring or worsening problem.

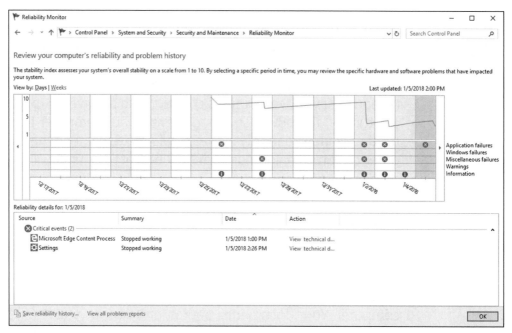

FIGURE 12-9

Speed Up Your Computer

1. Computers are like people — they tend to slow down with age. However, Windows 10 offers a couple of administrative tools that can make your computer work faster. To find out what these tools are, go to the desktop and type **administrative tools** in the Search box. Then select the Administrative Tools tile to open the Administrative Tools area of the Control Panel, as shown in **Figure 12-10.**

2. Select Defragment and Optimize Drives. The Optimize Drives screen opens, as shown in **Figure 12-11.** When you save a file, the new data you recently added gets placed on the hard drive wherever Windows 10 can find room for it. Consequently, a file is stored in many different places. If you've used your computer for a long time, files become fragmented — the bits and pieces are spread all over the drive and your computer has to work hard to assemble all the pieces to open a file.

3. Select the C drive and then select the Optimize button. Windows 10 optimizes your hard drive by moving the bits and pieces of files so that they are stored next to each other on the hard drive. It can take a few minutes or a few hours to optimize a hard drive, but no matter, because Windows 10 conducts this activity in the background and you can go on to do other tasks.

4. Return to the Administrative Tools screen (refer to **Figure 12-10**) and select Disk Cleanup. The Disk Cleanup for Windows dialog box appears, as shown in **Figure 12-12.** It tells you how much disk space you can make available on your hard drive by removing unnecessary files.

5. Select the types of files you want deleted, and then select the Clean Up System Files button. A message box appears as the files are deleted from your computer.

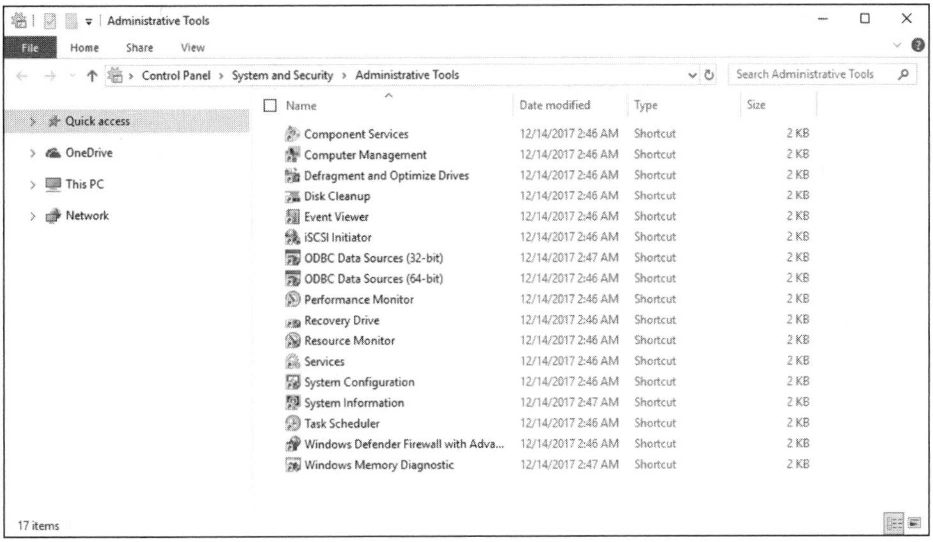

FIGURE 12-10

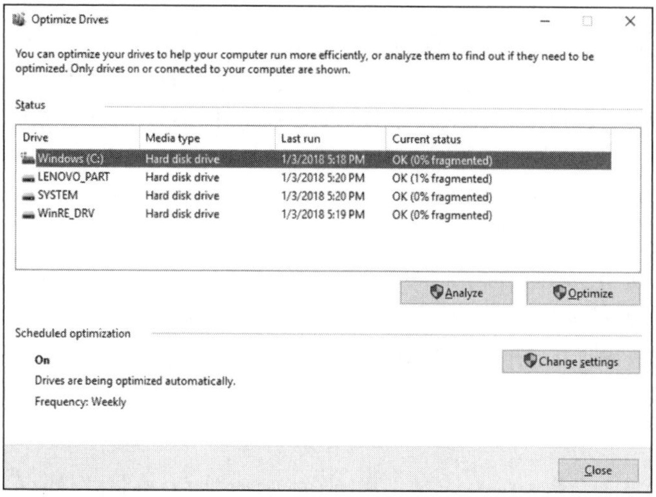

FIGURE 12-11

FIGURE 12-12

Protect Your Computer with Windows Defender

1. Windows Defender identifies and removes viruses, spyware, and other malefactors from your computer. To refine your use of Windows Defender, type **windows defender** in the Search box on the left side of the taskbar and then select the Windows Defender Settings tile in the Search panel. The Settings app opens to its Windows Defender page. Select the Open Windows Defender Security Center button to open the Security Center, as shown in **Figure 12-13.**

2. The Home tab of the Windows Defender Security Center tells you whether the defense mechanisms on your computer are up to date. If they aren't up to date, you can take actions in the Security Center to update your computer's defenses. Select Virus & Threat Protection to open the screen shown in **Figure 12-14, top.**

3. Windows Defender performs "quick scans" in the background each time you run your computer. From time to time, to make sure your computer is thoroughly clean of viruses and spyware, run a full scan. Select the Advanced Scan link to open the Advanced Scans window, shown in **Figure 12-14, bottom.** Then make sure that the Full Scan option is selected and select the Scan Now button.

4. A full scan can take a long time as Windows Defender examines all the files on your computer for viruses and spyware. You can do other tasks on your computer while the full scan is running. If Windows Defender finds a bad actor, the file with the virus or spyware is quarantined so that it won't harm your computer.

5. Close Windows Defender.

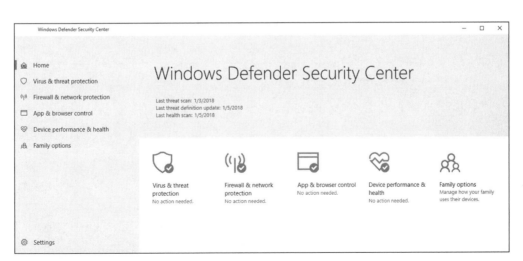

FIGURE 12-13

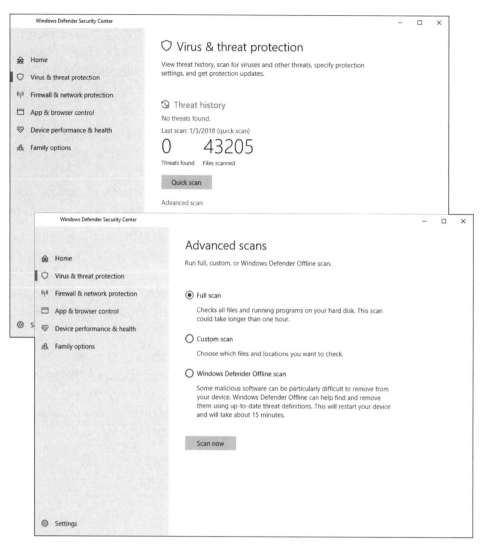

FIGURE 12-14

Chapter 13

Connecting a Printer and Other Devices

Every computer has a screen. Most computers, other than tablets, also have a keyboard and a mouse or other pointing device. You can add a mouse to a laptop that lacks one or replace the keyboard or mouse that came with your computer. Add a printer or a scanner to extend your computer's functionality.

For any hardware add-ons — which tech folk call *peripherals* — Windows 10 has a trick up its sleeve. Thanks to *plug-and-play* technology, which automatically identifies add-on devices, connecting new devices to your computer can be quite easy.

In this chapter, you explore the devices connected to your computer, as well as options available for those devices. You find out how to access devices connected to your computer and also calibrate a touchscreen to make it work better for you.

Trust USB Plug and Play for Hardware

You may find many kinds of add-on devices useful:

» A **printer** lets you, well, print documents and photos. Your choices for printers include black and white versus color, and inkjet versus laser printer. A multifunction printer also works as a copier, scanner, and fax machine.

» A **digital camera** captures photos that you can copy to your computer to enjoy and to share with others. See Chapter 10 for information on working with photos.

» A **scanner** enables you to make digital images of old photos or documents so that you can view them onscreen. Chapter 10 explains how to use a scanner.

» An **external hard drive** stores backup copies of your files. See Chapter 15 for information on adding an external hard drive to your computer.

» An additional or replacement **pointing device** (your mouse is a pointing device), including a trackball or a pen with a tablet, may be more comfortable to use than what came with your computer. Switching between pointing devices helps you avoid repetitive stress. A wireless mouse eliminates the hassle of dealing with a cord. Some people like to add a mouse as an alternative to their laptop's built-in touchpad.

» A **microphone** is crucial for communicating by voice with your computer, through speech recognition, or with your friends over the Internet. A combination headset with microphone may produce the clearest sound.

» A **video camera** (or *webcam*) is essential for video phone calls *à la* the Jetsons. See Chapter 10 for information on using a video camera.

The majority of these devices connect using *USB* (Universal Serial Bus) technology. When you connect a device to your computer using a USB cable to the USB port (see **Figure 13-1**), the device identifies itself to the computer. This identification process is called *plug and play*. Ideally, you connect your device, and it simply works.

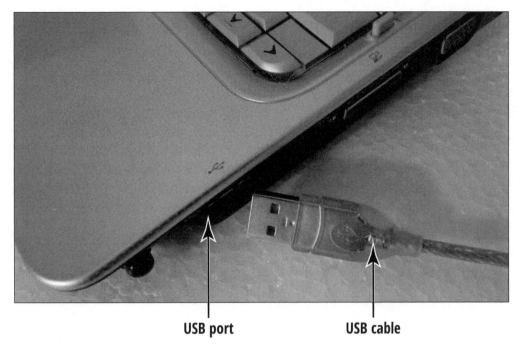

USB port   **USB cable**

FIGURE 13-1

Windows 10 uses a *device driver* to communicate with an add-on device. The driver is really a program that tells Windows 10 how to run the device. When you connect a device, such as a printer, Windows 10 looks for a driver (in this case, a *printer driver*). That driver may be built into Windows 10, come on a disc that's packaged with the device, or need to be downloaded from the Internet, either automatically by Windows 10 or manually by you.

TIP

Every computer has at least a couple of USB ports. Some are in the front; others are in the back or top of the computer and are harder to reach. If your computer doesn't have enough ports, you can add more by buying a USB hub, which is a small box with two to four USB ports. If a port is hard to reach with a device's cable, you can buy a USB extension cable. Office supply stores may have hubs and cables.

TIP

Bluetooth is a wireless technology for adding devices to your computer. If your computer has Bluetooth, you can use Bluetooth as well as USB to add some devices, especially a microphone or headset.

See All Devices

1. Choose Settings on the Start menu. The Settings window opens. Choose Devices (if it isn't already chosen) to open the Bluetooth & Other Devices category of the Devices window, as shown in **Figure 13-2, top.** Devices listed may include your monitor, speakers, headphones, keyboard, mouse, and more. Devices shared through your homegroup or network also appear here. For information on adjusting device settings, see the "Access Device Options on the Desktop" section, later in the chapter.

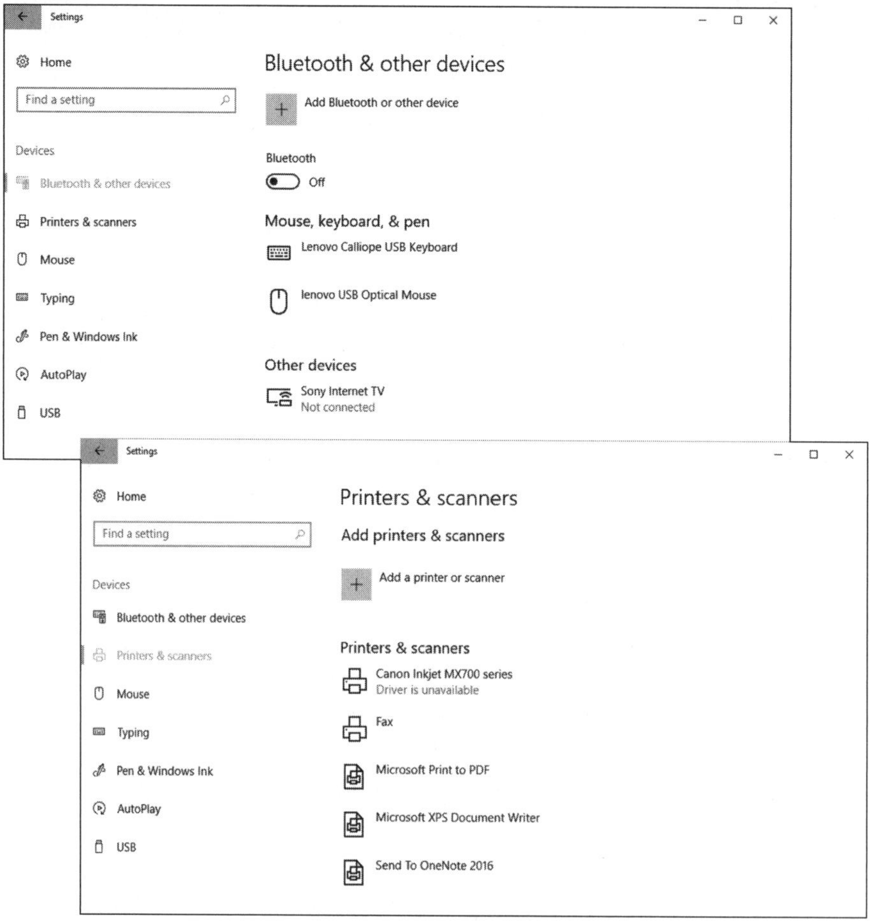

FIGURE 13-2

2. Select the Printers & Scanners category in the Devices window, as shown in **Figure 13-2, bottom.** This screen lists printers and scanners that are connected to your computer.

Some, but not all, devices display information below the device name. A network device may display *Offline* (not accessible) or it may display nothing if it is accessible. A printer may display *Ready* or it may display nothing if the printer isn't ready.

You are unlikely to need the Add a Bluetooth or Other Device button because most devices are added *automagically* (that's a word nerds like to use). However, if you select Add a Device, Windows 10 scans for additional hardware. No harm in doing so.

Connect a Printer or Other Device

1. Take your printer out of the box. Keep all the packing material together until you know you won't need to return the printer. Arrange all the components for easy access. In addition to the printer, you'll probably find ink cartridges or a toner cartridge, a power cable, and a CD with printer software. Read the setup instructions that come with your printer.

Some of these steps apply to other devices, such as a mouse, a webcam, or a microphone. Printers often have more packaging and require more assembly than other devices.

2. Remove all tape from the printer. Most printers ship with the print mechanism locked in place to prevent it from moving during shipping. Look for brightly colored tape, paper, or plastic indicating what you need to move or remove to release the print mechanism.

3. Put the printer within cable length of your computer. Insert the ink or toner cartridge before you turn on the printer for the first time. Place some paper in the paper drawer or tray. Connect the printer to the power supply. Plug the printer cable into the printer and into the computer.

Your printer may have come with a disc with a printer driver and other software. I recommend using the disc to install your printer. Allow Windows 10 to install a printer only if you don't have the disc.

4. Turn on the printer. A notification tells you that Windows is "setting up a device." If all goes well, you soon see this notification: *Device is ready,* your printer (the brand and model number of your printer) *is set up and ready to go.* You may see other informational messages as Windows 10 handles the configuration.

5. To confirm that your printer is installed properly, see the preceding section, "See All Devices."

Access Device Options on the Desktop

1. For more control over device setup, open the Control Panel to the Devices and Printers window. Enter **control panel** in the Search box on the taskbar. Then select Control Panel in the search results to open the Control Panel, and select View Devices and Printers (under Hardware and Sound) to display the window shown in **Figure 13-3.**

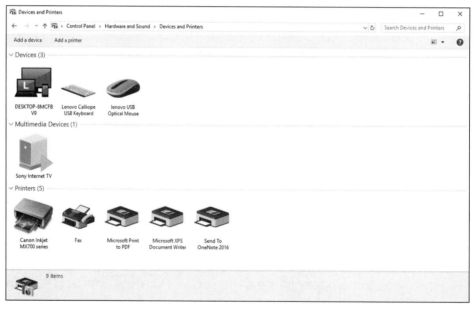

FIGURE 13-3

2. The Device and Printers window shows the devices attached to your computer, including the computer itself, the display (or monitor), external add-on devices (such as a hard drive, flash drive, or memory card), and the mouse.

TIP

Most of these devices also appear in the Devices category of the Settings app (refer to **Figure 13-2**). However, you'll find options under Devices and Printers that aren't available in the Settings app.

TIP

Windows 10 automatically installs the Microsoft XPS Document Writer. This device doesn't print but does create files that you can print later using a real printer. For example, if you're in a coffee shop and want to print a web page or an email message, you can use this device and then open the file it creates when your computer is connected to a printer. (That file will open in Acrobat Reader.)

3. Double-click or double-tap the device you want to examine. This action opens the device's properties in a window with options or in a smaller box with limited information and options. (Older devices have more limited information.) **Figure 13-4** shows information about a printer. When you're finished reviewing the information or selecting available options, return to the previous screen using one of these methods:

- If a small box is open, close it.

- If a full-screen dialog box is open, select the back arrow or select Devices and Printers near the top of the window.

FIGURE 13-4

4. Display the context menu of options for your printer (or any device) using one of these methods: Click the right mouse button, or tap and hold until you see a small box appear under your finger and then release. Select Printer Properties from the context menu. (Oddly, the menu also has a separate Properties option — be sure to select Printer Properties instead.)

5. In the Properties window, select the Print Test Page button. Another window opens indicating *A test page has been sent to your printer.* Select Close.

TIP

If a test page doesn't print, check that both ends of the cable are plugged in properly and make sure the printer is turned on. Try to print a test page again. For more help, contact the printer manufacturer or the store where you bought the printer, or search the web.

TIP

If you're having problems with any device, select the Troubleshoot option on the context menu to open a guided troubleshooting program that will walk you through options for resolving problems with the device.

TIP

The top of the Devices and Printers window has the Add a Device and Add a Printer buttons, but you need to use them only if Windows 10 doesn't automatically detect and install your device. With USB and plug and play, most devices install automatically.

Calibrate Your Touchscreen

1. If you have a problem accurately selecting objects on your screen using touch, you can calibrate your screen alignment. In this case, calibrating means to help Windows 10 understand what constitutes a tap on the screen. Enter **control panel** in the Search box on the taskbar, select Control Panel in the search results, and select Hardware and Sound in the Control Panel window. You see the Hardware and Sound window, shown in **Figure 13-5, top.**

2. In the Hardware and Sound window, select Calibrate the Screen for Pen or Touch Input, as shown in **Figure 13-5.** The Tablet PC dialog box appears (refer to **Figure 13-5, bottom**).

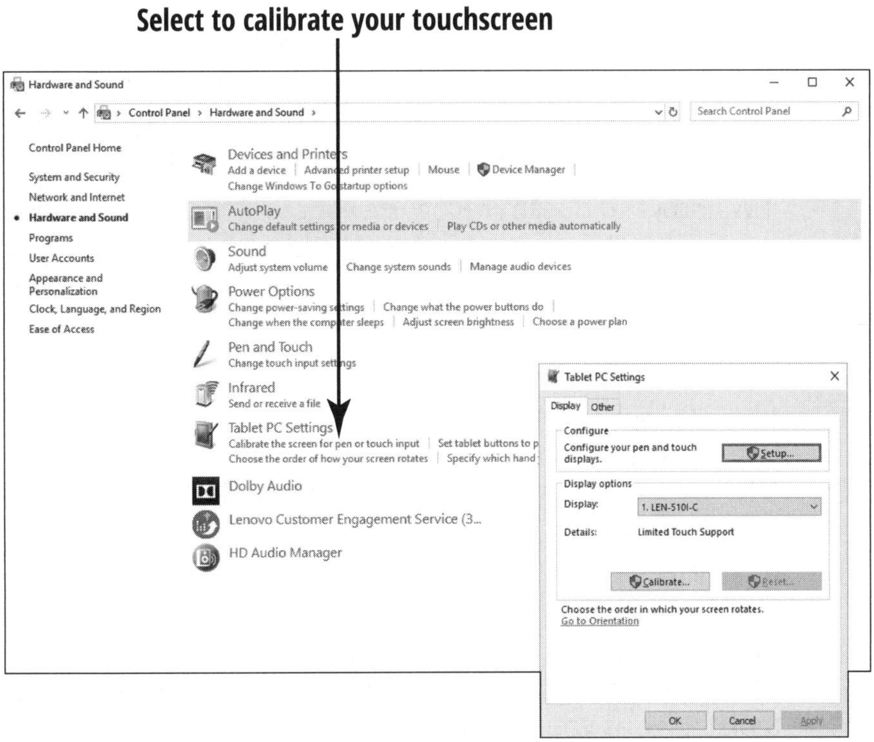

Select to calibrate your touchscreen

FIGURE 13-5

3. Select the Calibrate button. User Account Control may ask you to confirm that you want to run the Digitizer Calibration Tool. If so, select Yes.

TIP

If your touchscreen is badly calibrated, you may not be able to tap the Calibrate button. In that case, plug in a mouse to make the selection, and then continue using touch.

4. The screen displays lines around its perimeter, forming a box near the edge of the screen and a second box inside the first about half an inch from the edge. Lines connect these boxes near each corner. The result is 16 intersections. Starting at the upper-left corner, use your finger or a stylus to tap each intersection, which displays two short black lines forming crosshairs. As you touch each intersection, Windows 10 measures your touch and adjusts touch settings accordingly. After each touch is recorded, the crosshairs move to the next intersection to the right. (If the crosshairs don't move, tap the previous intersection again.) As the crosshairs move, tap the highlighted intersection, left to right, down, and then left to right again. The process takes much longer to read about than to do.

TIP

If Windows 10 doesn't recognize your touch, it won't continue with the process. The screen says *Right-click anywhere to return to the last calibration point*. What if you don't have a mouse? Tap and hold until you see the little box under your fingertip, and then release — that's the touch equivalent of a click of the right mouse button.

5. After you have selected each of the 16 calibration points in turn, a box pops up asking whether you want to save the calibration data. Select OK unless you think something went wrong. In that case, select Cancel.

TIP

It's unlikely but possible that you can't continue to the end of the process. If so, the screen says *Press the Esc button to close the tool*. What if you don't have a keyboard? In that case, press and hold the Windows button (the one with the four-part Windows logo) on the tablet edge as you also press the power button, and then release both. On the next screen, select Task Manager. In the Task Manager window, select Digitizer Calibration Tool, and then select the End Task button. (Makes one yearn for an Esc key.)

Chapter **14**
Working with Files

Ah the data inside your computer is stored on a disk. Your computer has a primary disk, formally called the internal *hard drive.* You may see this disk referred to as the C: drive. (The terms *drive* and *disk* are interchangeable.)

The contents of a disk are organized into individual files. When you create a file and save it for the first time, you create a file on a disk. Many other files on the disk belong to the programs you use, including the thousands of files that make up Windows 10.

Disks also are organized into *folders,* which are containers for files. For its own files, Windows 10 has a main folder that contains dozens of other folders (called *subfolders*). Inside or below that user account folder, Windows 10 creates more folders to help you organize your files by type. For example, by default all your photos go into the Pictures folder, and all your documents go into the Documents folder.

In this chapter, you discover how to save and open a file, search for files, and explore your disk, folders, and files. You work with File Explorer as you create new folders to organize documents and move files from one folder to another. You also copy files from your hard drive to other disks to take with you or give to other people. This chapter also explains how to rename and delete files and folders.

What if you delete a file or folder and you regret doing so? Don't worry, because this chapter shows how to get back a file or folder that you mistakenly deleted.

Save and Open a File

1. In computer land, nothing is more important than files. Computer programs are stored in files. Data is stored in files. To start working, you open a file. When you're finished working, you save and close your file. To experiment with files, open WordPad, the word processing app that comes with Windows 10.

TIP

Chapter 2 explains how to open apps. Chapter 8 looks into WordPad and how it can serve your word processing needs.

2. As shown in **Figure 14-1, top,** type a few words into WordPad and then save your file. Most apps (WordPad included) offer three ways to save a file:

- Select the Save button.

- Press Ctrl+S.

- Open the File menu and choose Save.

3. When you save a file for the first time, the Save As dialog box appears (refer to **Figure 14-1, bottom**). It invites you to give the file a name and to tell Windows 10 which folder to keep it in. Enter the name **My File** in the File Name text box. The Save As dialog box offers the means of choosing a folder for your file. For now, you can store your file in the Documents folder, the folder that Windows 10 selected for you (refer to **Figure 14-1, bottom**). Notice that the Documents folder is already selected in the navigation pane on the left side of the Save As dialog box.

4. Select the Save button in the Save As dialog box. Congratulations! You just saved your file. The title bar at the top of the WordPad window shows the name of your file, "My File." When you're not sure what a file is called, look at the title bar along the top of the screen.

5. Close WordPad. The fastest way to close an app is to select the Close button (the X) in the upper-right corner of the screen.

Save button

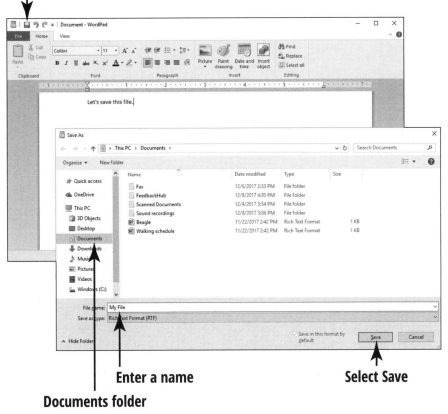

Enter a name

Select Save

Documents folder

FIGURE 14-1

6. Open WordPad as you did in Step 1. Where is My File, the file you saved and named in Steps 4 and 5?

7. Open the File menu (select the word *File* in the upper-left corner of the screen) and choose Open. The Open dialog box appears, as shown in **Figure 14-2.** This dialog box is the mirror image of the Save As dialog box that you saw earlier. Use it to locate the file you want to open. In this case, Windows 10 has opened the dialog box to its favorite folder, Documents, which also happens to be the folder where My File is stored.

8. Choose My File and then select the Open button (refer to **Figure 14-2**). My File opens onscreen.

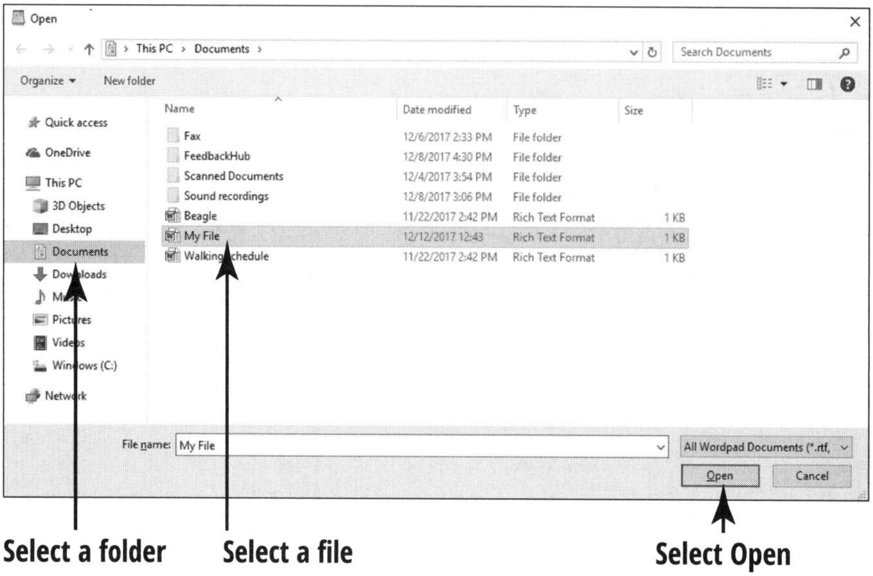

![Open dialog box screenshot]

Select a folder   **Select a file**   **Select Open**

FIGURE 14-2

TIP   Most apps offer shortcuts for opening files. In WordPad, for example, you see a list of files you recently opened on the File menu. You can select a filename on the list to open a file straightaway.

TIP   You can open files by selecting their names in File Explorer. See "Use File Explorer for Easy Access to Files," later in this chapter.

Find a Misplaced File

1. To search for a misplaced file, begin in the Search box. This box is located on the left side of the taskbar. Type the name of a document or photo you have on your computer. The search results panel appears, as shown in **Figure 14-3.**

TIP   Initially, the search panel shows all and sundry — settings, apps, files, websites, and other search opportunities — in the search results. If you don't see the item you want in a search, narrow the list of items by selecting one of the three Find Results buttons at the top of the search panel — In Apps, In Documents, or In Web. Find Results in Documents narrows the search to items on your computer.

Narrow the search

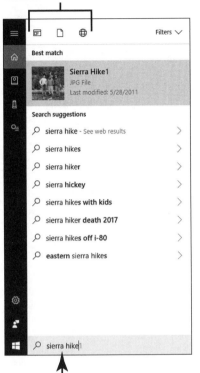

Enter a search term

FIGURE 14-3

2. To open a file, select it in the search results. If more than one application on your computer is capable of opening the file, you may see the How Do You Want to Open This File? dialog box, as shown in **Figure 14-4.** Select an application to open the file.

TIP

The How Do You Want to Open This File? dialog box offers a means of telling Windows 10 to always open files of a certain type with a particular application (refer to **Figure 14-4**). Selecting the Always Use This App to Open check box tells Windows 10 to open files of a certain type automatically with the app you chose.

3. Close the app that opens the file by using one of these methods:

- Click or tap the Close button (the X located in the upper-right corner of the screen).

- Press Alt+F4.

Choose an application

How do you want to open this file?

	Look for an app in the Store
	Adobe Reader
	Internet Explorer
	Notepad
	Office XML Handler
	Paint
	Windows Media Player

☐ Always use this app to open .dll files

OK

**Select to always open files of this type
with the application you choose**

FIGURE 14-4

TIP

Strictly speaking, if you find what you're looking for, stop looking. (No extra charge for pearls of wisdom.) In this case, however, keep looking because doing so reveals important information about how files are organized and how you can take control of that organization.

4. On the desktop, select the File Explorer icon (the yellow folder) in the taskbar. File Explorer opens. Note the *Ribbon,* which is the collapsible toolbar at the top of the window, as shown in **Figure 14-5.**

TIP

On the Ribbon, tools are grouped by tabs, which in File Explorer consist of File, Home, Share, and View, as well as other tabs that appear based on the selection. Tabs are further divided into sections, labeled below the related tools. (Note, for example, the Clipboard section on the Home tab.) To expand the Ribbon, select the up arrow at the far right of the tabs. Collapse the Ribbon by selecting the down arrow. Select a tab to display its tools, regardless of whether the Ribbon is expanded or collapsed.

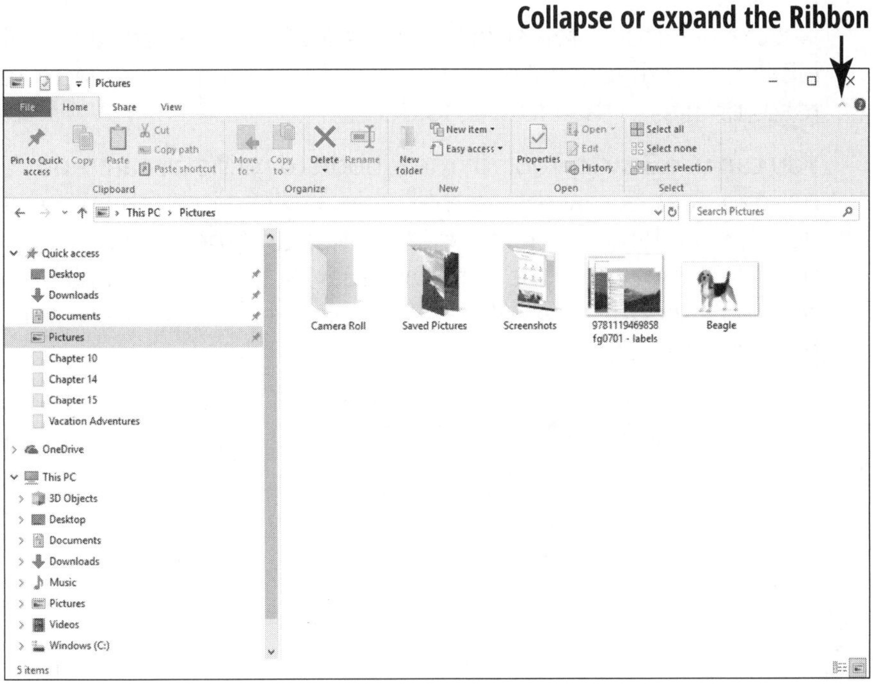

Collapse or expand the Ribbon

FIGURE 14-5

5. Select This PC on the left side of the File Explorer window, and then select the box labeled *Search* (probably followed by *This PC*), below the Ribbon and to the right. Type the same search term you used in Step 1. As you type, File Explorer displays any matching files, highlighting the text that matches. **Figure 14-6** shows the results of a search on my computer using the search term *sierra*.

TIP

On a touchscreen, the virtual keyboard doesn't appear on the desktop until you select the keyboard icon on the right side of the taskbar.

TIP

If the search results include too many files, making it hard to see the one you want, type more of the filename in the Search box. The number of matching files should decrease as you type more text in the box.

6. The *focus* of a search — where File Explorer searches — determines what files and folders are found. In Step 5, you selected This PC, making all the files on your computer the focus of the search. Accordingly, Windows 10 searched for files and folders throughout your computer. To change the focus of your search to the Pictures folder, select the Pictures folder in the navigation pane. Then select the box labeled Search and enter your search term again. The search results focus on files in the Pictures folder.

TIP

You can use Search Tools in the Ribbon to refine a search, as needed. Start a search and then select the Search tab. In the section labeled Refine, select Date Modified and then select a time period ranging from Today to Last Year. Select Kind to limit the search to specific types of files. You can even select by size and other properties.

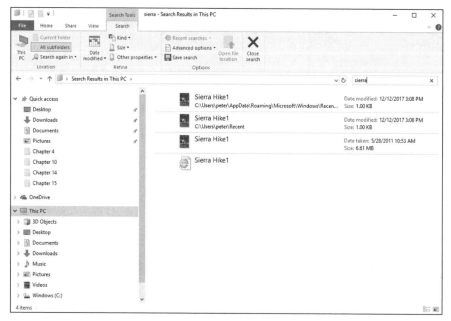

FIGURE 14-6

Add a Location to Quick Access

1. If you frequently access a specific location using File Explorer, you might want to add that location to the Quick Access section of the navigation pane for easy access. The Quick Access section is located at the top of the navigation pane. It lists folders in alphabetical order that you visit frequently. Windows 10 places some folders in the Quick Access folder list automatically, including the Documents folder and the Pictures folder.

2. Display the Quick Access folders. To do so, click or tap the right-pointing arrow next to Quick Access in the navigation pane, as shown in **Figure 14-7**.

3. Select a folder that you access frequently. For example, if you're currently working on files you keep in a folder called My Work, select that folder in the navigation pane.

Display Quick Access folders

Select a folder and select Pin to Quick Access

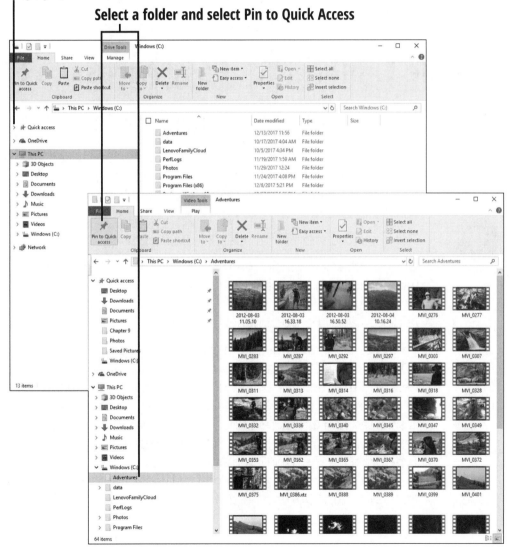

FIGURE 14-7

4. On the Home tab, select the Pin to Quick Access button (refer to **Figure 14-7**). The name of the folder you selected in Step 3 now appears in the Quick Access folder list. Notice the pin beside its name.

5. Select your folder in the Quick Access folder list. Next time you want to get to this folder, you can get there quickly by selecting Quick Access in the navigation pane and then selecting your folder.

To remove a folder from the Quick Access list, select the folder you want to remove. Then right-click the folder and choose Unpin from Quick Access on the shortcut list.

Use File Explorer for Easy Access to Files

1. On the desktop, select the File Explorer icon in the taskbar if File Explorer is not already open. The right side of Explorer is called the *content area.* The left side of Explorer is called the *navigation pane* and contains folders. Explorer starts with its focus on your Quick Access and This PC folders, and on your C drive and Network drives (if your computer is connected to a network).

The keyboard shortcut to open File Explorer is ⊞+E.

2. On the left, select Music, then Pictures, and then Videos, while noting the files in the content area on the right. Many Windows 10 apps store files by default in the Documents, Music, Pictures, and Videos folders. Select the Documents folder again.

3. To create a practice document that you can use in later sections, select the Home tab in the Ribbon. In the New section, select New Item and then select Text Document, as shown in **Figure 14-8.** (If you don't see this option, make sure that the Documents folder is selected.) An empty text document is created and the words *New Text Document* are highlighted so that you can type a new name. Type **practice file.** (You'll rename this file in a later section.) Feel free to repeat this step to create additional items for practice, such as Microsoft Word Documents or Bitmap Images.

Select New Item to create an empty document

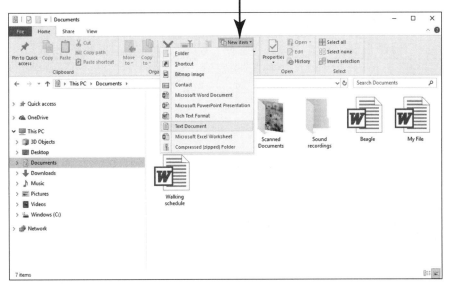

FIGURE 14-8

TIP

On a touchscreen, the virtual keyboard doesn't appear on the desktop until you select the keyboard icon on the right side of the taskbar.

4. Select the View tab in the Ribbon. In the Layout section, select each option, such as Extra Large Icons and Large, Medium, and Small Icons. If you see a downward-pointing triangle on the right edge of the Layout options, select that triangle to display even more options. Try them all, if you like.

TIP

Certain layouts are better for certain purposes. For example, photos are easier to recognize as Extra Large Icons than as a List. **Figure 14-9** shows my documents using the Details view, which includes the date the file was modified.

TIP

The more time you spend in File Explorer, the more worthwhile it is to explore the Ribbon as you need it.

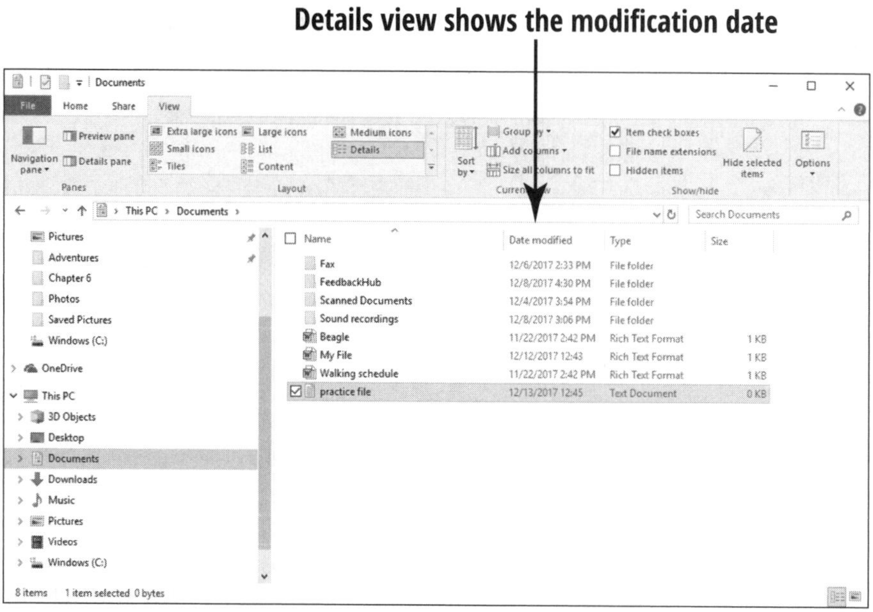

Details view shows the modification date

FIGURE 14-9

Create a Folder to Organize Your Files

1. In the File Explorer navigation pane, select the Documents folder.

2. On the Home tab, select the New Folder button. An icon for the new folder appears in the content area on the right, with the name *New folder* next to it and already selected (see **Figure 14-10**).

TIP

On a touchscreen, the virtual keyboard doesn't appear on the desktop until you select the keyboard icon on the right side of the taskbar.

3. Type **practice folder** as the new name. Don't move the cursor or mouse before you start typing. Your new text will replace the high-lighted text automatically. Press the Enter key to make the new name stick. (If you have a problem naming the folder, see the "Rename a File or a Folder" section, later in this chapter.)

4. Open your new folder by double-clicking or double-tapping its icon. Notice that the content area is empty.

5. To return to the Documents folder, select Documents in the naviga-tion pane.

TIP

Don't worry too much about creating folders, because the folders that Windows 10 provides may be all you ever need. As you accumulate more files, however, placing them into other folders can help you stay organized. In the Documents folder, for example, you might create a subfolder called Finances for files related to income, expenses, and investments, and another subfolder called Family for family-related documents. Which folders and subfolders to create and how to name them depends entirely on your own sense of order.

Select the New Folder button

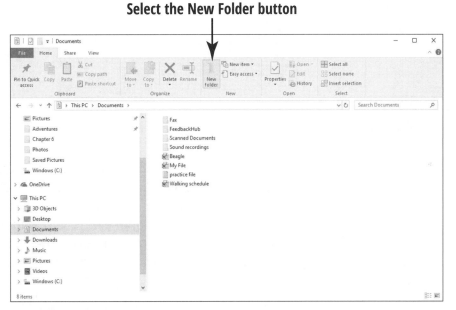

FIGURE 14-10

Use Check Boxes to Select Files

1. In File Explorer, you select files to move, copy, rename, or delete. You can add a check box to make selecting multiple files easier. In Explorer, select the View tab and then select the Options button. The Folder Options window appears. Select the View tab (in the Folder Options window, not in the Explorer Ribbon), as shown in **Figure 14-11.** Scroll through the Advanced Settings box until you see Use Check Boxes to Select Items, and then select that check box. Select the OK button.

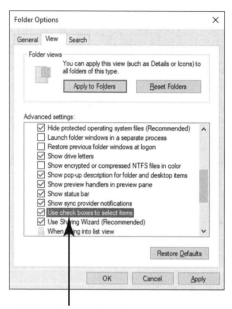

Select this option

FIGURE 14-11

2. Select the Documents folder (or any folder that contains more than one file). To select a file, click or tap its filename. (You won't see the check box until you select it with a tap or a click, or hover over it with the mouse pointer.) Repeat to select additional files. If you want to deselect a file, select the check box again to remove the check mark. Close the window after you've seen how these check boxes work. **Figure 14-12** shows three selected files.

TIP

If you want to select only a single file, you can select anywhere on the filename. You use the check box when you want to select more than one file at a time.

The Home tab has other methods for selecting. Select All does just what it says — selects all objects in a folder or library. Select None works similarly. Invert Selection switches the selection. For example, if I chose Invert Selection in the context of **Figure 14-12,** the three selected files would be deselected and all the other files would be selected. Sometimes it's easier to select the files you don't want and then invert the selection.

Select a file by using its check box

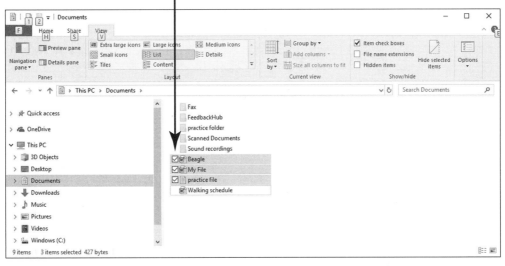

FIGURE 14-12

Add the Undo Button to File Explorer

1. You can add a button to File Explorer to undo an action, such as moving, renaming, or deleting a file. Above the Home tab, select the rather small down-pointing arrow to display the Customize Quick Access Toolbar list, as shown in **Figure 14-13.**

2. Select the Undo option from the drop-down list. The Undo button, which sports a blue arrow curving to the left, appears immediately to the left of the arrow you clicked in Step 1. You can undo most — but not all — actions in File Explorer by clicking or tapping this button immediately after the action. (Time isn't the issue. You can do something and then undo it a year later if you don't do anything in the meantime.)

TIP

The keyboard shortcut for undo is Ctrl+Z. This shortcut works regardless of whether the Undo button is on the screen.

Sometimes, you can undo a series of actions by repeating the undo function.

3. Select the Customize Quick Access Toolbar button again. Note that you can also add the Redo button, which, as you would expect, undoes the undo. All the other options appear also on larger buttons on the Home tab, so you don't need to add them to the Quick Access toolbar.

Customize Quick Access Toolbar list

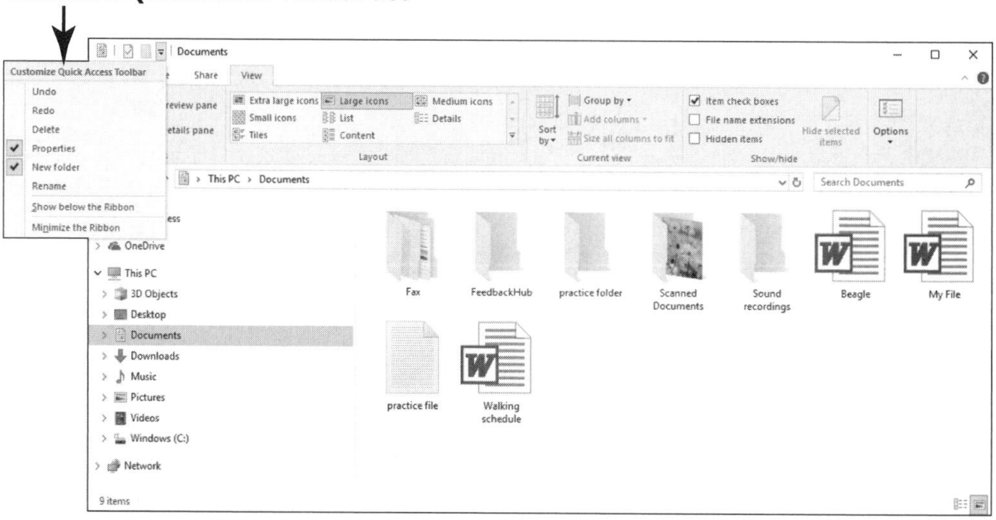

FIGURE 14-13

Move a File from One Folder to Another

1. You can move files to organize them. For this exercise, select the Documents folder in File Explorer. Select one of your documents.

TIP

To move more than one file at a time, see the section "Use Check Boxes to Select Files."

On the Home tab, select the Move To button, as shown in **Figure 14-14.**

2. If you see the location you want in the drop-down list, you can select that location. However, for practice, select Choose Location. A window opens, showing every possible location, as shown in **Figure 14-15.** Select Documents and then select the practice folder I tell you how to create in the section "Create a Folder to Organize Your Files," earlier in this chapter. (You can also select the Make New Folder button and name that folder.) Finally, select the Move button.

TIP

Unless you move many files or large files, you may not see any indication that the move was completed.

3. In Explorer, select the folder to which you moved your file. There it is!

TIP

Note that the Copy To button in File Explorer works similarly, except that the original file stays where it is and a copy is created in the new location.

TIP

Use these same steps to move a subfolder from one folder to another. However, don't move folders that Windows 10 creates.

TIP

You can move a file in a single step. Click and drag or tap and drag the file to the desired folder. When the file is over the folder, release the mouse button or lift your finger. Although this method can make moving easier, it can also make moving a file to the wrong destination easier. Double-check that the file ends up where you want it before going on to other things.

Select the Move To button

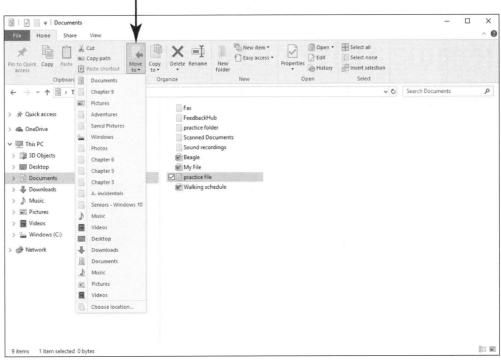

FIGURE 14-14

Select a location

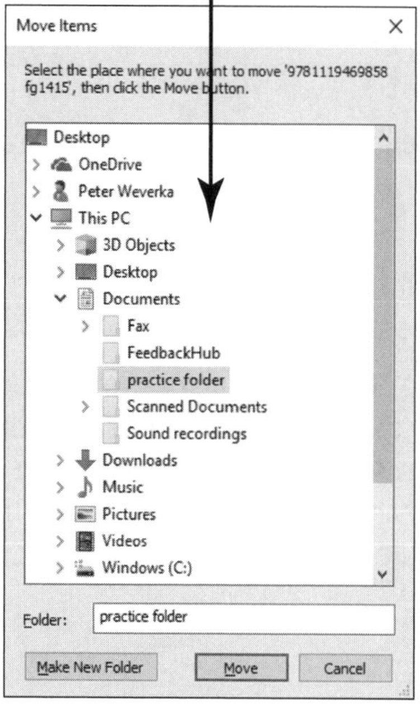

Move Items   ×

Select the place where you want to move '9781119469858
fg1415', then click the Move button.

Desktop   ∧
> ☁ OneDrive
> 👤 Peter Weverka
∨ 💻 This PC
    > 💿 3D Objects
    > ▦ Desktop
    ∨ 📄 Documents
        > ▢ Fax
          ▢ FeedbackHub
          ▢ practice folder
        > ▢ Scanned Documents
          ▢ Sound recordings
    > ⬇ Downloads
    > 🎵 Music
    > 🖼 Pictures
    > 🎞 Videos
    > 💾 Windows (C:)   ∨

Folder: practice folder

Make New Folder   Move   Cancel

FIGURE 14-15

Rename a File or a Folder

1. You can change the name of any file or folder you create. (Don't rename files in the Windows or Program Files folders.) For this exercise, select the Documents folder in File Explorer. Then select one of your files.

TIP

To rename more than one file at a time, see the section "Use Check Boxes to Select Files," earlier in this chapter. On completion of the rename operation, the files you selected will share the name you provide; each file will have a unique number added to the name, starting with *(1)*.

2. On the Home tab, select the Rename button. In the content area, the current name of the file or folder is selected, as shown in **Figure 14-16.** If you type anything while the text is selected, you erase the current name, which is convenient if the new name is completely different from the old name. If you want to keep most of the current name and edit it, select inside the name or press the left- or right-arrow key to move to the place in the name where you want to type new text.

3. Type the new name, which can be more than 200 characters long (although a dozen characters may be more than enough). You can capitalize letters and use spaces and dashes, but you can't use slashes or asterisks, which Windows 10 reserves for other purposes.

On a touchscreen, the virtual keyboard doesn't appear on the desktop until you select the keyboard icon on the right side of the taskbar.

4. When you've typed the new name, press the Enter key to finish the process.

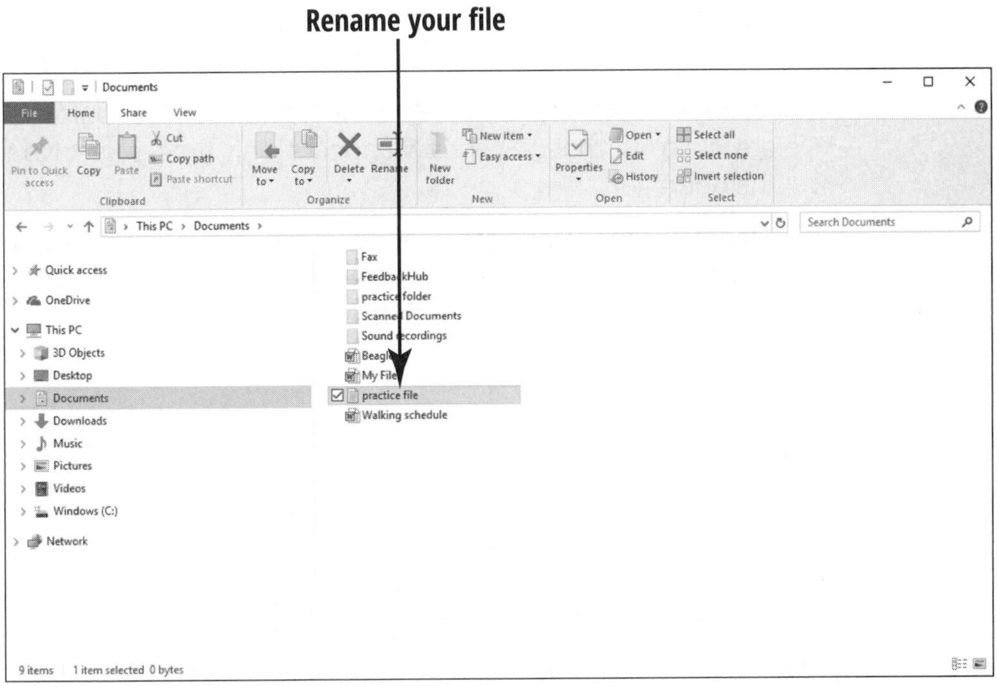

FIGURE 14-16

Delete a File or Folder

1. You can delete any of your files that you no longer need. (Don't delete files in the Windows or Program Files folders.) For this exercise, select the Documents folder in File Explorer. Then select one of your files.

TIP

To delete more than one file at a time, see the section "Use Check Boxes to Select Files," earlier in this chapter.

2. On the Home tab, select the X on the Delete button.

TIP

The keyboard shortcut to delete the selected file is the Delete key (surprise!).

3. A confirmation dialog box appears and asks whether you really want to delete the file, as shown in **Figure 14-17.** Here's your chance to change your mind, if you want. However, for this exercise, select Yes in the dialog box to delete the file.

TIP

If you don't see a confirmation dialog box like the one in **Figure 14-17,** tell Windows 10 that you want to see this dialog box when you delete files and folders. Select the bottom third of the Delete button to display the drop-down list and then select Show Recycle Confirmation.

4. Select another file, and then select the X on the Delete button. The Delete File confirmation window appears. This time, select No to cancel the operation.

TIP

You can permanently delete a file, in which case it will not be sent to the Recycle Bin. Select the file, select the bottom of the Delete button, and then select the Permanently Delete option.

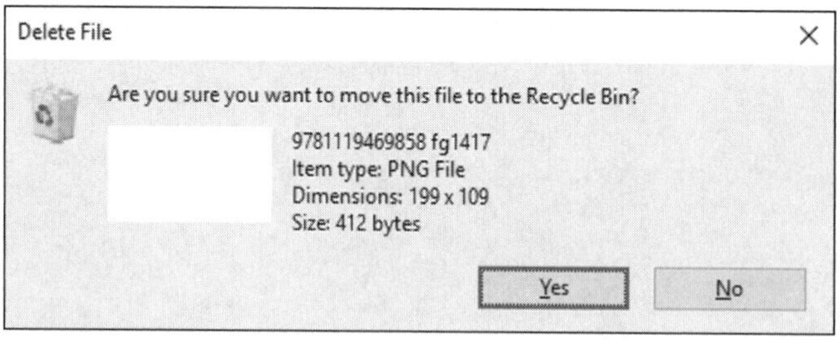

Delete File	✕

Are you sure you want to move this file to the Recycle Bin?

9781119469858 fg1417
Item type: PNG File
Dimensions: 199 x 109
Size: 412 bytes

[Yes]   [No]

FIGURE 14-17

Get Back a File or Folder You Deleted

1. Normally, when you delete a file or folder, Windows 10 moves the object to the Recycle Bin. Objects remain in the Recycle Bin indefinitely, allowing you to restore something you deleted long after you did so. To open the Recycle Bin, go to the desktop and double-click or double-tap the Recycle Bin icon. The Recycle Bin opens, as shown in **Figure 14-18.**

2. If many files or folders are listed in the Recycle Bin window, type the name of the item you want in the Search box in the top-right corner of the window. If any files match what you type, they appear in the content area.

Note that on a touchscreen, the virtual keyboard doesn't appear on the desktop until you select the keyboard icon on the right side of the taskbar.

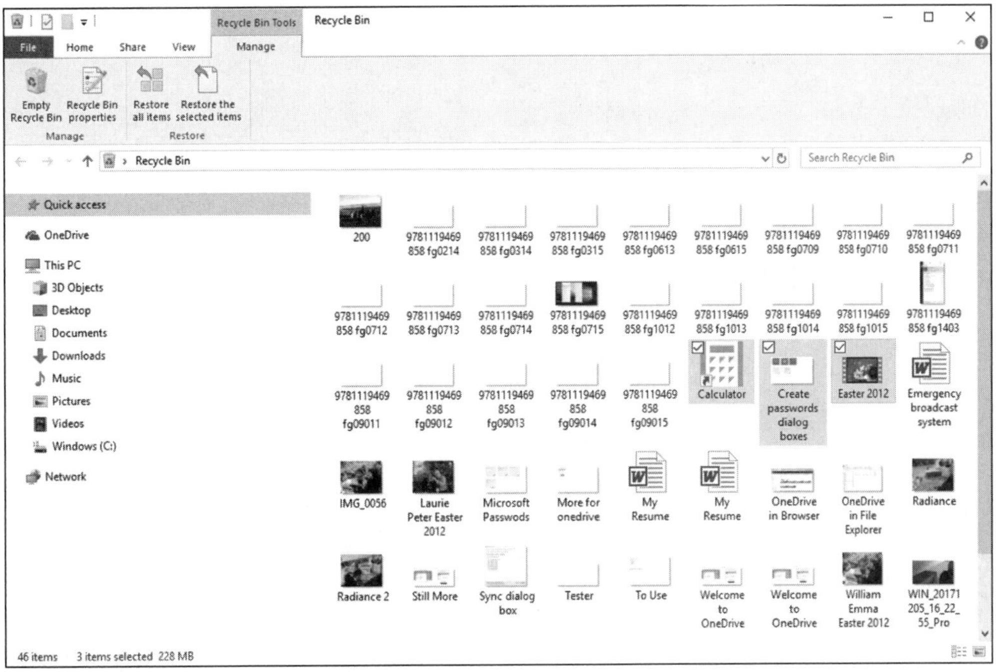

FIGURE 14-18

3. To restore a file or folder to its original location, select the file or folder in the Recycle Bin window. On the Manage tab, select Restore the Selected Items (refer to **Figure 14-18**). The selected file or folder returns to the folder it was in before it was deleted.

If Windows 10 needs disk space, it will automatically clear out the oldest files in the Recycle Bin first. If you want to get rid of everything in the Recycle Bin, select the Manage tab and then select Empty Recycle Bin. After you empty the Recycle Bin, you can't undo your action.

Don't select the Restore All Items button, because doing so puts every single item in the Recycle Bin back in its original location. Most of the files in the Recycle Bin are probably files that you really meant to delete. Choosing this command would be like dumping the trash can on your living-room floor to find a penny you threw away.

See Chapter 15 for information on backing up and restoring files.

Chapter **15**

Backing Up and Restoring Files

Some of your files — photos and documents — are priceless. If you accidentally delete a treasured file, what can you do but cry? You can insure your well-being by creating copies of your documents and photos.

The best insurance involves storing copies of files on devices separate from your computer. Such devices include the following:

» **Flash drive and memory card:** Carry your files when you're away from your computer by storing them on a portable storage device. For example, you can store files on a USB *flash drive* (also called a *thumb drive*), which is about the size of a disposable cigarette lighter, or a *memory card,* which is the size of a postage stamp and is most often used in laptop computers and digital cameras. Common capacities for flash drives and memory cards range from 2 to 128GB.

TIP

A *gigabyte* (GB) of storage can hold thousands of files, but you'll be amazed by how quickly you can fill that space.

» **External hard drive:** This type of drive has a much higher capacity than a flash drive, making it ideal for backing up all your files — the best insurance. Affordable external hard drives range from 500GB to 3TB.

A *terabyte* (TB) of storage is equal to a thousand gigabytes, which should be enough room to back up everything on your computer.

» **Network drive:** If your computer connects to a home network, you may be able to copy files to other devices on the network. For example, you can use a large-capacity network drive to back up files from more than one computer.

» **OneDrive:** Your Microsoft Account comes with 5 gigabytes of free storage in the cloud (on the Internet). Anything stored in OneDrive is duplicated on additional computers you log in to with the same Microsoft Account.

OneDrive provides storage but not a backup (duplicate). If you delete a file from OneDrive, any copies stored on linked computers are also deleted.

In this chapter, you copy files to a flash drive and hard drive so that you can transport files between machines and back up your files. You also find out how to store files in the Microsoft cloud with OneDrive. As well, you use the Backup function, which automatically copies files as a backup. Consider this scenario: You write a letter to a friend and save it to your Documents folder. Later that day, you delete part of the letter and save it again, replacing the original document. The next day, you wish you still had the deleted text. The Backup function comes to your rescue because it saves versions of files; you can recover the latest version or an earlier version of a file. As I wrote this book, I saved it hundreds of times — the Backup function could save every version, allowing me to roll back to an earlier copy, to before I had made some big goof. (That's purely hypothetical, of course.)

Finally, in this chapter you explore the Reset function, a tool you may need if you have problems with your computer. The Reset function reinstalls Windows 10 but preserves your personal data.

Add an External Hard Drive or Flash Drive

1. Before you attach a flash drive or hard drive to your computer, consider the following options that Windows 10 automatically offers for using the newly attached drive:

   - **Configure Storage Settings** opens the Settings app so that you can configure the storage settings on your computer.

   - **Open Folder to View Files** displays the contents of the disk in File Explorer on the desktop. You select this option to copy files to or from the drive you're attaching.

   - **Take No Action** dismisses the notification.

   TIP

   Notifications appear for the amount of time specified in PC Settings. If the notification disappears before you can select it, you can redisplay it by removing and then reinserting the drive or USB cable.

2. Locate an unused USB port on your computer. A *USB port* is a small rectangular slot on the front or back of a desktop computer or along any edge of a laptop or tablet computer. USB ports are often marked with a symbol that looks like a trident, as shown in **Figure 15-1.**

   TIP

   If a USB port is hard to reach, you can buy an extension cable from any office supply store. You can also buy a *hub*, which adds ports to your computer.

3. If you're using a flash drive, insert it into the USB slot. USB fits one way only. If you're using an external hard drive, plug it into a power source, if one is required, and then connect a cable to the USB port. Turn on the external drive, if it has a separate power switch. (Flash drives and some external hard drives don't have separate power supplies or switches.)

4. Windows 10 displays a notification to *Select to choose what happens with removable drives*. (You can click the mouse instead of tapping.) If you select the first notification, a list of choices appears, as shown in **Figure 15-2.** If you know which action you want to take, you can select that action. Otherwise, select Take No Action or wait until the notification disappears on its own.

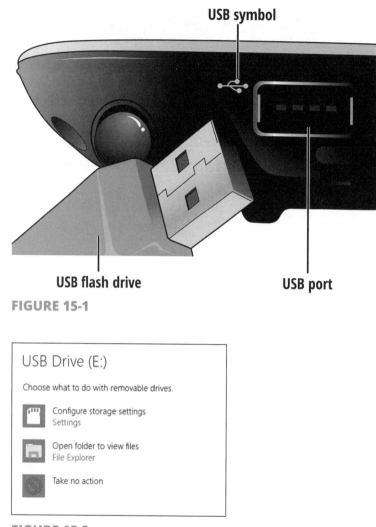

USB symbol

USB flash drive

USB port

FIGURE 15-1

USB Drive (E:)

Choose what to do with removable drives.

Configure storage settings
Settings

Open folder to view files
File Explorer

Take no action

FIGURE 15-2

Copy Files to or from a Flash Drive

1. To copy files or folders to a flash drive, insert the flash drive into one of your computer's USB ports.

TIP

Laptops, like cameras, often have a slot for a memory card. Want to turn your memory card into a flash drive? Simply buy a device called a dedicated or single-purpose memory card reader. Strictly speaking, a multipurpose card reader also works, but multicard readers cost more and are often larger than single-card readers.

In addition, a dedicated memory card reader doesn't need a cable to connect a camera to a computer. You can just download your pictures to your hard drive from the card.

2. If Windows 10 displays a notification (refer to **Figure 15-2**) when you insert the flash drive or memory card, select Open Folder to View Files, which will open File Explorer on the desktop. If File Explorer doesn't open automatically, go to the desktop and then select the yellow folder icon in the taskbar to open File Explorer.

The keyboard shortcut to open File Explorer is ⊞+E.

3. In File Explorer, navigate on the left to the folder that contains the files you want to copy. See Chapter 14 for information on navigating in File Explorer. Select the folder.

4. On the right side of File Explorer, select the folder or file you want to copy. If you see a check box to the left of each object you want to copy, you can select each check box to copy multiple files simultaneously. (If you don't see check boxes next to files, see Chapter 14 for information on enabling this function for file selection.)

To select every object on the right simultaneously, use the Select All button on the Home tab. You can also select the files you don't want to copy and then use the Invert Selection button on the Home tab; deselected files become selected and vice versa. You can select files in other ways as well.

The keyboard shortcut to select all files in File Explorer is Ctrl+A.

5. In the Ribbon, select the Home tab and then select the Copy To button, as shown in **Figure 15-3.** Select Choose Location from the menu that appears.

You can move files if you want them gone from their original location. To do so, select the Move To button. Follow the remaining steps, but substitute the word *Move* for *Copy*.

6. In the Copy Items window, under the This PC heading, locate the flash drive or memory card. The drive will not be Local Disk (C:), where Windows 10 resides. Select the removable flash drive or memory card to which you want to copy the files, as shown in **Figure 15-4,** and then select the Copy button. If the files copy quickly, you may not see any indication of progress; otherwise, a progress bar is displayed until copying is complete.

Select the Copy To button

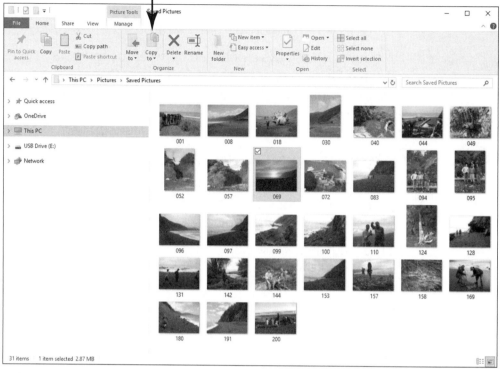

FIGURE 15-3

TIP

If you select your user name in the Copy Items dialog box, you may see OneDrive listed in the expanded list. Files you copy to OneDrive are automatically copied to the cloud and to linked computers.

7. If you copy a file that is already on the destination disk, the Replace or Skip Files window appears, as shown in **Figure 15-5.** (Perhaps you're copying a newer version of a file you copied before.) Note the available options:

- **Replace the File in the Destination:** Selecting this option replaces one file with another. Be certain that you don't need the replaced file (as you might if you want to keep different versions of files).

- **Skip This File:** Selecting this option does nothing with this file.

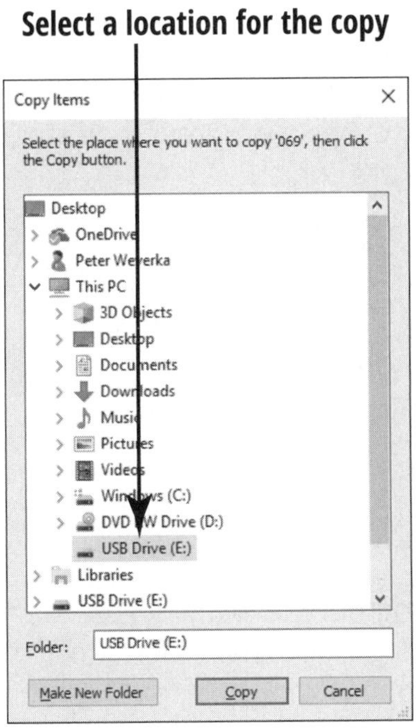

Select a location for the copy

FIGURE 15-4

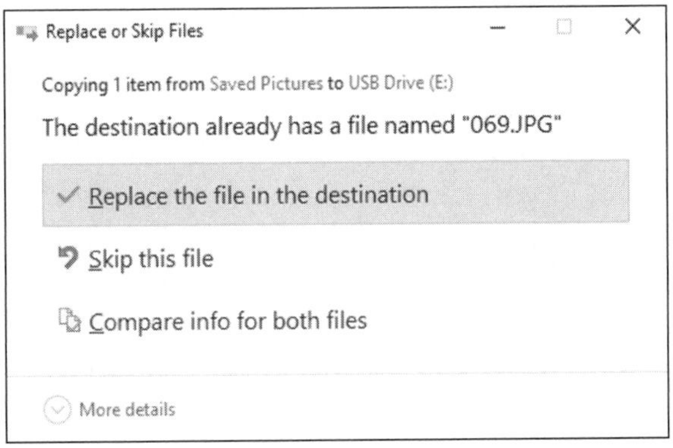

FIGURE 15-5

- **Compare Info for Both Files:** Selecting this option opens another window in which you can select files on the left to replace those on the right, and select files on the right to keep. Selecting the same file on the left and right creates a second file with a number added to the name, such as *my file (2).* This option enables you to have the original and the new file.

Select one of the previous options. If you selected Compare Info for Both Files, select the files to replace or skip, and then select the Continue button. You may or may not see a progress indicator, depending on how quickly the files are copied.

8. Confirm that the copy worked by navigating on the left to the location you selected as the destination in Step 6. If the files are there, congratulations; you're done. If not, try Steps 4 through 6 again.

9. Remove the flash drive or memory card you inserted in Step 1. You're good to go.

TIP If you have files or folders that you'd be devastated to lose, follow the steps in this task to create backup copies of those items on a portable storage device. Then keep that device in a safe place.

TIP To copy files from a flash drive or memory card, follow these same steps but select the flash drive in Step 3 and the folder or other destination to which you want to copy or move files in Step 6.

Use OneDrive to Store File Copies

1. Use OneDrive to back up and store files on the Microsoft cloud — in other words, to back up and store files on servers that Microsoft maintains on the Internet. If you have a Microsoft Account, you are entitled to 5 gigabytes of free storage space on the Microsoft cloud. If you have an Office 365 subscription, you are entitled to 1,054 gigabytes. Here's the big advantage of OneDrive: You can access files that you keep on the cloud from any computer connected to the Internet, whether you're in Tallahassee or Timbuktu. Use one of these techniques to open the Set Up One Drive dialog box and tell Windows 10 that you want to use OneDrive:

   • Select the OneDrive icon in the notification area.

   • Enter **onedrive** in the Search box and select the OneDrive desktop app in the pop-up menu.

TIP If you're signed in with a Microsoft Account, Windows 10 already knows your password. Skip to Step 3.

2. In the Set Up OneDrive dialog box, enter your email address and select the Sign In button. In the dialog box that appears, enter the password to your email account and select the Sign In button.

3. As shown in **Figure 15-6,** the next dialog box welcomes you to OneDrive or tells you where your OneDrive folder is located (which dialog box you see depends on whether you are signed in with a Microsoft or a local account). Click the Next button or Close button as necessary. You're ready to copy the folders you want to back up or store into your OneDrive folder in the Microsoft cloud.

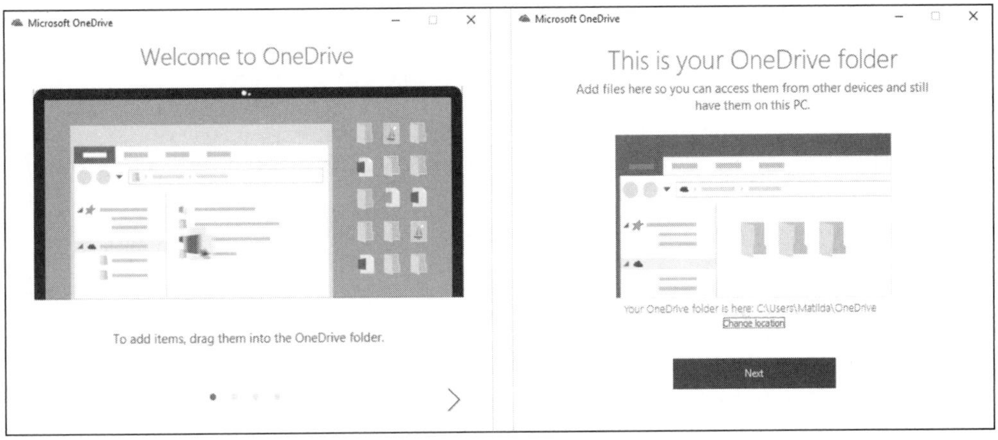

FIGURE 15-6

4. Open File Explorer and copy the folders you want to back up or store into the OneDrive folder. As shown in **Figure 15-7,** this folder appears in the folder panel on the left side of the File Explorer window. Don't let appearances fool you. Although the OneDrive folder appears alongside the other folders in the folders panel, that folder lives in the Microsoft cloud, not on your computer. Folders and files on OneDrive show a green checkmark to let you know they're on OneDrive (refer to **Figure 15-7**).

TIP

Chapter 14 explains how to copy and move files with File Explorer. As well, it explains how to create and save files.

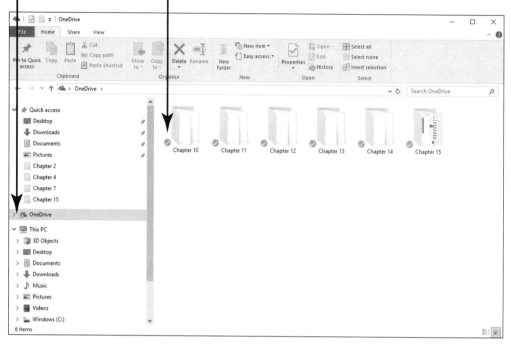

OneDrive folder

Check marks indicate files and folders stored on OneDrive

FIGURE 15-7

5. In File Explorer, open one of the folders on your computer that you copied to OneDrive, create a new file, and save the new file under the name **Sync** in the folder you opened.

6. In File Explorer, select the OneDrive folder and then, in OneDrive, open the folder with the same name as the folder you opened in Step 5. You see the Sync file on OneDrive. When you save a file in a folder that is also kept on OneDrive, a copy of the file is made to OneDrive automatically. Microsoft calls this *syncing* (for synchronizing). Thanks to syncing, you don't have to copy files to OneDrive on your own because the copies are made automatically.

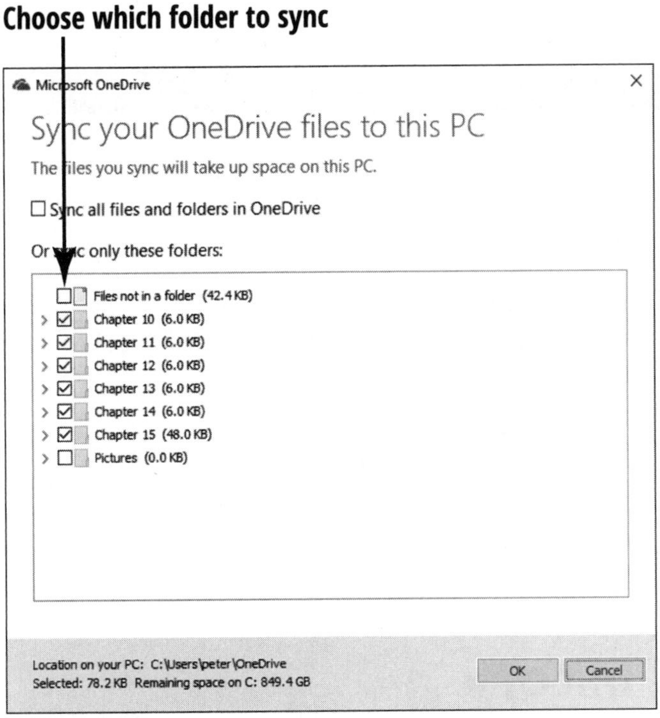

Choose which folder to sync

Sync your OneDrive files to this PC

The files you sync will take up space on this PC.

☐ Sync all files and folders in OneDrive

Or sync only these folders:

☐ 🗋 Files not in a folder (42.4 KB)
> ☑ 📁 Chapter 10 (6.0 KB)
> ☑ 📁 Chapter 11 (6.0 KB)
> ☑ 📁 Chapter 12 (6.0 KB)
> ☑ 📁 Chapter 13 (6.0 KB)
> ☑ 📁 Chapter 14 (6.0 KB)
> ☑ 📁 Chapter 15 (48.0 KB)
> ☐ 📁 Pictures (0.0 KB)

Location on your PC: C:\Users\peter\OneDrive
Selected: 78.2 KB Remaining space on C: 849.4 GB

[OK] [Cancel]

FIGURE 15-8

TIP

To see which folders from your computer are synced to folders in OneDrive, display the context menu on the OneDrive folder icon in File Explorer and select Choose OneDrive Folders to Sync. The Sync Your OneDrive Files to This PC dialog box appears, as shown in **Figure 15-8.** You can deselect a folder in this dialog box to prevent OneDrive from syncing a folder on your computer to its counterpart folder on OneDrive.

7. Start the Edge browser and go to the OneDrive online website at this addresss: `onedrive.live.com`. If necessary, enter your password. You see the folders from your computer that you store on OneDrive, as shown in **Figure 15-9.** You can manage your files and folders starting here. For example, you can delete, move, and download files and folders.

TIP

Chapter 6 shows how to use Edge, the official web browser of Windows 10.

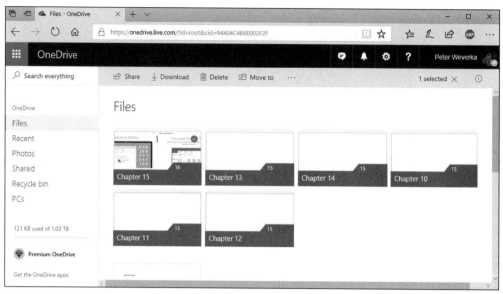

FIGURE 15-9

Turn On File History

1. To enable Windows 10 to create backup copies of your files, first make sure that an external drive such as a hard drive or flash drive is connected to your computer. Then select the Start button and choose Settings on the Start menu.

2. In the Settings window, select Update & Security. Then select Backup in the Update & Security window. The Backup screen opens, as shown in **Figure 15-10, top.** Which screen you see depends on whether you have told Windows 10 where you want to keep backup copies of your files. If your screen looks like **Figure 15-10, bottom,** Windows 10 already recognizes where your backup drive is located; skip to Step 4.

3. Select Add a Drive, and in the Select a Drive window, choose a backup drive on the list (refer to **Figure 15-10**).

TIP

Another way to access the Back Up Using File History screen is to select Configure This Drive for Backup when you attach an external hard drive.

TIP

File History stores information on an external drive or a network location. After you turn on File History, it will automatically create copies of your documents and photos on the drive you identify. If you lose, delete, or change your mind about changes to a file, you can restore the backup copy created by File History following the steps in the "Restore Files with File History" section, later in this chapter.

4. Turn on the Automatically Back Up My Files setting (shown in **Figure 15-10, bottom**) if this setting isn't already turned on.

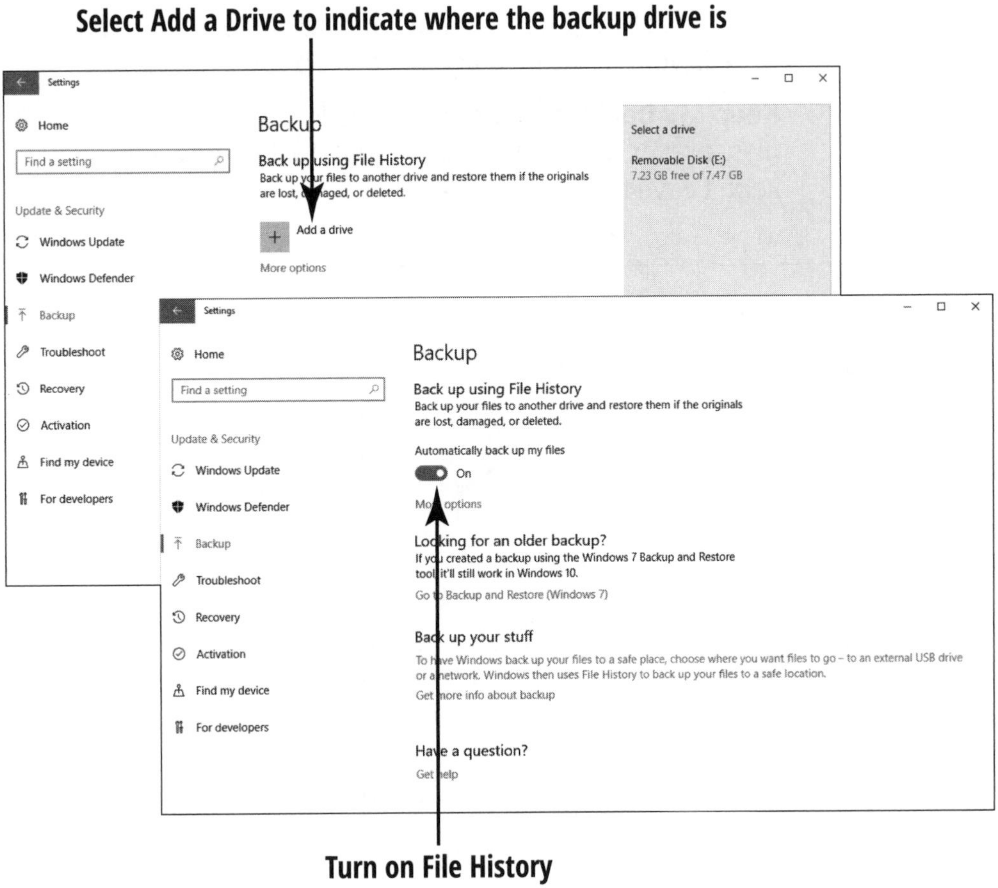

Select Add a Drive to indicate where the backup drive is

Turn on File History

FIGURE 15-10

5. Select More Options to tell Windows 10 which folders to back up and how often to back up the folders. The Backup Options screen opens, as shown in **Figure 15-11.** By default, Windows 10 saves copies of files every hour, but you can change this and other file history settings, as follows:

- **Back Up My Files:** This option controls how frequently File History checks for new or changed files. I recommend that you select Every 10 Minutes to minimize the chances of losing new or changed documents.

TIP

When you go on vacation, consider disconnecting the external drive and storing it in a fireproof safe or a safe deposit box. The drive is your insurance against theft or destruction.

- **Keep My Backups:** By default, File History keeps copies of your files forever. This option allows you to limit how long copies are kept. Leave this set as Forever.

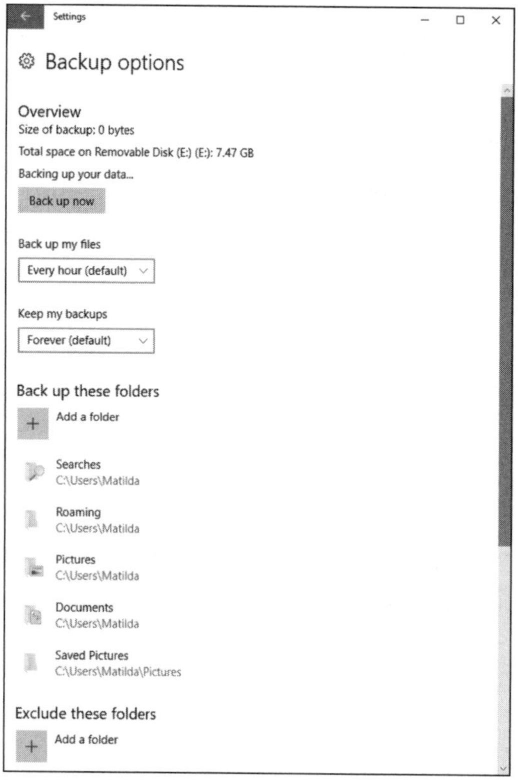

Settings — □ ×

⚙ Backup options

Overview
Size of backup: 0 bytes
Total space on Removable Disk (E:) (E:): 7.47 GB
Backing up your data...

Back up now

Back up my files

Every hour (default) ∨

Keep my backups

Forever (default) ∨

Back up these folders

+ Add a folder

Searches
C:\Users\Matilda

Roaming
C:\Users\Matilda

Pictures
C:\Users\Matilda

Documents
C:\Users\Matilda

Saved Pictures
C:\Users\Matilda\Pictures

Exclude these folders

+ Add a folder

FIGURE 15-11

- **Back Up These Folders:** File History provides a laundry list of folders to back up.

  To remove a folder, select it in the list. The Remove button appears. Select this button.

  To add a folder, select the Add a Folder button. Then select the folder in the Select Folder dialog box.

- **Back Up to a Different Drive:** Select the Stop Using Drive button and repeat Steps 1 through 3 to choose a different external drive for keeping backup copies of your files.

Restore Files with File History

1. In the Search box on the taskbar, type **file history**. On the search results screen, select Restore Your Files with File History – Control Panel. File History opens on the desktop.

2. Select the Restore Personal Files link. You see a screen similar to the one in **Figure 15-12.**

3. The most recent backup versions created by File History appear in the window. To see other versions of backups, select the left-pointing arrow at the bottom of the window. To return to the most recent backup, select the right-pointing arrow.

   Don't select the Restore button until you select the specific file(s) you want. Otherwise, all files will be restored simultaneously.

   Generally, you want to restore the most recent version of a file. However, if you want to restore content that you changed prior to the most recent version, browse to an earlier backup.

4. If you know the location of the file you want to restore, you can open that location with a double-click or double-tap. If you're not sure of the location, select the Search All box in the upper-right corner and type the document name. Matching results appear as you type. Select the file you want to restore.

5. Select the Restore button. If you restored a file you previously deleted, you can close File History. Skip the remaining steps.

FIGURE 15-12

6. If the Replace or Skip Files window opens (refer to **Figure 15-5**) in the preceding step, a different version of the file exists in the original location. If you're sure you want to restore the previous version of the file, you can choose Replace the File in the Destination Folder. However, to see additional options, select Let Me Decide for Each File. The File Conflict window appears, as shown in **Figure 15-13.**

7. In the File Conflict window, consider the following selections:

- Select files on the left to replace files in the destination with the backup files. (This is the same as selecting Replace on the Replace or Skip Files screen.)

- Select files on the right to cancel restoring those files. (This is the same as selecting Skip on the Replace or Skip Files screen.)

- If you select the same files on both sides of the window, File History will leave the original as is and restore the backup version with the same name plus *(2)*, allowing you to have both versions. (You need this option only if you're uncertain about which version you want.)

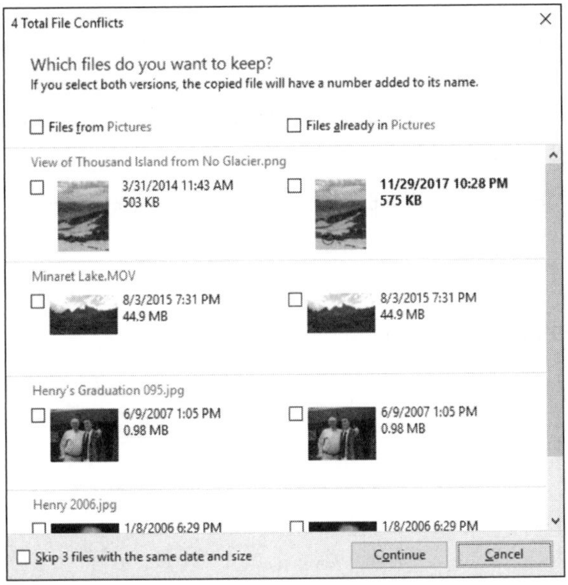

4 Total File Conflicts ✕

Which files do you want to keep?
If you select both versions, the copied file will have a number added to its name.

☐ Files from Pictures ☐ Files already in Pictures

View of Thousand Island from No Glacier.png

☐ 3/31/2014 11:43 AM
503 KB

☐ 11/29/2017 10:28 PM
575 KB

Minaret Lake.MOV

☐ 8/3/2015 7:31 PM
44.9 MB

☐ 8/3/2015 7:31 PM
44.9 MB

Henry's Graduation 095.jpg

☐ 6/9/2007 1:05 PM
0.98 MB

☐ 6/9/2007 1:05 PM
0.98 MB

Henry 2006.jpg

☐ 1/8/2006 6:29 PM ☐ 1/8/2006 6:29 PM

☐ Skip 3 files with the same date and size   Continue   Cancel

FIGURE 15-13

TIP

If you're restoring multiple files at the same time, you can select different options for each: replace one, skip another, and have File History create a copy for another. That's a lot of choices in one little window.

8. Select Continue, and Windows 10 completes the operation based on your choices in Step 7. The location of the restored files opens in File Explorer.

Reset a Misbehaving Computer

1. Glitch happens. The computer misbehaves, a program crashes, or the machine becomes unexpectedly slow. If your computer is misbehaving, try resetting it. Click the Start button and choose Settings. In the Settings window, select Update & Security. In the Update & Security window, select Recovery.

TIP

Before you reset your PC, see Chapter 12 for information about updating and maintaining Windows 10. Updating Windows may resolve some problems.

TIP

The Reset function should leave your data alone and unchanged. However, consider following Steps 1–4 in the section "Restore Files with File History" to confirm that your external drive contains all your files. Better safe than sorry.

2. Under Reset This PC, select the Get Started button, as shown in **Figure 15-14.**

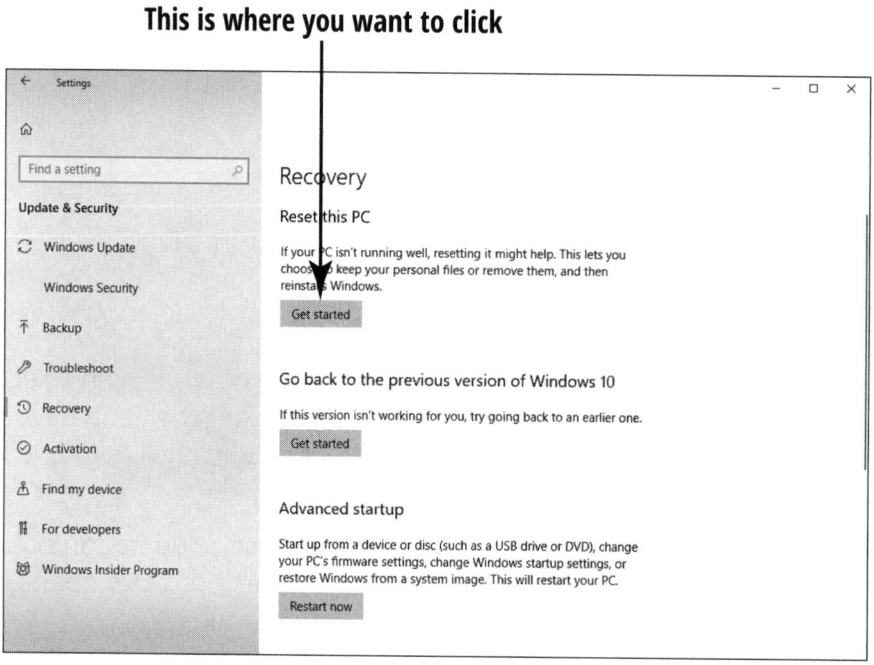

This is where you want to click

FIGURE 15-14

TIP

The Reset function doesn't remove apps installed through the Microsoft Store but does remove any apps you installed any other way. This safety feature is based on the assumption that something you installed from some other source is causing a problem. Be certain that you either don't need a desktop app or you have the materials necessary to reinstall a desktop app, such as Microsoft Office. Windows 10 will create a file on the desktop after the fact, identifying the programs it removed.

3. In the Choose an Option dialog box, select Keep My Files. (Or select Cancel, if you're just exploring this feature and don't want to continue with it.)

4. Reset runs, and your computer will restart at least once. When the reset process is complete, the Lock screen appears. Sign in as usual. If you see a file named *Removed Apps* on the desktop, double-click or double-tap it to open that file in your browser. The removed apps are listed. If you're aware that one of these apps created a problem, don't reinstall it.

TIP

Don't be intimidated by the Reset function — it's easy, quick, and worthwhile if it makes a problem computer run better.

Index

bulleted list, 137

burning, defined, 216–218

Business category, 170

C

Calculator app, 42–43

Calculator icon, 106

Calendar app, 149–153

Calibrate button, 249

calibration point, 250

Camera app, 57, 186, 189–192

carbon copy (CC). *See* courtesy copy

CDs (compact discs), 204–208, 216–218

Change Camera option, 186

Cheat Sheet, 6

Check Boxes, 263–265

Chrome, 114

clock, 94

Close button, 98, 117, 252, 255

Code text box, 86

Color Filters setting, 61

compact discs (CDs), 204–208, 216–218

complex apps, 27

computers, resetting, 289–291

Connect button, 69

contacts, deleting, 148–149

content area, 260, 271

context menu, 35, 46–47, 93

control keys, 16

Control Panel, 62, 226–227

Copy button, 277

Copy To button, 267

Cortana, 28, 47–50, 62

courtesy copy (CC), 135

Crop & Rotate method, 196

cropping, 196

Ctrl button, 191

Ctrl key, 13

Ctrl+Z, 265

cursor, 14, 135

Custom aspect ratio, 196

D

data, accessing, 9

Data button, 89

dates, 94–96

daylight savings, 95

default location, 29

Defender, Windows, 224, 234, 238–240

Delete button, 269

Delete key, 14

Delete Note button, 160

desktop, 91–110

  apps, 28, 91

  backgrounds for, 105–106

destruction, 286

deuteranopia, 61

Developer Tools category, 170

device driver, 243

device options, 244–248

devices, connecting, 241–250

dialog boxes, 53, 149, 278

digital cameras, 242

digital images, 242

Digitizer Calibration Tool, 249, 250

Directions button, 155

Discard button, 135

Disconnect button, 72

disconnecting from Internet, 71–73

Disk Cleanup, 237

documents, 89, 199–200

Documents icon, 42

double-clicking, 262, 287

double-headed arrow, 99

DPI (Resolution), 200

drafts, 133

dragging, 11, 12

drop-down menu, 82, 195

DVDs, 203–204

E

Ease of Access screen, 59–62

Edge app

  features of, 124–127

  icon for, 34

About the Author

Peter Weverka is the best-selling author of many *For Dummies* books, including *Office 2016 All-in-One For Dummies*, as well as four dozen other books about various topics. Peter's humorous articles and stories (not related to computers, thankfully) have appeared in *Harper's*, *SPY*, and other magazines for grown-ups.

Dedication

For Ireneo Funes

Author's Acknowledgments

Thanks to Mark Justice Hinton for writing the first edition of this book. Much of Mark's work lives on in this edition. I would also like to thank Amy Fandrei at Wiley for giving me the opportunity to write this book and Susan Christophersen for editing it. Thanks as well go to Russ Mullen, the technical editor, who made sure all instructions were accurate.

Publisher's Acknowledgments

Executive Editor: Amy Fandrei

Project Manager and Copy Editor: Susan Christophersen

Technical Editor: Russ Mullen

Editorial Manager: Mary Corder

Proofreader: Debbye Butler

Production Editor: G. Vasanth Koilraj

Cover Image: © Jose Luis Pelaez Inc/ Getty Images